DARK MIRROR

DARK MIRROR

The Sense of Injustice
in
Modern European and American Literature

by
RICHARD CLARK STERNE

FORDHAM UNIVERSITY PRESS
New York
1994

Library of Congress Cataloging in Publication Data

Sterne, Richard Clark, 1927—
Dark mirror : the Sense of injustice in modern European
amd American literature / by Richard Clark Sterne.
p.   cm.
Includes bibliographical references and index.
ISBN 0–8232–1509–1 : $32.00
ISBN 0–8232–1510–5 (pbk.) : $18.00
1. Fiction—19th century—History and criticism.
2. Fiction—20th century—History and criticism.
3. Trials in literature. 4. Justice in literature.
5. Natural law in literature. I. Title.
PN3499.S73   1994   93–17963
809.3'9355—dc20   CIP

PUBLICATION OF THIS BOOK
WAS AIDED BY A GRANT FROM
THE HENRY AND IDA WISSMANN FUND

For my family

CONTENTS

Acknowledgments   ix

Introduction   xi

1. **Idealistic *vs*. Realistic Conceptions of Justice from Homer to George Eliot**   1

2. **The Sense of Injustice in Modern Religious Fiction**   67

    Tolstoy, "God Sees the Truth, But Waits"
           Resurrection
    Dostoevsky, *The Brothers Karamazov*
    Mauriac, *Thérèse Desqueyroux*

3. **The Sense of Injustice in Modern Social Fiction**   108

    Martin du Gard, *Jean Barois*
    Dreiser, *An American Tragedy*
    Brecht, *The Caucasian Chalk Circle*
    Koestler, *Darkness at Noon*

4. **The Sense of Injustice in Modern Absurdist Fiction**   168

    Melville, *Billy Budd*
    Kafka, *The Trial*
    Camus, *The Outsider*
    Kundera, *The Joke*

5. **A "Dissenting" Perspective**   218

    Cozzens, *The Just and the Unjust*
    Snow, *The Sleep of Reason*

Conclusion: Toward a Renewal of the Dialogue   243

    Betti, *The Landslide*
    Wright, *Native Son*
    Glaspell, "A Jury of Her Peers"

Porter, "Noon Wine"
Anouilh, *Antigone*
Muschg, "Reparations or Making Good"
Forster, *A Passage to India*
Lee, *To Kill a Mockingbird*

List of Works Cited   263
Index   273

ACKNOWLEDGMENTS

It is a pleasure to thank friends and colleagues who in various ways have helped me in my thinking about the theme of injustice in literature, and in the creation of this book. The late Wylie Sypher, mentor and friend, whose scholarly accomplishments lent particular weight to his judgments, commented on a segment of *Dark Mirror* in terms that have buoyed me through difficult years. The encouragement of David Friedrichs and David Papke, former editor and current editor, respectively, of *Legal Studies Forum*, to which I contributed two articles (in 1988 and 1992) that derived from my work on *Dark Mirror*, has been invaluable. David Papke's criticism of a portion of the book manuscript was astute; and though I do not refer in my text to his *Framing the Criminal: Crime, Cultural Work, and the Loss of Critical Perspective, 1830–1900* (1987), I have learned much from it.

My kind, polymath cousin, Jonathan Clark, made suggestions about the Introduction that led me to improve it. Myron Sharaf, who read several portions of the manuscript, combined expressions of respect for what I was doing with persistent houndings to do it better: may he be pleased—at least relatively—with the final text.

I appreciate very much the written commentary that Charles L'Homme, my late colleague in the Simmons College English Department, made several years ago on an extensive portion of the manuscript. I am also grateful to Beth Kowaleski-Wallace, formerly of the Simmons English Department, for an excellent idea concerning the Introduction; to several members of the Department who raised questions about it and made criticisms of that segment of the work; to Artemis Kirk, Director of the Simmons College Libraries, for providing me with a review of W. Wolfgang Holdheim's *Der Justizirrtum als literarische Problematik: Vergleichende Analyse eines erzählerischen Themas* (1969); and to Jenifer Burckett-Picker of the Simmons College Department of

Foreign Languages and Literatures for aid in transliterating a title from the Russian.

I must also acknowledge my debt to the anonymous reviewer for Fordham University Press whose helpful observations on the natural law tradition affected my shaping of the final chapter.

Two books on literature and the law, though not cited in the text, had an impact on my thinking as I revised the manuscript in recent years: Richard Weisberg's *The Failure of the Word: The Protagonist as Lawyer in Modern Fiction* (1984) and Brook Thomas's *Cross-Examinations of Law and Literature: Cooper, Hawthorne, Stowe, and Melville* (1987). Some time before Richard Weisberg's book was published, he kindly sent me a copy of his *Rutgers Law Review* (Winter, 1976) article, "Comparative Law in Comparative Literature: The Figure of the 'Examining Magistrate' in Dostoevski and Camus."

As a seminar leader in the Humanities and the Professions Program since its founding (1981) at Brandeis University by Sanford M. Lottor and Saul Touster, who have remained its co-directors, I have had the opportunity to discuss with state and federal judiciary members, and with law school professors, several of the texts that I treat in *Dark Mirror*. I hope that my listening to the observations of men and women engaged in the day-to-day procedures of the law has helped to save this work from too abstract an approach to its subject.

Finally, thanks to friends not named here, and to my family—especially my wife, Ruth; my sons, Larry and Dan; my father, Eugene Sterne; and my aunt Helen Clark, for help and sustenance all along the way.

INTRODUCTION

This book was born of my concerned realization that modern European and American literature, which almost always treats criminal trials negatively, rarely points to clear ethical criteria of justice. Believing that imaginative literature reveals, in a complex way, cultural attitudes prevalent at the time of its creation, I revisited Western fiction from Homer to the late Victorians in order to determine to what extent perspectives on trial justice during that long era agree with or differ from those of the modern age. I did not find many trials in ancient literature after the *Eumenides*, or during the medieval period—until the late Middle Ages, when trial by jury had at last superseded the oath and ordeal as a means of "proving" innocence and guilt.[1] Still relatively rare in literature before the dramas of the late sixteenth and early seventeenth centuries, trials do not occur frequently until the nineteenth century, when they begin to be important in many novels and tales. Conclusions that I hesitated to draw solely from trial fictions written during the pre-modern era appeared to be valid, however, when based in addition on the extensive treatment of social justice in pre-modern imaginative and discursive literature. For what emerged from my reading was a sense of a continuing battle—a battle which, significantly, has no counterpart in the imaginative literature of the period since about 1880—between evolving conceptions of ethical natural law and variations on the theme of Thrasymachus's definition of justice, in the *Republic*, as "the interest of the stronger."[2]

Aristotle, articulating the idea of the "law of nature" as "a natural justice . . . that is binding on all men, even on those who have no association or covenant with each other," finds this ethical law in Antigone's defense of her burial of Polyneices, in disobedience to Creon's edict, and in Empedocles's prohibition of the killing of any living creature.

Aristotle remarks that "everyone to some extent divines" the natural law;[3] in the words of the twentieth-century philosopher Yves R. Simon, it is "known by way of inclination before it is known by cognition."[4] Although Aristotle was unfriendly to democracy, the notion of a law that all human beings to some extent divine has egalitarian implications that were to be spelled out in later pre-modern literature.

The realistic Thrasymachean perspective on justice, which opposes the idealism of both Plato's Socrates and Aristotle, is most vividly set forth by the despairing King Lear:

> . . . The usurer hangs the cozener.
> Through tatter'd clothes small vices do appear;
> Robes and furr'd gowns hide all. Plate sin with gold,
> And the strong lance of justice hurtless breaks;
> Arm it in rags, a pigmy's straw does pierce it. (IV.vi.168–173)

Lear's cry that justice is a sham is one we can also find in idealistic censures, during the pre-modern period, of the corrupt trial. But the difference in these censures from Lear's indictment is that they implicitly or explicitly set an ethical standard that "everyone to some extent divines" and that could serve as a rallying point for persons in quest of "true" justice. Consider the dissimilarity between a cynical Thrasymachean farce like the fifteenth-century French play *Patelin*—with its crooked lawyer, his equally corrupt client, and an inept judge—and Langland's fourteenth-century allegory *Piers the Ploughman* (inspired in part by the British peasants' economic misery), in which the king, although attracted to the glittering Lady Fee, finally discovers that she is trying to bribe her way to a courtroom acquittal. The king's counselors in this idealistic work are Conscience and Reason, guardians of natural law who would be as out of place in the nihilistic *Patelin* as in a modern piece of fiction.

The notion of ethical natural law evolved during its long history, and moral imperatives must sometimes have derived in part from prudential interests. The particular stress, for example, that the Greek Stoics placed on brotherhood—the fundamental unity of mankind—may have been largely determined "by needs resulting from an unprecedented amount of communication" among various ethnic groups after the Macedonian conquests.[5] Similarly practical considerations doubtless influenced Cicero when he declared that natural law, or "right reason," " 'applies to all men and is unchangeable and eternal. . . . It will not lay down one rule at Rome and another at Athens. . . .' "[6] This sounds quite fair. But Julius Stone, a modern historian of natural law, points out that although in the Greco-Roman idea of the law of nature there was "horizontal" universalism, "across peoples," this universalism did not penetrate "vertically down to the subject classes, for instance, of slaves."[7] In practice, the universalism of Christian natural law—despite its emphasis on the Golden Rule—was not to penetrate down either, until economic circumstances began to make slavery unprofitable.

An important difference in the Greco-Roman conception of natural law from that of early Christianity was the belief that human beings and gods constituted what Cicero called "one commonwealth"; hence, religious faith did not conflict with "pagan" obedience to natural law. St. Augustine, however, considered the law of nature to be part of the divine order of things from which the Fall had alienated mankind. A great gulf separated Augustine's "City of God" from the "City of Earth," where human beings were doomed unless God, out of His infinite love, granted them grace. As the Roman Empire, with its legal system based on a combination of natural law and customary law, gradually crumbled, Augustine's anti-civic idea of sharp conflict between spiritual and earthly life became dominant throughout Christendom. Only after St. Thomas Aquinas harmonized Aristotle's thought with Christian faith did natural law—now defined as the rational creature's participation in God's eternal law—again become pertinent to social life. It also became prominent in the works of Dante, Langland, and Thomas More, all of whom, in effect, reaffirmed Aristotle's conception of human beings as political animals. While More's contemporary Machiavelli Thrasymacheanly teaches Renaissance rulers, in *The Prince*, how to gain and keep power, More depicts in his *Utopia* a true commonwealth, where theft is forestalled by a general sharing of goods, and the people "live together lovingly, for no magistrate is either haughty or fearful. Fathers they be called, and like fathers they be themselves. . . . Nor the prince himself is not known from the other by princely apparel or a robe of state . . . but by a little sheaf of corn carried before him."[8]

During the sixteenth century, however, the emerging egalitarian idea (which More shared with Langland) that natural law applied to kings as well as commoners was assailed not only by outright Machiavellianism—the view that "justice" was always defined by the "stronger"—but also by the assertion of the divine right of kings. The fifth book of Edmund Spenser's *The Faerie Queene*, though supposedly celebrating the Aristotelian virtue of justice, actually subverts the idea of natural law by subordinating the allegorical figure of Justice in the trial of Duessa—who represents Mary, Queen of Scots, a Catholic—to the imperial will of Mercilla, the Protestant Queen Elizabeth.

Shakespeare's plays articulate a wide range of Renaissance attitudes toward justice: a bitter Thrasymacheanism in Lear's outburst; natural law idealism in Portia's "quality of mercy" speech in *The Merchant of Venice*; a curious mélange of cynicism and idealism in *Measure for Measure*; and divine-right doctrine—transcendental Thrasymacheanism—in Ulysses's declaration in *Troilus and Cressida* that unless the cosmic and social hierarchy is maintained, in which a king rules his people as the sun rules the "other" planets, justice loses its very name.

Corneille's *Cinna*, and plays by other writers in absolutist seventeenth-century France, advance the divine-right idea that ascent to the monarchy automatically expunges any crimes that a man may have committed en route. But in Spain of the Inquisition, ironically, natural law retained great prestige. Various sixteenth-century Spanish political theorists emphasized that "the king receives his power from the people."[9] And Lope de Vega's *Fuenteovejuna* (*The Sheep Well*) illustrates a king's eventual acquiescence in a harsh justice that "the people" have wrought. In killing a brutal military commander who has raped many women, they have acted in accord with a principle that Aquinas had recognized: the right to overthrow an intolerable tyrant.

A Protestant contemporary of Lope's, the Dutch jurist Hugo Grotius, declared that natural law would hold " 'even if it should . . . wickedly be supposed that God does not exist, or takes no concern in human affairs.' "[10] Despite that "wickedly," Grotius's observation was a step away from divine-right doctrine and toward the secularization of the ethical law of nature. Locke took an additional step in his *Essay Concerning Civil Government*—a justification of the Whig revolution of 1688–89—when he said that "princes . . . owe subjection to the laws of God and nature," and defined natural law as the rule of "common reason and equity."[11] Many French enemies of Locke's liberal political ideas considered Racine's drama *Athalie* (produced in 1691, under the nose of the "Sun King") to be nothing but "the English Revolution [of 1688–89] tricked out in an elaborate stage-disguise."[12] The newly crowned monarch in *Athalie* promises, in the constitutional Lockean manner—altogether in opposition to the idea that "I am the state"—to follow always "what the Law commands" (IV.iii.1409).[13]

By the turn of the eighteenth century, the remarkable discoveries made by such men as Galileo, Harvey, Boyle, and Newton had resulted in widespread use of "natural law" as a scientifically descriptive term as well as, in other contexts, an ethically prescriptive one. Perhaps, because of what a French writer referred to in 1751 as "a certain fermentation of universal reason,"[14] it was not always clear in which of the two senses "natural law" was being used. But no ambiguity mars Voltaire's observation on the term in his *Philosophical Dictionary*. His sense of injustice had been quickened by painful personal experiences: he had served time in the Bastille after being beaten at the behest of a nobleman who was offended by one of his witticisms. But Voltaire did not doubt (despite his patronizing attitude toward the lower classes) the universality of natural law: "Show me a country where it was honourable to rob me of the fruit of my toil, to break one's promise, to lie in order to hurt, to calumniate, to assassinate, to poison, to beat one's father and mother when they offer you food." In the *Essay on Toleration*, which was inspired by his defense of a persecuted Protestant, Voltaire observes: "Human law must in every case be based on natural law. All over the earth the great principle of both is: Do not unto others what you would that they do not unto you. Now, in virtue of this principle, one man cannot say to another: 'Believe what I believe, and thou canst not believe, or thou shalt perish.' "[15] Thus Voltaire derives the natural right of freedom of religious belief from the natural law principle of the Golden Rule. Before the American Revolution, according to A. P. d'Entrèves, the expression "natural rights" had widely supplanted "natural law";[16] the change must have been due in part to Voltaire's influence.

Natural rights proponents on both sides of the Atlantic Ocean shared the view articulated by Diderot in his novel *The Nun*: opposition to the church–state alliance that prevented a woman whom circumstances had forced to become a nun from obtaining release through a civil lawsuit from her vows. Diderot's protagonist, whose attorney has been defeated in court, finally escapes from her convent, becoming an "outlaw" under a regime whose legitimacy Diderot effectively denies.

A more complex Diderot fiction, *Rameau's Nephew*, gives expression, through characters named "Moi" and "Lui," to sharply opposed idealistic and Thrasymachean views of the law and the polis. "Moi" makes essentially Voltaire's distinction between natural laws of general equity and laws that only circumstances dictate. He points out that Socrates, condemned by circumstantial law, is now greatly admired, while dishonor has fallen upon the judge who condemned him to drink hemlock. "Lui" retorts that by showing contempt for a bad law Socrates encouraged "madmen" to despise good laws. "Lui" favors—ominous phrase—the "well-policed city."[17] The argument between "Moi" and "Lui" presaged the nineteenth-century conflict between supporters of the "higher law," like Thoreau, and Benthamite exponents of laws that would achieve the "greatest good" for the greatest number. But the argument in *Rameau's Nephew* also prefigured the battle between twentieth-century totalitarians, with their particular notions of the "greatest good," and those anti-totalitarians who could ground their political commitment not in mere pragmatic preference, but in what they believed to be natural law.

Natural rights theory, which provided an intellectual basis for the American and French revolutions, also underlay the anti-slavery and women's movements, as well as the campaigns to secure more humane treatment for prisoners and the mentally ill. Taken together with the doctrine of laissez-faire, however, the individualistic idea of natural rights worked against the natural law concept of communities knit together by reciprocal obligations. The French minister of state, Guizot, became famous for his encouragement to nineteenth-century entrepreneurs: "Messieurs, enrichissez-vous!" In opposition to such unbridled economic egotism, there was nevertheless a longing in the early nineteenth century for fraternity—a watchword, along with liberty and equality, of the French Revolution. It is this longing that to a considerable extent informs fictional works like Heinrich von Kleist's "Michael Kohlhaas," Sir Walter Scott's *The Heart of Midlothian*, and Honoré de Balzac's "The Red Inn." The protagonists of these works either violate or are accused of violating positive laws; but Michael Kohlhaas, Jeanie Deans, and Prosper Magnan are more deeply faithful to communitarian natural law than are most members of the societies they live in.

In the later nineteenth century, the tradition of ethical natural law virtually succumbed to several powerful challenges: the Darwinians', which assimilated human beings to a nature governed by impersonal laws that differed strikingly from ethical natural law; the Marxists', which combined realistic Thrasymachean analysis of the world as it was with a vision of a truly "just" classless society, made possible for the first time in history by a proletarian revolution; and the Nietzscheans', which depicted human beings as either slaves to a contemptible Judeo-Christian morality or as bold nonconformists capable of building a bridge to the "superman." To Darwinians, Marxists, and Nietzscheans, ethical natural law served merely as an obstacle to the acceptance of the "struggle for existence," or the "class struggle," or the coming of the transcendent Übermensch.

Chapter 1 of this book, which prepares the way for my discussion of the sense of injustice in modern Western literature, treats the conflict in pre-modern literature between idealistic and realistic concepts of justice. That chapter ends with an analysis of George Eliot's *Felix Holt*, which can be read as a kind of elegy for natural law by a writer strongly influenced by Darwinism. The very integrity of Felix Holt, who aspires to improve the miserable lives of his fellow-workers, makes him vulnerable to his enemies and helps to convict him of a crime that he has had no intention of committing.

Dark Mirror focuses on the virtual collapse in Western literature, after Eliot and Dostoevsky, of the idea of man as a political animal aware of universal law. Such religiously oriented modern writers as Tolstoy, Dostoevsky, and Mauriac—works by whom are the subject of Chapter 2—bring to mind Péguy's observation that the sinner is at the very heart of Christianity.[18] Judicial error figures prominently in "God Sees the Truth, But Waits," *Resurrection*, *The Brothers Karamazov*, and *Thérèse Desqueyroux*, but all three writers imply that miscarriages of justice are inevitable in a world where erring or sinful human beings are judged by others who are equally botched. In these works, it is the spiritual effect on the defendants—and, in *Resurrection*, on a juror as well—that is most strongly emphasized. Even Tolstoy, who hoped to bring about a moral revolution within society, desires chiefly the conversion of sinners from their poisonous or "worldly" preoccupations to agape in the spirit of the Gospels.

The modern social writers discussed in Chapter 3 are all strongly influenced by Darwinism, but differ in their interpretations of it and, hence, in their implicit assessment of its relationship to the idea of justice. In *An American Tragedy* Dreiser presents Darwinism as the survival of the fittest and points to no social alternative to the Darwinian trial that results in Clyde's conviction for murder not so much because of his guilt as because he cannot afford to buy the services of the "best" lawyers. The law most sedulously observed in the world of Dreiser's novel—where "money makes the mare go"—is not ethical natural law, but the natural law of the jungle.

Contrasting with this extreme pessimism is the belief in moral evolution that Martin du Gard, in *Jean Barois*, attributes to the most courageous member of an intellectual group that attempts to overturn Captain Alfred Dreyfus's conviction as a traitor. Unlike other Dreyfus supporters in the novel, who are disillusioned by the eventual "pardon" and "rehabilitation" of the framed Jewish army officer—one of them calls justice and truth "pompous words that mean nothing"—Senator Marc-Élie Luce takes heart from his faith that present conceptions of truth and justice will someday be superseded. This notion, however, seems vague. It is true that a fundamental concept of natural law, that of brotherhood, came only recently in history to be understood as embracing women and ethnic groups previously treated as inferior by their European and American "masters." And twentieth-century philosophers like Jacques Maritain and Yves R. Simon have envisioned a continuing improvement in our comprehension of natural law. But the substitution by Martin du Gard of belief in the progressive revelations of "science" for belief in natural law results in murky thinking about justice.

Brecht's *The Caucasian Chalk Circle* combines with its pungent satire on courtroom and social injustice a revolutionary prescription for change. A Prologue to the play, set in Stalin's Soviet Union just after World War II, dramatizes the equitable settling of a land dispute between two collective farms. The standard of justice is the utilitarian one of the "greatest good" for the larger community of which both collectives are a part. The body of the play then implicitly contrasts with this rational resolution of a problem the perpetual injustice of the ages preceding a violent Marxist revolution. The thorniest question raised in our minds by the drama concerns Brecht's assumption that after "axes" have destroyed the unjust old order, a just new one will take its place. Another question concerns the rules that will be applied in disputes unlike the one dramatized in the Prologue. Will these rules, presumably established by "the people," accord or not with a "natural law" that—from a Marxist viewpoint—had previously served only the advantage of "ruling classes"?

Koestler's *Darkness at Noon*, inspired by the Moscow show trials of the 1930s, takes a clearer view than Brecht's of the relationship between revolution and natural law. The "old Bolshevik," Rubashov, who as a last service to the Party has collaborated in his own conviction as a traitor, asks himself while awaiting execution exactly what he is dying for. Finding no answer, he recalls having once written, "our sole guiding principle is that of consequent logic; we are sailing without ethical ballast." Then he imagines the eventual formation of a new Party that would wear monks' cowls and preach "that only purity of means can justify the ends." While understanding "economic fatality," this Party would also respect the complexity and dignity of individuals. *Darkness at Noon* articulates both a sense of injustice with respect to Stalin's society and judicial system, and the idea that only a revolution guided by ethical natural law can attain humane ends. Koestler grants human beings an autonomy that Dreiser's Darwinism in *An American Tragedy* denies them, and his ethical viewpoint is more lucid than either Martin du Gard's moral evolutionism in *Jean Barois* or Brecht's Marxism in *The Caucasian Chalk Circle*.

The agony of the absurdist writers I discuss in Chapter 4 results from their inability to conceive of an alternative to the injustices they depict. Captain Vere, in Melville's *Billy Budd*, tells the drumhead court he has summoned to try the young sailor that Billy is innocent of a mutinous murder as far as "natural justice" is concerned. At God's Last Assizes, says Vere, Billy will be acquitted. But the drumhead court's loyalty, the Captain emphasizes, is not to nature, but to "the King." *Raison d'état*, in short, decrees that Billy must die. Melville implies that both natural law and God are inert notions, words rather than realities, in a world where innocence is crucified in the name of utility. In Kafka's *The Trial*, Camus's *The Outsider*, and Kundera's *The Joke*, natural law has no place whatever, although there is a complacent show of "rationality" by lawyers and judges in the trials and hearings that these works depict.

Chapter 5 deals with the positive perspective on the criminal trial—clearly a "dissenting" one in modern literature—of Cozzens in *The Just and the Unjust* and Snow in *The Sleep of Reason*. Unlike the great majority of modern depicters of fictional trials, Cozzens and Snow indicate that the collaboration, though sometimes antagonistic, between judges and juries can produce at least an approximation of what we intuitively perceive as justice. But if these novels recall the tradition of natural law, they do so at the price of presenting courtrooms that seem almost hermetically sealed against the turbulence and irrationality of society. Neither *The Just and the Unjust* nor *The Sleep of Reason* points to the miserable social conditions that promote many of the acts we classify as crime; nor do Cozzens and Snow seem greatly troubled by the economic inequities that deny justice to some people while permitting others to get more than their due.

It was my concern over the general absence of clear ethical criteria of justice in modern trial fiction that impelled me to write this book. I agree, however, with Orwell's point in "Inside the Whale" that it is foolish to expect fiction in a bad time to be "positive" and "constructive." The widespread denigration of reason in modern literature, and the emphasis in fiction on a survival-of-the-fittest Darwinism, or a vague moral evolutionism, or an ethically ambiguous idea of revolution; the depiction of existence, in much of the best imaginative writing of our age, as absurd—all are understandable responses to social phenomena such as the technologizing of reason, the "absurd" persistence of poverty and famine amid plenty, the brutal extermination of millions of people in wars, and the mindless devastation of our natural environment. If the dominant perspectives in literature are to change, the world will have to shake itself into what Orwell called "its new shape."[19] In this reshaping, will the world resuscitate and reinterpret—in the light of what we know about the squalid circumstances in which so much crime is spawned—natural law? That law is not dead. It continues to live in our judicial system—in the idea, for example, of *malum in se* (that which is wrong in itself) as contrasted with *malum prohibitum* (that which is wrong because it is prohibited by positive law). Thrasymachus, with his compelling notion that justice is simply the interest of the stronger—in short, that all wrongs are merely acts that the stronger prohibits—we shall always have with us. But perhaps the natural law that all men and women "to some extent divine" will gradually become again a focus of discourse in society and literature. Increasingly, one may hope, fictional trials will evoke the possibility of ethical justice in a complex but not completely lost and absurd world.

A few comments, finally, about the relationship between Chapter 1 and the rest of the book, and about my criteria for choosing particular trial fictions for analysis in *Dark Mirror*.

The chapter on "Idealistic *vs.* Realistic Conceptions of Justice from Homer to George Eliot" is essentially a prelude to the chapters on modern trial literature. My theme in this prelude is the evolving conflict in pre-modern literature between the realistic, or cynical, notion of justice articulated by Thrasymachus and the idealistic conception adumbrated by Sophocles's Antigone—whom Jacques Maritain called the "eternal heroine of natural law."[20] Even if I had the knowledge to analyze thoroughly all the works I discuss or mention briefly in Chapter 1, I would need far more space in order to do so. My aim, however, is modest: to set the stage for a treatment of trial fiction since about 1880, fiction in which the conflict I underline in the prelude has virtually disappeared because the idea of ethical natural law has faded in the modern mind. In the chapters on modern literature, I refer repeatedly to writers discussed in Chapter 1, for the contrast between the spirit of the modern era and that of the pre-modern ages is at the heart of *Dark Mirror*.

The concluding chapter indicates more clearly than could the chapters devoted to particular writers the scope of modern trial literature, and it ends by expressing a hope about the direction that serious trial fiction will take. Throughout the chapters on modern works, my criterion has been a combination of artistic seriousness (not solemnity) and pertinence to the problem of the relationship between justice and the law. It is my concern with that problem which leads me, in the chapters on modern trial literature, to examine Tolstoy's *Resurrection* rather than *Anna Karenina*, Martin du Gard's *Jean Barois* rather than *The Thibaults*, Melville's *Billy Budd* instead of *Moby-Dick*. I must also make clear that the works I analyze do not necessarily "represent" their authors' oeuvres. Camus's *The Outsider*, for example (I use Joseph Laredo's translation called *The Outsider,* rather than *The Stranger*, when it was published in Great Britain in 1982), does not convey, as *The Plague* does, his idea of rebellion. But it does give expression, brilliantly, to an absurdism prevalent in Western literature of our time. And this is what matters to me, in the context of my general argument.

NOTES

1. References to the law in medieval literature, as a bibliographic note in Richard A. Posner's *Law and Literature: A Misunderstood Relation* (Cambridge: Harvard UP, 1988) 7 indicates, are frequent, but descriptions of trials in imaginative works before the thirteenth century seem to be very rare. Magnuss Magnusson and Hermann Pálsson, translators of the powerful Icelandic epic *Njal's Saga* (Harmondsworth: Penguin, 1960), "written by an unknown author . . . somewhere around the year 1280, as nearly as can be deduced," refer to "a long thrust-and-parry court drama (surely the first courtroom drama in European literature?)" (p. 29).

2. Plato, *Republic, The Portable Plato: Protagoras, Symposium, Phaedo, and the Republic*, ed. Scott Buchanan, trans. Benjamin Jowett (New York: Viking, 1948) 298–99.

3. Aristotle, *Rhetoric*, trans. W. Rhys Roberts, in *Rhetoric and Poetics*, trans. W. Rhys Roberts and Ingram Bywater (1954; New York: Modern Library, 1984) 78.

4. Yves R. Simon, *The Tradition of Natural Law: A Philosopher's*

Reflections, ed. Vukan Kuic (1965; New York: Fordham University Press, 1992) 133. Simon points out (41, 42) that when Aristotle speaks of the "natural just" and opposes it to the "legal just," the notion of the just is not exclusively ethical. That is, "the 'natural just' of Aristotle—and the same remark holds . . . for the natural right and the natural law of Thomas Aquinas—ignores the particular meaning that we often attribute to the contrast between the physical and the moral worlds."

5. Simon 31.

6. *De republica* 3.22, quoted in Julius Stone, *Human Law and Human Justice* (Stanford: Stanford UP, 1965) 41.

7. Stone 43.

8. Thomas More, *Utopia* [trans. Ralph Robinson], *Utopia and a Dialogue of Comfort* (London: Dent, 1951) 103.

9. Dian Fox, *Kings in Calderón: A Study in Characterization and Political Theory* (London: Tamesis, 1986) 12–13.

10. Quoted by Edward Dumbauld, *The Life and Legal Writings of Hugo Grotius* (Norman: U of Oklahoma P, 1969) 73.

11. John Locke, *An Essay Concerning the True Original, Extent, and End of Civil Government*, *The English Philosophers from Bacon to Mill*, ed. Edwin A. Burtt (New York: Modern Library, 1939) 483, 406.

12. Paul Hazard, *The European Mind: The Critical Years (1680–1715)*, trans. J. Lewis May (1953; Fordham UP, 1990) 63.

13. Jean Racine, *Athaliah*, *Complete Plays*, trans. Samuel Solomon, vol. 2 (New York: Random, 1967) 441.

14. Charles Frankel and Donald O'Connell, "The Enlightenment," in *Chapters in Western Civilization*, ed. Contemporary Civilization Staff, Columbia College, Columbia University, vol. 1 (New York: Columbia University Press, 1948) 345–46.

15. Voltaire, "Natural Law," in *Philosophical Dictionary*, trans. H. I. Woolf (New York: Knopf, 1924), and Voltaire, *Essay on Toleration*, trans. Joseph McCabe (New York: Putnam, 1912), both rpt. in *Introduction to Contemporary Civilization in the West: A Source Book*, ed. Contemporary Civilization Staff, Columbia College, Columbia University, vol. 1 (New York: Columbia UP, 1946) 834, 840–41.

16. A. P. d'Entrèves, *Natural Law: An Introduction to Legal Philosophy* (London: Hutchinson, 1951) 60.

17. Denis Diderot, *Le Neveu de Rameau, Oeuvres Romanesques*, ed. Henri Bénac (Paris: Garnier, 1964), 401–02, 404; my translations.

18. Quoted in Graham Greene, *The Heart of the Matter* (New York: Viking, 1948), epigraph; my translation.

19. George Orwell, "Inside the Whale," in *A Collection of Essays* (1946; San Diego: Harcourt, 1981) 252.

20. Jacques Maritain, *The Rights of Man and Natural Law*, trans. Doris C. Anson (London: Bles, 1958) 34.

1

Idealistic *vs.* Realistic Conceptions of Justice from Homer to George Eliot

DISGUISED IN BEGGARLY RAGS after returning to Ithaca, Odysseus praises his wife Penelope, whose fame, he tells her, goes up to heaven itself:

> as does the fame of some blameless king, who with the fear of the gods in his heart, is lord over many mighty men, upholding justice; and the black earth bears wheat and barley, and the trees are laden with fruit, the flocks bring forth young unceasingly, and the sea yields fish, all from his good leading; and the people prosper under him.[1]

What seems strange to our minds is Homer's assumption that when a ruler upholds "justice," the gods make nature teem for his subjects. To us there is no causal link between fair or equitable governing and the appearance of good harvests. Indeed, the notion of a "blameless" king who upholds "justice" seems almost quaint in the late twentieth century. We are not agreed on what justice is, and we suspect that nobody, least of all a head of state, can be blameless. We might be able to agree as to the injustice of certain acts and conditions: premeditated murder, the torture of persons held prisoner, the gnawing hunger of hundreds of millions of human beings. But most of us have no clear standards that enable us to deal adequately with murderers or political torturers; nor, remarkable as our century has been for its technological innovations, do we have any solution to the problem of the children with swollen bellies who are dying as I write these words. Our imaginative literature, when it does not avoid, as it generally does, such a problem, tends to reflect the helplessness that is characteristic of our era. Earlier ages, such as that of the ancient Greeks, had far less information about the world than we do, far less ability to do anything about the suffering that they did know about, and apparently little sense that members of one ethnic group owed succor or support to another. As late as the fourth century B.C., Plato distinguished between two kinds of human beings, Hellenes and barbarians. Homer, several centuries earlier, was not more universalistic. What he had that we do not, and that many Greeks who came after him retained, was the sense of an ordered cosmos, with gods in heaven who rewarded righteous kings below, whose subjects benefited materially from kingly justice. Every reader of the *Iliad* and the *Odyssey* must be struck by the author's repeated use of formulae that evoke a communal, ritualistic daily life. Men's passions, of course, were constantly violating boundaries, but the boundaries seem pretty clear. In Book 1 of the *Odyssey*, Zeus speaks to the other Olympian gods of men's bringing upon themselves, through their own folly, "sorrows beyond that which is ordained," and gives as an example Aegisthus, who "beyond that which is ordained," took to himself Agamemnon's wife, Clytemnestra, and slew Agamemnon on his return from Troy, "though well he knew of sheer destruction, seeing that we spake to him before, sending Hermes, . . . that he should neither slay the man nor woo his wife. . . ." Athena then agrees with Zeus that the vengeance that Orestes, when he comes to manhood, will take for his father is Aegisthus's " 'due' " (*Od.* 1.5–7).

It is notable that in this scene the taking of a life for a life is considered by the gods to be altogether fitting. In another Homeric scene involving "criminal justice," however—the trial depicted by Hermes on the shield he has made for Achilles in Book 18 of the *Iliad*—murder is dealt with in a different way. The killer has offered a "blood-price" to a kinsman of the slain man, but the kinsman has refused to accept any money. Although both men hope to "win the issue" on the decision of an umpire or mediator, the umpire has evidently referred the matter to the "elders:"

> And heralds held back the folk, and the elders were sitting upon polished stones in the sacred circle, holding in their hands the staves of the loud-voiced heralds. Therewith then would they spring up and give judgment, each in turn. And in the midst lay two talents of gold, to be given to him whoso among them should utter the most righteous judgment.

That is, a small sum is to be awarded to the elder whose judgment as to how the dispute should be settled meets with the greatest approval of "the folk."[2]

The reference to the "sacred circle" in which the elders were sitting indicates the close connection in Homeric society between "holiness" and the doing of justice. If we consider this scene together with that of the gods' conversation in the *Odyssey* about Aegisthus, we could reasonably conclude that at least three ways of dealing with the crime of murder were considered acceptable to the gods: private revenge; the payment of a blood-price; or some other solution, proposed by an elder in a trial, that was approved by the people.

Hesiod, whose *Works and Days* depicts an agricultural society unlike the aristocratic, bellicose one evoked by Homer, links justice as closely as Homer does to the gods. Justice (*Dikē*), described as a young maiden, Zeus's daughter, "brings a curse" upon "bribe-eating men"

> who drive her out, who deal in her
> and twist her in dealing.

On the other hand, when "men issue straight decisions / to their own people / and to strangers, and do not step at all / off the road of rightness,"

> their city flourishes, and the people
> blossom inside it.
> Peace, who brings boys to manhood, is in their land,
> nor does Zeus
> of the wide brows ever ordain that hard war
> shall be with them.[3]

After accusing his own brother, Perses, of having cheated him of his share of their father's inheritance by bribing "barons"— judges, evidently—Hesiod proposes a final settlement of their quarrel

> with straight decisions, which are from Zeus,
> and are the fairest. (23)

Even though Hesiod depicts the age he lives in as an "iron" one, greatly deteriorated from the "golden generation" when men "lived as if they were gods," he still believes that both men's injustice and their righteous dealings will be duly requited by deities.

Several hundred years later, a court for the trial of criminal cases, the Areopagus, was established in Athens. Aeschylus's trilogy, the *Oresteia*, which begins with the murder of Agamemnon that Homer speaks of in the *Odyssey*, evokes symbolically the evolution of criminal justice from revenge sanctioned by the gods to a public trial conceived by the goddess Athena and participated in by representatives of the polis. Clytemnestra declares, after killing Agamemnon in the first play of the trilogy, that her motive was revenge: he had sacrificed "his own child, our daughter [Iphigenia], / the agony I labored into love,"[4] in order that Artemis might provide a fair wind for his Argive fleet to sail to Troy. In the second play, the *Libation-Bearers*, Orestes comes home at the instigation of Apollo to exact revenge by slaying first Aegisthus, Clytemnestra's lover-accomplice, and then, after hesitating, his mother. That hesitation—"What will I do, Pylades—dread to kill my mother?" (238)—is a more significant change from Homer's version of the story than is the shift of direct responsibility for Agamemnon's death from Aegisthus to Clytemnestra. The hesitation anticipates the civilizing influences that will be brought to bear upon the bloody history of "the house of Atreus" in the final play of the trilogy, the *Eumenides*. Here Apollo, at whose shrine Orestes has sought sanctuary from the Furies, bids Hermes escort Orestes to the Areopagus, where Athena presides, to be tried. Apollo then serves as Orestes's attorney, presenting a blatantly patriarchal argument to refute the demand of the prosecuting Furies, ancient female nature-deities whose function is to avenge the slaying of blood-relatives, that Orestes pay with his life for matricide:

> The woman you call the mother of the child
> is . . . just a nurse to the seed,
> the new-sown seed that grows and swells inside her.
> The *man* is the source of life—the one who mounts.
> She, like a stranger for a stranger, keeps
> the shoot alive unless god hurts the roots.
>
> I give you proof that all I say is true.
> The father can father forth without a mother.
> Here she stands, our living witness. Look—
> [Exhibiting Athena]
> Child sprung full-blown from Olympian Zeus. . . . (288)

Athena confirms Apollo's account of her motherless birth and announces that if the twelve-man Athenian jury's vote produces a tie—which it turns out to do—she will break it by voting for Orestes's acquittal.

Absurd as Apollo's and Athena's arguments seem to us, they are presented by Aeschylus as part of an historical process in which the primitive justice represented by the Furies, "everlasting children of the Night," is at least formally superseded by the enlightened public justice of the criminal court. In addition to the civilized verdict that ends at last the dreary wild justice of revenge, there is an additional emblem of social progress in the *Oresteia*. Persuasion ("Peitho"), which in the first two plays of the trilogy is put at the service of revenge—first by Clytemnestra, who induces Agamemnon to walk on rich tapestries before she kills him, and later by the Chorus, which tricks Aegisthus into meeting face-to-face with his slayer-to-be, Orestes—is employed in the *Eumenides* for a civilized purpose. Very patiently, Athena persuades the Furies, who bitterly resent Orestes's acquittal and their own defeat by the youthful god Apollo, to accept her invitation to abide forever in Athens. Their special honor is to be that without their blessing no Athenian house shall thrive. Their acceptance of Athena's offer represents, along with the establishment of the Areopagus court, the victory of reason and community spirit over the primal thirst for revenge.

The gods play a variety of roles in Homer, Hesiod, and Aeschylus with respect to the doing of "justice." They reward the just behavior of a "blameless" king by enabling his people to thrive under him; they punish "bribe-eating" men or instigate the taking of revenge; they preside in spirit over a sacred assembly of elders who are asked to pronounce judgment in what modern jurists would treat as a "criminal" case; and they establish, or at least Athena establishes, a formal judicial process that supersedes private vengeance by enabling community judgments on a presumably rational basis. But if it is clear that the gods do justice, or see that it is done, it is not clear in the works we have considered what the criteria of justice are. Beyond the "revenge-justice" of an eye for an eye, in what exactly does rational judgment consist in particular cases? The *Eumenides*, after all, while it points to a means of resolving private enmities that is more civilized than revenge, does not spell out laws or commandments. Sophocles's *Antigone* provides some guidance in this respect. King Creon justifies his proclamation that Polyneices is to be left unburied on the battlefield where he fell by asserting that he has been a traitor to Thebes. Antigone, when she is brought before Creon after having sprinkled dust on her brother's body, does not deny that Polyneices betrayed Thebes. This is simply irrelevant to her. To Creon's declaration that she is honoring a traitor as much as her loyal brother, Eteocles, she replies, "His own brother, traitor or not, and equal in blood." And to Creon's "He made war on his country. Eteocles defended it," she retorts, "Nevertheless, there are honors due all the dead."[5] The central moral issue here, as Hegel pointed out, is whether the "right" of the state to punish disloyalty, or the "right" of the family to bury its dead, is to take precedence.[6] Antigone adumbrates the notion of "natural law" when she says to Creon that although his edict was strong, his strength "is weakness itself against"

> The immortal unrecorded laws of God.
> They are not merely now: they were, and shall be,
> Operative for ever, beyond man utterly. (203)

Whatever arguments can be made "outside the play" in support of Creon's viewpoint, there is no doubt that in the text of *Antigone*, the heroine's principle is vindicated. Creon heeds the prophet Teiresias's warning too late to save the life of his son, Haemon, who after Antigone's suicide has killed himself, or of his wife, who has hanged herself upon hearing of Haemon's death. Creon's final broken words in the play, "Fate has brought all my pride to a thought of dust," are in effect affirmed by the Chorus, which has the last line: "And proud men in old age learn to be wise" (238).

After reading of the grave transactions concerning justice between gods and human beings in the works of Homer, Hesiod, Aeschylus, and Sophocles, it is astonishing to come upon the irreverence and cynicism of Euripides. Werner Jaeger observes in *Paideia* that the great difference in Euripides's values from those of Sophocles, his contemporary, is that Euripides was greatly influenced by Sophistic ideas.[7] According to the Sophists, of whom Callicles in Plato's dialogue *Gorgias* is representative, law was

simply "an artificial bond, a convention agreed on by the orga-
nized weaklings to repress their natural masters, the strong, and
make them do their will" (Jaeger 322). The world of Euripides's
dramas—think of *Medea* and *The Trojan Women*—is one of unmiti-
gated injustice, in which men are mere sports of cruel gods.
Euripides' version, in *Orestes*, of what happened in Argos after the
murder of Clytemnestra travesties the *Eumenides.* Apollo, who in
Aeschylus's account of that killing (and Sophocles's account as
well—his *Electra* corresponds to the *Libation-Bearers*) appears jus-
tifiably to incite Orestes to revenge, is a criminal in Euripides's
play. Opening the drama with a bitter speech, Orestes's sister,
Electra, speaks of the "old charge" against Apollo:

> The world knows all too well
> how he pushed Orestes on to murder the mother
> who gave him birth, that act of matricide
> which wins, it seems, something less than approval
> in men's eyes. But persuaded by the god, he killed. . . .

Now, a week after that murder, Orestes is "wasted by raging fever
/ and whirled on to madness by his mother's blood."[8] Meanwhile,
the city of Argos is assembling to vote on whether Orestes and
his sister-accomplice shall live or die.

Euripides's Argos, unlike that of Aeschylus's and Sophocles's
versions of the story, has a criminal court. But Orestes and Electra
have not, before killing Clytemnestra and Aegisthus, attempted to
bring their own case before it. For this failure, Clytemnestra's
father, Tyndareus, sternly denounces Orestes. When Agamemnon died, he says, Orestes should have taken legal action—charged
Clytemnestra formally with murder "and made her pay the penalty prescribed, / expulsion from his house." Now that Orestes
has killed her, "what difference is there between him and his
mother?"

This sounds sensible. The reader supposes that Tyndareus will
represent reason, moderation, in a climate of violence. But a bit
later Tyndareus warns Menelaus to do nothing to prevent Orestes
from being stoned to death (40–41). In this play, nobody proves
admirable. Menelaus, cowed by Tyndareus, proffers only empty
words when Orestes asks for his help. Pylades, Orestes's friend,
does remain loyal even after the Argives condemn Orestes and

Electra to death; but he proposes the insane project of killing
Helen in order to punish her husband, Menelaus:

> . . . we punish her in the name of all Hellas
> whose fathers and sons she murdered, whose wives
> she widowed [in the Trojan War].
> > Mark my words, Orestes.
> There will be bonfires and celebrations in Argos;
>
> . . . .
> > No longer
> shall they call you "the man who murdered his mother."
> No, a fairer title awaits you now,
> the better name of "the killer of Helen
> who killed so many men." (74–75)

Embracing this nutty plan with wild enthusiasm, Orestes does
not see that by killing Helen he would be dishonoring the memory
of his own father, who led so many Argives to death on her
behalf. Electra, equally unaware of this, agrees, suggesting that
after Helen's murder, her daughter, Hermione, be taken hostage.
Then, says Electra, if Menelaus tries to avenge his wife, Orestes
will threaten to kill the girl. (The reader may decide here that an
up-to-date translation of *Orestes* should be called *The Argos Terror-
ists*.)

The drama ends with a phantasmagoric scene. Menelaus arrives,
to find Hermione standing on the palace's smoking roof, between
Orestes and Pylades, with Orestes's sword at her throat. Holding
blazing torches behind these three stands Electra. Orestes tells
Menelaus that heaven, by stealing Helen away, has robbed him of
the pleasure of killing her. But he threatens to murder Hermione
unless Menelaus persuades the Argives to let Orestes and Electra
live. As the desperate, fatuous Menelaus hesitates, Orestes orders
Electra to set the palace on fire. Amid a general alarm caused by
Menelaus's cry for the Argives' help, Apollo appears "ex machina" above the royal dwelling. Behind him is Helen, who, the
god explains, is immortal and sits enthroned in the sky forever,
"a star for sailors." This faintly obscene metamorphosis of Helen
is less bizarre than Apollo's prophecy that Orestes will be acquitted at the Areopagus in Athens and will then marry Hermione,
"the girl against whom your sword now lies." Eventually, recon-
ciled to the Argives by Apollo himself, Orestes is to reign over

them. After hailing Apollo as a "true prophet," Orestes deviates into sanity:

> And yet when I heard you speak,
> I thought I heard the whisper of some fiend
> speaking through your mouth. (103–04)

The prophecy that Orestes will marry the girl he has been about to kill, and will rule over the city that has decided to execute him, reduces life to a cruel joke—which is what Euripides may have concluded it is. Certain episodes of the Peloponnesian War could have helped to induce such an attitude. In 416 B.C., after capturing the island of Melos, whose sole offense had been its neutrality in the war, the Athenians massacred the adult male population and sold the women and children as slaves. Three years later, after besieging the city of Syracuse, an Athenian force was routed by the Syracusans and their allies. It was a few years after these episodes that Orestes equated "justice" with bloody, triumphant power. Thrasymachus would make the same equation in Plato's *Republic.*

Behind Plato's greatest dialogue lay a long Greek tradition that equated justice (*dikē*) with obedience to the law (*nomos*) of the city-state in which one lived. But an event like the massacre of the Melians gave particular point to the argument of the Sophists that there was in men a brutal "nature" that was more powerful than any civil laws. In the *Republic,* after Socrates has proposed that he and his acquaintances attempt to discover the nature of justice, the Sophist Thrasymachus confidently asserts that "in all states there is the same principle of justice, which is the interest of the government; and as the government must be supposed to have power, the only reasonable conclusion is, that everywhere there is one principle of justice, which is the interest of the stronger."[9]

Socrates's refutation of this argument, which emerges from Thrasymachus's grudging answers to his questions and from comments by the other interlocutors, is, of course, idealistic: governing is one of the arts; the proper concern of any art is the interest of the subject matter, not of its practitioner—the art of medicine, for example, considers the interest of the patient, not the doctor; in consequence, the art of government enjoins the interest of the governed, not of the governor. Thrasymachus tries

to regain the initiative now by changing his terminology: instead
of defining the just man as the strong one, he calls the just man a
simpleton; the unjust man

> is lord over the truly simple and just: he is the stronger, and his
> subjects do what is for his own interest, and minister to his own
> happiness, which is far from being their own. . . . Consider,
> further, most foolish Socrates, that the just is always a loser in
> comparison with the unjust. . . . where there is an income tax, the
> just man will pay more and the unjust less on the same amount of
> income; and where anything is to be received the one gains nothing
> and the other much.

Indeed, Thrasymachus declares, when injustice is done on a large
enough scale—"When a man besides taking away the money of
the citizens has made slaves of them"—the perpetrator is called
happy and blessed. Thrasymachus is essentially maintaining that
injustice, "a man's own profit and interest," *becomes* justice, "the
interest of the stronger," whenever the doer of injustice is able to
impose his will on society (305–07).

Socrates's most piercing counter-thrust against Thrasymachus
is that injustice tends to arouse hatred wherever it exists, setting
even those who practice it at variance with one another, exactly as
the unjust person is "incapable of action because he is not at unity
with himself" (319). This reference to the disunity or disharmony
of the unjust man anticipates the definition of justice that Socrates—who is seeking justice in the ideal polis, where it is "writ
large," in order to find it in individuals—will later give. It is
notable that Plato uses, not the traditional Greek word for justice,
dikē (which originally meant "custom" or "usage," and came to
mean acts that were "right"), but *dikaiosunē*, which signifies the
disposition to do justice, "justice-mindedness," as well as the acts
that proceed from this disposition.[10] Ultimately, Socrates finds
social justice in an harmonious interrelationship among three
classes in the polis, each of which would faithfully perform its
own tasks: the philosophers, who have learned to see "the beautiful and just and good in their truth" (554), would teach other men
the difference between the shadows they take for reality and reality
itself; the auxiliaries would be prepared to defend the polis against
its enemies; the husbandmen and craftsmen would sustain the

polis, day by day. There would be no class warfare within this rigorously ordered state, which corresponds to the justly "ordered" person in whom, Socrates says, reason rules; passion, or spirit, is brought into accord with reason by education; and concupiscence, "the largest part of the soul and . . . most insatiable of gain" (447), is carefully controlled by reason and spirit.

It is essentially this idea of the just man that Hamlet will express in praising Horatio as one who "is not passion's slave," and whose "blood and judgment are so well co-meddled / That they are not a pipe for Fortune's finger / To sound what stop she please." A significant difference, however, in Socrates's perspective from Hamlet's is a firm belief in the gods and an afterlife. Thus he can resist the strong argument of one of his interlocutors: that a man with a magic ring capable of making him invisible would not feel obliged to act justly. Socrates's riposte is that a man must learn during his earthly existence to distinguish good from evil, so that when in the afterlife he is given a "choice" among various lives for "a new cycle of life and mortality" (691), he will be able to choose well. Since the soul, according to Socrates, is immortal, the unjust user of the magic ring would forever be choosing an "unjust," hence an unhappy, life.

Seductive as Socrates's idealism is—his notion of the metempsychosis that keeps the just man just, and of justice as a harmony in both polis and person—his utopia is totalitarian. Ideas incompatible with his conception of what is right or true would not be permitted to circulate. For example, only a rigorously vetted literature would be used in the education of children: "the first thing will be to establish a censorship of the writers of fiction, and let the censors receive any tale of fiction which is good, and reject the bad; and we will desire mothers and nurses to tell their children the authorised ones only" (353). Thrasymachus's cynical voice would be welcome at this point in the *Republic*. Who, we wish he would ask, is to prevent Socrates's censors from advancing their own selfish interests under the cover of lofty references to "law and the reason of mankind," which Socrates invokes in defense of his policy? And it seems ironic that Socrates, who, at least according to Plato in the *Republic*, conceived the "just" society as one sealed against heresy, should have been condemned to death for subversive teaching. His refusal to escape from jail after this condemnation is, however, movingly consistent with his idealistic conception of justice. For, as he explains to Crito in another Platonic dialogue, it is less important to him to save his own life than to respect the Athenian laws, which have "nurtured and educated" him.[11] What Socrates is upholding, of course, is not the application of a particular law, but the idea of civil law, which he believes to be ordained by the gods.

For Homer, Hesiod, Aeschylus, Sophocles, and Plato, justice is a religious imperative. Homer's human-like Olympian gods are very different from Plato's distant deities; Aeschylus's conception of an evolution from revenge—justice to civic justice—is not found in either Homer or Hesiod; and Sophocles's adumbration of natural law in *Antigone* seems to anticipate Grotius's declaration that natural law would hold even if there were no God. Yet for all these Greek writers, justice is ordained or "done" by the gods— just as, for the ancient Cretans, Jupiter was the original lawgiver who had instructed Minos; and for the Spartans, Apollo rather than Lycurgus was the source of their laws.[12] Euripides, however, who boldly depicts Apollo as a criminal, has a radically different perspective, as does Thrasymachus in the *Republic*. Their "realistic" view is that, whatever myths men have created, "justice" consists essentially in the decrees of the strongest. Thrasymachus, defeated though he is by Socrates, is a forerunner of Machiavelli, Marx, and Nietzsche, all of whom will identify justice, as it is actually administered, with established power.

THE OLD TESTAMENT AND EARLY CHRISTIAN LITERARY TRADITION

There is no conflict in the Old Testament corresponding to the one in ancient Greek literature between the idealistic and the realistic, or cynical, views of justice. Completely unlike the Greek people, who tolerated irreverent portrayals of their gods—Dionysus defecates in Aristophanes's *Frogs*—the Hebrews single-mindedly worshiped an awesome God whose Law must be obeyed, lest the people perish. The Decalogue is ascribed in Exodus directly to Yahweh, who is depicted as dictating it to his amanuensis, Moses. And the Book of Deuteronomy "implies that all the commands contained therein were given directly to Moses by

Jahweh" (Robson 31, 32). There are, however, two stories that, to the modern "absurdist" mind, reveal a radical discontinuity between man's understanding and feelings, on the one hand, and God's mysterious justice, on the other. These are the stories of the binding of Isaac and the sufferings of Job. Yet both were written, not in order to question God's ways, but to enforce obedience to Him. The modern reader of the former tale experiences terror whcn Abraham binds Isaac, lays him upon the wooden litter, and "stretche[s] forth his hand, and t[akes] the knife to slay his son." Yet we know that the story has a happy ending: Isaac's life is spared, and God's angel tells Abraham of God's vow:

> That in blessing I will bless thee, and in multiplying I will multiply thy seed as the stars of the heaven, and as the sand which is upon the sea shore; and thy seed shall possess the gate of his enemies;
> And in thy seed shall the nations of the earth be blessed; because thou hast obeyed my voice.[13]

The aspect of the story most strongly emphasized in medieval Christian literature was the obedience to God of both Abraham and Isaac. Among the surviving Middle English dramatizations of the tale, the York "Abraham and Isaac" is especially notable because its Isaac is a thirty-year-old man rather than a child. Far from rebelling against what modern readers tend to see as God's injustice, Isaac is well pleased—since he knows it is God's will— to be "cut up and burned in fire." But because he knows that his flesh will fear the brand and overcome his desire to submit, he urges Abraham to bind him:

> For father, when I am bound,
> My might may not avail,
> Here shall no fault be found
> To make your promise fail.[14]

The other five extant Middle English dramatizations evoke, more or less, the pathos of the situation, but in none does it occur to either father or son to disobey God's command. In the Brome version, Isaac tries to comfort Abraham by reminding him that he has other children, "one or two, / The which you should love well by nature"; and an epilogue tells the audience it should not "grudge against" God, whatever He sends:

> For when he will, he may it amend,
> His commandments truly if you keep with good heart. . . . (90, 98–99)

What is most arresting in all these plays is the expansion of Isaac's role from that of the Old Testament character who is silent after saying "Behold the fire and the wood: but where is the lamb for a burnt-offering?" (Gen. 22:7) to that of a son so devoted that he not only consents to his own sacrifice but also wishes to spare Abraham undue difficulty or pain. The present-day reader of the Biblical story may well imagine a look of dread in Isaac's eyes that intensifies Abraham's agony as he clutches the knife. But audiences of the medieval dramas must have perceived the impending sacrifice as an altogether submissive collaboration between father and son.

From an "absurdist" perspective, the Book of Job presents an even more urgent problem than the Isaac story does, because it is closer to the texture of our everyday life. That Job, a decent, kindly man, could be tormented with God's permission is absurd in Camus's sense: there is an unbridgeable gap between our reason, which asks "Why?" and the evident irrationality of what is happening. The early readers of the Book of Job, however, were undoubtedly chiefly impressed by the fact of God's ultimately replying to Job, actually speaking to him, as His angel speaks at the end of the Isaac story to Abraham. Job himself seems to believe, in the depth of his suffering, that God will reply to his agonized questions. Dismissing the homilies of his "comforters," who make "all the shop-worn arguments for the existence of a direct relationship between suffering and sin,"[15] Job declares that God destroys both the innocent and the wicked, and he passionately interrogates the Lord:

> I will say unto God, Do not condemn me; shew me wherefore thou contendest with me.
>
> Is it good unto thee that thou shouldest oppress, that thou shouldest despise the work of thine hands, and shine upon the counsel of the wicked? (10:2–3)
>
> . . . .
>
> Though he slay me, yet will I trust in him: but I will maintain my own ways before him. (13:15)

The Lord's eventual reply to Job, "out of the whirlwind," does not, of course, answer Job's questions. It consists, rather, of counter-questions that accentuate mortal man's ignorance of God's ways:

> Where wast thou when I laid the foundations of earth? declare, if thou hast understanding.
> Who hath laid the measures thereof, if thou knowest? or who hath stretched the line upon it? (38:1, 4–5)

Job exults now—not because he has received an "answer" from God, but because God has "appeared" before him:

> I have heard of thee by the hearing of the ear: but now mine eye seeth thee.
> Wherefore I abhor myself, and repent in dust and ashes. (42:5–6)

Biblical scholar Isaac Rabinowitz has referred to the "quasi-palpable dimension of words" in the Old Testament.[16] The words that Job has *heard* here he identifies with the experience of *seeing* the Lord. This is the really convincing "happy ending" of the Book of Job in comparison with which the didactic happy ending— God's giving Job twice the wealth he once had and the same number of sons and daughters he has lost—is paltry stuff. So is the "very late Hebrew" prose introduction (Albright 33), where God grants Satan permission to test Job's loyalty. But both the didactic ending and the prologue serve the Biblical purpose of teaching man to submit and be faithful to a God whose justice transcends his own limited powers of comprehension. During the Middle Ages, Christians considered the Book of Job edifying, as they did the Isaac tale. In Chaucer's translation, "The Tale of Melibee," of a French translation of a twelfth-century Latin work, Melibeus's noble wife urges her husband not to grieve excessively after three of his foes have seriously wounded his daughter. Rather, she advises, Melibeus should emulate "patient Job," who, after his far greater tribulations, said: " 'Oure Lord hath yeve it me; oure Lord hath biraft it me; right as oure Lord hath wold, right so it is doon; blessed be the name of oure Lord!' "[17]

To the modern absurdist mind, the injustice of Job's suffering is plain. In Christian as well as Jewish tradition, however, it is Job's loyal patience, rather than his excruciating perplexity over God's apparent injustice, that became proverbial.

ROMAN AND EARLY AND MEDIEVAL EUROPEAN LITERATURE

The early Christians, much like the Hebrews, saw themselves as a chosen people. Their overwhelming concern was the God "above" who loved, punished, and rewarded them. The Greeks, on the other hand, whether idealists like Aeschylus or realists like Euripides, had been, in Aristotle's terms, "political animals." They were intensely concerned with the meaning and doing of justice in the polis they inhabited. The Romans, inheritors and translators of Hellenic culture, also understood justice in political terms. Ennius, fragments of whose Latin adaptation of Aeschylus's *Eumenides* survive, propagated the Greek story in which Athena surpasses revenge-justice by establishing the Areopagus court. Two centuries later, Cicero, who gave Platonic titles to his own dialogues—the *Republic*, the *Laws*—had his spokesman, Marcus, say of the laws:

> Can you imagine any other field of debate that provides as much scope for considering the topics of man's natural endowments, the capacity of the human mind to realize those noble projects we were created to initiate and perfect, the relationships of men to one another as individuals, and the natural groupings of men into communities? In trying to explain these phenomena we may discover the first principles of law and justice.

Marcus defines "natural law," a concept that had earlier been expressed dramatically in *Antigone* and discussed by Aristotle, as "innate reason in the highest form, which tells us what we ought to do and forbids the contrary . . . , the measuring stick of right and wrong." Man, says Marcus, has in common with God, his creator, "the sense of right," and he adumbrates a universalist ideal of justice:

> As [the sense of right] is, in reality, law, we should think of men and gods as linked together by law. Furthermore, those who are partners in law are necessarily also partners in justice, and those who share the same law and the same justice must be considered members of the same commonwealth. . . . the whole universe should be regarded as one commonwealth of men and gods.[18]

The phrase "one commonwealth of men and gods," inconceivable in a Hebrew or Christian context, vividly illustrates the

Romans' politico-social sense of justice. A similar notion of human fraternity, derived from Greek and Roman Stoic thinkers, appears in Lucretius's philosophic poem, *On the Nature of Things*. But since Lucretius was a materialist, his commonwealth was one created by men themselves. According to Lucretius, early mankind exhausted itself in feuds, then submitted freely to laws and codes. In consequence of that submission, it is not easy "for him who by his deeds transgresses the terms of the public peace to pass a tranquil and a peaceful existence. For though he eludes God and man, yet he cannot but feel a misgiving that his secret can be kept forever. . . ."[19] The reference to God here is merely conventional Epicurean rhetoric, for in Lucretius's atomic theory of the universe, "the gods" are completely inert. Yet Lucretius's materialism differs from that of Euripides and Thrasymachus; his reference to "the terms of the public peace" suggests a kind of contract based on a common human sense of justice. And the transgressor troubled by his "misgiving" is no Thrasymachean strong man, brutally defining justice in terms of his own interest. Although Lucretius does not speak of natural law, there seems little difference between such a law as defined by idealistic Cicero and the "laws and codes" to which, in Lucretius's materialistic view, mankind has submitted.

Significantly different from both Lucretius's ethical materialism and Cicero's idealism is the quietist Christian idealism of St. Augustine. A stark contrast between the earthly city—where both Cicero and Lucretius thought justice could be done—and the celestial city is the theme of Augustine's *City of God*, written shortly after the Visigoths sacked Rome in A.D. 410. The first earthly city, Augustine observes, was built by the Biblical murderer Cain; but his brother Abel, being only a "sojourner" here below, built none:

> For the city of the saints is above, although here below it begets citizens, in whom it sojourns till the time of its reign arrives, when it shall gather together all in the day of the resurrection; and then shall the promised kingdom be given to them, in which they shall reign with their Prince, the King of the ages, time without end.[20]

Though sufficiently Roman to use the city as a metaphor, and believing in a natural law prescribed by God that some "citizens" here below obeyed, Augustine had faith only in the heavenly polis that could never decay. Faithful followers of Augustine rendered unto Caesar what was Caesar's: they observed Roman laws. But the only judgment they were truly concerned with was the Last one. This is the spirit that informs the English poem "Dooms-day," adapted from a Latin poem evidently composed in the eighth century. While a "doom" was, historically, a law or decree applicable to a particular situation, the term "doomsday" is used figuratively in this work—as it gradually came to be used in everyday speech—to signify the day of God's final verdict on "the whole world." Then,

> the secret thoughts of all shall be revealed to all, all that the heart thought of evil, or the tongue uttered in malice, or the hand of man wrought of wickedness, of things on earth, in dark caves. . . . There the poor and the wealthy shall have one law. . . . Nor can any man there be bold near his Judge because of honourable works, but terror shall run alike through all. . . .[21]

A similar contrast between earthly injustice and heavenly justice informs the late medieval "mystery" drama *The Play of Coventry*. Jesus's condemnation to death and crucifixion in the part of the drama called "The Trial of Christ" are compensated for by the final judgments of men in "Doomesday."[22] What most strikingly differentiates this Augustinian Christian perspective from the per-spectives of idealistic Greeks and Romans is its concern with "secret thoughts . . . of evil," its denigration of "honourable works" that are performed out of pride, not humility. The Greeks and Romans were political beings precisely because they were interested in, and rewarded and condemned, not what people secretly thought or intended, but the acts they performed. But Augustine's insistence on a great gulf between the sinful earthly city and the flawless heavenly one dominated Western thought for eight centuries after the fall of Rome. Only in the thirteenth century did Aquinas's wedding of Christian faith to Aristotelian ideas rediscovered by Moslem and Jewish thinkers restore the possibility of justice to the polis. Man, though still perceived by Christians as a being with a soul to be saved, was also seen, once again, as a political animal. Aquinas's commentary on Book 5 of Aristotle's *Nicomachean Ethics* emphasizes the importance of natural law—the immutable ethical imperatives to which Cicero had referred—as thc basis for human law: "Every human law has just so much of the nature of law, as it is derived from the law of nature. But if in any point it deflects from the law of nature, it is no longer a law but a perversion of law."[23]

It has not been a simple matter, historically, to use the law of nature as a standard for positive law. Basil Willey observes that while Aristotle considered slavery to be in accordance with natural law, this view was contested in the Middle Ages. Willey also notes the contradictory invocations of natural law, through the ages, in defense of and in opposition to the private holding of property.[24] A twentieth-century exponent of natural law, Jacques Maritain, is undoubtedly thinking of just such conflicts when he writes that "the knowledge men have had" of the unwritten law "has passed through more diverse forms and stages than certain philosophers or theologians have believed." He adds that the knowledge "which our own moral conscience has of this law is doubtless itself still imperfect, and very likely it will continue to develop and to become more refined as long as humanity exists."[25]

Maritain's view that natural law itself is immutable, but that human knowledge of it becomes ever more refined clearly does not meet all objections to inconsistencies in interpretation of "the law of nature." His view does, however, accord with the evident belief of such thinkers as Aristotle, Cicero, Aquinas, Grotius, and Kant in the capacity of human reason to distinguish between natural law and its "perversion."

Dante, who knew well the works of Aquinas, including the commentary on the fifth book of Aristotle's *Nicomachean Ethics*, had no doubts about men's ability to know natural law. Banished from Florence in the middle of his life's journey, he reflected passionately upon the nature of justice and injustice in the polis. For he shared the traditional Greek and Roman belief that human beings realize themselves fully only by participating in politics. The heart of his treatise *De monarchia* is the idea of removing all temptations to cupidity—the greatest source of public injustice—from the monarch: "It must first be noted that the worst enemy of Justice is cupidity, as Aristotle signifies in the fifth book of Nicomachus. When cupidity is removed altogether, nothing remains inimical to Justice . . ." (Gilbert 36). Dante's most scathing judgments in the *Inferno* are not of private sins, but of betrayals of the city. For Brunetto Latini, the Florentine philosopher who had been his teacher, and whom he finds in Hell among the sodomites, he has only affectionate words:

> Still in my heart stays, memory's dear inmate,
>   The fatherly kind image, paining now,
>   Of you, when in the world early and late,
> You taught me how man may eternal grow.

And he attributes to Latini himself the language in which Florence is denounced in this scene as "that nest of malice and of greed."[26]

In the *Purgatorio*, Dante contrasts the vibrant city-spirit of Sordello's greeting to his fellow-Mantuan, Virgil, with present-day civil discord in Italy. City-dwellers, Dante declares, now spend their days in quarrel: "each one doth the other wound / Of those whom one wall and moat defend." He sarcastically praises Florence for its professions of justice, amid its corruption:

> Athens and Lacedaemon, famous still
>   For law-making and civil discipline,
>   Showed but a small hint of the Commonweal
> Compared with thee. . . . (216, 218)

For Dante, the love that moves the sun and the other stars is the source of justice, and his intense idealism impels him to bitter anger against those whom he sees perverting natural law in the polis. His Christian perspective differs as markedly as Aquinas's from that of Augustine.

Like Dante, William Langland was a political animal. His late fourteenth-century poem *Piers the Ploughman*, aspires as the *Commedia* does toward earthly justice as well as toward spiritual redemption. Part I, "William's Vision of Piers the Ploughman," begins with the narrator's dream of a splendid tower; the dream is reminiscent of a passage in the *Purgatorio* in which Dante, nostalgic for the Christianized Roman empire of the sixth century, when Justinian codified the laws in the *Corpus Juris Civilis*, called for a king who can discern "of the true city at least the tower" (270)— that is, see human law in relation to eternal law. Beneath the tower in "William's vision" is a great gulf with a dungeon in it, inhabited by Wrong. And between tower and gulf is "a smooth plain, thronged with all kinds of people," many of whom lead lives of labor or of prayer and penance, though some of them frequent what Bunyan would later call "Vanity Fair."[27] The sin that Langland will particularly attack is avarice, which Dante had also focused on in *De monarchia*.

William sees in his dream a dazzlingly dressed maiden, Fee, granddaughter of Wrong and daughter of Falsehood, who is about to wed Fraud. Another allegorical villain, Civil Law, authorizes a marriage deed drawn up by Falsehood. But Theology's indignant objection to this shocking union impels Civil Law to lay the case before the king's court. The monarch, reproving Lady Fee for accepting Fraud, asks her to wed Conscience if he will have her. Conscience, however, would "rather be damned" than marry such a faithless woman: " 'Christ! How her jewels mow down the magistrates! How she perjures herself in the law-courts, and chokes up the course of justice! Her florins fly so thick, that truth is smothered with them. She bends the law as she likes.' " Nevertheless the king is swayed by Fee's defense that she had "cheered his men up" during the recent "French wars" (49–50) and that a monarch must "fee those who serve him." Conscience must explain to the king what many politicians have perennially had trouble understanding: the difference between a "fair wage," which Conscience declines to call a fee, and a bribe (51). A spokesman for natural law in Langland's allegory, Conscience is not solely an allegorical figure. Equity courts arose in England around 1340 to permit "a disappointed litigant at common law to lay his plight before the sovereign." The king habitually referred such a litigant's petition to his Chancellor, a cleric who became known as the "Keeper of the King's Conscience."[28]

Only after a trial at law in which Fee seeks acquittal through bribery does the monarch see Fee's wickedness. Although he is determined to have "honest lawyers" from now on, Conscience warns him that he will need the common people's support if he is to govern according to justice. Whereupon the king grants to Conscience's friend, Reason, the power he requests to command obedience throughout the realm.

William now sees, in his dream, Reason preaching to the folk in a fair field. Reason's evangelistic effectiveness would impress a Billy Graham, for the Deadly Sins themselves—Pride, Lechery,

Envy, Anger, Avarice, Gluttony, and Sloth—confess their pec-
cancy. Avarice, however, to Langland as to Dante the most re-
doubtable enemy of justice, remains conspicuously unrepentant.
In a lively comic scene, Avarice solemnly swears that he will stop
selling short weight, and swindling customers, then assures Re-
pentance—who asks if he has ever made any "restitution"—that
he has: " 'I was staying at an inn once, with some merchants, and
while they were asleep I got up and burgled their bags.' " Repen-
tance corrects him: " 'That wasn't restitution, that was robbery.' " Avarice retorts, sounding like a medieval W. C. Fields,
" 'I thought restitution meant robbery. . . . I never learned to
read, and the only French I know comes from the wilds of
Norfolk' " (60, 61, 68).

The people of the realm decide, after hearing Reason preach, to
seek Truth. Piers Ploughman now appears, offering to guide them
if they will first help him sow his field. He symbolizes, at this
point, the peaceful industrial world envisioned by the prophet
Isaiah: "And they shall beat their swords into ploughshares, / And
their spears into pruning-hooks." The people accept Piers's offer,
but some of them prove to be shirkers, or truculent vagabonds.
Piers calls upon Hunger to drive these rogues, but as soon as
Hunger is satisfied, they again refuse to work. A more just society,
it seems, cannot be achieved until men are morally transformed.

In consequence, Part II of the poem, "William's Vision of Do-
Well, Do-Better, and Do-Best," concerns the attempts by Piers
Ploughman—whose first name, Piers or Peter, has become a
Christian symbol—to establish a Christian society. Justice, one of
the four Cardinal Virtues that Piers sows in men's souls, does not
fear "to correct even the king himself if he breaks the Law" (239).
Clearly, Langland is contrasting the justice of natural law with the
"divine right" of the king (a "right" which would become increasingly prominent in European political discourse) to rule as he
wished. The king asserts, indeed, that he is "the head of the Law,"
that he may seize whatever he wants. But Conscience warns him
that he may take only within *reason* what he needs (244).

Langland was plainly aware of the difficulty of keeping human
behavior, both kings' and commoners', within reason. His time
was one of frightful plagues and famines; the Black Death of
1348–49 had killed at least a third of the population, so much land

was long left untilled. In the final chapter of *Piers the Ploughman*, the narrator, now hungry and miserable, is told by Need that "in great necessity, Need may help himself, without consulting Conscience or the Cardinal Virtues—provided he keeps the Spirit of Moderation. For no Virtue can compare with this, not even justice or fortitude." The tough-minded compassionate Langland knows that people cannot act justly when they have neither land nor food. He reminds us of Thrasymachus when he has Need say that "the spirit of Justice is bound, willy nilly, to judge according to the king's policy or the people's measure" (246). But Langland is also deeply concerned to conform society to ethical natural law.

His idealism contrasts diametrically with the cynicism of the anonymous author of the French *Farce of the Worthy Master Patelin, the Lawyer*. The relationship of this fifteenth-century satire to *Piers the Ploughman* and the *Commedia* is similar to that of Aristophanes's ribald plays to Aeschylus's and Sophocles's noble dramas. The laughter of both Aristophanes and the author of Patelin comes from man's desire to thumb his nose at his own imperious moral sense. It is appropriately discordant that the earliest actors of Patelin were clerks of the Paris Palais de Justice. Like their superiors, the lawyers, the clerks formed a "corporation." One of its activities was the production of farces, as well as religious and morality plays, before legal confreres and the public. At Mardi Gras especially, the *basochiens*—members of the corporation—enacted grotesque trials of ridiculous cases.[29]

Patelin is a "Thrasymachean" variation on the themes of avarice and corruption which Dante and Langland treat as serious perversions of natural law. The lawyer-protagonist, Patelin, tricks a draper, Joceaulme, into selling him a beautiful cloth on credit, at what Joceaulme smugly considers an excessive price. When the draper comes for his money, Patelin feigns illness: his wife tells Joceaulme, with stylish chutzpah, that her husband has been in bed, on the point of death, "for thirteen weeks," and could not possibly have made a business deal. Joceaulme's bewildered insistence that he has spoken with Patelin that very morning evokes her retort, "Are you cracked or have you been drinking?"[30] Thwarted, Joceaulme leaves and vents his frustration on a shepherd, Lambkin, whom he accuses, quite accurately, of having stolen his sheep over a period of years. Lambkin denies the charge, then goes to Patelin to ask him to be his attorney. Pleasantly surprised by the high fee that Lambkin offers, Patelin takes the case, advising the shepherd to say nothing at all during the trial, except "Ba": "Only bleat like your sheep. No matter what they talk to you. Just say Ba. . . . Even if they call you an ass, an idiot, . . . don't answer anything but Ba. . . ."

Joceaulme finds the trial a nightmare. Whenever he begins discussing the stolen sheep, Patelin distracts him with outrageous mugging. At one point the confused draper accuses the shepherd of having taken "six yards of cloth. . . . I mean, sheep. . . ." Patelin delivers a malicious coup de grâce when he earnestly tells the judge that there is "surely something strange about this poor man's talk, and I would advise that a physician be consulted. At times, though, it seems as if he were talking about some money he owes this poor shepherd" (*Farce* 488, 491).

The farce ends with Lambkin's canny refusal to say anything but "Ba!" when Patelin demands the high fee he had offered. Thus, after one middle-class rogue has duped another, both are duped by a shepherd, whose name suggests a wolf in sheep's clothing (493–94).

In addition to being funny, this cynical play has the merit of keeping us on the *qui vive* for what is unconsciously amusing in the idealistic literature of justice. Dante, for example, puts Ulysses in the eighth circle of Hell for "fraudulently" using the wooden horse to capture Troy. Dante's reasoning obviously is that the Trojans were ancestors of the Romans (for he subscribes to this legend), whose great period he reverently remembers. But his pietistic punishment of Ulysses has nothing to do with ideal justice.

NATURAL LAW AND ITS ADVERSARIES IN RENAISSANCE LITERATURE

From the perspective of a Florentine later than Dante, Machiavelli, Ulysses's stratagem would merit praise. Chapter 40 of the *Discourses*, called "Deceit in the Conduct of a War Is Meritorious," commends Hannibal for feigning flight "on the lake of Perugia . . . for the purpose of hemming in the Consul and the Roman army," and for attaching "blazing fagots to the horns of his cattle to enable him to escape from the hands of Fabius Maximus."[31] Nature, for Machiavelli, and life itself, were "a perpetual struggle of one kind with another for prepotence,"[32] a struggle in which all means were justified by the end in view. His *The Prince* was a treatise for aspiring rulers, dedicated to Lorenzo the Magnificent and based on close observation of ruthless careers like that of Cesare Borgia. A prudent ruler, Machiavelli counsels, ought not to keep faith when to do so would be against his interest: "If men were all good, this precept would not be a good one; but as they are bad, and would not observe their faith with you, so you are not bound to keep faith with them" (Machiavelli 64).

This ruthless rejection of natural law both accorded with and encouraged the cynical practices of Renaissance monarchs. When Machiavelli pleads in *The Prince* with Lorenzo to liberate Italy from a "barbarous domination" by foreign powers that "stinks in the nostrils of everyone" (98), he speaks with no *moral* authority at all, but simply with a yearning for a powerful, independent Italian state.

That the idea of natural law was, nevertheless, vigorously alive at the beginning of the sixteenth century is indicated by the tone and substance of Sir Thomas More's *Utopia.* Clearly inspired by Plato's *Republic,* the work depicts a society whose good king, Utopus, had brought a "rude and wild people" to excellent perfection in all good fashions, humanity, and civil gentleness.[33] Among these people, who live together "lovingly," the magistrates are called "fathers," and the prince is distinguished from other persons only "by a little sheaf of corn carried before him" (103). More's narrator, Raphael Hythloday, calls Utopia the sole society deserving the name of commonwealth. For in Utopia (playing on Greek prefixes, More hopes that his "ou-topia," or "no place," will inspire the creation of an actual "eu-topia,"a good place), all things are owned in common: "though no man have anything, every man is rich." In other so-called commonwealths, however, "who knoweth not that he shall starve for hunger, unless he make some several provision for himself, though the commonwealth flourish never so much in riches?" (130–31).

The Utopians, in addition to practicing common ownership, make no use of money except for foreign trade and the hiring of foreign soldiers in emergencies. It is true that More, speaking for himself after recording Hythloday's tale of his sojourn in Utopia, apparently objects to "the community of their life and living without any occupying of money." But he is being ironic. After the expression "occupying of money," there is the following parenthetical phrase: "(by the which thing only all nobility, magnificence, worship, honour, and majesty, the true ornaments and honours, as the common opinion is, of a commonwealth, utterly be overthrown and destroyed)" (135). The phrase "as the common opinion is" is a smiling giveaway. Perhaps More's joke is intended to remind us of the most charming aspect of his Utopia: that, there, reason "stirreth and provoketh" the inhabitants to lead life "out of care in joy and mirth" (85).

The conflict between More's idealistic approach to statecraft and justice and Machiavelli's cynical one recalls the dispute between Socrates and Thrasymachus. But one respect in which the six- teenth century A.D. differed from the fourth century B.C. was that strong monarchs in France, Spain, and England were equating the law with their own wills in defiance of traditional natural law, which accorded with common reason. Another difference in the sixteenth century from Plato's era was the spiritual predominance of a church that subscribed to the concept of natural law, but which was beginning to be torn by schisms. The Catholics who killed Protestants during the Reformation, and the Protestants who killed Catholics as well as other Protestants, all professed to believe in natural law. Amid the tumults of his age, Montaigne asked, "How many condemnations have I seene more criminall, than the crime it selfe?" He commented on justice in terms at least as subversive of natural law as Machiavelli's had been. For he recalled the Stoics' opinion "that Nature her selfe in most of her workes, proceedeth against justice"; the idea of the "Cyre- naiques," that nothing is just of itself—that customs and laws "frame justice"; and the notion of the Theodorians that a "wise man" may justly practice "theft, sacriledge and paillardise, so he thinks it profitable for him."[34]

Edmund Spenser reflects in a way that differs from Montaigne's a weakening of the universalist ideal of natural law. His The Faerie Queene is directly related to the increased power, in the sixteenth century, of the national state. When Spenser began writing it, he thought of depicting twelve "Aristotelian virtues," each one to be symbolized by a different knight serving the "faerie queene," Gloriana—Elizabeth I. The virtues actually represented in the six books that Spenser completed are not all Aristotelian (nowhere, for example, does Aristotle mention "Holiness," the subject of the first book). But Justice, the virtue celebrated in Book 5, "The Legend of Artegall," is discussed by the Greek philosopher, who defines it in the *Nicomachean Ethics*: "Just conduct is a mean between committing and suffering injustice; for to commit injustice is to have too much, and to suffer it is to have too little."[35] Spenser's Proem to "The Legend of Artegall" echoes this definition. After lamenting the world's decline from the golden age to the present "stonie one," Spenser recalls how, anciently, "good was onely for it selfe desyred, / And all men sought their owne, and none no more."[36] There is a marked difference, however, between Aristotle's discussion of two kinds of political justice, "one natural and the other legal,"[37] and Spenser's celebration in "Artegall" of an "imperial" justice (277) that monarchs—or at least, one infers from Book 5, Protestant monarchs like Elizabeth—are given by God the power to dispense. Aristotle distinguishes between a natural justice which is valid everywhere and a legal justice which may take one form or another, but which, "once laid down, is decisive." Although everything is subject to change in the world, natural law does exist, and it is easy to see "what sort of thing . . . is so by nature and what is not, but is legal and conventional" (*Ethics* 190). Aristotle's tone is rational and impersonal. Spenser's apostrophe to Justice, on the other hand, compares this "sacred virtue" to "God in his imperiall might," who both does justice and lends to Princes the power to do it,

> And makes them like himselfe in glorious sight,
> To sit in his owne seate, his cause to end,
> And rule his people right, as he doth recommend. (Spenser 277)

Spenser's language resembles that of James VI of Scotland in his famous defense of divine right, the "Trew Law of Free Monarchies," issued in 1598, two years after the publication of the second half of *The Faerie Queene*. Just as Spenser says that God makes kings "to sit in his own seate," James cites the Biblical David's reference to kings as Gods "because they sit upon God his

Throne in the earth." James then demonstrates that the ancient Scottish kings were "the authors and makers of the Lawes, and not the Lawes of the kings."[38]

In an arresting article on "Spenser and British Imperialism" (one seems to hear, while reading this Edwardian piece, the strains of "Land of Hope and Glory"), Edwin Greenlaw calls Spenser "the laureate of the new England, defending that national policy which, however cruel and narrow in some of its applications, was to enable her to thwart the foes that threatened her destruction." According to Greenlaw, Spenser "conceives of the State as Machiavelli conceived it; to him the Prince is the State."[39]

This, however, seems an oversimplification. Spenser's language is not Machiavellian, but rather a conflation of the language of classical-Christian idealism with that of the divine-right theorists. Divine right theory, though not typical of medieval thought, had been adumbrated in Duns Scotus's insistence on the primacy of God's will, as distinguished from Aquinas's insistence on His reasonableness. Wycliffe, in the fourteenth century, had espoused the divine-right theory, calling the king "the vicar of God."[40] But only in the sixteenth century did this voluntaristic theory of kingship become widely accepted. Spenser's combination of divine-right language with the language of idealism is exemplified in the trial of Duessa before Mercilla. Duessa here represents Mary, Queen of Scots, Elizabeth's Catholic cousin and rival for the throne. Mercilla symbolizes the sovereign Elizabeth under the sway of mercy. Before the trial begins, Mercilla is described as sitting

> in souerayne Maiestie,
> Holding a Scepter in her royall hand,
> The sacred pledge of peace and clemencie,
> With which high God had blest her happie land.

Attending the sovereign are three "lovely daughters of high Jove," whose role is to intercede with mortal princes in behalf of supplicants. The daughters are Eunomie (Good Law), Eirene (Peace), and Dice (Justice) (318). As an attendant, Justice is symbolically subordinated to the monarch's will. One is reminded of Frank Kermode's observation that Elizabeth I insisted upon her role "as head of a church founded by Joseph of Arimathaea and a State that inherited the powers of the Constantinian Empire."[41] Machiavellian cynicism is not Spenser's attitude; he simply assumes that Christian (Protestant) Mercilla sits on God's throne.

Zele, a prosecuting attorney, proceeds to give evidence of the beautiful Duessa's treacherous designs. The first of the "many grave persons" who substantiate Zele's charges is silver-haired Kingdomes care. Immediately after him, Authority testifies (319). Only after those allegorical figures representing the State itself do the traditional figures Religion and Justice plead against Duessa. Spenser's tone thus differs markedly from that of the medieval Langland, who made Reason the dominant figure in the trial of Lady Fee. The change in tone between Langland and Spenser accompanied the rise of rival European monarchs whose conceptions of justice were quite pragmatic. Machiavelli shocked his contemporaries by breaking brutally with the idealistic tradition. Spenser, on the other hand, makes it easy for his patriotic Protestant countrymen to identify Mercilla-Elizabeth with all virtue and Duessa-Mary with all vice. When the trial ends, Mercilla plainly sees Duessa's guilt, yet refuses to

> let iust vengeance on her light;
> But rather let instead thereof to fall
> Few perling drops from her faire lampes of light. (320)

Thus Spenser reduces to pure pity the complex moral and political reasons for Elizabeth's hesitancy in 1587 to order Mary's execution.

From a Catholic viewpoint, Spenser's depiction of Mercilla-Elizabeth as the incarnation of God's will, and of Justice and Mercy, would have seemed hypocritical. Mary Queen of Scots was a legitimate heir of Henry VIII; indeed, her son, author of the "Trewe Law of Free Monarchies," would succeed Elizabeth on the English throne as James I. Elizabeth, on the other hand, was the child of a marriage annulled by the Anglican Church just before the beheading—arranged by her father, Henry VIII—of her mother, Anne Boleyn. Two centuries after *The Faerie Queene*, Schiller's *Maria Stuart* would arouse sympathy for Elizabeth's rival by showing the doomed woman not only as a repentant sinner but also as a defendant denied the common right of confronting witnesses testifying against her.[42]

The chief interest of Spenser's handling of justice in *The Faerie Queene* is that it helps to undermine the ideal of natural law. On what basis, one wonders, would he have opposed Mary Stuart's divine will if she had won the war with Elizabeth for the crown? Christopher Marlowe, and other Elizabethans fascinated by Machiavelli, might have had less difficulty than the idealistic Spenser in accepting Mary as queen. Think of the Prologue to Marlowe's *The Jew of Malta*, spoken by "Machiavel":

> Many will talk of title to a crown:
> What right had Caesar to the empery?
> Might first made kings, and laws were then most sure
> When like the Draco's they were writ in blood.[43]

Machiavellian villainy is punished in the fifth act of the play. But in *The Jew of Malta* as in other Elizabethan-Jacobean dramas, the punishment is less important than the crime which precedes it. Harry Levin remarks in a discussion of Ben Jonson's *Volpone* that although the final courtroom scene "reverses the decision of the fourth act," "by that time our faith in lawyers and judges and Venetians and human beings has become corroded."[44]

The wealthy "magnifico," Volpone, assisted by his "parasite," Mosca, pretends in this comedy to be dying in order to extort bribes from persons with greedy expectations. One such character forces his own wife to visit Volpone; only the intervention of a young man, Bonario, who happens to be on the premises, prevents her from being raped by the vulpine grandee. At a rigged trial, clever Mosca transforms Bonario's intervention into an assault, in which the woman was an accomplice, upon Volpone and himself. When one of the crooked trial judges asks the defendants to name their witnesses, Bonario replies, "Our consciences," and the woman adds, "And Heaven, that never fails the innocent." But they are told that "[t]hese are no testimonies." To which Bonario bitterly retorts, "Not in your courts, / Where multitude and clamour overcomes"(IV.2, p. 263). We should recall at this point the cynical advice about comportment in Venice which Sir Politic Wouldbe, an English traveler, has earlier in the play given a young compatriot:

> . . . beware
> You never speak a truth—

. . . .
And, for your part, protest, were there no other
But simply the laws o' the land, you could content you.
Nick Machiavel and Monsieur Bodin both
Were of this mind. (IV.1, p. 246)

The repudiation of natural law attributed to "Machiavel" and Bodin must have sent a guilty thrill through audiences torn, like Jonson himself, between traditional faith and contemporary relativism.

The frame-up of the two innocents is reversed in Act V after Volpone discovers that Mosca has betrayed him. This falling-out of knaves is reminiscent—perhaps this was the classicist Jonson's intention—of Socrates's argument that injustice sets even those who practice it at variance with each other. But there is a mechanicalness about the distribution of punishments at the end of the play which depreciates them. One's most vivid memory of a good performance of *Volpone* is the villain's zest.

SHAKESPEARE'S PLAYS

The Elizabethan-Jacobean conflict between a realistic or cynical view of justice and an idealistic view based on a belief, however weakened, in natural law is reflected in a very complex way in Shakespeare's dramas. His famous "trial" play, *The Merchant of Venice*, has inspired innumerable lawyerly discussions, some of which express contempt for Shakespeare's legal knowledge. To focus on legal procedure, however, is to misconstrue the play's concerns. For the fundamental issue between Shylock, the Jewish usurer, and Antonio, the Gentile merchant, is not resolvable in a law court. Shakespeare's essential subject is a battle in a war between two communities that had been enemies since the first Crusades. The Jews had been expelled from Christian England in the thirteenth century, Christian France in the fourteenth, Christian Spain and Portugal in the fifteenth. Where they were tolerated in Europe, they were virtually restricted to commercial occupations. Their ghettoization, which was partly their own choice, partly Gentile policy, confirmed their alien status. At the folklore level, *The Merchant of Venice* is about a cruel moneylender whom audiences are glad to see refused his pound of flesh. But although Shylock is in part a stereotype, he also articulates a viewpoint that Elizabethan audiences, habituated to plays like *The Jew of Malta*, rarely heard: that of a Jew opposing the Gentile power elite. When on behalf of his friend Bassanio, the Venetian merchant Antonio asks Shylock to lend him three thousand ducats, for which his own property is to be collateral, Shylock scathingly reminds him of some personal history:

> You call me misbeliever, cut-throat dog
> And spit upon my Jewish gaberdine,
> And all for use of that which is my own.
> Well then, it now appears you need my help.
> Go to then, you come to me and you say,
> "Shylock, we would have moneys," you say so—
> You that did void your rheum upon my beard,
> And foot me as you spurn a stranger cur
> Over your threshold.[45]

Because the "stranger cur's" hatred of Antonio exceeds his desire to make money, he will take no interest on the sum he agrees to lend the merchant. But if the ducats are not returned within three months, Shylock is to cut a pound of flesh from Antonio's body. The moneylender's tone throughout the scene clearly indicates that he would rather lose the loan than the chance to avenge himself physically upon the Gentile who has spat upon him.

At the trial occasioned by Antonio's inability, owing to the apparent loss of his ships, to repay the loan, the Duke, sitting as judge, professes to believe that Shylock's insistence upon the pound of flesh is a mere game. Shylock's reply evinces his absolute seriousness: it is solely out of "loathing" for Antonio that he is following what he describes as a "losing suit." Whether a "losing suit" means a lawsuit in which he has nothing to gain, or one in which the cards are stacked against him, Shylock's impassioned attitude is that of a lover rather than a merchant. The pound of flesh, he declares, belongs to him as much as the Venetian Gentiles' purchased slaves, "which . . . *you* use in abject and slavish parts" (IV.i.91–92) belong to them.

This mordant equation does him no good. The Duke threatens to dismiss the court, failing the appearance of a scholar he has summoned to determine the issue. The scholar, of course, proves to be Portia, disguised as a male Doctor of Laws. It does not matter whether it is as a supposed amicus curiae or a supposed judge that she now takes over the trial. What should matter to us is that the "scholar" is not disinterested, that she is the fiancée of Bassanio, whose desire to woo her had led him to ask Antonio for financial aid. In addition, she is sheltering in her house Shylock's daughter, Jessica, whose love for the Gentile Lorenzo has led her to run away from her father's home. Portia's blatantly inappropriate courtroom role does not militate against the general human truth of her "quality of mercy" speech; it does, however, cast doubt on the moral lucidity of her plea that Shylock should consider, when he demands justice,

> That in the course of justice, none of us
> Should see salvation. We do pray for mercy
> And that same prayer, doth teach us all to render
> The deeds of mercy. . . . (IV.i.199–202)

Portia gives no indication of regretting Antonio's mercilessly contemptuous behavior toward Shylock. We must listen to her "mercy" speech with a third ear that detects what Shakespeare is saying to compassionate auditors. He is asking not simply for mercy on Shylock's part, but also for reciprocal forbearance between Jews and Gentiles, the mitigation of the ancient conflict in which "justice" has been used as a weapon by both communities. Such forbearance is commanded by the Golden Rule, a central tenet of both Jewish and Christian natural law.

Shylock's harsh insistence on "[t]he penalty and forfeit of my bond" (IV.i.207) evokes a judicial ruling that the nineteenth-century German jurist Rudolph von Ihering has censured. He calls Portia's decision—that if in cutting the pound of flesh Shylock sheds "one drop of Christian blood," his property will be "confiscate unto the state of Venice" (IV.i.309–12)—mere trickery. It violates, says Ihering, the spirit of the Roman law of the Twelve Tables, which imposed no such restriction on a creditor authorized to operate on his debtor's body.[46] But this legal argument misses the central point of *The Merchant of Venice*, which is that only charity can overcome hatreds that the law perpetuates. Portia's words to Shylock about "the deeds of mercy" condemn, though she does not realize this, the very penalties imposed on the moneylender after she has turned his civil suit against Antonio into a criminal trial of Shylock himself. The Duke remits the penalty of death to which, according to Portia, the "alien" Shylock is subject for having sought the life of the "citizen," Antonio. But this pardon becomes conditional: the moneylender must, as Antonio has urged, convert to Christianity and will all his possessions to his son-in-law and daughter. Such coercions mock justice.

The ideal of charity, beyond Portia's skewed charity, is exemplified not in the trial scene, but in the tender colloquy between the married lovers, Jessica and Lorenzo, at the beginning of Act V. Especially resonant is Lorenzo's speech beginning, "How sweet the moonlight sleeps upon this bank!"

> Here will we sit and let the sounds of music
> Creep in our ears. Soft stillness and the night
> Become the touches of sweet harmony.
> Sit, Jessica. Look how the floor of heaven
> Is thick inlaid with patens of bright gold.
> There's not the smallest orb which thou behold'st
> But in his motion like an angel sings,
> Still quiring to the young-ey'd cherubins;
> Such harmony is in immortal souls,
> But while the muddy vesture of decay
> Doth grossly close it in, we cannot hear it. (V.i.54–65)

Shakespeare finds in nature emblems of a concord that contrasts with the dissonance in the Duke's courtroom. Is it the "muddy vesture of decay" that has prevented both Shylock and the Christian enforcers of a biased positive law from apprehending an "immortal" harmony? Or can the inveterate hostility between two communities be healed? The question seems open at the end of *The Merchant of Venice*. It is the absence from such later plays as *Measure for Measure* and *King Lear* of a truly hopeful or persuasive evocation of natural law that makes them so dark.

Measure for Measure is a disturbing puzzle. The Duke of Vienna's behavior in the last three acts, and especially in the final one, is strangely inconsistent with his announced concern with civil justice at the beginning of the play.

The Duke has a twofold purpose in authorizing Angelo to rule in his place during his own pretended absence from the city. He wants to observe, in disguise, his deputy's conduct in order to learn how pure this apparent puritan actually is. And what is more important from the standpoint of the public weal is the Duke's desire to reform dissolute Vienna, where "liberty plucks justice by the nose" (I.iii.29), by enabling a sterner man than he to enforce laws long unused.

Angelo immediately implements a draconian law against fornication by ordering the arrest and condemnation to death of Claudio, whose fiancée is pregnant. Claudio's sister, a novice in a religious order, visits Angelo to plead for her brother's life. Her plea, in response to the deputy's curt remark that Claudio is "a forfeit of the law," recalls Portia's "mercy" speech to Shylock:

> Why, all the souls that were were forfeit once,
> And He that might the vantage best have took
> Found out the remedy. How would you be
> If He, which is the top of judgment, should
> But judge you as you are? O, think on that,
> And mercy then will breathe within your lips,
> Like man new made. (II.ii.71.73–79)

There is, it is true, an important difference between Portia's appeal and Isabella's. Portia is begging a private person to put mercy above harsh justice in a matter that concerns him and another private person. Isabella, on the other hand, is pleading with a public officer whose charge is the enforcement of law, to act in the spirit of Jesus's injunction "Judge not, that ye be not judged." Renaissance theorists, attempting to resolve the conflict between justice and mercy for government leaders, tended to turn not to the Pentateuch or the Gospels but to classical texts, Cicero's *De officiis* and Seneca's *De clementia*, which emphasized the "*via media* of equity founded upon reason."[47] And indeed, not only a modern audience, but a Jacobean one as well, would find the death penalty for Claudio unreasonable. For Claudio is all but formally married to his fiancée: the "true contract" (I.ii.145) between them to which he refers is a form of betrothal—"*de praesenti*"—that was "recognized by English common law as a valid marriage" (Lever lxv). Hence Angelo, were he a different sort of deputy, would not even have arrested Claudio, but would have found ample opportunity to enforce, against actual criminals, laws long flouted in

Vienna. The deputy, however, is a puritan for whom any civil law must be applied to the letter. His problem, when the virgin novice, Isabella, asks him to treat her brother as an exception, is that his lust is stirred by her very purity. He asks her to visit him a second time, and when she does, he turns her plea for Claudio to his own ends. "Might there not be a charity in sin," he asks, "[t]o save this brother's life?" Joyfully misinterpreting this, Isabella thinks Angelo intends to "sin" by being merciful (II.iv.63–64, 66). He disabuses her by declaring that only her sexual surrender to him can prevent Claudio's execution. Isabella's indignant threat to tell the world of his villainy elicits both Angelo's assertion that nobody would believe her and a terrible ultimatum: either she consents, by the following day, to yield to him or Claudio will be tortured to death. Thus the magistrate who has condemned a betrothed man to die for fornication is prepared either to commit a vicious crime against him or virtually to rape his sister.

Isabella, in soliloquy, is certain that Claudio would rather die than have her submit to "pollution." She is wrong. When she visits him in his prison cell, he begs her to do what Angelo has demanded, in order that he may live. As icily virtuous as the deputy is reputed to be, Isabella calls Claudio a coward, telling him with contempt that she will say a thousand prayers for his death (III.i.136–45).

Up to this point, *Measure for Measure* is structurally coherent: Angelo has revealed, and discovered—for in soliloquy he is honest with himself—his cruel concupiscence. Isabella, who does not articulate to herself the contradiction of refusing to save, by fornicating with Angelo, the life of the brother whose fornication she had asked the deputy to pardon, simply affirms that she will not violate God's law. But the play now takes an odd turn. The Duke, disguised as a friar, tells Isabella, after eavesdropping on her conversation with Claudio, that she may redeem him "from the angry law." His plan calls for her to agree ostensibly to Angelo's *quid pro quo*, thus tricking him into a nighttime meeting with his own fiancée, Mariana, whom he had deserted years before but who loves him the more violently for his "unjust kindness." If this scheme succeeds, Angelo will possess Mariana, thinking she is Isabella; and when their intercourse becomes publicly known he will be compelled to marry his fiancée, Claudio will be spared, and Isabella's honor will be safe (III.i.197–258).

Now, the "bed trick" was a Renaissance literary convention; a Jacobean audience might be expected to enjoy the idea of Mariana's "catching" her faithless man. But the Duke's project—which is carried out without a hitch—is bizarre in the light of both Isabella's religious vocation and the high moral intentions that the Duke has declared at the beginning of *Measure for Measure*. For what is involved is a collaboration between a "friar" and a nun-to-be in urging a woman to fornicate with a man not yet her husband. It is pertinent to note here that the "spousals" of Angelo and Mariana differ from those of Claudio and his Juliet: the former pair have simply made a sworn declaration of their intention to marry at some time in the future (their betrothal comes under the head of *sponsalia per verba de futuro* rather than *sponsalia per verba de praesenti*), and this declaration is not absolutely binding. It is true that sexual intercourse between the parties to such a betrothal automatically converted it into absolute marriage (Lever liii–liv), but from the perspective of the Duke, who has been concerned about excessive "liberty" in Vienna, as well as from the viewpoint of the "friar" he pretends to be, the bed trick seems strange.

The moral fog in the play thickens from here on. Angelo, after falling into the "friar's" trap, and assuming that Mariana is actually Isabella, fears that Claudio will someday avenge his sister's defloration. The deputy therefore orders Claudio killed and gives instructions that the dead man's severed head be sent to him as proof of the execution. The Duke, however, still disguised as a friar, persuades the warden to spare Claudio and to send the deputy the head of another prisoner, who has just died. This trick prepares a confrontation between the Duke, supposedly returned from abroad, and Angelo. But the confrontation proves bizarre, and its outcome disturbing.

The Duke's plan for publicly exposing Angelo's corruptness involves keeping up the pretense, even after Angelo's confession of guilt and a request for his own execution, that Claudio is actually dead. This deception seems unnecessarily cruel to Isabella, or at least it would be if Isabella's reaction were "normal." But as troubling as the Duke's declaration that "The very mercy of the law cries out / . . . 'An Angelo for Claudio; death for death! / . . .

Like doth quit like, and *Measure* still for *Measure*' " is Isabella's
response when Mariana begs her to plead for Angelo's life. She
asks the Duke to look upon the condemned deputy "as if my
brother lived," then concentrates on the difference between Claudio's crime of fornication and Angelo's failure to commit the
fornication he intended:

> . . . My brother had but justice,
> In that he did the thing for which he died;
> For Angelo,
> His act did not o'ertake his bad intent,
> And must be buried but as an intent
> That perish't by the way. . . . (V.i.448–53)

In this speech there is an incoherent "charity" toward Angelo and
an odd impersonality toward Claudio. The moral vacuum at this
point in the play is not filled once the Duke brings forth the living
Claudio; for after setting him free for the sake of Isabella, to
whom he almost parenthetically proposes marriage, the Duke also
frees Angelo. Although it has earlier been made clear that Claudio
loves the woman he has made pregnant, while Angelo had abandoned his own fiancée, the Duke urges Claudio to "restore" her
whom he has "wrong'd" and enjoins Angelo to love Mariana.
Finally—curiouser and curiouser—Angelo is asked to "forgive"
the substitution of the dead prisoner's head for Claudio's (V.i.525–
39).

    Measure for Measure has been read by some critics as a Christian
play in which mercy ultimately triumphs over harsh legalism.[48]
The mercy shown to Angelo, however, seems mindless. Having
authorized the deputy to enforce hard laws, the Duke now evokes
cynical laughter throughout Vienna—we would hear it if the play
had a sixth act—by smiling upon the subverter of the common
weal. In a sense, the "cleanest" character in *Measure for Measure* is
the bawd, Pompey, who asks if the new regime, determined to
extirpate fornication, intends to "geld and splay all the youth of
the city" (II.i.230–31). This query seems less far removed from
ethical natural law than is the Duke's inexplicable subversion in
Act V of the civil order he had declared endangered in Act I.

    There is a sort of moral wasteland in *Measure for Measure* and
other plays that Shakespeare wrote near the beginning of the

seventeenth century. It is true that the locus classicus of the Elizabethan belief in an interdependent cosmic and social harmony is Ulysses's speech on degree in *Troilus and Cressida* (I.iii.75–137). This belief, however, is subverted by the tenor of the play itself. Hector, the one admirable character, is treacherously killed by Achilles, and the past words of the drama are spoken by a bawd. In *Hamlet*, on the other hand, there are some intimations of natural law: Claudius knows that the murder of his brother "smells to heaven" and is convinced that though he may escape earthly punishment, there is "no shuffling" above (III.iii.36–61). Furthermore, at the end of the play, with the arrival of Fortinbras, order is restored in Denmark. Yet the play is haunted by Hamlet's "to be or not to be" soliloquy, which evokes both the injustices and pains of this life and a frightening uncertainty about what follows death.

King Lear, the most nearly despairing of the early seventeenth-century tragedies, calls profoundly into question the concept of natural law, or, as Robert Heilman calls it, "a normal, ordered functioning of the moral world, a final principle to which all moral phenomena are to be referred."[49] Expecting Regan to act kindly toward him, Lear tells her she knows better than Goneril the "offices of nature, bonds of childhood" (II.iv.177–78). And Gloucester, thinking of Lear's unreasonable treatment of Cordelia, says,". . . the King falls from bias of nature; there's father against child" (I.ii.110–12). Yet it is upon natural lawlessness that Lear reflects when, after Regan and Goneril have refused him shelter, he is led by Kent to a hovel on the storm-tossed heath:

> Poor, naked wretches, whereso'er you are,
> That bide the pelting of this pitiless storm,
> How shall your houseless heads and unfed sides,
> Your loop'd and window'd raggedness, defend you
> From seasons such as these? O, I have ta'en
> Too little care of this! Take physic, pomp,
> Expose thyself to feel what wretches feel,
> That thou mayst shake the superflux to them,
> And show the heavens more just. (III.iv.28–36)

Lear says that by giving of his superfluous wealth to hungry wretches, he may make the heavens appear more just than they actually are. But if the very heavens are unjust, then Lear's sense of cosmic injustice cannot be based on "natural" law. It must be the result of a divorce between his moral sense and the nature from which it has sprung. Implicit, therefore, in his moving speech is the idea of man as a creator of moral values, not as part of a morally ordered universe.

Lear's expression of his sense of heavenly injustice is soon followed by his exposure of social injustice in the "trial" he conducts of Regan and Goneril. No sooner has he begun the trial conceived by his disturbed imagination than he thinks that Regan has escaped with the aid of one of the judges:

> Arms, arms, sword, fire! Corruption in the place!
> False justicer, why has thou let her scape? (III.vi.55–56)

The corruption of justice evoked by Lear is being exemplified at that moment—a movie could split the screen between Lear's farmhouse "law court" and Gloucester's castle—by Regan's husband, Cornwall, who after ordering his servants to find and bring back "the traitor Gloucester," observes Machiavellianly:

> Though well we may not pass upon his life
> Without the form of justice, yet our power
> Shall do a court'sy to our wrath, which men
> May blame, but not control. (III.vii.3, 24–27)

Accordingly, when Gloucester, who has just informed Kent of a plot against Lear, is brought to the castle, Cornwall puts out his eyes.

Meeting the blinded Gloucester, Lear cries that a man may see without eyes how the world goes: the protection of the law, unavailable to the destitute, is purchased by the wealthy:

> . . . Plate sin with gold,
> And the strong lance of justice hurtless breaks;
> Arm it in rags, a pygmy's straw does pierce it. (IV.vi.165–67)

At the end of this terrifying play, there is no requital for the cosmic and social injustice of which Lear has become aware. There is some compensation, in his reunion with Cordelia, for his earlier injustice to her. But her violent death, at the hands of Edmund's henchman, seems like the crucifixion of goodness itself. The most fitting comment on the tragedy as a whole is Lear's question: "Is there any cause in nature that make these hard hearts?" (III.vi.77–78).

The idea of nature as a rational moral order, though seriously brought into question in Shakespearean drama, does at least linger there. But in seventeenth-century literature, nature will come increasingly to connote a "mechanistic physical world . . . indifferent to all morality,"[50] which Francis Bacon and René Descartes evoke. Bosola, in Webster's *The Duchess of Malfi* a spokesman for the Jacobean age, points out to the Duchess, who would "curse the stars" for the injustices she has suffered, that "the stars shine still."[51] Later in the play, echoing a despairing utterance by Gloucester in *Lear*, Bosola cries,

> We are merely the stars' tennis-balls, struck and
> bandied
> Which way please them. (V.iv.537)

SPANISH GOLDEN AGE DRAMA

Since the early sixteenth century the idea of natural law had been assaulted in Europe by Machiavellian realism; by the Protestant Reformation, which exalted God's will rather than His "reasonableness"; and by the new science of Copernicus, Kepler, and Galileo, which shattered scholastic assumptions about a fixed, unchanging physical universe. In deeply Catholic Spain, however, Spain of the Inquisition and the Counter-Reformation, natural law retained its prestige. Such sixteenth-century writers as Mariana, Suárez, Molina, de Soto, Vitoria, and Rivadeneira, all of whom based their arguments to some extent on Aquinas, carefully countered "both Machiavellian pragmatism and the divine right of kings." All of them emphasized the importance of a ruler's conscience and religious faith. Mariana, the most "democratic" of the group, placed the king at the bottom of a hierarchy of authority, and accountable to the people, who themselves answered to God. Since the king ruled in the service of the people, he could, according to Mariana, be legally overthrown and even killed by the citizens if he became a tyrant. This Lockeanism "avant la lettre" was not shared by the other theorists, who were "exceedingly chary about when it is licit to remove a ruler from office" and who considered tyrannicide justifiable only under the most extreme and specific circumstances. But they agreed with Mariana "that the king receives his power from the people."[52]

According to Robert L. Fiore, the concept of natural law exercised a "pervasive influence" on Spanish drama of the Golden Age.[53] Lope de Vega's *The Sheep Well* (*Fuenteovejuna*, c. 1613) is one of the plays on which Fiore focuses in demonstrating that influence.[54] Based on a fifteenth-century episode in an Andalusian village, the drama centers on the tyrannous lechery of Fernán Gómez, Commander of a feudal military order. He and his underlings seduce and rape both virgins and married women in Fuente Ovejuna; and when the dignified mayor protests against lewd references to his daughter and to a councillor's wife by Gómez, the Commander contemptuously remarks, "Oh, what rustic virtue! Here, . . . get him the book of *Politics*, and let him perfect himself in Aristotle."[55] The significance of the jibe is that Aristotle had been cited as an authority in Aquinas's condemnation of precisely the kind of tyranny which the Commander, knowingly, practices. A tyrannical government, wrote Aquinas, "is not just, because it is directed, not to the common good, but to the private good of the ruler, as the Philosopher states." Significantly, Aquinas goes on to say that "there is no sedition in disturbing a government of this kind, unless indeed the tyrant's rule be disturbed so inordinately, that his subjects suffer greater harm from the consequent disturbances than from the tyrant's government."[56]

The Commander obviously has no fear of the people he is abusing. He and his men interrupt the wedding of the mayor's daughter, Laurencia, to a youth who had prevented Gómez from raping her; Gómez then proceeds to have the bridegroom jailed. When the mayor warns him that the king and queen (Ferdinand and Isabel) will not permit "arrogance to overpower their towns and villages" (II, 328), Gómez directs that he be beaten with his own staff of office.

The humiliated men of Fuente Ovejuna are eventually shamed into action by Laurencia's contempt for their cowardice: "Oh, well-named Village of Fuente Ovejuna, the Sheep Well! Sheep, sheep, sheep! Give me iron . . ." (III, 333). The women of the village join the men in their descent upon the Commander's castle, where they defenestrate Gómez and deface him after his death. The villagers then resolve to tell the judge sent by the king to affix blame for the murder that "Fuenteovejuna did it" (Ill, 344). This resolution to accept only communal responsibility they bravely adhere to, despite the tortures inflicted on three hundred men, women, and children in an effort to extract the names of individual killers. Reporting to the king and queen his failure to affix personal responsibility, the judge declares, "Either you must pardon the village or wipe it out to the last man" (Ill, 353). Spokesmen for the village, who have accompanied the judge, then testify to the Commander's extreme brutality—the sole cause, they stress, of their violent acts. Pertinent here is Fiore's observation that the judgment that the Commander's rule was tyrannical has been "accepted by a large and well-distributed number of citizens" (21): Fuente Ovejuna as an organic entity has indeed passed judgment upon a tyrant. Fortunately, from the vilagers' standpoint, Gómez has angered King Ferdinand by attempting, on behalf of the Portuguese king, to wrest power from him in Castile. Ferdinand thus has no reason to regret Gómez's death, and he knows that legality has been assiduously served by the judge's merciless investigation. The king's decision in the case is that since "no indictment is set down" (Ill, 355), Fuente Ovejuna's grave fault in killing the Commander shall be pardoned. This language, even if the pardon is due in part to a royal grudge against Gómez, indicates respect for a reasonable law independent of the monarch's will. And certainly the king's judgment is consonant with Aquinas's view that "there is no sedition in disturbing" a tyrannical government "unless indeed the tyrant's rule be disturbed so inordinately, that his subjects suffer greater harm from the consequent disturbance than from the tyrant's government." Avoidance of such harm is virtually ensured by the king's now taking Fuente Ovejuna under his own protection, at least until a new Commander inherits the village.

A concern with natural law also permeates a complex drama by Calderón, *The Mayor of Zalamea* (*El alcalde de Zalamea*, c. 1642). During the thirty years between Lope's *The Sheep Well* and this play, Spain had suffered defeats in the Thirty Years War and major revolts in Portugal and Catalonia. Spanish society was also riven by the Inquisition's attempt, through statutes of "purity of blood," to distinguish "true" or "old" Christians from "new" Christians—Jews and Moors who had converted in order to escape persecution. In about 1640, the year of the Portuguese and Catalonian revolts, King Philip IV gloomily told his chief minister that "these evil events have been caused by your sins and by mine in particular." Five years later the author Francisco de Quevedo was to write to a friend: "From all sides come very bad news of utter ruin. . . . I do not know whether the end is coming or whether it has already come. God only knows. . . ."[57]

This dark mood envelops *The Mayor of Zalamea*, which is set in 1580, during Philip II's progress to Lisbon to claim the Portuguese throne. As in *The Sheep Well*, the dramatic focus is the irruption of brutal force in a pastoral community. An army captain, Don Álvaro, obsessively attracted to the daughter of a wealthy farmer who is housing him during his regiment's stay at Zalamea, is astonished when this "mere peasant girl" resists him "as though she were a lady!"[58] He kidnaps Isabel and rapes her. Overwhelmed by shame, she repeatedly begs her father, Pedro Crespo, to win back his honor by killing her. His reaction she finds shocking: instead of seeking to expunge the "stain" on his honor, he calmly says that "this is the lot of man," which both he and she must bear "deep within our hearts" (III, p. 196). The farmer does intend, however, to kill Don Álvaro—until he learns that he himself has been made mayor of Zalamea. Deciding now that he cannot exceed the law, since he is committed to "keeping others within its bounds" (III, p, 197), Crespo performs an extraordinary act: assuring Don Álvaro that what he seeks is a remedy rather than revenge, he asks the captain to marry Isabel and to take all his own property at once. Crespo and his son will, if necessary, beg on the streets. Even if Don Álvaro decides he wishes

> to brand us as slaves and sell us
> immediately, you may add
> those proceeds to the dowry
> I have offered you. . . .

The mayor adds, however, that if the Captain refuses to "restore the honor you deprived me of," he can seize it by force (III, pp. 201–02). Don Álvaro, reflecting a contemptuous attitude toward civilian authority widespread among the seventeenth-century

Spanish military, retorts that Crespo has no legal power over him. Clearly convinced at last that he cannot move the Captain, Crespo jails him, and shocks Isabel again——for she thinks (as contemporary Spanish audiences of the play undoubtedly did) that the only alternative to private revenge is silence—by telling her to sign a complaint against Don Álvaro. Don Lope, the choleric commander of Don Álvaro's regiment, now arrives, and announces to Crespo that the Captain comes under his military jurisdiction; the mayor, Don Lope angrily declares, has "trespassed on my authority." After Crespo retorts that his own good name is beyond Don Lope's authority, and that he is "drawing up the evidence of this trial" (III, p. 210), the commander announces his intention to burn down the jail where the Captain is being held "[i]f they refuse to let him go" (III, p. 2ll). The king's arrival in Zalamea prevents this holocaust, and Crespo presents evidence to him to prove that "the trial"—which must have occurred with preternatural rapidity—was fair, and that the death sentence is clearly called for. The king, without looking further into the matter, declares the "verdict" justified; he adopts, however, the military viewpoint by adding that actual execution of the verdict depends upon "another court's decision and jurisdiction." Whereupon Crespo, observing that "[w]e have only / one tribunal here, which executes / whatever verdict has been passed," causes a door to be opened, "*and the Captain is revealed garroted in a chair.*"

Once the king regains his composure, he grants the merit of Crespo's argument that all royal justice "is contained in one body with many hands," that the jurisdictional issue is of no importance as long as the "broader purpose" of justice is served. The monarch calls the execution "fully justified" and appoints Crespo permanent mayor of the town (III, pp, 212–14).

The king's volte-face here makes him seem far less self-assured than the monarch in Lope's *The Sheep Well*. And sympathetic as we may be to Crespo, in view of the humanity and restraint he has shown before the arrival in Act III of Don Lope, we question whether he has done justice or simply taken revenge. That the latter is the case is the conclusion of José M. Aguirre, who finds Crespo's sentencing and execution of the Captain "radicalmente ilegal y injusto."[59] What seems clear is that Calderón was deeply troubled by the problem he conceived in *The Mayor of Zalamea*;

that he is, in a sense, seeking but not finding a "natural law" solution and ultimately falling back upon a traditional "Augustinian" *contemptus mundi*: when Don Lope suggests to Crespo toward the end of the play that the Captain, if he had been released to military jurisdiction, would have been forced to marry Isabel, the mayor replies that she has just entered a convent, to become the bride of One "who cares nothing for the differences / in social origin among us" (III, p. 214).

Seventeenth-Century French Drama

While Spanish drama of the Golden Age tends to seek, even if it does not find, a basis in natural law for judicial decisions rendered by the king, French classical plays typically reflect the "divine right" absolutism of Louis XIII and Louis XIV. Pierre Corneille's *Cinna* (first performed in 1640) is described by Martin Turnell as important "for the passion for order which inspires it."[60] This order is imposed in the play by a Roman emperor's will. Declaring "I am master of myself as of the universe,"[61] Augustus pardons Cinna, who has led a conspiracy to assassinate him. Thus, the emperor restores harmony in Rome. The absolutist notion of royal authority is vividly exemplified in the scene preceding that of the pardon. Augustus's wife, Livia, speaking to the woman who had instigated the conspiracy in order to avenge her own father's murder by Augustus, explains that this murder, "the memory of which ignites thy fury," had been committed not by "Augustus," but by "Octavius," which was the future Augustus's name when, as Consul, he was maneuvering toward the crown. All state crimes, Livia serenely declares, are pardoned by Heaven once It grants the crown to him who has striven for it: "The past becomes just and the future—unimpeachable" (V.ii.1612). Thomas Corneille, Pierre's younger brother, has the protagonist of one of his own plays, *The Earl of Essex*, express the same idea of absolution from sin and crime through ascent to the throne:

> . . . To rise to that high station
> Would have absolved me of the sin of doing so,
> And those who seek to ruin me when guiltless
> Would have beheld my crimes but to applaud them.[62]

Jean Rotrou's *Wenceslaus*—adapted, as was many a seventeenth-century French play, from a Spanish drama[63]—provides still another variation on the same theme. The rash, passionate Prince Ladislaus kills his own brother by mistake in the dark, taking him for a man he believes to be the lover of Cassandra, whom Ladislaus himself is pursuing. His father, King Wenceslaus, persuaded by the people of the realm that their beloved Prince Ladislaus is exempt from the laws, abdicates in his favor to avoid having to punish him. To Cassandra, unwilling to accept a marriage proposal from the brother of the dead man, who ironically actually was her lover, Wenceslaus says:

> The sceptre which I place there [in Ladislaus's hand]
>   blots his crime out.
> In a new reign let us forget the past.
> Let him lose with the name of prince, thy hate.
> When I give thee a king, give us a queen. (Lockert, V, p. 264)

Despite her scruples, Cassandra will probably succumb to this plea.

Belief that divinity hedged about a king was general in seventeenth-century Europe. England at the time of Charles I's beheading in 1649 had evolved much further than France and other continental nations toward representative government. Yet in many English minds that regicide was tantamount to deicide. In France, of course, Louis XIV ruled like Jupiter. It was only in the late 1600s, the time of Locke's two treatises on civil government (1690) and Pierre Bayle's *Dictionnaire historique et critique* (1698), all written in Dutch exile, that French imaginative literature began to express the subversive ideas about limited monarchy which would eventually be used to justify a revolution. Racine's *Athaliah* (*Athalie*, 1690; first performed in 1691) sets forth in a striking passage the notion that a king must follow God's law—which John Locke was calling "the law of Nature." The passage occurs in Act IV, when the Hebrew High Priest warns young Jehoash, whom he has just told of his identity as King David's descendant, that he must beware of flatterers who

> will soon tell you that the holiest laws
> Bind subjects, but must bend before their kings. . . .

The High Priest has the child-monarch swear on the Bible before witnesses,

> That God will always be your first devotion;
> Scourge of the wicked, refuge of the righteous,
> So you will make God judge between king and poor,
> Remembering, concealed beneath this robe,
> Like them you were once poor, and orphan once.

Jehoash's responsive promise to "follow what the Law commands" seals a "Lockean" contract between himself and the Jewish people.[64] Paul Hazard observes that hostile contemporaries of Racine accused *Athalie* of being "nothing more nor less than the English Revolution [of 1688–89] tricked out in an elaborate stage-disguise."[65]

MODULATION OF NATURAL LAW INTO NATURAL RIGHTS IN ENLIGHTENMENT LITERATURE

Racine's self-exiled countryman Pierre Bayle did not disguise his own iconoclasm. Although he was a Christian, like most rationalists of the late seventeenth and early eighteenth centuries, he demonstrated in his philosophic works that history abounded with religious scoundrels and decent atheistic rulers.[66] Bayle subordinates Biblical revelation and ecclesiastical tradition to the reason which, according to Locke, is " 'natural Revelation, whereby the Father of Light, and Fountain of all knowledge, communicates to mankind that portion of truth which he has laid within the reach of their natural faculties.' "[67] Locke's "natural Revelation" is Aquinas's Law of Nature (natural law), "that part of the Law Eternal which is made known to man through his reason" (Willey 15). The climate of thought, however, of Locke and other Enlightenment intellectuals differed radically from Aquinas's, for the thirteenth-century theologian had wedded reason, in the form of authoritative commentaries on Aristotle's works, to faith in a God whom men were expected to make it the chief end of their lives to love and fear. To Aquinas, as to his classical predecessors in the natural law tradition, and to a successor like Grotius—who said that natural law would be valid even if there were no God—this law was closely linked to order, both cosmic and social. We have noted that Aquinas considered rebellion against a tyrant justifiable under certain conditions. His emphasis, however, was on the need to protect the common good against a demonstrably mischievous, selfish ruler. Nowhere does Aquinas speak of a natural right to liberty. The idea of natural rights was born of the political revolutions of the seventeenth century, and nurtured by men like James Harrington, Pierre Bayle, and John Locke. But it was not to come to maturity until the later eighteenth century. Such writers as Pope and Swift, early in the century, associated natural law primarily with order rather than liberty. The king of Brobdingnag, obviously expressing Swift's viewpoint, tells Gulliver that

> he knew no Reason, why those who entertain Opinions prejudicial to the Publick, should be obliged to change, or should not be obliged to conceal them. And, as it was Tyranny in any Government to require the first, so it was Weakness not to enforce the second: For a Man may be allowed to keep Poisons in his Closet, but not to vend them about as Cordials.[68]

Nevertheless, Montesquieu and Voltaire, who familiarized themselves with Locke's writings and with English institutions, saw no incompatibility between natural law and a considerable degree of religious liberty. During "a momentary relaxation in the censorship,"[69] Montesquieu published anonymously his satirical *Persian Letters* (*Lettres Persanes*, 1721), supposedly written by two Persians visiting Paris. One of the letters boldly articulates a belief in natural law:

> . . . if there were no God, we would still be obliged to venerate justice, that is, we should do everything possible to resemble that being of whom we have such an exalted notion and who, if he exists, would necessarily be just. Free though we might be from the yoke of religion, we should never be free from the bonds of equity. (Torrey 86)

The sentence referring to freedom from "the yoke of religion" is a restatement, with a distinctly "libertine" twist, of Grotius's remark that natural law would hold, even if there were no God. Another "Persian" letter clearly alludes to the revocation of the Edict of Nantes by telling of the project formed by "a number of ministers of Shah-Soliman" to force "all the Armenians in Persia to leave the realm or become Mohammedans, with the idea that our empire would be polluted as long as it kept these infidels in our midst" (87).

After declaring, certainly with a wink to his French readers, that the great Shah "would have preferred to cut off his two arms rather than sign such an order," the writer argues that the toleration of several religions within a State is to the sovereign's advantage, and he concludes with this libertarian sally: "The man who wants to make me change my religion surely does so only because he would not change his, even if forced: he thinks it strange, then, that I do not do something he would not do himself perhaps for the whole world" (89).

Voltaire, as firm a believer in natural law as Montesquieu, defines it in his *Philosophical Dictionary* (1764) as "the instinct which makes us feel justice," and elaborates by distinguishing it from conventional law and arbitrary customs: ". . . the essential remains always. Show me a country where it was honourable to rob me of the fruit of my toil, to break one's promise, to lie in order to hurt, to calumniate, to assassinate, to poison, to be ungrateful towards a benefactor, to beat one's father and mother when they offer you food."[70]

Thirty years earlier, Voltaire had published in England (1733) before it appeared and was barred in France (1734) his *Letters Concerning the English Nation*, which has been described as "the first bomb hurled against the Old Regime." Cool to the government that had put him in the Bastille and released him only upon his promise to go to England, he came to admire the religious freedom the English had won through the Toleration Act of 1689 (Torrey 53). He implicitly advocates such freedom both by indicating in the *Letters* the variety of sects among the British and by discussing them all with his characteristic irreverence. It is his tone at least as much as the substance of this argument which must have frightened the French censors. Consider the passage in which he tells of talking with and questioning an elderly Quaker, as "good Catholics" often questioned Huguenots. Told by Voltaire that the Quakers are not Christians because they have not been baptized, the Quaker replied that they do not believe that sprinkling water on a child's head makes him a Christian. To Voltaire's objection that Christ was baptized by St. John, he retorted that

Christ Himself never baptized anyone. "We are disciples of Christ, not of John." Voltaire then fires this twisting bullet at the adversaries of toleration: "I pitied very much the sincerity of my worthy Quaker, and was absolutely for forcing him to get himself christened" (54–55).

The change of emphasis, from Locke's time to the mid-eighteenth century, in the interpretation of natural law, is interestingly exemplified in Henry Fielding's novel *Tom Jones* (1749). Tom, the ward of Squire Allworthy, had given to another child, the lovely Sophia Western, a bird that he had "nursed up and taught to sing." Allworthy's sanctimonious nephew, Master Blifil, resents Sophia's preference of Tom to him; she calls the bird "little Tommy" and makes it "her chief business . . . to feed and tend it." One day Blifil asks her to let him hold it; when she does so, he slips the string from its leg, and tosses it into the air. Despite Tom's attempt to recapture the bird by climbing the tree to which it has escaped, it flies away, only to be seized by a hawk. Blifil defends his own act to Squire Allworthy by saying that because he had thought the bird to be languishing for liberty, "I own I could not forbear giving it what it desired; for I always thought there was something very cruel in confining anything. It seemed to be against the law of nature, by which everything has a right to liberty; nay, it is even unchristian, for it is not doing what we would be done by."[71]

It is obvious that Blifil has acted maliciously and is now defending himself with the language of natural law and natural rights. John Locke had written nothing about the natural rights of domestic animals, but had considered "natural," within limits, the right of men to own property. Since the bird had belonged to Sophia, he would have agreed, as Fielding obviously does, with the angry condemnation of Blifil's act by Sophia's father. What is arresting about the passage, from our viewpoint, is its indication of the cultural weather: the association of natural law with the right to liberty was evidently so familiar to Fielding's public that he could make satirical use of it in his novel.

According to A. P. d'Entrèves, the theory of natural law had become, by the eve of the American and French Revolutions, a theory of natural rights. He quotes a work published as early as 1741 as evidence of the metamorphosis: "whenever we speak of natural raw (*ius naturae*), we never intend the law of nature, but rather the right which belongs to man on the strength of that law, that is naturally."[72]

Denis Diderot, co-editor of the *Encyclopédie* (1751–72), which epitomized Enlightenment skepticism and rationalism, was one of the intellectuals most responsible for the change that d'Entrèves describes. Unlike Montesquieu and Voltaire, and like Rousseau—a member of his circle, who contributed music articles to the *Encyclopédie*—he wanted to transform political institutions, not simply modify them. A striking episode in his life was his attempt to persuade Catherine the Great, whom he met during a visit to Petersburg in 1773–74, to undertake a radical codification of Russian law. The manuscript of his "observations of Catherine the Great to her deputies" went to Russia with his library after Diderot's death in 1784; but the czarina, alarmed by the revolutionary tide in France, considered his ideas unrealistic and out of place (Torrey 217–18). American and British readers will find at least one of those ideas quite familiar. The first line of a well-drawn code, says Diderot, should bind the sovereign, and should begin thus:

> "We, the People, and We, the Sovereign of this people, take solemn oath to uphold these laws, by which we are to be equally judged; and if it happens that We, the Sovereign, change or break them, as an enemy of our people it is just that they should be our enemy and be freed from their oath of allegiance, that they should pursue us, depose us, and even condemn us to death if the circumstances so require." (Torrey 218–219)

The language, of course, recalls that of Locke and of the American Declaration of Independence.

Diderot, like Voltaire and other *lumières*, was especially concerned to defend men's natural rights against the oppressive alliance of state and church. *La Religieuse* (*The Nun*), apparently written during the 1780s but published posthumously, is both a psychologically penetrating novel of "distress" in the manner of Samuel Richardson and a natural rights *roman-à-thèse*.

Marie-Suzanne Simonin, the first-person narrator, tells of her fruitless attempts to renounce religious vows that she has taken under heavy parental pressure and of her eventual "illegal" escape from a convent. She had agreed to enter this "prison" only after learning that she was the illegitimate child of a man other than her supposed father; that her two sisters were to become their father's sole heirs; and that the nunnery was her only refuge from indigence. Deeply unhappy at the convent, she contrived, with the courageous help of a sympathetic nun, to disclose her desire to leave to a lawyer. The best he could do for her in the civil courts, however, was to obtain her transfer to another convent, where the tumultuously disturbed Mother Superior made sexual advances that confused and horrified her. Eventually, this woman having died insane, Marie-Suzanne escaped from the nunnery and found employment as a house servant. Now an isolated outlaw, she has written a memoir, the novel we are reading, to an aged marquis who has taken an interest in her case.

Diderot's psychological acumen and superb dramatization of Marie-Suzanne's circumstances lift *The Nun* far above the level of the anti-clerical gothic fictions so prolifically produced in the late eighteenth century. Diderot also treats convincingly the state's refusal to respect the young woman's right to liberty, which she can obtain only by breaking a man-made law. Her lawyer, though resourceful, cannot win the case because, as Marie-Suzanne says, "claims like mine are always treated unsympathetically by politicians, who fear that if one nun succeeds in renouncing her vows, innumerable others will attempt to do the same: it is secretly sensed that if those jail doors were permitted to open for one unhappy woman, a throng would try to break them down."[73]

Diderot clearly implies that only radical social change can end the tyrannous alliance between church and state, and ensure the natural rights of a woman like Mlle Simonin.

Le Neveu de Rameau (*Rameau's Nephew*), another posthumous Diderot work, is much more intellectually complex than *The Nun*. A vivacious dialogue, supposedly occurring in the social atmosphere of the Parisian Café de la Régence, it pits "Moi," a rationalist exponent of natural law, against "Lui," a Thrasymachean cynic described as "a bit of yeast that leavens and that restores to everyone a portion of his natural individuality" (397). During a discussion of genius, "Moi" avers that the genius who decries a general error may fall victim to prejudice and to the laws. But, he says, there are two kinds of laws, "those of an absolute and general equity, and those that are bizarre, deriving their sanction only from blindness or from the force of circumstances." Violators of the "bizarre" kind of law, he says, incur only a transitory dishonor, which time eventually reverses and casts forever on the judges themselves. "Is it," asks "Moi," "Socrates or the judge who condemned him to drink hemlock, who is now dishonored?" "Good for Socrates!" retorts "Lui." "Wasn't he condemned anyway? Wasn't he put to death? In showing contempt for a bad law, didn't he encourage madmen to despise good laws?" (401–02). For "Lui," the locus of justice is the "well-policed city" (404).

As epigraph to *Rameau's Nephew*, Diderot quotes Horace: "Vertumnis quotquot sunt natus iniquis" (395), which may be freely translated: "To the man who unceasingly goes from one extreme to another." The epigraph evokes not only Diderot's own temperamental conflicts but a conflict in the thought of his age. Idealistically espousing the cause of Socrates and linking it to "laws of an absolute and general equity," "Moi" implicitly supports the revolutionaries who will, after Diderot's death, assault the Bastille in the name of universal human rights. "Moi's" voice is that of the writer who made Marie-Suzanne Simonin plead for liberty in *The Nun*. But the voice of "Lui"—cynic, actor, bohemian "good-for-nothing," and would-be artist—is already undermining the French Revolution. Its tone is that of Thrasymachus, and its language recalls David Hume, the eighteenth-century philosopher who attacked rationalism by dissolving mind into a bundle of perceptions. "Lui's" hard-boiled pragmatism anticipates the modern rejection of both natural law *and* natural rights. The extreme political right wing was to reject those concepts in the name of "fatherland" or "Führer." A certain brutal left was to deny them in the name of the "masses." And the center was to abandon them in the name of "positivism" and "realism." By the end of the eighteenth century, the conflict between idealistic and realistic conceptions of justice had become part of a tremendous historic upheaval, which would bring temporary victory to natural-rights idealism, but eventual triumph—one to which Dostoevsky and Kafka bear witness—to the established disorder.

NATURAL LAW AND THE BOURGEOISIE
IN EARLIER NINETEENTH-CENTURY LITERATURE

Wherever the French Revolution's shock waves were felt, the victory of natural rights, derived from natural law, affected the legal status of numerous persons. Large groups previously disenfranchised—Catholics in England, for example, and Jews on the continent—were eventually integrated into the political community. The movement to abolish Negro slavery gathered momentum, and agitation for women's rights intensified. The greatest beneficiary of the Revolution, however, was the middle class. Its freedom to acquire property and profits had been defended by John Locke, Adam Smith, the Physiocrats, all of whom rejected a traditional denigration of commerce based in part on the hostility of Christian natural law to profit-making.[74] Fiction after the French Revolution reflects the consolidation of bourgeois rights and influence, and tends to locate natural law in the conscience of exceptional individuals rather than in the polis, which is perceived as erring or corrupt.

Heinrich von Kleist's protagonist in the historically based "Michael Kohlhaas" (1810) is a sixteenth-century Brandenburgian horse-trader who repeatedly attempts to gain legal redress for wrongs done to his horses and his groom by an arrogant Junker's subordinates. Each of Kohlhaas's legal initiatives fails, owing chiefly to the nobleman's political connections. After the horse-trader's wife dies of injuries inflicted when she tries to present a petition in his behalf, the grief-stricken Kohlhaas turns to violence. With a rapidly assembled "revolutionary army" he attempts to flush out the hiding Junker by setting fires in cities—first Wittenberg, then Leipzig—where he has reportedly been seen. Kohlhaas also issues eccentric but moving manifestos, one of which, signed "Given at the seat of our Provisional World Government," appeals to the people to join him in establishing "a better order of things."[75] This language recalls that of Immanuel Kant, with whose writings Kleist was familiar, and who in his treatise "Perpetual Peace" (1795), had argued that in order to end the international anarchy which perpetuated war, a "federation" of nations must be established under a "covenant of peace." Natural law

would then, according to Kant, apply for the first time in history
to international relations.[76]

Eventually, after Martin Luther, who at first had been shocked
by Kohlhaas's incendiary campaign, intervenes on the horse-
trader's behalf, he gains recognition from Saxony as a "foreign
power" which has attacked it: he is no longer considered a mere
"rebel" against the throne. Then, through a complex series of
betrayals of Kohlhaas and political negotiations involving Bran-
denburg, Saxony, and the Emperor of the Holy Roman Empire,
the horse-trader is criminally arraigned for breaking the emperor's
peace but is permitted to sue in a civil court for redress of his own
grievances. The upshot of these simultaneous proceedings is that
the Junker is condemned to two years' imprisonment, Kohlhaas's
horses—restored to good condition—are, to his delight, returned
to him, and the horse-dealer himself is beheaded. The story, a
favorite of Kafka's, can be read as embodying the tragic absurdity
of history. From another perspective, it presents an honorable
bourgeois who becomes a quixotic incarnation of natural law, and
in doing so reminds us of the Old Testament prophets who
envisioned a time when nation would neither lift up sword against
nation nor learn war anymore.

The heroine of Sir Walter Scott's *Heart of Midlothian* (1818) is an
eighteenth-century Scottish farmer's daughter, Jeanie Deans, who
refuses to tell a lie in court, even to save her sister from condemnation to death under a "Child Murder Act." The Act presumes
that if a woman tells nobody of her pregnancy, then bears a baby
that cannot subsequently be proven to be alive, she is guilty of
killing it. Jeanie is convinced that her sister Effie, though unaware
of her baby's whereabouts, has not murdered it. In contrast to
Claudio's sister in *Measure for Measure*, Jeanie is compassionate,
but she cannot be persuaded to testify falsely that Effie has
disclosed the pregnancy to her. God, Jeanie believes, " 'has given
us a law for the lamp of our path; if we stray from it we err against
knowledge—I may not do evil, even that good may come out of
it.' "[77]

Once Effie is condemned to die, Jeanie attempts indefatigably
to obtain a pardon for her. After traveling alone to England, she
makes an impassioned appeal to Queen Caroline, which finally
triumphs over a law based on "abstract, arbitrary principles."[78]

Almost as striking as Scott's characterization of the resourceful Jeanie is his treatment of other socially undistinguished Scots, some of whom are more closely attuned to natural law than are many notable members of the legal profession. Thus, a shopkeeper's wife, replying to her husband's remark that Effie's crime of " 'murder presumptive,' " has actually been created by the law itself, avers that if the law makes murders, the law should be hanged for them: " 'or if they wad hang a lawyer instead, the country wad find nae faut' " (60).

Scott, like Kleist, was politically conservative—Leslie Stephen once remarked that *Waverley* was fictionalized Burke—but Revolutionary currents of feeling flow through *The Heart of Midlothian.* It is notable that both this novel and "Michael Kohlhaas" evoke historical eras before the French Revolution, when the middle class was seeking to establish its rights. Honoré de Balzac, whose *Comédie Humaine* depicts a triumphant bourgeois society that apotheosizes materialism ("Messieurs, enrichissez-vous!" was the watchword of Louis Philippe's minister of state, Guizot), takes a darker view of the middle class. For while Balzac, himself a kind of fiction factory, admired the energy of money-hungry industrialists, he looked back nostalgically to pre-Revolutionary days when, he thought, justice and equity (natural law) had not yet succumbed to self-aggrandizing "liberty." A central figure in his story "The Red Inn" ("L'Auberge Rouge," 1833), a doctor in the French Revolutionary army in 1799, is significantly named Prosper Magnan. A bourgeois desire to "prosper" inspires his plan to murder and rob of his gold and diamonds a manufacturer with whom he is sharing a room at a German inn. His moral sense, however (indicated by his surname, which suggests "magnanimity"), prevents him, at the last moment, from killing the sleeping man. Awakened in the morning by an uproar, he finds the manufacturer decapitated, and discovers blood on himself and his sheets. The dead man's valise, and an army doctor traveling with Magnan, have both disappeared. Magnan declares his innocence at a court-martial, but witnesses falsely testify that they have seen him burying gold and diamonds. Knowing that he has been framed but feeling that his conscience has lost its " 'virginity,' "[79] he declines a pardon after the court-martial finds him guilty and sentences him to death.

The whole story is told by an unnamed narrator who himself experiences a conflict between egoistic concerns and a desire to adhere to natural law. He has learned, many years after Magnan's execution, that the murderer and thief who had framed the doctor is the father of a young woman whom he loves. If the narrator were to marry the girl, who knew nothing of her father's guilt, he would share her blood-soaked inheritance. To aid him in his moral quandary, he convokes a "sanhedrin" composed of his friends, whom he asks to vote anonymously for or against his proposing marriage. When he counts the votes, he finds nine against such a proposal and eight for it. It then occurs to him to count the number of his contemporaries in the sanhedrin—young men whose values have been formed during what the narrator (like Balzac himself) obviously thinks of as the low, dishonest decades following the French Revolution. The number is nine. He concludes that each of these "casuists" has voted "no" with the same *arrière pensée*: a yearning to propose to the heiress (235–36).

Less cynical than Balzac about post-Revolutionary bourgeois values, and sympathetic, as Scott had not been, to the extension of political rights to British working men, George Eliot presents in *Felix Holt* (1866) an intelligent, honorable weaver's son who wants to improve "the life of the miserable, the spawning life of vice and hunger."[80] He does not, however, share the bitter disappointment of many of his fellow-laborers over the provisions of the 1832 Reform Bill, which has not met their demand for universal manhood suffrage.[81] He insists in a public speech that it is not political power but the ability to use the vote wisely that is of chief importance to the workers. Later, attempting to restrain (by leading it) an election day mob that has become violent, he unintentionally but mortally wounds a constable. Tried and jailed for homicide, he is eventually pardoned through the collaborative efforts of bourgeois and aristocrats of diverse political persuasions. Eliot admires, as we do, Holt's Orwell-like insistence on pure political means as well as pure political ends. Clearly, however, Eliot, like most of her intellectual contemporaries, worries more about the dangers that Holt runs by associating with mobs than about the social and economic conditions that breed political violence.[82] Reflecting the cautious attitudes of a middle class that has consolidated its own "natural rights" revolution, Eliot finally sides with the Establishment against the "animal" passions of the uneducated. Her protagonist, though he incarnates natural law much as Jeanie Deans does, or Prosper Magnan, or Michael Kohlhaas, is ultimately left hanging between the workers for whom he is too independent and the middle class to which in spirit he can never belong.

The early nineteenth-century culture in which Kleist, Scott, and Balzac composed their fiction retained at least a memory of classical-Christian natural law. All three writers evoke, in the works we just discussed, some kind of transcendental intervention on behalf of what they imply is equity or justice. One aspect of the plot of "Michael Kohlhaas" is the horse-dealer's encounter, at a fair attended by the Elector of Saxony, with a gypsy woman who writes out that prince's "fortune," then gives it, sealed, to Kohlhaas. Although he has never met her, she tells him that if the Elector wishes to know his fortune, "'he will have to ask you about it.'" Months later, while being escorted to Berlin to stand criminal trial, Kohlhaas meets a man whom he tells of the strange incident, and who turns out to be the Elector. So eager is the prince to obtain the still sealed paper from Kohlhaas that he sends a knight in pursuit of him, with an offer to help him escape criminal proceedings should he turn it over. But the horse-dealer refuses to do so because of the unjust treatment he has received from the government of Saxony. Though he were sent to the scaffold, he informs the knight, he means to make the Elector suffer. After Kohlhaas's trial, and while he is in jail awaiting execution, the gypsy—now bearing an uncanny resemblance to his dead wife—reappears, and urges him to give up the paper to the Elector, in return for life and liberty. Again he refuses. On the day set for his beheading, he receives a written warning from the gypsy that the Elector intends, immediately after Kohlhaas's burial, to disinter the paper. With panache the horse-dealer forestalls this move: striding up to the Elector he unseals the Fortune, reads it through, swallows it and—the Prince having fainted—turns to the scaffold, where his head is lopped off.

The whole gypsy episode is embarrassingly Romantic from a twentieth-century point of view. Kleist, however, plainly wants to indicate that a supernatural power is aiding Kohlhaas, whose quest for justice has become violent only after the death of his beloved, peacefully inclined wife.[83]

Transcendental intervention in *The Heart of Midlothian* consists in grim punishment of both Effie Dean's illicit sexual intercourse with her lover, Staunton, and Staunton's various transgressions. These include the seduction and abandonment—before his affair with Effie—of a young woman whose mother has avenged her by kidnaping Effie's baby. The pardon that Jeanie Deans obtains for her sister is conditional on Effie's exiling herself from Scotland for fourteen years. She leaves with Staunton, who, after learning that their child is still alive, assiduously searches for him. The search succeeds, but the boy, having become a ruffian, kills his father. Scott thus suggests that the sins of a father and mother have been terribly requited by their illegitimate son.

Balzac's Prosper Magnan—standing with a surgical instrument raised above the sleeping manufacturer in "The Red Inn"—suddenly hears an inner voice, and fancies that he sees a "light" (207–08). He throws the weapon on his bed, leaves the inn, and walks rapidly along a bank of the Rhine. Beneficent nature—the night air, the rippling of the waves, the sight of the stars—dissipates his "momentary madness" (208). Thus, evidently with help from a higher power, his conscience quashes his criminal plan. The court-martial is, of course, deceived by circumstantial evidence planted by Magnan's doctor "friend," Taillefer. Taillefer is never tried in a court of law, but the recurrent headaches, or " 'gout in the head' " (231), which afflict him after the crime presumably constitute what one character in the story refers to as " 'divine justice' " (227).

George Eliot, a mid-century agnostic, stands apart from these Romantic writers. As strongly influenced by the new "sociology" as by a moral code that derived from the Western religious tradition, she introduces no transcendental element into *Felix Holt*. A fundamental difference in her subtly positivist view of human behavior from the still theistic outlook of her Romantic predecessors is indicated in the following passage from the novel: "As [Holt] was pressed along with the multitude . . . his very movement seemed to him only an image of the day's fatalities, in which the multitudinous small wickednesses of small selfish ends . . . had issued in widely-shared mischief that might yet be hideous"

(270). Eliot's complex concept of destiny does not prevent her from believing that individuals make moral choices. It is evident, indeed, that she can conceive a community more justly, more compassionately ordered than the parish, and the country, in which Felix Holt lives. Somewhat astringently she comments on nineteenth-century material progress:

> As to all that wide parish . . . it has since prospered as the rest of England has prospered. Doubtless there is more enlightenment now. Whether the farmers are all public-spirited, the shop-keepers nobly independent, . . . the Dissenters quite without narrowness or asperity in religion and politics, . . . —these things I have not heard, not having correspondence in those parts. . . . (399)

What Eliot is bearing witness to in her post-Romantic way Kleist, Scott, and Balzac also point to: the enfeeblement of a communal sense of justice. Exceptional individuals, all these nineteenth-century writers suggest, retain a belief in natural law and attempt to live by that belief. But society's positive laws and legal processes are inferior to these exemplary consciences.

Our voyage from Homer to the late nineteenth century, in this discussion of the conflict between idealistic and realistic views of justice, ends at a point at which "objective" idealism has virtually ceased to be a tenable perspective. Kleist, Scott, Balzac could still look to the heavens, or to gypsies, for some manifestations of natural law. Eliot's fiction, while it recalls Wordsworth's Duty, "stern daughter of the Voice of God," helps usher in an age when duty will be an orphan and Thrasymachus's definition of justice will sound to many ears like blunt truth.

NOTES

1. Homer, *The Odyssey*, trans. A. T. Murray, vol. 2 (Cambridge: Harvard UP, 1975) 237.

2. Homer, *The Iliad*, trans. A. T. Murray, vol. 2 (Cambridge: Harvard UP, 1976) 325–27.

3. Hesiod, *Works and Days*, trans. Richmond Lattimore (Ann Arbor: U of Michigan P, 1959) 45.

4. Aeschylus, *The Oresteia*, trans. Robert Fagles (New York: Bantam, 1977) 172.

5. Sophocles, *Antigone, The Oedipus Cycle: An English Version*, trans. Dudley Fitts and Robert Fitzgerald (New York: Harcourt, n.d.) 205.

6. George Steiner, *Antigones* (New York: Oxford UP, 1984) 27–28. Steiner remarks that throughout much of the Antigone tradition, Creon is "left in hideous solitude." But not in Anouilh's version. Toward the end of it, a page-boy enters, and not only "is Creon's punitive isolation broken, but the contact with childhood is, inevitably, suggestive of a larger re-entry into life" (193–94). See my own discussion of Anouilh's "absurdist" modern *Antigone* in the "Conclusion" of this book.

7. Werner Jaeger, "Euripides and His Age," *Paideia: The Ideals of Greek Culture*, trans. Gilbert Highet, vol. 1 (New York: Oxford UP, 1945) 329.

8. Euripides, *Orestes*, trans. William Arrowsmith, *The Complete Greek Tragedies*, ed. David Grene and Richmond Lattimore, vol. 7 (New York: Modern Library, n.d.) 12.

9. *Republic* 298.

10. See Erik A. Havelock, *The Greek Concept of Justice, from Its Shadow in Homer to Its Substance in Plato* (Cambridge: Harvard UP, 1978) 312. Havelock says that two generations before Plato, the term "dikaiosunē" had appeared in Herodotus, but only exceptionally (296). In Plato's substitution of "dikaiosunē" for "dikē," says Havelock, the field of meaning of justice "became richer and more complex by including the double reference to the polis and to the individual" (312).

11. Plato, *Crito, Apology, Crito, Republic I–II* (Chicago: Great Books Foundation, n.d.) 41.

12. William A. Robson, *Civilization and the Growth of Law: A Study of the Relations Between Men's Ideas About the Universe and the Institutions of Law and Government* (New York: Macmillan, 1935) 32.

13. Gen. 22:10, 17–18.

14. *Earlier English Drama from Robin Hood to Everyman*, ed. Thomas Whitfield Baldwin (New York: Thomas, 1929) 78.

15. William Foxwell Albright, *From the Stone Age to Christianity: Monotheism and the Historical Process* (New York: Doubleday, 1957) 331.

16. Isaac Rabinowitz, "Towards a Valid Theory of Biblical Hebrew Literature," *The Classical Tradition: Literary and Historical Studies in Honor of Harry Caplan*, ed. Luitpoid Wallach (Ithaca: Cornell UP, 1966) 318. Robert Gordis, in "Natural Law and Religion," observes that in Job's "great confession of innocence" in chapter 31, where he sets forth the code of conduct by which he has lived, all the fourteen elements of the code—except for his avoidance of the pagan worship of heavenly bodies—are "ethical." Developing the theme of links between the Biblical tradition and ethical natural law, Gordis says that "Leo Strauss has shown

that Judah Halevi equates the law of reason which underlies all codes with the law of nature." But, Gordis notes, "With the growth of secularism in the last few centuries, . . . the Greco-Roman source of natural law has continued to be cited, while the Judeo-Christian element has tended to be relegated to theologians." John Cogley et al., *Natural Law and Modern Society* (Cleveland: World, 1963) 261, 264–65.

17. Geoffrey Chaucer, "The Tale of Melibee," *The Poetical Works of Chaucer*, ed. F. N. Robinson (Boston: Houghton, 1933) 202.

18. Cicero, "On the Laws," *Selected Works of Cicero* (Roslyn, NY: Black, 1948) 225, 226, 228–29.

19. Lucretius, *On the Nature of Things*, trans H. A. J. Munro (London: Bell, 1929) 209.

20. St. Augustine, *The City of God* 15.1, trans. Marcus Dods in *Introduction to Contemporary Civilization in the West: A Source Book*, ed. Contemporary Civilization Staff, Columbia College, Columbia University, vol. 1 (New York: Columbia UP, 1946) 124.

21. *Anglo-Saxon Poetry*, trans. R. K. Gordon (London: Dent, 1926) 316–17.

22. *Earlier English Drama* 200–24.

23. Allan A. Gilbert, *Dante's Conception of Justice* (Durham, NC: Duke UP, 1925) 43.

24. Basil Willey, *The Eighteenth Century Background: Studies on the Idea of Nature in the Thought of the Period* (New York: Columbia UP, 1940) 15–17.

25. Maritain 36–37.

26. Dante Alighieri, *The Divine Comedy*, trans. Laurence Binyon, in *The Portable Dante*, ed. Paolo Milano (New York: Viking, 1947) 82.

27. William Langland, *Piers the Ploughman*, trans. J. F. Goodridge (Harmondsworth: Penguin, 1966) 25–26.

28. Henry J. Abraham, *The Judicial Process: An Introductory Analysis of the Courts of the United States, England, and France*, 3rd ed. (New York: Oxford UP, 1975) 15.

29. *La Farce de Maistre Pierre Pathelin*, ed. C. E. Pickford (Paris: Bordas, 1967) 6–7.

30. *The Farce of the Worthy Master Pierre Patelin, the Lawyer*, trans. Moritz Jagendorf, *The World of Law*, ed. Ephraim London, vol. 1 (New York: Simon & Schuster, 1963) 482.

31. Nicolò Machiavelli, *The Prince and the Discourses* (New York: Modern Library, 1940) 526–27.

32. Ralph Roeder, *The Man of the Renaissance: Four Lawgivers—Savonarola, Machiavelli, Castiglione, Aretino* (New York: Viking, 1935) 161.

33. More 56.

34. Michel de Montaigne, "Of Experience," *The Essays of Montaigne*, trans. John Florio (New York: Modern Library, n.d.) 968–69.

35. Cited by William Fenn DeMoss, *The Works of Edmund Spenser: A Variorum Edition*, ed. Edwin Greenlaw, vol. 5 (Baltimore: Johns Hopkins UP, 1936) 281.

36. *The Poetical Works of Edmund Spenser*, ed. J. C. Smith and E. de Selincourt (London: Oxford UP, 1916), 276.

37. Aristotle, *The Ethics of Aristotle: The Nicomachean Ethics*, trans. J. A. K. Thompson, rev. Hugh Tredennick (New York: Penguin, 1976) 189.

38. James I, *The Trew Law of Free Monarchies; or, The Reciprock and Mutuall Dutie Betwixt a Free King and His Naturall Subjects*, repr. in *Introduction to Contemporary Civilization in the West: A Source Book*, ed. Contemporary Civilization Staff, Columbia College, Columbia University, vol. 1 (New York: Columbia UP, 1946) 695, 700.

39. Edwin Greenlaw, "Spenser and British Imperialism," *Mod. Philol.* 9 (Jan. 1912) 347–70, rpt. in *Spenser's Critics: Changing Currents in Literary Taste*, ed. William R. Mueller (Syracuse: Syracuse UP, 1953) 131, 145.

40. Marshall Clagett, "The Medieval Heritage: Political and Economic," in *Chapters in Western Civilization*, ed. Contemporary Civilization Staff, Columbia College, Columbia University, vol. 1 (New York: Columbia UP, 1948) 40.

41. Frank Kermode, "*The Fairie Queene*, I and V," *Bull. of the John Rylands Library* 47 (1965) 123–50, rpt. in *Essential Articles for the Study of Spenser*, ed. A. C. Hamilton (Hamden, CT: Archon, 1972) 275.

42. Calvin Thomas, *The Life and Works of Friedrich Schiller* (New York: Holt, 1901) 356, 357. See also the free adaptation-translation of Schiller's *Maria Stuart*, Stephen Spender, *Mary Stuart* (New Haven, CT: Ticknor & Fields, 1980).

43. Christopher Marlow, *The Jew of Malta*, *Five Plays*, ed. Havelock Ellis (New York: Hill & Wang, 1956) 198.

44. Ben Jonson, *Selected Works*, ed. Harry Levin (New York: Random, 1938) 17.

45. William Shakespeare, *The Merchant of Venice*, *The Riverside Shakespeare*, ed. G. Blakemore Evans (Boston: Houghton, 1974), (I.iii) 111–19.

46. Rodolphe Ihering [Rudolf von Ihering], *Le Combat pour le droit*, trans. François Maydieu (Paris, 1875) 35 fn.

47. J. W. Lever, introduction, *Measure for Measure*, by William Shakespeare (London: Methuen, 1965) lxiv.

48. See Anne Barton, introduction, *Measure for Measure*, *Riverside Shakespeare* 545.

49. Robert Bechtold Heilman, *This Great Stage: Image and Structure in King Lear* (Seattle: U of Washington P, 1963) 119.

50. George C. Herndl, *The High Design: English Renaissance Tragedy and the Natural Law* (Lexington: UP of Kentucky, 1970) 151.

51. John Webster, *The Duchess of Malfi, Eight Famous Elizabethan Plays* (New York: Modern Library, 1932) 503.

52. Fox 12–13.

53. Robert L. Fiore, *Natural-Law Ethics in Spanish Golden Age Theatre* (Lexington: UP of Kentucky, 1975) 1.

54. Fiore, ch. 2.

55. Lope de Vega, *Fuente Ovejuna (The Sheep Well), Four Plays*, trans. John Garrett Underhill (Westport, CT.: Hyperion, 1978), 309 (Act II).

56. Fiore 21.

57. Henry Kamen, *The Spanish Inquisition* (1965; New York: NAL, 1975) 136.

58. Pedro Calderón de la Barca, *The Mayor of Zalamea, Four Plays*, trans. Edwin Honig (New York: Hill & Wang, 1961), 168 (*El alcade* II).

59. José M. Aguirre, "El alcalde de Zalamea: ¿'Venganza o justicia?' " *Estudios filológicos* 7 (1971) 121.

60. Martin Turnell, *The Classical Moment: Studies of Corneille, Molière, and Racine* (Norwalk, CT: New Directions, n.d.) 37.

61. Pierre Corneille, *Cinna, Théâtre choisi de Corneille*, ed. Maurice Rat (Paris: Garnier, 1961), 203 (V.iii.1696).

62. Thomas Corneille, *The Earl of Essex, The Chief Rivals of Corneille and Racine*, trans. Lacy Lockert (Nashville: Vanderbilt UP, 1956) II, p. 393.

63. Margaret Wilson, *Spanish Drama of the Golden Age* (New York: Pergamon, 1969) 193; and E. Martinenche, *La Comédie espagnole en France de Hardy à Racine* (Paris, 1900), passim.

64. Racine, *Athaliah*, IV.iii.1391–92, 1404–08, 1409–10.

65. Hazard 63.

66. *A History of the Western World: Early Modern Times*, ed. Shepard B. Clough (Lexington, MA: Heath, 1969) 698.

67. Quoted by Willey 7.

68. Jonathan Swift, "A Voyage to Brobdingnag," *Gulliver's Travels and Other Writings* (New York: Modern Library, 1958) 100.

69. Norman L. Torrey, ed. *Les Philosophes: The Philosophers of the Enlightenment and Modern Democracy* (New York: Capricorn, 1960) 85.

70. Voltaire, "Natural Law" 833–34.

71. Henry Fielding, *The History of Tom Jones, a Foundling* (New York: Modern Library, n.d.) 110–12.

72. D'Entrèves 60.

73. Denis Diderot, *La Religieuse, Oeuvres romanesques*, ed. Henri Bénac (Paris: Garnier, 1962) 310.

74. See Bernard Groethuysen, *Origines de l'esprit bourgeois en France* (Paris: Gallimard, 1927), passim, on the condemnation by the Church of profit-making in seventeenth- and eighteenth-century France.

75. Heinrich von Kleist, "Michael Kohlhaas," *The Marquise of O— and Other Stories*, trans. David Luke and Michael Reeves (Harmondsworth: Penguin, 1978) 148.

76. *Introduction to Contemporary Civilization*, I 886–88.

77. Sir Walter Scott, *The Heart of Midlothian* (London: Dent, 1956) 173.

78. Karl Kroeber, *Romantic Narrative Art* (Madison: U Wisconsin P, 1961) 186.

79. Honoré de Balzac, "The Red Inn", *Novels: The Unknown Masterpiece, The Maranas, A Seashore Drama, The Red Inn, Master Cornelius* (Philadelphia, 1899) 216.

80. George Eliot, *Felix Holt, the Radical*, ed. Fred C. Thomson (Oxford: Oxford UP, 1980) 222.

81. See E. P. Thompson, *The Making of the English Working Class* (New York: Knopf, 1966) 808–22, esp. 819–20.

82. Raymond Williams, "The Industrial Novels," *Culture and Society, 1780–1950* (New York: Doubleday, 1960) 110–18, discusses *Felix Holt*.

83. In a disenchanted modern version of "Michael Kohlhaas," the "Coalhouse Walker" episode in E. L. Doctorow's novel *Ragtime* (1975; New York: Bantam, 1976), no transcendental force, or civil court for that matter, aids an American black man who after the frustration of his many efforts to obtain legal redress for egregious injuries becomes the leader of a group of urban guerrillas. The difference in tone in Doctorow's version of the story from Kleist's is emblematic of a major shift, from the nineteenth to the twentieth century, in writers' conceptions of the world. See Richard Sterne, "Reconciliation and Alienation in Kleist's 'Michael Kohlhaas' and Doctorow's *Ragtime*," *Legal Studies Forum*, 12.1 (1988) 5–22.

2

The Sense of Injustice in Modern Religious Fiction

IT IS INSTRUCTIVE to contrast George Eliot's description in *Felix Holt* of a half-drunken mob, lurching toward the great house of the parish, with Sir Walter Scott's account of the disciplined mob which, in *The Heart of Midlothian*, lynches Captain Porteous of the Edinburgh City Guard. Some mobs, obviously, are more restrained than others, and Scott was being faithful to an historical source. But later nineteenth-century writers tended, as their Romantic predecessors did not, to assimilate human behavior to that of other animals. Thus Eliot's remark that the actions of the crowd, most of whom were excited with drink, "could hardly be calculated on more than those of the oxen and pigs congregated amidst hootings and pushings" (264) is the sort of observation one finds increasingly in literature as Darwin's ideas seeped into everyone's consciousness. The subtitle of Emile Zola's Rougon-Macquart series of novels (1871–93), "Histoire naturelle et sociale d'une famille sous le Second Empire," indicates his naturalistic purpose: to treat human behavior in a "scientific spirit" and "to use the realistic and symbolic possibilities of a hereditarily unbalanced family to portray critically certain aspects of a diseased society."[1] Unlike Balzac, who in the *Comédie Humaine* had played the role of "secretary" to a society for whose corruptions he held individuals responsible, Zola seems in his fiction to be the amanuensis of deterministic biologists, sociologists, and alienists.

Although naturalism undercuts the idea of ethical natural law by absorbing human beings into Darwinian nature, modern religiously oriented fiction subverts it by humiliating reason, in the spirit of Augustine and Pascal. Religious writers in the natural law tradition of Aquinas—one thinks of Dante, Langland, Lope—took for granted the importance of ethical rules that reason could discern. In works like the *Commedia*, *Piers the Ploughman*, and *Fuenteovejuna*, the avaricious character or the cruelly lustful one is forthrightly presented as a sinner or criminal. But such recent authors as Tolstoy, Dostoevsky, and Mauriac suggest in their fiction that what matters far more than obedience to ethical rules is the turning of the sinner's heart away from selfish and worldly things and toward a loving God. Tolstoy's "God Sees the Truth, But Waits," where a man is framed for murder and theft, and spends the rest of his life in a Siberian prison, indicates—through the words of the innocent prisoner to the criminal who belatedly begs his forgiveness—that only God can know which of the two is the better person. Equally antinomian in spirit is Tolstoy's novel *Resurrection*: the aristocratic protagonist resolves to change his life after realizing that his negligence as a juror has helped to convict of murder a woman he had ruined years ago and thus driven into prostitution. Nekhlyudov eventually learns that only those efforts to help victims of injustice which are animated by agape have a chance of success. If you feel no love, he decides, you should leave others alone. Dostoevsky, who reacted violently against the positivistic world view symbolized for him by Claude Bernard—one of Zola's intellectual models—dramatizes in *The Brothers Karamazov* the belief that human beings can overcome judicial and social injustice only through faith in and imitation of a loving God. The depiction of Dmitry's trial implies that the trial as an institution is irremediably flawed by the narrow rationalism that dominates it; what interests Dostoevsky more than the judicial error with which the trial ends is the positive spiritual effect upon Dmitry of the pain he has suffered and the faith in him that Alyosha has shown. Mauriac recalls Dostoevsky by indicating that Thérèse Desqueyroux, wrongly found innocent of an attempt to poison her husband to death, is closer to God in her confused, agonized quest for love than are the complacent, loveless, rationalist family members who condemn her. Tolstoy, Dostoevsky, and Mauriac treat criminal trials, in the works discussed in this chapter, as essentially "missing the point": the judicial error that occurs in each trial simply shows the incapacity of reason to deal with problems that can be resolved only through selfless love in the spirit of Jesus.

TOLSTOY'S "GOD SEES THE TRUTH, BUT WAITS" AND *Resurrection*

Leo Tolstoy, his biographer Henri Troyat remarks, was two men, "a sybarite and a saint—sewed up inside one skin, each loathing the other.''[2] Although the sybarite begot a thirteenth child by his wife when he was fifty-nine, the saint preached chastity to the disciples at his Yasnaya Polyana estate and renounced almost all the sybarite's literary works, including *War and Peace* and *Anna Karenina*. Among the few fictions to escape this auto-anathema was a story for children called "God Sees the Truth, But Waits" ("Bog Pravdu Vidyet, da Nye, Skora Skazhet," 1872). It concerns a cheerful young merchant, Aksyónof, who drives off to the Nizhni-Novgorod fair despite his wife's nightmare in which, as she has warned him, his hair suddenly turned gray. Stopping at an inn, he meets a merchant acquaintance whose room adjoins his own. Aksyónof awakens in the middle of the night, decides to leave while the air is cool, and later stops at another inn. There he is visited by a rural police chief who questions him about his early departure from the first inn, tells him the merchant has been found dead with his throat cut, and discovers a blood-stained knife in Aksyónof's bag. Aksyónof insists he is innocent, but his faltering voice and pale face convince the police chief of his guilt. Aksyónof's wife, when she visits him in jail, says that she has unsuccessfully petitioned the tsar in his behalf, and that his hair has indeed turned gray; then she softly says," 'Ványa, dearest, tell your wife the truth; was it not you who did it?' " He weeps. After she has left, he says to himself, " 'It seems that only God can know the truth; it is to Him alone we must appeal and from Him alone expect mercy.' "[3] He petitions no further, is found guilty at his trial of murder and robbery, and is condemned to hard labor in Siberia.

Twenty-six years later, his hair white, his gaiety gone, the constantly praying Aksyónof is venerated as a saint by his fellow-prisoners, who ask him to settle their disputes. He never hears, however, from his wife and children, has no idea what has happened to them. A new prisoner, Makár, who, though he comes from Aksyónof's home city, does not recognize him, reveals that the Aksyónof family are rich merchants; Makár also declares that he himself is in Siberia for a minor crime of which he is innocent, but that there are other crimes for which he should have been arrested long ago. Convinced that Makár, to whom he has disclosed his own identity, is the merchant's murderer, Aksyónof struggles against both a suicidal impulse and a rage for revenge. Two weeks later he accidentally discovers Makár digging a passageway to freedom; threatened by him with death should he reveal the plan, Aksyónof bitterly retorts, " '. . . you have no need to kill me; you killed me long ago! As to telling of you—I may do so or not, as God shall direct.' "

When after soldiers discover the passageway, and Aksyónof is summoned by the Governor to tell who had dug it, he refuses to name Makár, both because he does not want him to be whipped to death and because " 'maybe I suspect him wrongly. And, after all, what good would it be to me' " (8)?

The next night, Makár sits down at his feet, begs his forgiveness, confesses the murder of the merchant and the framing of Aksyónof, and promises to free him by making a public avowal. Although Aksyónof cuttingly replies that he now has no place to go, his wife having died and his children having forgotten him, he is softened by Makár's repeated weeping plea for forgiveness. He says at last: " 'God will forgive you. Maybe I am a hundred times worse than you!' " (9). By the time the order comes for his release, he is dead.

Tolstoy's plot resembles that of the murder story in Balzac's "The Red Inn." But the thematic difference between the two fictions is important. Balzac is chiefly concerned with the decay of morality, or sense of justice, between two historical periods: the pre-Revolutionary one, when a certain "purity"—a sense of natural law—prevailed, and the corrupt, commercialized post-Revolutionary one. Tolstoy, on the other hand, contrasts the fallibility of man's legal processes, and the extreme inadequacy of man's judgments of his fellows and himself, with God's omniscience and love. It is only when the once–self-sufficient Aksyónof accepts his own powerlessness and puts all his faith in God that he achieves a kind of peace. Balzac's perspective in "The Red Inn" is essentially a social one: he is nostalgic for what he thinks of as the pure provincial morality of the days of the Old Regime. Tolstoy's perspective is religious: rejecting, as Augustine did, Cain's unjust earthly city, he looks to the heavenly one for justice and mercy.

Tolstoy's Christianity in "God Sees the Truth, But Waits" differs significantly from the Romantic supernaturalism which, in a murky way, continues the natural law tradition. Aksyónof, having experienced an inner revolution during his jail term, comes to believe in and rely on God absolutely. But there is nothing in this

story like Kleist's reincarnation of a wife in the form of a mysterious gypsy, or Scott's punishment of a father's wrongdoing at
the hands of a son, or Balzac's introduction of a "light" that
prevents his protagonist from committing murder. Paradoxically,
all these heavenly interventions in "Michael Kohlhaas," *The Heart
of Midlothian*, and "The Red Inn" enforce traditional, rational
natural law. In "God Sees the Truth, But Waits," however, the
truth and justice that God sees are inaccessible to human reason.

Resurrection (*Voskressenye*, 1899), the last novel that Tolstoy
wrote, differs in tone from "God Sees the Truth, But Waits"; it
does not imply that only God can adequately know and judge
human actions. On the contrary, Tolstoy vigorously criticizes
legal and social injustices throughout *Resurrection*, which insists on
the necessity of a moral revolution within individuals, especially
those of the privileged upper class, as a condition of the transformation of society. It is accurate to say of Tolstoy, as Isaiah Berlin
does, that like "the believers in natural law, Tolstoy was convinced
that men have certain basic material and spiritual needs in all
places, at all times," and that moral values are "objective and
eternal."[4] What distinguishes *Resurrection*, however, from such
fictional works in the natural law tradition as *Antigone*, *Piers the
Ploughman*, *Fuenteovejuna*, and "Michael Kohlhaas" is the virtual
fanaticism of Tolstoy's idea that if men will only obey Jesus's
"simple, clear, practical commandments"—in the Sermon on the
Mount (Matt. 5:21–48), "a completely new order of human
society, in which the violence that filled Nekhlyudov with such
indignation would not only cease of itself but the greatest blessing
man can hope for—the kingdom of heaven on earth—would be
attained."[5]

While Tolstoy's artistry is impressive in most of this didactic
novel, his insistence on literal adherence to a moral code that
forbids not only violent acts but anger, not only adultery but
enjoyment of a woman's beauty, and that enjoins us to offer the
other cheek when we are smitten, and to love, help, and serve our
enemies, constitutes a serious esthetic error as well as an exagger-
ation of what human beings can achieve, or wish to achieve.
Resurrection as a whole, however, is a powerful critique, from the
perspective of an antinomian, "primitive" Christianity, of the way
law works in czarist society. The protagonist, Prince Dmitri

Nekhlyudov, comes to understand through his long effort to atone for a great wrong "that society and order generally speaking existed, not thanks to those legalized criminals who judge and punish other men, but because in spite of their depraving influence people still pity and love one another" (565).

Two minor characters in the novel illustrate movingly this capacity for mutual pity and love. Fedosya, a peasant girl married without her consent at the age of sixteen, tried to poison her husband soon after the wedding. While out on bail awaiting trial, she asked him to forgive her " 'for that there silliness, I didn't know what I was doing.' " Her husband, Tarass, replied, " 'Don't talk so much, I forgave you long ago.' " Yet although she now called him " 'sweet'eart,' " Tarass recalls their returning home from the field one day to find a summons: " '*Appear in court*, it said. And we'd clean forgotten the business she were to be tried for' " (456–57).

Fedosya's subsequent trial and punishment represent the defeat of love and forgiveness by abstract human law. Augustine might have said that Fedosya and Tarass, whose love for each other is of the City of God, are prisoners of the earthly city. Tolstoy, however, emphasizes continually in *Resurrection* that injustice in the earthly city is the consequence of control of the law by the rich and the powerful. Repeatedly in the story, serious wrongs committed by the wealthy go unpunished, while the peccadilloes of the socially obscure are severely penalized. The revolution within Prince Nekhlyudov begins when he suddenly realizes that a defendant in a murder trial in which he is serving as a juror is

> the same girl, half ward, half servant [of his two aunts], with whom he had once been in love, . . . whom he had seduced, and deserted, and then never thought of again because the memory would have been too painful. . . . it would have proved that he who was so proud of his "good breeding" not only was not a gentleman but had treated this woman disgracefully. (54–55)

The outcome of the trial intensifies Nekhlyudov's remorse. For the woman, Maslova, now a prostitute, is, through the negligence of both the presiding judge and the jury, declared guilty. Actually, she had been tricked by two confederates, who wanted to rob a merchant she was entertaining, into poisoning the merchant's soup with a powder she believed to be a mere soporific. But because the judge, hurrying to end the day's work and join his mistress, forgets to explain to the jury that unless they add the words "without intent to take life" (117) to a verdict of guilty, the defendant will be declared guilty of intentional murder; and because the jurors, owing to his careless omission and their own fatigue, neglect to specify that Masloya did not intend to kill; and because the presiding judge, though empowered to set aside a jury decision that the court finds unjust, is dissuaded from doing so by one of the two other judges sitting on the case—because of this compound of unseemly haste (recalling Pope's "Wretches hang, that jurymen may dine"), error, and judicial deference, Maslova is deprived of her civil rights and sentenced to four years of penal servitude in Siberia.

A well-informed Russian reader at the turn of the twentieth century might have been particularly struck by the judge's failure to instruct the jury to add "without intent to take life" to a verdict of guilty. For one of the provisions of the great Judicial Reform of 1864, which established trial by jury, was that the jury had to respond to written questions submitted to it by the bench with the words "yes, guilty," or "no, not guilty," or "yes, but deserves indulgence." An historian of the Russian legal system of the nineteenth century points out that "the right of indulgence toward the accused is a very important one."[6] Thus, the presiding judge and, in consequence, the jury in Maslova's case make an error that is especially egregious in a judicial system that encourages compassionate corrections of the letter of the law. Yet Tolstoy's emphasis on the compounding of mistakes in this trial clearly indicates that he finds great slovenliness in the implementing of the Reform, and that he believes a significant change in human behavior itself is what is really needed.

Nekhlyudov feels overwhelmingly responsible for the jury's negligence, undoubtedly because it was his own earlier abandonment of Maslova—who had subsequently, he has learned, had a baby—that turned her into a prostitute. As a first step toward appealing her conviction to the Russian Senate, he puts the case into a lawyer's hands. But he realizes that he cannot atone for his fault by paying a lawyer to save her from undeserved hard labor in Siberia. He must, he decides, ask her forgiveness, do everything he can to ease her lot, even marry her if necessary. He must also tell his fiancée, Princess "Missy" Korchagin, that he cannot marry her because he is a libertine; and he must break off his affair with a married woman with whose husband he is friendly. But that is not all. Years earlier, his reading of Herbert Spencer's *Social Statics* had persuaded him that the private ownership of property was unjust. He had therefore given his peasants 500 acres inherited from his father. Now, his mother having died, he tells himself that, in accord with his principles, he will dispose of the extensive property that she has left him. Tolstoy deftly indicates Nekhlyudov's mixed emotions after he has taken these resolutions: "His eyes filled with tears as he was saying all this to himself, good and bad tears: good because they were tears of joy at the awakening of the spiritual being within him, the being that had slumbered all these years; and bad tears of tender emotion at his own goodness" (142).

His spiritual awakening leads to his quitting the jury after one more trial, that of a young apprentice for petty burglary; the Prince has concluded that instead of considering how to eliminate the cause of a youth's becoming a thief, society unfairly punishes him. At this point Tolstoy's position on the relationship between formal legal processes and the structure of society becomes completely clear: trials are held essentially in order to permit all of us—since we are society—to punish scapegoats for our own failures.

Nekhlyudov goes to the Public Prosecutor, announces that he had seduced Maslova, wants to marry her, and can no longer serve on the jury because he considers " 'all law-courts not only useless but immoral' " (170). But before the Prince can feel the full horror of what he has done to "Katusha" (whose surname, Maslova, that of the mother who had borne her out of wedlock, reminds him of his own guilt), his "tender emotion at his own goodness" must be dispelled. When he visits her in jail, she tells him "curtly and spitefully" (197) that their child had died soon after its birth; he declares during a second visit that he wants to marry her to atone for his wrong, but she lashes out: " 'You had your pleasure from me in this world, and you want to get your salvation through me in the world to come! You disgust me—with your spectacles and your fat, ugly mug. Go away, go away! . . .' " (219). Until this point, Tolstoy comments, Nekhlyudov had been "dallying with his feelings of remorse, delighting in himself"; now, however, "he was quite simply filled with horror." He realizes what he has "done to the soul of this woman" and "could not imagine what would come of his relationship to her" (220).

It is true, as Isaiah Berlin observes, that Tolstoy, like Rousseau, "rejected the doctrine of original sin" ("Tolstoy" 30), but in a passage like this one he shows a vivid awareness of the psychological consequences of the wrongs that persons do to each other. Indeed, because of Tolstoy's sense of the wrongs he himself had committed against others—*Resurrection* derives largely from his own life—he is preoccupied in this novel with the abyss into which we can fall. Unlike the natural law writers, who stressed the importance of obedience to transcendent moral laws, Tolstoy emphasizes the need for a spiritual transformation that will enable such obedience.

The actions that Nekhlyudov takes after Maslova's scornful rebuke alter her attitude toward him. He inquires, as she had asked him to, into the case of two fellow-prisoners, the Menshovs, who were apparently innocent of the crime of arson for which they had been convicted. Then he arranges for Katusha's transfer to the prison hospital where a great many workers are needed to care for the patients. Although at first Maslova turns down the transfer, she proves to be strongly affected by his intercession on behalf of the Menshovs. Suddenly she both accepts the transfer and promises not to " 'touch any more drink either.' "

Here is an important moment in *Resurrection*. When Nekhlyudov first visited Maslova in jail, she thought only of how she could make use of this man who had used her. She borrowed money from him, and when he spoke of helping her she urged him to get the best possible lawyer. Now, however, she believes in his sincerity. " 'Yes, yes, she is an entirely different person,' " Nekhlyudov reflects, "experiencing after all his former doubts a feeling he had never known before—the certainty that love is invincible" (255).

He discovers, nonetheless, that it is one thing to begin to change both Maslova's life and his own, another thing to remedy the myriad social injustices that he now attributes to the absence of love in people's relationships. In jail along with Maslova are 130 stonemasons who have been locked up for nearly two months because, as a prison official explains, " 'they had no identity papers, and they ought to have been sent back to their own province, but the prison there was burnt down, and the local authorities appealed to us not to send them on' " (234–35). The government official, a former army acquaintance of Nekhlyudov's, through whom the Prince arranges Maslova's hospital transfer, eventually agrees to investigate the stonemasons' situation; but there are limits to what he will do: he calls Nekhlyudov "too inquisitive" for asking whether, as he has heard, some of them had received corporal punishment.

By the end of the first of three parts of *Resurrection*, Nekhlyudov feels personally accountable for social evils of which he had been unaware during his self-indulgent youth. This change in him is due to remorse over the wrongs that both he and the legal institutions of the country in which he occupies so privileged a place have done to Katusha. His French-speaking fellow aristocrats know nothing of the lower depths with which he has become familiar. And he now keeps one of these aristocrats—Missy Korchagin, his fiancée—at a distance. As for his married mistress, he has prudently neglected to correct her mistaken assumption that inspired her letter "releasing" him so that he could marry Missy. His central concern is to help Maslova, on whose behalf he intends to visit Petersburg to " 'do all I can about your—about our—case, and God willing, get the sentence revoked' " (254).

Anticipating, nevertheless, that her sentence will not be revoked, he prepares to follow her to Siberia. Before leaving, he feels he must settle matters on his estates in accordance with his recently reawakened belief that private landholding is sinful. He will not give the peasants the land outright, as he earlier had done with the estate left him by his father. Rather, he will let them rent it cheaply. Although he knows that this approach resembles the old one under serfdom of charging serfs quit-rent in lieu of labor, he thinks it is at least a change from a harsh "to a less harsh form of tyranny" (262). Though less idealistic than he was in his student days, the Prince now seems more deeply determined to change his life.

At Kuzminskoye, the estate that provides most of his income, he rediscovers how poorly paid the peasants are. He also learns how difficult it is to persuade people over whom he exercises complete economic control that a new arrangement will benefit them: the law that abolished serfdom has not abolished their traditional ways of thinking. Some of the peasants mutter that under the system he proposes, Nekhlyudov will have nothing to do but let the money come in—in contrast to " 'the worry and trouble there is now!' " (269). Nekhlyudov's "overfed" bailiff, however, blames the peasants for causing the "trouble" and tells the Prince that one of them regularly steals wood from the forest. An old man retorts, " 'Didn't you smash my jaw for me last summer, and did I get any damages?' " But the bailiff, confident of his own power, complacently warns him not to break the law (268–70).

This discussion of law makes Nekhlyudov uncomfortable. He is doubtless aware of the similarity between his own past exploitation of Katusha and his bailiff's treatment of those poor farmers, who, if they "go to the bad," are punished by a "law" that is altogether in the landowner's interest.

Despite the peasants' dissatisfaction, and his own, with the compromise property arrangement, he plans to implement it also at Panovo, an estate he has inherited from his aunts, where he first met Katusha. There, however, he has experiences that make him even more intensely conscious of his own responsibility for the peasants' misery. Two boys whom he meets tell him, for example, of a peasant jailed for cutting down a couple of beech-trees in the forest, " 'cos the forest belongs to the gentry, you see . . .' " (280). "Gentry," of course, means Nekhlyudov, who is soon to discover feelingly his own close kinship with these peasants. After finding the hut of Matriona, Katusha's aunt, and inquiring about "the child," he learns that the aunt herself had christened it—since Katusha had been so ill she seemed unlikely to survive—then paid a woman who " 'made a business of it' " to take the baby to the Foundlings' Hospital in Moscow. But the child—" 'the image of the father,' " says Matriona with a wink—had died as soon as the woman reached Moscow. Nekhlyudov asks if the baby had sickened because it was not fed properly. " 'Fed properly? It only got a lick and a promise. It wasn't her child. All she cared about was to get him there alive . . .' " (282–83).

Nekhlyudov's reaction to this moral nightmare is evoked through the description of a scene in the street immediately after he emerges from Matriona's hut. He recognizes an "emaciated woman holding her bloodless infant," learns that she lives by begging, and gives her ten rubles. "Before he had gone two steps another woman with a baby caught him up, then an old woman, then another young one. All spoke of their poverty and asked him for help. Nekhlyudov distributed the sixty roubles in small notes that he had in his pocket-book and, terribly sick at heart, returned home, that is, to the bailiff's house" (284).

The grief that he now shares personally with peasants whose children are dying of hunger enables him to see clearly that ". . . the chief and most immediate cause of the people's suffering sprang from the fact that the land which should feed them did not belong to them but was in the hands of men who take advantage of their ownership to live by the labours of the people" (286–87).

Henry George's doctrine comes vividly back to his mind: land ought not to be bought and sold, any more than water, air, or sunshine (287). He had been deceiving himself by giving the Kuzminskoye peasants only part of something which he had no right to. He now decides to renounce his right to the private ownership of the Panovo land and to recognize the rents he would receive for letting it as actually belonging to the peasants. These rents he would use to pay taxes and help the community in general. When the bailiff understands this plan, he concludes that the Prince is a little mad. And when the peasants finally accept it, it is chiefly because of an aged woman's opinion that "the master," anxious about his soul, is doing good in the hope of salvation (304).

Resurrection is partly autobiographical; just as Tolstoy's idealism estranged him from his family, Nekhlyudov's estranges him from his older sister, Natalia. It is all too schematically congruent with the "reformed" Tolstoy's asceticism that Natalia has deteriorated since her marriage to "a man whom she loves with a sensual love" (404). Her husband, a lawyer contemptuous of the altruistic aspirations she had once shared with Nekhlyudov, accompanies her to Moscow to see the Prince just before he leaves for Siberia with Maslova. Nekhlyudov's appeal to the Senate on her behalf has failed, and his mind is full of what he has seen and learned at Panovo. The luxurious hotel room of his brother-in-law, Rogozhinsky, becomes the scene of a hot argument in which Nekhlyudov depicts both Katusha and the peasants as victims of oppression. Rogozhinsky scornfully retorts that innocent persons are rarely convicted of crimes and that it is "socialism" to contend that the landed proprietors had long ago seized what should be common property. Since, as far as Rogozhinsky knows, his children by Natalia might become Nekhlyudov's heirs, the argument is not merely theoretical. When Nekhlyudov denounces the judicial courts as " 'only an instrument for upholding the existing order of things, in the interests of our class' " (414), he presents an immediate threat to his lawyer brother-in-law. In the light of this scene alone, it is difficult to understand John Bayley's complaint that Tolstoy

> does not distinguish between the system and the given case [Maslova's]. Is the system, corrupting and deforming the individuals who attempt to work it, always unjust, or has an exceptional miscarriage occurred here? It is a point of some importance, but Tolstoy ignores it. He has to, because he believes all government procedures to be inherently bad.[7]

But Tolstoy does not ignore the point. Nekhlyudov's comment on the class bias of the court system makes it plain that both he and Tolstoy consider the miscarriage of justice in Maslova's case frighteningly "normal." Bayley's question about the "system" is anticipated by Nekhlyudov's declaration that " 'over half the people sentenced by the courts are innocent' " (410). *Resurrection* indicts the Russian legal system not on the grounds that it is "always" unjust but that it is *fundamentally* so.

What probably annoys most readers of *Resurrection*, however, is Tolstoy's extreme asceticism, that of the "saint" (in Troyat's terminology) loathing the "sybarite" within himself. A striking illustration of this asceticism, which is quite opposed to the natural law tradition of measured reason, is Nekhlyudov's response to the change in his sister since her maidenly youth. When she comes to the railroad station to see him off for Siberia, he apologizes for the way he had talked to her husband, and he adds that since he himself intends to have no children even if he should marry, everything he owns except the Kuzminskoye land will eventually go to her children. " 'Dmitri, please don't say that,' " she pleads; but Nekhlyudov knows she is pleased, and he feels "that the

Natalia who had been so dear to him no longer existed, leaving only the slave of her husband, that unpleasant, dark, hairy, alien man" (445–46).

This is not art, but propaganda. Yet there is an indissoluble link in the novel between Nekhlyudov's rejection of sexual love, which seeks primarily to possess its object, and his rejection of the private ownership of land. Just as the Prince becomes convinced that the land belongs to all men, so he has arrived, through his experience of debauchery and guilt, at the conclusion that only agape can bring human beings together. In short, he believes that while sex and the law put us all asunder, love devoid of sex creates community.

It is characteristic of the converted or "resurrected" Nekhlyudov that he compares his own "unloving" outburst at his brother-in-law to the way in which governors, inspectors, and policemen treat those accused of crime. In the train carrying him and Katusha and the other convicts to Siberia, he reflects:

> "The whole trouble is that people think there are circumstances when one may deal with human beings without love, but no such circumstances ever exist. . . . And it cannot be otherwise, because mutual love is the fundamental force of human life. . . . a man cannot force himself to love in the way in which he can force himself to work, but it does not follow from this that men may be treated without love, especially if something is required from them."

He concludes—and this is virtually the key to the novel—" 'If you feel no love—leave people alone' " (450).

Tolstoy's attack in *Resurrection* on the Orthodox Church, whose power in Russia was buttressed by the law, was based precisely on his conviction that it did not act out of love. In jail with Maslova, before her departure for Siberia, were some religious sectarians who complained to Nekhlyudov that they had been sentenced to deportation for reading the Gospels. The Prince's lawyer subsequently told him that severe punishment could be incurred for expounding the Bible in a manner critical of the Church's interpretation. To detract "in public from the Orthodox Faith" means, in accordance with the law, exile to Siberia. Nekhlyudov managed to discuss the sectarians' plight with a high official of the Holy Synod who, wanting to avoid harmful publicity to the Church, had agreed to grant their petition—but had smiled condescendingly when the Prince asked how families could be broken up in the name of religion. Nekhlyudov recalls some time after this conversation the remark of Thoreau's—whose antinomian perspective resembles Tolstoy's in *Resurrection*—that " 'the only proper place for an honest man in a country where slavery was legalized and protected was the gaol' " (392).

Honest men abound, Nekhlyudov discovers, among the political prisoners with whom he has arranged for Maslova to travel to Siberia. Many of them have a higher standard of morality than he has found among judges, lawyers, priests, and government administrators. It is true that some of the revolutionary prisoners are detestable; one of them, Novodvorov, who believes only in power, could be a character in Dostoevsky's *The Possessed*. Tolstoy underlines the miserable social conditions that have led such men to violent activity; but the "politicals" to whom he is most sympathetic are two ascetic idealists, Marya Pavlovna and Simonson. Marya, an aristocrat turned revolutionary out of hatred for the way the upper classes lived, had pleaded guilty, solely in order to protect a comrade, to a charge of shooting during a police search of her lodgings. She and Katusha are drawn together by their common kindness and by—here again, Tolstoy's ascetic extremism is evident—their common loathing for sexual love: "One hated it because she knew all its horrors, while the other, having never experienced it, regarded it as something incomprehensible and at the same time repugnant and offensive to human dignity" (473).

Simonson, exiled for teaching dangerous ideas about justice to the peasants, has formulated an organic theory of life that opposes killing of every kind, of animals as well as human beings. Believing that to serve existing life is a higher function than to increase and multiply, he holds that celibates like himself and Marya Pavlovna resemble phagocytes, whose mission is to destroy diseased parts of the organism. Simonson loves Katusha, but platonically, so he feels he can propose marriage to her without endangering his phagocytic function in the world. Katusha ultimately accepts his offer, both because she feels she would be a burden to Nekhlyudov, whose marriage proposal is due not to love but to generosity, and because Simonson "loved her as she was now" (474–75).

Before she makes this decision, Nekhlyudov has had news from a highly placed Petersburg juror who had influenced the czar's Appeals Committee in Maslova's favor. Her sentence to hard labor is to be commuted to one of exile to some less remote region of Siberia (543). When Nekhlyudov visits her in the Siberian jail to convey this good news, he is jolted by her declaration that she intends to follow Simonson wherever he goes. While the Prince senses that she is refusing him for her own sake, he regrets " 'all that he would lose when he lost her' " (552–53). It is clear that he himself has been "saved" in the course of his efforts to help her and others. But Tolstoy indicates that the Prince's battle against his own egotism—evidently like that of an alcoholic against the urge to drink—must be unremitting.

As for the terrible social problems that give rise to cruel and futile imprisonments, Nekhlyudov still can see no solution; in his imagination "he beheld hundreds and thousands of degraded human beings locked up in noisome prisons by indifferent generals, prosecuting attorneys and superintendents . . ." (561). Suddenly, however, after opening a New Testament at random, and beginning to read the Gospel according to St. Matthew, he finds "the whole answer": " 'Shouldest not thou also have had compassion on thy fellow-servant, even as I had pity on thee?' " Nekhlyudov now realizes

> that the only sure means to salvation from the terrible wrongs which mankind endures is for every man to acknowledge himself a sinner before God and therefore unfitted either to punish or reform others. . . . Now he knew the cause of all the horrors he had seen, and what ought to be done to put an end to them. The answer he had been unable to find was the same that Christ gave to Peter: to forgive everyone always, forgive an endless number of times, because there was no man living who was guiltless and therefore able to punish or reform. (564–65)

This "revelation" of Nekhlyudov's recalls Aksyónof's forgiving attitude at the end of "God Sees the Truth, But Waits." Nekhlyudov is rejecting not only the unjust legal and penal system of czarist Russia, but also all institutional prosecutions and imprisonments. His antinomianism would abolish penitentiaries and lodge penitence within every human heart. It makes a much more extreme demand on everyone of us than does a call to obey natural law, for while a sense of fraternity is at the heart of the natural law tradition, that tradition has never attenuated the crime of murder.

Anton Chekhov, who had helped to effect some prison reforms with his report "The Island of Sakhalin" (1893–94), on a Siberian prison settlement, found the conclusion of *Resurrection* disappointing: " 'To write and write, and then suddenly throw it all away on a piece of scripture, is a little too theological!' " (Troyat 551). This is acute literary criticism; the Orthodox Church, however, recognized more clearly than Chekhov the grave threat that *Resurrection* represented to the established order. The Church excommunicated Tolstoy, declaring in a document that was to be posted on the doors of all churches, that it "no longer recognizes him among her chldren and cannot do so until he has repented and restored himself to communion with her."

On Sunday (the Russian word for which is the same as the word for Easter and Resurrection—*Voskressenye*), February 4, 1901, when *Ecclesiastical News* published the excommunication, Tolstoy was hailed by joyful students and workers who surrounded him in Lubyanka Square, crying, " 'Three cheers for Leo Nikolayevich! Hail the great man!' " Alexis Suvorin, director of the *New Times*, commented: " 'We have two tsars, Nicholas II and Leo Tolstoy. Which is stronger? Nicholas II is powerless against Tolstoy and cannot make him tremble on his throne, whereas Tolstoy is incontestably shaking the throne of Nicholas II and his whole dynasty' " (Troyat 560–61, 564).

The eventual topplers of Nicholas's throne, the Soviets, had a mixed attitude toward Tolstoy. While revering him as a great pre-Revolutionary writer who exposed the evils of czarist society, they disapproved of his intensely antinomian criticism of "the law" and his insistence on a moral revolution within persons as a precondition for social transformation. In short, Tolstoy was as problematic from the standpoint of Soviet legality as he was from that of any positive legal system and from the perspective of natural law. In Vladimir Tendryakov's compassionately ironic post-Stalin story "Justice," a Soviet Prosecutor and his Assistant discuss uneasily an influential industrial developer, Dudyrev, who has come to them to insist on accepting his share of the blame for a man's death in a hunting accident. Actually, Dudyrev is entirely at fault and is seeking to salve his conscience with a partial confession. But both officials are embarrassed by what he says, for his high standing in the community "threatened the Prosecutor and his Assistant with 'complications.' " Unwilling to face their legal responsibilities in the matter—it is easier for them to let full blame for the accident fall on an obscure hunter—they agree after Dudyrev's departure that he is an idealist. " 'Damn it all, what a Quixote!' " says the Assistant Prosecutor. " 'More like Nekhlyudov,' " replies the Prosecutor—" 'another example of that Russian conscience which could drive a man to follow a prostitute to Siberia.' "[8]

DOSTOEVSKY'S *Brothers Karamazov*

Proust observes, in *À la recherche du temps perdu*, that Tolstoy often imitates Dostoevsky;[9] and I have said that Novodvorov, a violent revolutionary in *Resurrection*, could be a character in *The Possessed*. In addition to being influenced as an artist by Dostoevsky, Tolstoy shares with him a sense of the injustice of the criminal trial. But while *Resurrection* imputes the chief fault for the unjust verdict against Maslova to a negligence that Tolstoy indicates is endemic in Russian society, *The Brothers Karamazov* (*Brat'ya Karamazovy*, 1879–80) implies that Dmitry falls victim primarily to the machinations of the murderer, Smerdyakov, who symbolizes a hollow, atheistic rationalism. Tolstoy expresses considerable admiration in *Resurrection* for the "majority" of revolutionaries: they "differed favorably from ordinary people in that their moral standards were higher. Temperance, frugal living, honesty and unselfishness were binding principles for them, and they went farther and included a readiness to sacrifice everything, even life itself, for the common cause . . ." (480). Dostoevsky, on the other hand, indicates through Ivan that Smerdyakov is the "typical" forerunner of a revolution; and Ivan's "poem" about the atheistic Jesuit Grand Inquisitor suggests that the seeds of a rationalist revolution are present in the Inquisitor's condemnation of Jesus and His teaching.

Dostoevsky's idea of what the Revolution is all about differs markedly from the notion implicit in *Resurrection* that the revolutionaries envision the economic and social transformation of society. What impels Ivan to tell Alyosha the story of the Grand Inquisitor is Ivan's refusal to accept that the vile tortures inflicted on children in this life can ever be compensated by a divine "harmony." He says that he is giving back his "ticket" of admission to any such harmony—even if God has ordained it.[10] The "Grand Inquisitor" story turns on the contrast between a Jesus who has asked mankind to follow freely the path of love and faith to a "harmony" after death and the Inquisitor who would rather see human beings happy though enslaved than happy and free. In the story, Jesus returns to earth in Seville fifteen centuries after His crucifixion and is greeted by the people with great love. The Inquisitor, however, orders Him arrested, and tells Him he has no right to interfere with the work of the Church to which He had transmitted His power, and which has " 'corrected' " His teaching by founding it upon miracle, mystery, and authority (309). The Inquisitor says that although the people think they are free, the Church has actually lifted from them the burden of freedom; in place of it, the Church has given them bread and the security of a dogmatic religion and communal worship. After informing Jesus that tomorrow He will be burned at the stake as the wickedest of heretics, and that, " 'the very people who today were kissing Your feet will tomorrow, at a sign from my hand, hasten to Your stake to rake the coals' " (301), he reveals that he and a hundred thousand other ecclesiastics have accepted the task of lulling human beings—weak and dependent as they are—into dying " 'peacefully with Your name on their lips' "; " 'but beyond the grave they will find nothing but death. . . . for their own happiness we shall dangle before them the reward of eternal, heavenly bliss . . .' " (313).

That the Inquisitor yearns to be able to believe, as he once did, in Jesus's doctrine of freedom, is indicated by the ending of Ivan's story: Jesus responds to what the Inquisitor has told Him by suddenly kissing him gently on the lips; and the startled old man shudders, and releases Jesus from prison, telling Him to go away and never return. Toward the end of the "Grand Inquisitor" chapter, Dostoevsky draws an explicit parallel between Alyosha and Jesus and between Ivan and the Inquisitor by having Alyosha commit what his brother calls "plagiarism": he kisses the tormented Ivan on the lips.

What is clearly indicated by Ivan's story of the trial, condemnation, and "pardon" of Jesus, and by the kiss that Alyosha gives Ivan, is the great gap that Dostoevsky sees between the conclusions of reason and the attitude of agape. Writers in the natural law tradition like Dante, Langland, and More had posited a kind of community of reason in which men participated under God's governorship. Dostoevsky, however, in the tradition of Augustine and Pascal, presents human beings as utterly lost as long as they are guided chiefly by reason rather than by the light of divine love. Ivan, whose notion that "everything is permitted" in a world without God is at the heart of absurdist literature, faces a more difficult problem at the end of *The Brothers Karamazov* than does Dmitry, who has been wrongly convicted of murder. The suffering that Dmitry has gone through, and the faith in him that Alyosha has shown, may help him to repair the split between his spiritual and his animal nature. But how will Ivan deal with what Alyosha has called the "hell" in his head and heart?

More completely lost than Ivan, however, and than any other character in the novel, is Smerdyakov—the epileptic son of an idiot woman who had been raped by Fyodor Pavlovich, the father of Alyosha, Ivan, and Dmitry. Never acknowledged as a son by Fyodor Pavlovich, whom he serves as a cook, the rootless and conscienceless Smerdyakov finds in Ivan a master for his slavish soul. On the eve of Dmitry's trial for parricide, Smerdyakov tells the horrified Ivan that in addition to authorizing the crime philosophically by arguing that " 'everything is permitted,' " Ivan has actually signaled him, Smerdyakov, to proceed with the murder. The conscience-striken Ivan, who had indeed wished for Fyodor Pavlovich's death, now plans to produce Smerdyakov in court to clear Dmitry. The cook, however, hangs himself before the trial begins. Earlier in the novel, not knowing what horrors Smerdyakov is capable of, Ivan told his father that the cook, though a " 'flunkey,' " was also " 'a forerunner of progress.' " Fyodor Pavlovich was puzzled:

> "Forerunner of progress?"
> "Eventually there'll be better material, too, but some of it will be of this quality. First there will be the likes of him, then there'll be better ones."
> "And when will that be?"

"When the fuse is lighted. But perhaps it will fizzle out before anything happens. For the moment, the masses are none too eager to listen to what cooks like him have to say."

"That's just it, my boy. Balaam's ass broods in silence and then all of a sudden, he comes out with God knows what."

"He just stores up ideas," Ivan said with a crooked grin. (157)

This passage, with its reference to "the masses," associates the intellectual Ivan and the proletarian Smerdyakov with an incipient revolutionary movement. Although Ivan does not spell out its program, Dostoevsky links it "spiritually" with the program which, according to the atheistic Grand Inquisitor, the Roman Catholic Church follows in order to make its followers happy: the provision of bread, dogma, and communal worship. What all the foes of a true Christianity that are represented in the novel by Zosima and Alyosha have in common is a rationalism that prevents them from accepting the non-rational truth of a loving God's existence. But Dostoevsky opposes rationalism not only in its revolutionary and Roman Catholic manifestations but in its liberal, utilitarian form. In *Notes from Underground* (1864) his narrator declares that "a man's condition *sometimes* not only may, but even must, consist exactly in his desiring under certain conditions what is harmful to himself and not what is advantageous."[11]

This idea is strikingly exemplified in *The Brothers Karamazov* in the characterization of Dmitry, who has hated the father who, after abandoning him in his childhood, and cheating him of most of the inheritance from his mother, tried to seduce the woman Dmitry loved. Although innocent of the murder of Fyodor Pavlovich, Dmitry acts during the preliminary invcstigation that follows his arrest as if he desires "what is harmful to himself and not what is advantageous." For he tells the examining magistrate that although he has not killed his father, he has wanted " 'many, many times' " (556) to do so. This confession clearly expresses Dmitry's deep need—like that of the Underground Man—to punish and humiliate himself.

Fetyukovich, the brilliant lawyer who defends Dmitry at the murder trial, argues in his summation that a man who actually intended to kill his father would not, as Dmitry had done, threaten publicly to kill him, knock him down a few days before the crime, then write a letter saying he would kill him if he could not obtain three thousand rubles (which Dmitry had needed to pay a debt) in any other way. As far as Dmitry's conscious intention is concerned, Fetyukovich is of course right. These actions, however, are consonant with the murderous desire he has spoken of during the preliminary investigation.

Yet while Dmitry needs to be tried and humiliated, it is also extremely important to him to receive the public expression of Alyosha's belief in his innocence. On direct examination by Fetyukovich, Alyosha suddenly recalls Dmitry's gesture, the last time they had met before their father's death, of striking " 'the upper part of his breast.' " Then, Alyosha remembers, Dmitry said that he had "there" what was necessary to restore his honor. At the time Alyosha thought that Dmitry meant he could find in his heart enough strength " 'to escape some horrible disgrace' ": " 'I thought his gesture indicated his horror at the thought that he might do violence to his father.' "

Now, however, Alyosha believes Dmitry was " 'pointing at the fifteen hundred rubles sewn in the rag that he carried around his neck!' " " 'Right!' " shouts Dmitry, " 'It's true, Alyosha, it was the money that I was striking with my fist!' " (815). Alyosha's intuitive understanding seizes here the truth about the accused man that Fetyukovich's clear, altogether logical mind does not grasp. The celebrated lawyer, in fact, fails to comprehend both Dmitry's innocence and those murderous impulses in him of which Father Zosima had showed his understanding by bowing low before the young man.

It is pertinent to recall that Dostoevsky once remarked, "There is only one thing in the world: direct compassion. As to justice, that comes second."[12] A sense of injustice he surely has, and he conveys it through both the account of Dmitry's trial, and Ivan's evocation of the unjustified suffering of children. He suggests, however, in his characterization of Zosima and Alyosha, that only compassionate acts which proceed from feelings of love can in some measure compensate injustice. Tolstoy is much more concerned than Dostoevsky to transform society, but Nekhlyudov's realization in *Resurrection* that " 'if you feel no love,' " you should " 'leave people alone' " links Tolstoy closely to Dostoevsky. Writers in the natural law tradition, while stressing the importance of brotherhood, do not make the stringent emotional demands on individuals that the two Russian writers do. In Shakespeare's "natural law" play, *The Merchant of Venice*, Portia's plea to Shylock to show mercy to Antonio is fully as pertinent—although Portia herself does not seem to realize this—to the behavior of Gentiles toward Jews. What Shakespeare is emphasizing is the need for imperfect human beings to show forbearance for each other's errors and shortcomings. This is a social standard, a criterion for humane living in any community—as distinguished from the kinds of saintliness that Alyosha and Nekhlyudov aspire to.

To return to the coolly rational Fetyukovich, whom I think it is fair to say that Dostoevsky depicts as "soulless": the brilliant defense attorney asserts during his summation that psychology " 'is a knife that cuts both ways' " (876), then offers alternative explanations of evidence that the prosecutor has produced. Shrewdly and accurately accounting for an incident that seems especially damaging to his client, Fetyukovich remarks, with a complacency completely foreign to Zosima and Alyosha: " 'And now we have a different conclusion based on psychology. But I want you to understand, gentlemen of the jury, that the only reason I have dabbled in psychology here is to demonstrate to you that you can use it to arrive at whatever conclusions suit you best. It all depends on who uses it . . .' " (878).

Dazzled though everyone in the courtroom is by Fetyukovich's performance, the jury of government officials, peasants, artisans, and merchants probably find him too clever. Toward the end of his summation, he does something that undoubtedly damages his previous efforts to convince the jury of Dmitry's innocence. The lawyer argues that Dmitry is *essentially* guiltless, because Fyodor Pavlovich had been a horrible father—really no father at all; guiltless *even if* in a moment of passion he had actually struck his father dead. This attempt to arouse a kind of muddled compassion for Dmitry undercuts his earlier astute demonstration that the murderer could well have been Smerdyakov. In consequence of Fetyukovich's maladroit plea—which virtually concedes that Dmitry had in fact delivered the killing blow—there occurs a deeply moving scene: Dmitry, addressing the jury before they begin their deliberations, says after thanking his attorney," 'But he did not have to assume that I killed my father, since I did not kill him—he shouldn't even have assumed it' " (906).

In the trial the most arresting instance of the narrowness of rationalism is the verbal duel between Fetyukovich and the prosecutor, Kirillovich, concerning Smerdyakov. Before the trial begins, we know, because Smerdyakov has confessed to Ivan how he himself killed Fyodor Pavlovich, that Dmitry has been framed. But since Smerdyakov has killed himself on the eve of the trial, nothing said in the courtroom about the substance of his confession can be confirmed. Among other things that we know—but that neither Fetyukovich nor Kirillovich is aware of—is that Smerdyakov knew where Fyodor Pavlovich had concealed three thousand rubles with which he was hoping to seduce Grushenka (whom Dmitry loves) if she were to visit him in response to his invitation. We also know that in order to convince Ivan of the truth of his confession, Smerdyakov showed him three thousand rainbow-colored rubles and, in a gesture of ultimate resignation, gave them to him. Although it is true that Smerdyakov had evidently intended to use the money to go to France, the acquisition of money was clearly not his primary aim in committing murder. He was driven chiefly by a yearning to compensate, through discipleship to Ivan, for his own spiritual emptiness. The frustration of this yearning was evident in his contemptuous remark to Ivan about the latter's "weakness"—his revulsion from the crime of which Smerdyakov insisted Ivan had been the true author. At the trial, however, Kirillovich attempts to exculpate Smerdyakov by declaring, first, that the cook, unlike Dmitry," 'had no motives such as hatred, jealousy, and so on, for murdering Fyodor Karamazov, [but] could have conceivably done it for money' " (853), and then proceeding to demonstrate that if Smerdyakov had actually planned to kill for money, nothing would have induced him to tell Dmitry, as he had told him, about the envelope containing the rubles. Kirillovich's assumption that Smerdyakov had told Dmitry where the envelope was hidden is incorrect. But the prosecutor's more important error is his attribution to the cook of exclusively materialistic concerns. Kirillovich is the type of the rational, utilitarian nineteenth-century man in his failure to comprehend that Smerdyakov was driven to suicide by a sense of his own nothingness.

Fetyukovich's understanding of Smerdyakov is certainly keener than the prosecutor's. Having talked, as Kirillovich had, with the

cook, he has concluded that, although weak in health, Smerdyakov was neither timid nor weak-minded, and that he hated
and was ashamed of the story of his parentage:

> Knowing he was an illegitimate son of Fyodor Karamazov . . .
> Smerdyakov was bitter about his position as compared with that of
> [the] legitimate sons who, he felt, had everything while he had
> nothing, who would inherit their father's money while he . . . was
> doomed to remain a cook all his life. He also told me that he had
> helped Fyodor Karamazov put the hundred-ruble bills into that
> envelope. . . . The many rainbow-colored bills must have made a
> violent impression on his imagination. . . . (891)

This is shrewd analysis, which goes beyond Kirillovich's in that
it stresses the resentment, the sense of unjustified exclusion, which
undoubtedly underlay Smerdyakov's so-called "greed." And Fetyukovich's subsequent guess about the subtle method Smerdyakov must have used to murder Fyodor Pavlovich, steal the
money, and cast the blame on Dmitry closely approximates what
we know has actually occurred. Fetyukovich's interpretation of
the killer's failure to confess his crime in his suicide note is also
perceptive: Smerdyakov, he says, never felt repentant, but " 'was
filled with despair!' " Despair, he observes, may be combined
with irreconcilable resentment, and " 'at the moment of perishing
by his own hand, a suicide may find his hatred doubled for those
he envied during his life' " (893–94).

One could hardly ask for a more accurate reading by a lawyer
of Smerdyakov's nature and probable motivations. Yet Fetyukovich assumes, as Kirillovich does, that Smerdyakov, if he committed the murder, must have done it in order to obtain Fyodor
Pavlovich's money. It is plain to us, however, that although in a
strangely "obscene" passage the cook had asked Ivan to allow him
" 'one more look' " (761) at the rainbow-colored rouble notes
that Smerdyakov was giving his master, Smerdyakov had actually
killed out of perverted worship of Ivan. And the cook's despair,
which Fetyukovich discovers deductively after eliminating repen-
tance as a cause of his suicide, we know to have resulted from
Ivan's horrified rejection of him.

In defense of Fetyukovich, it may be argued that he could hardly
have known of Smerdyakov's psychological dependence upon

Ivan. This is true. But Dostoevsky takes pains to contrast Fetyukovich's thoroughgoing rationalism, his incapacity to understand
"mysteries," with Alyosha's intuitive sense of the kinds of persons
Smerdyakov and Dmitry are. Fetyukovich's personal limitations
as a rationalist are most clearly revealed by Dostoevsky toward the
end of the defense lawyer's summation, where he attempts to
show that Fyodor Pavlovich had not been a real father: Fetyukovich contrasts the "progressive" interpretation of "father" as a man
who has not only begotten a child but deserved his love, with the
traditional understanding according to which

> "a father may be a monster who treats his children viciously, but
> who must nevertheless always be respected as a father. . . . But that
> is a mystical attitude that my reason does not understand, that I can
> accept only on *faith*, so to speak, just as we are asked to accept so
> many things that we do not understand, but that our religion orders
> us to believe. . . ." (899)

The attitude dismissed by Fetyukovich as "mystical"—that even
a father who treats his children viciously must nevertheless always
be respected as a father—is exactly the attitude of Dostoevsky's
hero. Alyosha, according to the narrator, was not "a mystic"
(20), but when he came to live with his father after having been
brought up by guardians, he offered Fyodor Pavlovich "something that he had never had before—a complete absence of contempt for him. Indeed, Alyosha treated him with kindness and a
completely genuine and sincere affection which Karamazov little
deserved" (110).

From Dostoevsky's perspective, Fetyukovich and the prosecutor
make the same error. Both are chiefly interested in condemning
another man's evil: Kirillovich, the evil of presumed parricide;
Fetyukovich, the evil done by the father who is no true father.
Father Zosima, however, has said earlier in the novel, during a
discussion of criminal justice, that sentencing people to hard labor
does not reform criminals and, " 'more to the point, does not
deter them from committing crimes.' " Not only does the number
of crimes not diminish, it seems to increase: " 'If anything protects
society in our time, if anything can reform the criminal and make
a new man out of him, it is only the law of Christ, which manifests
itself in the awareness of a man's own conscience' " (73–74).

For Dostoevsky, the deepest import of the trial is that it brings to intense awareness the consciences of two men who feel morally responsible for their father's death—Dmitry and Ivan. The trial in *The Brothers Karamazov* thus serves chiefly a "private" purpose, unlike trials in Sophocles's *Antigone*, Shakespeare's *The Merchant of Venice*, and Scott's *The Heart of Midlothian* where an essential purpose is the "public" one of dramatizing the tension between the positive law that men mete out and a transcendent concept of justice.

For Ivan, the trial occasions the discovery that he cannot live by his own dictum that in a world without God, "everything is permitted." In the midst of his testimony, he takes out a bundle of money, hands it to the bailiff, and tells the astonished judge that it was given to him the day before by Smerdyakov, " 'who killed my father . . . on my instructions.' " " 'Why,' " he continues, " 'is there anyone who doesn't wish his father's death?' " When the judge asks him if he is in his right mind, he bursts out:

> "Yes, I am very much in my right mind, and that's the trouble, because my right mind is just as vile as yours and anyone else's— because just look at all those mugs! . . . A father has been killed and they pretend they're shocked," he snarled with immense loathing. "They're putting it all on for each other's benefit. The liars! They all long for their father's death, because one beast devours another. . . . If it were proved here that no parricide had been committed, they would be angry and would leave terribly disappointed. . . . A circus! That's what they want, bread and circuses! But I myself, I haven't got so much to brag about either! . . ."

Shock waves pass through the courtroom. Alyosha shouts, " 'Don't believe what he's saying. He's sick and feverish!' " And Dmitry stands up, "looking intently at his brother with a strange, wild, contorted smile" (825). The presiding judge, shaken, "seemed to come to himself" (this is superbly subtle "Freudian" writing) after a whispered conference with his two colleagues, and rules Ivan's words " 'inadmissible in court' " (826).

The attentive reader is as much shaken as the chief judge. For if we all long for our fathers' deaths, is not our guilt comparable to Ivan's or Dmitry's? Have Ivan's words recalled even to Alyosha velleities that only his exceptional capacity for love enables him to surmount? This moment in the novel is truly theater of the soul:

each psyche in the fictional courtroom, and in the community of Dostoevsky's readers, may play by turn the role of prosecutor, defense attorney, judge, and jury. The difference, however, between Ivan's psychological accusation of his auditors and himself and Freud's Oedipal theory is crucial. To Freud, the Oedipus complex is an inevitable stage in a male child's development toward mature sexuality. The child who learns to transfer his erotic interests from his mother to other women diminishes thereby his rivalry with his father. In Freud's view, it is only the immature adult who desires so intensely his father's death that he is crippled by feelings of guilt. To Dostoevsky, however, parricide appears to be a horrible universal—or at least universal male— temptation. And the direction of a child's development is of no importance if no God exists to love and pardon him. In God's absence, "crime" is but a name, and murder and suicide are as normal as eating and sleeping. Ivan's greatest torment is not his belief that he has incited Smerdyakov to kill Fyodor Pavlovich, but an inability to believe in a God who could absolve him of this sin. Ivan's breakdown in court—he becomes delirious after his outburst—eventuates from a despair so profound that only what he once called "'the strength of the Karamazov baseness' " has hitherto enabled him to endure it.

The effect of Ivan's astonishing speech on Dmitry's case is the opposite of what we expect. For Katerina Ivanovna, the woman to whom Dmitry owes 3,000 rubles and who has earlier testified in his favor—disclosing that he had once saved her father, a fellow army officer, from financial dishonor—now denounces him as a man who borrowed money from her in order to take the " 'creature,' " Grushenka, away with him, and who had explicitly described in a letter to her (a letter which the court clerk reads aloud): " 'how he'll kill his father and where he'll find the money his father was hiding. And I want you to note the sentence where he writes, "I'll kill him provided Ivan leaves." Doesn't that prove he'd worked out in advance how he'd go about the murder?' " (829)

This letter will prove an insurmountable obstacle to the defense. Despite Dmitry's stricken protest that he would not have written it had he not been drunk, and despite Fetyukovich's virtuoso attempt to convict Smerdyakov, the letter constitutes clear proof in the jury's eyes of Dmitry's guilt (827). But, in a sense, the judicial error that convicts Dmitry is almost irrelevant to Dostoevsky. Before the jury retires to consider the case, Dmitry is asked if he has anything to say; the narrator's comment at this point indicates the profound significance of the trial to the accused man: "It was as though what he had experienced that day had made him understand something of the utmost importance that would stay with him for the rest of his life, something that had been quite beyond him until then. . . . there was defeat and resignation in [his voice], and also a new kind of understanding." Despite Dmitry's declaration to the jury that he has not killed his father, and despite his plea to them to " 'show mercy and acquit me' " (906), he is found guilty of premeditated murder and robbery, and sentenced to twenty years in Siberia. He falls ill and is hospitalized—and at this point Alyosha plays a vital role. Katerina Ivanovna, remorseful over her betrayal of Dmitry in court, acts to save him; she tells Alyosha of a plan that Ivan, before his breakdown, had outlined for Dmitry's escape from the convoy to Siberia, and she asks Alyosha to persuade Dmitry to follow the plan. Alyosha not only agrees, and warns Dmitry that because he would not be able to bear imprisonment in Siberia, he would " 'rebel' " (921), but also says that if Ivan and Katerina had wanted him, Alyosha, to do so, he would have paid the bribes necessary to ensure Dmitry's escape.

What is striking about this turn of events is the serenity with which Alyosha, whose understanding of others is more reliable than that of any other character in the novel except Zosima, endorses the "lawless" escape plan. Unlike Tolstoy's Nekhlyudov, Alyosha has no program for social transformation. Like the regenerated Nekhlyudov, however, Alyosha values active love for others more than he does "the law." The trial that eventuates in Dmitry's conviction is to Dostoevsky emblematic of the fundamental error men commit by thinking of one another in terms of "innocence" and "guilt" rather than by attempting to overcome through agape the sins common to us all. Even less than *Resurrection* does *The Brothers Karamazov* treat human beings as rational creatures who attain their full development in a polis by obeying and upholding positive laws based on natural law. Dostoevsky's novel attempts to point the way to a transformation of our wayward hearts.

Mauriac's *Thérèse Desqueyroux*

François Mauriac, "the most profound of the Catholic novelists,"[13] grew up in a Bordeaux milieu where people called their chamber-pots "Zola."[14] Emile Zola was the renowned public supporter of Captain Alfred Dreyfus, the Jewish army officer court-martialed in 1894 and convicted of passing military secrets to the German high command. By proclaiming in an open letter in 1898, "J'accuse!" that army leaders and the Ministry of Defense had framed Dreyfus, Zola incurred the hatred of Frenchmen who believed either that the army could not be guilty or that it was above the law, and of anti-Semites who had been brought to a boil by works like Edouard Drumont's *La France juive* (1886). Although some Catholics—most notably Charles Péguy—joined in the call for a retrial of Dreyfus, Catholics generally upheld the court-martial's verdict. Many years passed before Mauriac, twenty-one years old when Dreyfus was "rehabilitated" in 1906, shook off the influence of what he came to call a "pharisaic Catholicism."[15]

Mauriac's treatment in his fiction of the Dreyfus case annoyed and offended Catholics who refused, long after the "Affair," to accept that Dreyfus was innocent. Mauriac, however, like Dostoevsky, was less interested in justice than in the Christian awakening of the heart. Some of his most powerfully drawn characters, while "justly" pro-Dreyfus, are depicted as deeply in need of faith in the God against whom they rebel, or whose existence they do not accept. The freethinking Dreyfus supporter, Louis, for example, in *Vipers' Tangle*, is a celebrated lawyer whose life turned to ashes when his wife revealed that she had married him only after rejecting for reasons of health the proposal of a man she loved. Now a bitter miser at sixty-eight, near death from heart disease, and determined to avenge himself on Isa and the children he believes she has alienated from him, he writes her a "confession"—virtually the entire novel comprises it—that recalls, among other episodes, a turbulent dinner-table discussion of Dreyfus. We have already learned that Isa was anti-Dreyfus: " 'To disorganize the army for the sake of a wretched Jew' " was one of her standard remarks. At dinner, Louis's sister-in-law, Marinette, who shared his Dreyfusard convictions, had asked the young abbé if it was permissible to hate the Jews. "That evening," Louis observes,

> to our greater joy [the abbé] did not resort to vague evasions. He spoke about the greatness of the Chosen People, their exalted role as a witness, . . . the forerunner of the end of time. And when [Louis's son-in-law] protested that one must hate the executioners of our Lord, the abbé replied that everyone of us had a right to hate but one executioner of Christ: "Ourselves, and nobody else."[16]

Though Louis sounds admirable here, he shows malice on the next page of his "confession" by telling Isa that he had been on the verge of seducing Marinette later in the evening of the dinner: ". . . what was infamous in me, at that moment, was that I thought of you, Isa; that I dreamt of a possible revenge: to make use of Marinette to make you suffer. Fleetingly as the idea flashed through my mind, it is nevertheless true that I conceived this crime" (85).

Shortly before his death, Louis experiences a religious conversion that his earler expressions of despair, and of hunger for love, have foreshadowed. It is typical of Mauriac's treatment of religion that a "sinner" and condemner of the Church like Louis should ultimately prove more deeply responsive to God than are his bigoted, conventional wife and in-laws, who participate in all the public Catholic rites.

Thérèse Desqueyroux is also a freethinking sinner, an intelligent, "emancipated" woman who, desperately unhappy in her marriage to a neighboring landowner, slowly poisons him. As the novel opens, she has been acquitted at the Assizes—in consequence of the lying testimony of her husband, Bernard—of attempted murder. Looking "like a woman condemned . . . to an eternity of loneliness"[17] despite the courtroom verdict, Thérèse is thinking, as she travels homeward, of the "defense" she must soon make to Bernard. For the sake of the family's "honor" he has collaborated with her to procure the acquittal. But between them, "from now on, would lie not fiction but reality" (11). Thérèse discovers to her dismay, in attempting to prepare her "defense," that she can articulate no clear truth:

What should she tell him? What should be her first confession?
Could mere words ever make comprehensible that confused, inevitable conglomeration of desires, determinations, and actions un-
foreseen? How do those act who *know* the crimes they are
committing? . . . "I *didn't* know. I never wanted to do that with
which I was charged. I don't know what I *did* want. I never had the
slightest idea to what that frantic urge inside me, yet outside too,
was working, what destruction it would sow in its frantic progress.
No one was more terrified of it than I was. . . ." (16)

Implicit in Thérèse's thoughts is the important difference between the confused nature of the feelings and acts that she remembers as leading up to her crime and the clearcut, "rational"
judgments made in criminal courts—and by such a downright
"judge" as her husband. Like Dostoevsky, Mauriac suggests that
judicial error is not simply a result of falsified or misinterpreted
evidence. In a larger sense, it is the inevitable consequence of the
gap between such simple, pragmatic judgments as "innocent" and
"guilty" and the complex reality of the persons being judged.

Thinking back to her girlhood, Thérèse contrasts herself, intelligent and studious, but "torn by passions"—she had "suffered
and made others suffer too" (19)—with her friend Anne de la
Trave, innocent through ignorance, the dutifully devout pupil of
the Sacred Heart Convent. Thérèse's marriage to Anne's half-
brother Bernard had been, from the neighbors' viewpoint, the
sensible fusion of two properties. Now, however, she sees the
marriage as the result of "a movement of panic" on her part: "She
wanted to be reassured, to feel that she was protected against
some danger the precise nature of which she did not understand.
. . . She embedded herself in the substance of her new family,
made it her object to 'settle down.' She had entered, as it were,
into an Order. She had sought safety, and found it" (30).

This "Order," however, quickly proved to be a jail. She found
Bernard's lovemaking selfish and coarse, his outlook on life devoid
of imagination—he always "worried lest the numbers of the
pictures did not correspond with those in his Baedeker" (34).
Toward the end of their honeymoon she feels "like a tranported
criminal, sick in her soul of transit prisons, and anxious only to
see the convict island where she would have to spend the rest of
her life" (36). Her depression was deepened by the arrival at her

and Bernard's Paris hotel of letters from Anne, exuding rapture over Jean Azévédo, a Jewish intellectual she had fallen in love with. Thérèse recalls having furiously pierced with a pin, "just where the heart should be," a photograph of Azévédo enclosed in one of the letters; then she flushed the photograph down the toilet, for she could not bear the thought that Anne had managed to escape from the "desert island" where Thérèse and she "should have been together to the end" (40, 41).

Mauriac's attribution to Thérèse of thoughts of herself on a "convict island" and a "desert island" indicates her renunciation of happiness at the very beginning of her married life, and suggests that at least semi-consciously she identified her own desolation with that of Dreyfus, who had been sentenced to exile on a horrible Caribbean convict island—L'Ile du Diable.

Rather than sharing the anti-Jewish prejudices of Bernard and his family, who now asked her to intercede with Jean Azévédo in order to separate him from Anne, she was pro-Semitic. The Azévédos, she pointed out to her husband, belonged to an old Portuguese Jewish community in Bordeaux, and " 'were somebody when our ancestors were a miserable lot of shepherds shaking with fever in the marshes.' " But although—by referring to a history of tuberculosis in Bernard's and her own family—she cuttingly dismissed his sneer about consumption among the " 'degenerate' " Azévédos (42), she agreed for her own reasons to serve as the family envoy to Jean: the "little fool," Anne, "who was so sure that happiness was possible, must be made to see with her eyes, be made to understand that no such thing as happiness existed" (45).

Her hopeless loneliness intensified by pregnancy soon after the honeymoon—Thérèse wanted to pray (though she had been reared in an anti-religious family) that the baby might never be born—she was dazzled by Azévédo's flaunted unconventionality. Contrary to Bernard's view of him as a utilitarian schemer, she found him uninterested in marrying Anne—a " 'delightful child' " with whom, for he had not taken her virginity, he had simply been amusing himself. Anne, all set for a dull provincial life, had at least acquired from him what he called " 'feelings and dreams to hoard up against her old age.' " To this airy self-justification he added a touch of estheticism—one should " 'suck the last drop of pleasure from each fleeting moment' " (63) and a mixture of Nietzsche and murky religiosity: there was no " 'depravity worse than the denial of self,' " and " 'If one is to find God one must transcend one's limitations' " (69–70).

Easily persuaded by Thérèse to compose with her help a letter breaking off with Anne, Azévédo later arranged that Thérèse and he should meet in a year. He said he hoped that she would meanwhile find " 'some way of freeing' " herself (71).

Once Azévédo left for Paris, she felt even more isolated than before meeting him. Considered a traitor by Anne, looked upon essentially as a womb by Bernard's family, she began, because of a remark by Azévédo, to pay close attention to the local curé, whose intense religious ardor disturbed his parishioners. He had chosen, Thérèse thought, "the way of tragedy" (78). Mauriac is implicitly contrasting him with the pedestrian curé, Bournisien, in *Madame Bovary*, whom Emma briefly looks to as a savior from her deadly boredom. Thérèse is more intelligent, more spiritually dissatisfied with "the world," and also more wary of public opinion than Flaubert's protagonist. Although she would have liked to attend the priest's weekday masses, she refrained because this would have caused gossip about her "conversion" (79).

After the birth of her child, Marie, she found life completely unendurable. Bernard had developed heart disease, but this did not mitigate her hatred of "his fat paunch, . . . his peremptory way of talking, his self-complacency" (81). A terrible drought made him fear a forest fire that would destroy his pine trees. Thérèse, however, liked to imagine "that one of these nights she would . . . leave the house, reach the most inflammable part of the forest, throw away her cigarette, and watch the great column of smoke stain the dawn sky. . . ." An accident provided the impetus for her efforts to free herself from a stultifying existence. Recalling that crucial moment, Thérèse sees Bernard listening one summer day to a servant's report on a forest fire—listening so intently that, as he held his "Fowler" heart medicine over a glass of water, the drops fall in "all unnoticed": "He swallowed the medicine at a single gulp, before Thérèse, overpowered by the heat, could warn him that he had taken twice his usual dose" (82). Still preoccupied by the fire, Bernard returned to the room to ask if he had taken his drops; then he shook some into his glass, and she said nothing.

When he fell ill that night, the doctor, Pédémay, asked what had happened. But Thérèse remained silent about the dining-room scene: a crime had been conceived in her mind.

Bernard suffered several puzzling attacks of illness that summer. To a specialist finally summoned from Bordeaux, Pédémay confided that the local pharmacist, worried about having filled two prescriptions presented to him by a family servant for powerful doses of drugs, had shown them to him. They were plainly forgeries. Bernard began to improve immediately after being removed to a Bordeaux hospital; and Thérèse improvised a story of having met a stranger on the road who, because he owed money to the pharmacist, had asked her to have a prescription made up for him, which he would later fetch from her house. She said that he had later come for it. But it turned out that nobody in the house had seen him.

At this point in Thérèse's memories, her train stops at a station where she is met by Bernard and her father's sister, Clara. To Thérèse's forced, cheery greeting, " 'Case dismissed,' " her deaf, anti-clerical aunt, confused about what Thérèse has been tried for, responds by attacking the "enemy": "She said . . . that it was the Dreyfus case all over again. 'Throw enough mud and some of it is bound to stick.' *They* were very powerful. The Republicans had been fools. They ought to have watched their steps more closely. Give the beasts half a chance and they'd be on top of you" (89).

Clara obviously assumes that Thérèse is as innocent as Dreyfus has been shown to be. The only actual similarity, however, between Dreyfus's conviction and Thérèse's acquittal is that both are instances of judicial injustice. Nevertheless, it is clear that Clara, despite her muddle over the facts, is more "right" in her love for and loyalty to Thérèse than are the local gossips who call Thérèse a monster; and more right than Thérèse's own father, concerned chiefly with winning a seat in the Senate, and the members of her husband's family—all of them desperate to hush the scandal she has caused.

The paradox of Clara's being emotionally right, though wrong about the facts, is somewhat analogous to the paradox of her believing more sincerely in a God against whom she passionately rebels than do any of Thérèse's church-going in-laws. Clara "waged incessant warfare against the Eternal Being who had let her become deaf and ugly, who had decreed that she would die without ever having been loved or possessed by a man" (59).

This is a key passage in *Thérèse Desqueyroux* and in Mauriac's work, for it stresses the injustice, or at least apparent injustice, of God. From Mauriac's perspective, love of God—of which hatred like Clara's is clearly the bitterly angry expression—is a non-rational human need rather than the corollary of a belief in an ethical natural law. It is significant of Mauriac's rejection of the idea of a moral order comprehensible to humans (as it was comprehensible to writers in the natural law tradition) that he quotes, in a Foreword to *Thérèse Desqueyroux*, the following passage from Baudelaire:

> Seigneur, ayez pitié, ayez pitié des fous et des folles! O Créateur! peut-il exister des monstres aux yeux de celui-là seul qui sait pourquoi ils existent, *comment ils se sont faits*, et comment ils auraient pu ne pas se faire?
>
> (Lord, have mercy on madmen and madwomen! O Creator! Can monsters exist in the eyes of him who, alone, knows why they exist, how they have come into being, and how they might never have been created?)

Both Clara, whose metaphysical rebellion recalls that of Ivan Karamazov, and Thérèse, the "monstrous" poisoner who desperately seeks meaning in life, are among the "sinners" who, in Péguy's words, are "at the very heart of Christianity."[18]

It is notable that Clara "looked after and watched over" poor country folk with a disillusioned devotion; and that Thérèse, whom she loved, requited that love by taking over for her when Clara had an attack of rheumatism (this during the very period when Thérèse was slowly poisoning Bernard) her visitations to the poor: "She went round the farms, saw that the doctor's instructions were obeyed, and bought the necessary medicines out of her own pocket" (85).

Bernard, on the other hand, though he participated in the Corpus Christi procession, was respected as a "gentleman" by his tenants, and was never accused of a crime, was "incapable" of love (95).

Shortly before being met by Bernard at the railroad station, Thérèse wonders how she could ever persuade him to believe that she was not in love with Azévédo: " 'I'm sure he thinks I adored him. Like all those who really know nothing whatever about love, he imagines that a crime of the sort with which I was charged could have had its motive only in sexual passion.' " Mauriac clearly indicates that Thérèse is honest and lucid in thinking that, "at the period in question," no man other than Bernard (whom she had still been far from hating) "would have been of the slightest use to her" (57). Yet Bernard associates her, later in the novel, with a picture he had seen as a child, in a newspaper: "the Woman Prisoner of Poitiers." Like that prisoner, Thérèse has come to represent to him a frightening, criminal, female lust. It is, however, a *different* stereotypical idea—that Thérèse had attempted to poison him in order to obtain his property—which he now voices, once they are alone together. Thérèse has realized, immediately upon seeing Bernard at the railroad station, that she unconsciously created during her homeward journey an "understanding" Bernard who did not exist. Nevertheless, she is not prepared for his announcement that in order to protect both Marie and the property she will eventually inherit, the child will be kept away from Thérèse: " 'Once I am dead and she has turned twenty-one, the property will go to her. First the husband, then the child. . . . Why not?' " Contemptuously interrupting her cry of astonishment, he goes on to tell her that " 'as soon as the fact of our reconciliation has been fully established,' " and as soon as the parents of Anne's conventional fiancé (for she has fallen in line after the Azévédo episode) are persuaded that his marriage to the sister-in-law of the infamous Thérèse Desqueyroux would not be imprudent, Thérèse will " 'settle down' " by herself. Bernard will reside with his own family, and a story will be circulated about Thérèse's " 'neurasthenia.' " Mauriac's evocation of Bernard's pride in his own rationality and self-sufficiency again recalls Dostoevsky's perspective: "He realized, not without surprise, that nothing can resist the man of upright character who has a mind which can reason logically. . . . what was there so particularly humiliating in having married a monster? Nothing mattered so long as one had the last word" (94–95).

Thérèse contemplates running away from the house in which she is to be imprisoned. But she realizes that under French property law she has no money: "Thousands of pine trees might be hers in law, but without Bernard's agency she could not touch a single penny of her fortune" (100).

While Mauriac indicates here how "legality" helps to imprison Thérèse, his chief emphasis is on the glimmering of religious truth that may come to a sinner like her once she has been reduced to desperation. For now she thinks of suicide, and even of taking Marie to the grave with her. But in a memorable scene, after touching with her lips one of her sleeping child's hands, she finds herself, a woman who never cries, weeping. She goes to her own room, hesitates among the small boxes of poison which she has found—has Bernard, she wondered, discovered them?—in an old coat:

> The countryside lay soaked in dawn. How could she bring herself to abandon so much light? . . . Thérèse did not feel any certainty of annihilation. She could not be absolutely sure that Nothing and Nobody awaited her. . . . How humiliating cowardice can be! If that Being really did exist . . . since He *did* exist, let Him prevent the criminal act while there was still time. . . . (102)

A little earlier, Aunt Clara, who learns much by looking into people's eyes, has looked into Bernard's after his bitter discussion with Thérèse, and evidently read there the truth of her niece's crime. Now, as Thérèse thinks of suicide, a servant cries out to her that " 'Mademoiselle is dead!' "

Gazing at her aunt's body, "which had lain down in front of her feet just as she was about to take her leap to death," Thérèse thinks of "chance, coincidence." Mauriac says that she would have shrugged her shoulders had anyone spoken of a "special intention" (103). But his own language suggests that the God she has defiantly made entreaty to has prevented her self-murder. At church on the Sunday following the funeral, Thérèse is hedged in on three sides: the crowd of worshipers is behind her, Bernard is on her right hand, his mother is on her left. Only in front of her "was there a free and open space, empty as is the arena to the bull when he comes from the darkness into the light—space where, flanked by two small boys, a man in fancy dress was standing, his arms a little spread, whispering" (104).

This passage, in which Mauriac symbolically transforms the priest into a matador and Thérèse into a bull, recalls ancient rites involving the emblematic slaying of Dionysus in the form of a bull.[19] As a sacrifice, Dionysus is sometimes regarded as a forerunner of Jesus, and Mauriac may be suggesting that Thérèse must lose her life in order to enter the light of God's love. *The End of the Night* (*La Fin de la nuit*, 1935), a novel which continues her story, concludes as the dying Thérèse says to her young Platonic lover that she is waiting for the " 'end of life, the end of the night.' "[20] In *Thérèse Desqueyroux*, shortly after the church scene, she has a feverish reverie in which, while at a Paris restaurant with Azévédo and others, she becomes aware of someone "in her life who made the rest of the world seem meaningless": "someone completely unknown to the rest of her circle, someone very obscure and very humble. But her whole existence revolved about this sun which she alone could see, the heat of which she only could feel upon her flesh. . . ." Embracing this companion, she makes, in effect, the sign of the cross: "She clasped her left shoulder with her right hand. The nails of her left hand dug into her right shoulder" (109).

At several points in the novel, Thérèse's spiritual hunger is evoked by images of fire and light. The "someone completely unknown," in the passage quoted above, is a "sun." Earlier, as we have seen, the priest performing the Mass occupies space, "empty as the arena to the bull when he comes from the darkness into the light." And when Bernard before leaving Thérèse, at the end of the novel, in Paris—where she is to live apart from the family—asks her when she had taken the first step toward poisoning him, she replies, " '. . . it was on the day of the great fire . . .' " (127). Mauriac's language referring to that fire—he says that the smell of burning resin from the pines "filled the stifling air," and that "the sun looked dirty" (82)—accords with the hideousness of the crime that Thérèse was conceiving. An undeceived court of justice would have found her guilty as charged of attempting to kill her husband. If, however, the passage on the forest fire is taken together with other passages that evoke fire, heat, and light, we become vividly aware of a tormented spirit's yearning toward an enduring love.

During her final talk with Bernard on the terrace of a Paris café, Thérèse suddenly fears the solitude that will follow his departure, and she tries to charm him into staying with her. She describes herself to him as two persons, one of whom is " 'the Thérèse who instinctively stamps out cigarettes because the tiniest spark will set heather on fire.' " This prudent, profit-reckoning Thérèse, she insists to her practical husband, is " 'just as real, just as much alive, as the other' " (129–30). But when he asks her what "other" she means, she is silent. Clearly, however, that Thérèse is the soul on fire—burning bright as Blake's tiger—who has so desperately sought to escape from the respectability that Bernard incarnates.

The criminal that Thérèse has been must continue to seek a light with which men's conventions and legal procedures have nothing to do. Not even that natural law that Aristotle thought "everyone to some extent divines" could, as Mauriac depicts Thérèse, help her. In the world of this novel, as in the worlds of *The Brothers Karamazov*, "God Sees the Truth, But Waits," and *Resurrection*, there is a radical discontinuity between "the laws" and the ways of God.

NOTES

1. *The Penguin Companion to European Literature*, ed. Anthony Thorlby (New York: McGraw-Hill, 1969) 839–40.

2. Henri Troyat, *Tolstoy*, trans. Nancy Amphoux (New York: Doubleday, 1967) 69. Troyat's work is the source of the biographical information in this chapter.

3. Leo Tolstoy, "God Sees the Truth, But Waits," *Twenty-Three Tales*, trans. Louise and Aylmer Maude (London: Oxford UP, 1906) 4.

4. Isaiah Berlin, "Tolstoy and the Enlightenment," *Mightier Than the Sword* (London: Macmillan, 1964); rpt. in *Tolstoy: A Collection of Critical Essays*, ed. Ralph E. Matlaw (Englewood Cliffs, NJ: Prentice, 1967) 37.

5. Leo Tolstoy, *Resurrection*, trans. Rosemary Edmonds (Harmondsworth: Penguin, 1966) 565–66.

6. Samuel Kucherow, *Courts, Lawyers, and Trials Under the Three Tsars* (New York: Praeger, 1953) 63.

7. John Bayley, *Tolstoy and the Novel* (New York: Viking, 1967) 250.

8. Vladimir Tendryakov, "Justice," trans. Olive Stevens, *Three, Seven, Ace, and Other Stories*, trans. David Alger, Olive Stevens, Paul Falla (New York: Harper & Row, 1973) 145–46.

9. Marcel Proust, *La Prisonnière, A La Recherche du temps perdu*, ed. Pierre Clarac and André Ferré, vol. 3 (Paris: Gallimard, 1954) 380–81.

10. Fyodor Dostoevsky, *The Brothers Karamazov*, trans. Andrew MacAndrew (New York: Bantam, 1970) 295–96.

11. Fyodor Dostoevsky, *Notes from Underground, and The Grand Inquisitor*, trans. Ralph E. Matlaw (New York: Dutton, 1960) 19.

12. George Steiner, *Tolstoy or Dostoevsky: An Essay in the Old Criticism* (New York: Knopf, 1959) 179.

13. André Maurois, *From Proust to Camus: Profiles of Modern French Writers*, trans. Carl Morse and Renaud Bruce (1966; Garden City, NY.: Doubleday, 1968) 159.

14. François Mauriac, Preface, *Cinq Années de ma vie (1894–1899)*, by Alfred Dreyfus (Paris [?]: Fasquelle, 1962). 15.

15. François Mauriac, *The Inner Presence: Recollections of My Spiritual Life*, trans. Herma Briffault (Indianapolis: Bobbs, 1968) 92–95, 102, 108.

16. François Mauriac, *Vipers' Tangle*, trans. Warre B. Wells (Garden City, NY: Doubleday, 1957) 73, 84.

17. François Mauriac, *Thérèse Desqueyroux, Thérèse: A Portrait in Four Parts*, trans. Gerard Hopkins (New York: Farrar, 1974) 14.

18. Quoted in French by Graham Greene as epigraph for *The Heart of the Matter* (New York: Viking, 1948); my translation.

19. Sir James George Frazer, *The Golden Bough: A Study in Magic and Religion*, abr. ed. in 1 vol. (New York: Macmillan, 1942) 468.

20. François Mauriac, *The End of the Night, Thérèse: Portrait* 383.

3

The Sense of Injustice in Modern Social Fiction

I WANT TO EMPHASIZE two points about the modern religiously oriented trial fiction discussed in the preceding chapter. The first is that its perspective on justice is much closer to Augustine's than to Aquinas's. Aquinas considered human beings capable, on the whole, of obeying ethical natural law. Augustine had found them weak and corrupt, utterly dependent on a loving God to free them from the bondage of sin. It is that combination of corruptness and debility that Augustine saw as the central reality in the City of Earth which brings about the judicially erroneous murder convictions of Aksyónof, Maslova, and Dmitry and the erroneous acquittal of Thérèse on a charge of attempted murder. Human beings, it is implied by Tolstoy, Dostoevsky, and Mauriac, generally lack the strength to follow natural law, but some persons, through the suffering unjustly imposed on them, acquire profound spiritual insight. Tolstoy's Aksyónof and Maslova ultimately learn the truth of agape, Dostoevsky's Dmitry will strive to become what Alyosha calls "a new man," and Thérèse comes to a partial awareness that the love she has been seeking on the "desert island" of this world can be found only in God.

The second point is that it is doubtful that many readers of modern religiously oriented fiction share the authors' perspectives. I have frequently taught Thérèse Desqueyroux, in English translation, to American undergraduates. Rarely has any of them been aware, at least on a first reading, that Mauriac is writing from a religious viewpoint. I believe this unawareness reflects chiefly the absence of religious sensibility—not of religious zeal, for dogmatisms abound—in our time. Readers of The Brothers Karamazov usually identify themselves far more readily with Ivan, to whom in a world without God "everything is permitted," than with the imitator of Jesus, Alyosha, whom Dostoevsky's narrator calls the "hero" of the story. And Nekhlyudov, the protagonist of *Resurrection*, who attempts to practice agape in both his personal life and his relationships with the peasants, strikes most of us moderns as extremely impractical. We assent far more readily to the "realism" of "laughing all the way to the bank" than to Tolstoy's quixotic notion of living by the injunctions of the Gospel according to St. Matthew.

Realism in the arts is also accepted as a matter of course by the modern mind, which finds it difficult to believe that Madame Bovary was prosecuted for immorality in mid–nineteenth-century France. Subtitled "Provincial Mores," the novel shocked contemporary readers not because its protagonist commits adultery, but because it was written from an irreligious and virtually amoral perspective. Flaubert presents Emma's adulteries as the revolt of a tempestuous romantic temperament against a dull husband and a drab existence in the boondocks. The most scandalous scene for readers in the late 1850s was the one in which Emma, dying after swallowing arsenic, bestows upon a crucifix the most passionate kiss she has ever given.

Two years after the publication of *Madame Bovary*, Darwin's *Origin of Species* appeared (1859), with its clear indications of a family relationship between human beings and other animals. During the last third of the nineteenth century, the dominant literary tendency in the Western world was a naturalism strongly indebted to Darwin's theory of natural selection, or "the survival of the fittest." Thus, Émile Zola wrote in the preface to *Thérèse Raquin* that his protagonists were "completely dominated by their nerves and their blood, utterly without free will, impelled to perform every act of their lives by the fatalities of their flesh. Thérèse and Laurent are human brutes, nothing more. . . . It will be seen that each chapter is the study of a curious case of physiology. . . ."[1] Hippolyte Taine, as influential a critic as Zola was a novelist, considered justice and truth to be simply "products, like vitriol and sugar."[2] Zola, however, was not consistently deterministic even in his Rougon-Macquart novels; and in his late work, *Vérité* (part of the series *Les Quatre Évangiles*), he dealt with the Dreyfus case in a spirit—to paraphrase Harry Levin—more socialistic than "scientific."[3] Martin du Gard's *Jean Barois*, which also focuses on the Dreyfus Affair," evokes a turn-of-the-century intellectual milieu that is animated in the early days of the case by a hopeful scientific humanism, but that turns pessimistic as a sort of moral gangrene infects French political life. Martin du Gard's central character reverts, before dying at middle age, to the Catholic faith that he had renounced in favor of the scientific pursuit of truth and justice. The one character who clearly continues to believe that science can eventually resolve moral problems says that present-day conceptions of truth and justice will one day be "superseded." The relationship between this vague moral evolutionism and the concept of ethical natural law is unclear. And *Jean Barois* as a whole seems to show the limitations of science as a guide in the ethical domain.

Dreiser's *An American Tragedy*, with its emphasis on the "chemisms" within and the environmental forces outside Clyde Griffiths that combine to destroy him, recalls Darwin's remark that by "Nature," he means "only the aggregate action and product of many natural laws, and by laws the sequence of events as ascertained by us."[4] In the world that Dreiser depicts, the imperatives of ethical natural law serve chiefly to prevent Clyde from acting ruthlessly enough to break off with the woman he no longer loves and, after he has brought about her death, from fighting effectively as a witness in court to save his own life. Dreiser's survival-of-the-fittest perspective is much closer to Zola's in *Thérèse Raquin* than to the moral evolutionism that Martin du Gard seems partly to subscribe to in *Jean Barois*.

Brecht's *The Caucasian Chalk Circle* dramatizes a Marxist version of Darwin. The body of the play shows how a zany judge, Azdak, manages to mitigate, through judgments that in a fantastic way "do justice," the pervasive injustice of a medieval Transcaucasian society. The Prologue to the play, set in a Caucasian village in the summer of 1945, indicates that a society that had been brought to birth by a violent revolution is capable of rendering rational justice for the first time in history. Brecht's drama does not tell us, however, how the transformation from an unjust to a just society was accomplished; and one's reaction to *The Caucasian Chalk Circle* depends partly on whether or not one can accept, on faith alone, that revolutionary change.

Koestler's disenchanted "old Bolshevik," Rubashov, in *Darkness at Noon*, is more believable as a character than is any of the rational

Kolkhoz members in Brecht's Prologue. Awaiting execution after he has done the Party the final service of collaboration in his own show trial for treason, Rubashov decides that the Party's great mistake has been its discarding of all "ethical ballast." He imagines the eventual emergence of a new Party that might wear monks' cowls and preach that the ethical ends of revolution could be attained only through the practice of ethical means. Koestler suggests, in short, that unless ethical natural law serves as a guide to revolutionaries as they transform society, the transformation is likely to end in a cruel dictatorship. Koestler is a rarity: a fiction writer who combines a sense of injustice in existing societies—both "capitalist" and "communist"—with a clear ethical perspective. He is in the line of Langland, More, and Kleist.

MARTIN DU GARD'S *Jean Barois*

When Roger Martin du Gard received his baccalaureate, his father offered him a hunting rifle. Young Martin du Gard, however, said that he preferred a Larousse dictionary—which he was given six months later, after "his furious father had calmed down."[5] The hunting rifle and the dictionary are appropriate symbols for the opposing sides in the Dreyfus Affair, of which Martin du Gard has been called "the most faithful imaginative portrayer."[6] The rifle evokes the French army and its ardent nationalist supporters, for whom the honor of the military and the maintenance of order were more important than whether Captain Alfred Dreyfus, whom a court-martial had condemned to life imprisonment for treason, was actually guilty or innocent. The dictionary calls to mind the "intellectuals," who believed that Dreyfus had been framed, and who cared more that language be used to convey the truth than that the army's prestige be saved at the cost of perpetuating lies.

The protagonist of Martin du Gard's *Jean Barois* (1913) edits a magazine—it recalls both Charles Péguy's *Cahiers de la Quinzaine* and Marc Saignier's *Le Sillon*[7]—that comes to take Dreyfus's side. The novel shows the eventual disenchantment of Barois and his Dreyfusist allies with the judicial handling of the Affair, especially the long-delayed quashing of the original court-martial verdict not by a military court but by a civil one. *Jean Barois* also evokes the degradation of what Péguy called a "mystique"—an ardent, generous revolt against judicial injustice—into "politics"[8]—a bitter, dogmatic anti-clericalism that opposed but corresponded in its narrowness to the savage chauvinism of the French right wing.

Contrasting with the disillusionment, at the end of the Dreyfus Affair, of most of the intellectuals grouped around the *Sower* magazine, is the continued hopefulness of Senator Marc-Élie Luce, who has risked his reputation to establish the former captain's innocence. He takes heart from the belief that in the course of time present ideas of truth and justice will be "superseded."[9] It is not clear, however, whose ideas he is referring to—does he make a distinction between those he himself holds and those that resulted in Dreyfus's "rehabilitation" but not vindication? And what relationship is there between traditional, ethical natural law and Luce's conception of evolving notions of truth and justice?

Martin du Gard's own uncertainty about the very possibility of making the law conform to justice—however justice is defined—seems to be represented in the contrast between Luce and Jean Barois. Barois, after fighting hard for the exoneration of Dreyfus, is impelled by both discouragement and poor health to return to the conventional wife from whom he has long been separated and to the security of the Catholic faith that he thought he had definitively abandoned. The tension between Barois' "retreat" to religion and Luce's socialist humanism is well suggested by Martin du Gard's original title for the novel, one he regretted changing under pressure from his editor, André Gide. That title, *S'Affranchir?* (*To Free Oneself?*), indicates in words the same uncertainty about man's capacity to conquer his ignorance and terror that is symbolized pictorially by the frontispiece of the first edition of *Jean Barois*: Michelangelo's sculpture of a captive attempting to break his chains.[10]

Martin du Gard's orientation toward the Dreyfus case and the problem of justice is thus quite different from Mauriac's, which I have discussed in Chapter 2. Mauriac shows in *Thérèse Desqueyroux* and in *Vipers' Tangle* his detestation of the anti-Semitic anti-Dreyfusism of so many members of the French bourgeoisie. His central concern, however, is not the judicial and social injustice done to Dreyfus, but what he depicts as a complacently rationalist resistance to belief in a loving God on the part of persons of various political persuasions. His fundamental position is Pascal's: *Raison, humiliez-vous!* Mauriac sees not a continuity, but a gulf between religious faith and the reason that discerns ethical natural law. Martin du Gard, on the other hand, intimates in *Jean Barois* that religious faith is a crutch the strong do not need; and his strongest character is an unreligious man committed to putting reason at the service of moral progress. As I have indicated, the relation between natural law and the moral evolution that Luce believes in is problematic; but it is clear that Martin du Gard departs, in a very different way from Mauriac, from the allegiance to natural law we have found in so many pre-modern writers.

The most moving character in *Jean Barois* is a Jewish chemist, Woldsmuth, who belongs to the intellectual group that starts publishing the *Sower* as a liberal-radical journal. During a night of discussion in November 1895 about the articles to be included in the first number, he says he intends simply to copy out

> "a very sad letter I've just received from Russia. Six hundred Jewish families have been expelled from a little town in the Kiev district. Why? Because a Christian child had been found dead, and the Jews were accused of killing him—a ritual murder, you know—for making their unleavened bread! Incredible, isn't it? But that's how things are over there." (132)

In June, 1896, while members of the *Sower* group are talking in a *brasserie* about the Dreyfus case, Woldsmuth enters. Barois and three of his colleagues have rejected the idea, advanced by a lawyer, Portal, that Dreyfus may be innocent. Woldsmuth says that although he has never met Dreyfus, he was present at the "degradation" ceremony in 1895 when Captain Dreyfus was dismissed from the army. He adds gnomically, " 'And I saw.' " Although he remains silent when Barois irritably asks, " 'Saw what?' " (146), several months later he invites Barois to his flat. There he discloses that he has seen a photograph of a letter that Dreyfus had been directed to write at the War Office in order to determine whether his handwriting corresponded to handwriting on the memorandum—the notorious *bordereau*—supposedly found in a German Embassy wastebasket. The *bordereau* was a list of French military documents that its author said he was making over to the

addressee, and suspicion had fallen on the Jewish captain from
Alsace. At the War Office, Dreyfus was told to take a letter from
dictation, " 'so phrased as to include some passages' " from the
bordereau. They meant nothing to him, but the dictating officer's
voice, and the tension in the air, affected his nerves and, consequently, his handwriting.

> "The Major looks over his shoulder and exclaims, 'Ah, your hand
> is trembling!' Dreyfus, who has failed to grasp the reason for this
> remark . . . apologizes. [He] tries to write more steadily. The Major
> breaks in irritably. 'Take care! It's serious.' Then, suddenly, 'I arrest
> you, in the name of the law!' " (153–54)

According to Woldsmuth, the traces of emotion in Dreyfus's
handwriting in the photographed letter are both slight and easily
explicable. Yet solely, he asserts, because of the alleged identity of
Dreyfus's handwriting with that on the *bordereau*, the captain had
been court-martialed *in camera*, found guilty, and sentenced to
prison for life. To the highly skeptical Barois, who cannot believe
that a board of officers would have found a man guilty of treason
on skimpy evidence, Woldsmuth then reads passages from a
pamphlet—" 'a verbatim report of all that happened' "—by a
virtually unknown journalist, Bernard Lazare. Lazare argues that
since the German Embassy, in one of whose wastebaskets an
office-boy had allegedly found the *bordereau*, knew of the office-
boy's contacts with the French Intelligence Service, it would
hardly have permitted its employees " 'to tear into four pieces and
drop into a wastepaper basket a document so compromising to a
highly valuable agent.' " The *bordereau*, Lazare concludes, must
have been concocted by a forger collaborating with a German
Embassy servant, " 'thanks to whose assistance' " the forged
document was dropped into the basket, then taken from it and
transmitted to the War Ministry (156, 158).

Disturbed by Lazare's argument, Barois asks Luce, a distinguished senator and professor at the Collège de France, to investigate the matter. Luce does so, and persuaded by his own inquir-
ies that the army's case against Dreyfus had been flimsy, calls on
an old friend now highly placed at the War Ministry. Luce later
tells Barois that after he had presented all the facts he had collected, his friend had asked him how senators, university profes-

sors, scientists, and others whom Luce knew, felt about the case. Realizing that the War Ministry official wanted to size up the potential opposition before taking a stand, Luce had begged him to act on the strength of their friendship and " 'in the cause of justice.' " If the army had blundered, the only decent course was to confess the mistake, then make amends. But the friend remained silent, and finally showed him out (167–68).

What Luce says to Barois after recounting this episode reveals the conflict concerning the Affair in the minds of many Frenchmen of integrity—like Senator Scheurer-Kestner from Alsace, on whose character Luce's is partly based. Luce had wondered, he admits, whether his friend was not in the right. To the startled Barois he explains that one consequence of a public attack on the Dreyfus verdict would be " 'a bitter conflict between the claims of strict justice and the whole structure of the nation.' " For if Dreyfus were shown to be innocent, " 'his place in the dock' " would be taken by the General Staff of the French Army; and behind the General Staff was " 'that established order to which we have owed our national life for a quarter of a century' " (168). Luce is referring to the Third Republic, born of the Prussian victory over Napoleon III's Empire and never accepted by the monarchists—who would surely exploit against it a reopening of the Dreyfus case.

Luce's sense of the injustice that has been done to Dreyfus finally outweighs both his feelings of obligation to the Republic and his fear—he has nine children to support—of the personal risks he will be running. Barois has less to lose. Living apart from a Catholic wife, who under the terms of a separation agreement has charge of their daughter's upbringing, he finds in the Dreyfus Affair an opportunity to fight for justice while injuring a Church whose " 'despotism' " he despises. Luce's inner struggle, however, vividly illustrates the theme of "one humanity," or human brotherhood, which counterpoises in *Jean Barois* the theme of conflict between justice and *raison d'état*. For the range of Luce's allegiance, to the Republic as well as to an ideal of fairness in whose name he must attack the Republic's representatives, permits him compassionately to understand men against whom he must now battle.

Martin du Gard illustrates the "one humanity" theme not only at this intellectual-emotional level, but, in a more ironic way, at the sensual level as well. The pertinent scene occurs at the *Sower* office shortly after the newspaper *L'Aurore* has published in January 1898 Zola's bombshell of a letter under the headline, "J'AC-CUSE!" to the President of the Republic. The letter charges high army officials with having framed Dreyfus and accuses the Ministry of War of "having conducted a foul campaign in the press, with the object of misleading public opinion and covering up its misdeeds" (177).[11] Woldsmuth's niece, Julia, bursts terrified into the *Sower* office to tell Barois of a demonstration going on in the street below. He closes the shutters after hearing the mob's invective against him, the *Sower*, and Dreyfus. Suddenly, as a walking-stick hurtles through the window-pane, he is covered with splintered glass. Stones and sticks break the windows, rattle against the shutters. The violence erotically stimulates both Barois and Julia:

> Her features are convulsed, her skin is ashen-gray, her face has curiously coarsened, and is now like that of a much older woman. Its expression is frankly bestial, instinct has come to the surface. . . .
>   That, he thinks, is how she must look in the act of love. And the glance he throws her now is brutal, violent as rape, and she accepts it, like a woman yielding to her ravisher. (180)

Julia and Barois are thus brought together physically—they will become lovers—by a mob whose attitude they despise, but whose violence excites them. This illustration of brotherhood "under the skin" calls to mind Freud and the unconscious rather than Schiller's "Alle Menschen werden Brüder," or the Stoics' interpretation of fraternity. But the two "one humanity" episodes, taken together, seem to indicate an attempt on Martin du Gard's part to discover a basis for universal ethical laws in men's ambivalences and conflicts with one another. Martin du Gard does not affirm natural law in *Jean Barois*—Luce's notion of moral evolution is, as I have pointed out, ambiguous—but perhaps he is groping his way toward a new formulation of it.

The bitter trial of Émile Zola, which occurs shortly after the *Sower* scene, is essentially a new Dreyfus trial. Martin du Gard focuses on the assertion in the witness box by General de Pellieux, one of the military men denounced in "J'ACCUSE," that " 'conclusive proof' " has come to light, since Dreyfus's conviction, of his guilt (182). Georges Clemenceau, Zola's attorney, mockingly asks de Pellieux whether, until recently, only *inconclusive* proof has existed (191). Despite this thrust, however, de Pellieux's testimony seems impressive to the jury. He speaks solemnly of a signed document in the War Ministry's possession, which clearly implicates Dreyfus. The defense attempts to extract specific information from de Pellieux about his "document" and to have it produced in court; but a portentous evasiveness carries the day: Zola is convicted of libel.

The *Sower* group's suspicion that the "secret document" was a forgery is confirmed several months later. Lieutenant-Colonel Henry, arrested under suspicion of having fabricated the material that de Pellieux described at the Zola trial, confesses his guilt, then kills himself. A year later, nevertheless, during the new military trial of Dreyfus that Henry's confession has made inevitable, right-wing Yahooism wins again. It has expressed itself during the Zola trial in cries of " 'Traitors! . . . Down with the Jews!' " and in successful pressure to end Luce's lectures at the Collège de France (200, 204). On the eve of the new Dreyfus trial before the Council of War at Rennes in August 1899, Woldsmuth warns the excessively optimistic Barois that despite the revelations of forgeries and other illegalities by the military, the nationalist press is avenging itself. The latest rumor about the Affair is that a whole series of letters between Dreyfus and Kaiser Wilhelm II was somehow stolen:

> "According to this legend, the real *bordereau* formed part of the correspondence. It was written by Dreyfus on ordinary notepaper and the German Emperor made some notes in the margin in his own hand. When Wilhelm II learnt of the theft he insisted on the return of the stolen letters, threatening to declare war if they were not restored. So as to have documentary evidence of Dreyfus's guilt, the [War] Ministry had a tracing made of the *bordereau* on thin paper, before complying with the Kaiser's request. The marginal comments in his handwriting were, of course, omitted. Thus the whole affair was built up on this tracing of the original—a counterfeit in one sense, but a faithful reproduction of the incriminating original." (213–14)

Woldsmuth, just returned from Germany, has prepared material on this "diplomatic" issue which he urges Barois to publish

immediately; it will, he is sure, blow the "State Secret" argument
sky-high. But Barois fears that such publication might provoke
the use of the diplomatic issue as a reprisal (215). A week later he
admits in a letter to Woldsmuth that the chemist had been right.
The public has " 'interpreted the reticences of the General Staff
exactly as you foresaw. Which was what the General Staff
intended . . .' " (217).

Dreyfus's physical and psychological condition works to his
disadvantage at the Rennes trial. Having imagined him a hero, his
supporters find him, upon his return from Devil's Island, an
invalid shivering with fever. As a counterweight to Dreyfus's poor
image in the public mind, and to the military judges' extreme
sensitivity to the honor of the army as they conceive it, the
German government's statement that it never had any relations at
all with Dreyfus proves ineffectual. The strangely worded verdict
at Rennes, "Guilty of treason with extenuating circumstances,"
does, however, open the way to the offer of a "pardon" to the
condemned man. Anticipating such an offer, members of the
Sower group disagree as to whether Dreyfus should accept it.
Barois is opposed. Woldsmuth, on the other hand, thinking of the
ten years of additional imprisonment just imposed on the former
captain, asks, " 'Should he go back to that island and endure that
hell on earth again? To what purpose?' " Luce agrees with him
(230–31).

Martin du Gard does not mention Marcel Proust in *Jean Barois*,
but a letter from Proust to his mother indicates that he would have
agreed with Woldsmuth and Luce. After remarking that he has
just seen the "shameful verdict" posted, "to the great joy of the
Casino Staff," at the Évian-les-Bains Casino, Proust urges his
mother, who is Jewish, not to be too sad about the Rennes
decision:

> It is sad for the Army, for France, for the judges who have had the
> cruelty to ask Dreyfus, exhausted as he is, once more to make the
> effort of being brave again: But this physical torture, this appeal to
> moral strength in a man who really is already shattered, will be the
> only one he will have to undergo and that is already over. Hence-
> forth, things can only go well for him, morally in the estimation of
> the world, physically in that freedom that I suppose has been
> granted by now. As for the verdict itself, it will be legally quashed.

Morally it has been done. . . . Certainly "extenuating circumstances" for a traitor is odd. But it is not incomprehensible. It is the obstinate and vile admission on the part of the judges of their own doubts.[12]

One year later, at the Paris Exposition of 1900 (the same Exposition at which Henry Adams saw the towering dynamo as a symbol of terrific power but devoid of such human meaning as he thought the Virgin had had for the Middle Ages[13]), Luce and his fellow Dreyfusites gather to commemorate what he calls the last " 'unsullied hours of the Affair' ": those immediately before the Rennes verdict. Luce distinguishes " 'Dreyfusites' " from " 'Dreyfusards,' " who falsely " 'identify militarism and the army, nationalism and France.' " He is afraid that " 'in some respects they are no better than the men whom we defeated' " (235). From his perspective, a disheartening result of the campaign to clear Dreyfus's name has been the triumph of a bigotry of the left.

In the spring of 1908, when the remains of Émile Zola are transferred in an official ceremony to the Pantheon, both Barois and Luce are disgusted "with this theatrical parade, from which they have been excluded; with these vulgar demonstrations in the so-called honour of a man of Zola's stamp; with this exploitation of a name that stands for probity and justice as cover for political self-advancement" (266). Talking with Luce in the latter's Auteuil garden the day after the ceremony, Barois tells him of an experiment he had performed after a number of people had canceled their Sower subscriptions because of its campaign " 'against the nonsense talked by our rabid anti-militarists' ": for three months he had stopped sending the review to twenty subscribers who had been with the journal and given it active support from the beginning. None of them had even noticed the stoppage; the Sower had not received a single letter of complaint (266–67).

Woldsmuth, who has entered the garden with two other Sower members, sadly recalls Zola's real funeral, at which Anatole France had spoken—as Barois also remembers—of France as " 'the motherland of Justice.' " Cresteil, one of their colleagues, bitterly refers to the " 'fools' paradise' " in which they had all lived for a while: " 'We lanced the abscess, we counted on a cure—but now gangrene's set in . . .' " (269). He goes on to denounce, among the breaches of the law in the Dreyfus case, that " 'grotesque sentence given at Rennes and the equally grotesque pardon' "—and then the final judicial act in the Affair: the "rehabilitation" of Dreyfus by a civil court in 1906:

> "all the ideals for which we'd fought so hard and worked ourselves until we dropped—everything fell to pieces when that final illegality closed the Affair for good; the quashing of the sentence by a Court of Appeal which had no legal right to set aside the verdict but did not hesitate, in the interests of justice, to play fast and loose with the provisions of the law. What a miserable farce!" (270)

What was needed to annul the injustice done at Rennes, he says, was " 'a straight verdict of acquittal' " by another military court. For the lack of that, the Affair would always remain " 'a stain on our public life, a festering wound that nothing can ever heal'" (271).

Cresteil's comments are more persuasive, because of their specificity, than Luce's assertion that even though the Dreyfusists had not accomplished as much as they had once expected, " 'we're making headway slowly but surely,' " in a moral sense.

Barois, though not as hopeless as Cresteil, who will commit suicide soon after telling him that Justice and Truth are " 'pompous words that mean nothing' " (272–73), is deeply discouraged. On the left, he finds a vindictive anti-clericalism, manifested in the government's harsh legislation; on the right, a resurgence among young people of a belief in force, and a new pragmatic Catholicism, a civil religion for the sake of "order."

The recurrence of tuberculosis which he had contracted in his early years helps to sap Barois's will to continue an apparently futile fight for social justice. He gives up control of the *Sower* to a cynical colleague, for whom Julia has deserted him. And although he had written in vigorous middle age a last will and testament espousing agnosticism, and discounting in advance any death-bed conversion, his last conscious act is to crush to his lips the crucifix held out to him by an abbé.

Luce, true to the symbolism of his name and of his birth in the revolutionary year 1848, retains at his own dying moment the rationalist faith that he had expressed even after the Rennes trial, in " 'the slow but glorious progress of humanity towards a better world' " (237). As if giving the lie to this view, Barois's widow, the pious woman to whom he had returned after years of commitment to the scientific pursuit of truth, throws his rationalist testament into the fire.

In sum, Martin du Gard's novel conveys both a sense of injustice with respect to the course and outcome of a judicial and social *cause célèbre* and a mixture of hope and doubt as to the eventual development among human beings of a higher sense of justice. In contrast to writers in the natural law tradition, who believed in ethical imperatives that all men to some extent divine, Martin du Gard adumbrates the notion of "one humanity" which might gradually come to transcend previous, limited ideas of equity.

DREISER'S *An American Tragedy*

The idea that Martin du Gard at least entertains in *Jean Barois*, that human beings will acquire a higher sense of justice in the course of evolution, is absent from Dreiser's *An American Tragedy*. Human behavior in this novel is evidently determined by a combination of biological drives, psychological needs, social pressures, and chance. Battles like the trial of the protagonist, Clyde Griffiths, are counterparts of the animal warfare of jungle and swamp.

Dreiser, one of many children born to a poor immigrant couple, discovered the struggle for existence at an early age. He sometimes went to bed hungry, and with one of his brothers he picked up coal along the tracks of the Terre Haute and Evansville Railroad in order to help heat the family's home.[14] An ardent temperament, rebelling against his father's literal, superstitious Catholicism, led him on a quest for sexual pleasure and material success. His tendency to see life as governed by "forces," or by natural laws of the mechanistic kind, rather than by traditional ethical natural laws, was strengthened by both his journalistic experiences and his reading. Herbert Spencer, the popular Social Darwinist philosopher, destroyed—Dreiser wrote in *A Book About Myself*—the last vestiges of his belief in immutable, supernaturally sanctioned laws.[15] In the writings of the biologist Jacques Loeb, Dreiser found human behavior likened to the tropistic reactions of plants. From

Freud, he may have derived the term "chemism," and probably acquired a sense of the relationship between an adult's attitudes toward sex and the experiences he has had as a child.[16] He had little respect for the conventional morality consisting chiefly of fulminations against the indulgence of appetite, which is articulated in Dreiser's fiction by characters like the minister in *Jennie Gerhardt* and Clyde's parents in *An American Tragedy*. Yet, despite the generally mechanistic cast of his thought, he did evoke now and then in fiction written before *An American Tragedy*—Bob Ames's idealistic advice to Carrie in *Sister Carrie* constitutes one example—a moral sense based on "sympathy." Sympathy makes the Dreiser characters who possess it appealing, though not necessarily "fit" from a Darwinian point of view: Jennie Gerhardt, lovingly loyal to a man who has married a woman more socially polished than she, stays with him during his fatal illness, then envisages a bleak, lonely old age.

Perhaps Dreiser was influenced up to a point by Spencer's observation that "sympathy is the root of both justice and beneficence." Implicit in this formulation is a fundamental precept of ethical natural law—the Golden Rule, which is based on a capacity for sympathetic identification with one's fellows. Taken together with comments on the prospects for an "advance" of the sentiment of justice during "peaceful phases" of history,[17] Spencer's remark about sympathy makes him something of a moral optimist. Dreiser was not to adopt a comparable perspective until he arrived, in the 1930s and 1940s, at a kind of fusion of communism and Elias Hicks's Quakerism. Several years before beginning to work on *An American Tragedy*, he wrote in a newspaper piece that there was "really only the golden suggestion (not a golden rule) which softens life greatly and makes it more endurable, but it is not a law." The "first law" Dreiser said, "(in so far as humanity is concerned) is self preservation. . . . only the fit, or those favored by accident or chance, regardless of moral or inherent worth, can or do survive."[18]

Clyde Griffiths, the anti-hero of *An American Tragedy*, is plainly not one of the fit. He is neither resolute nor ruthless enough to seize what he wants in a sensate, materialistic society. At the same time, although capable of feeling sympathy for others who are in distress, he is so weakly guided by "the golden suggestion," so mastered by his dream of a glamorous, successful marriage, that he plans and causes the death of a woman without money whom he has made pregnant. Dreiser's account of his short life, with its climax in Roberta Alden's drowning and Clyde's trial for murder, emphasizes the hypocrisy of a society that lives chiefly by the law of the jungle, but preaches morality and uses the legal system to punish those too weak or clumsy to conceal or explain away their particular "crimes."

The final scenes in Clyde's life, involving his virtually filial relationship to the Reverend Duncan McMillan, indicate that Dreiser, despite the "hardness" of his Darwinism—in comparison to that of Martin du Gard—is in a way haunted by the ghost of traditional, ethical natural law. Yet Dreiser is essentially faithful, in *An American Tragedy*, to his view that the law of the jungle prevails in human life; he cannot, therefore, go beyond articulating compassion for his botched and bungled fellow-creatures: he cannot really express a sense of "injustice."

Clyde Griffiths is haphazardly raised by parents who wander from city to city conducting an evangelical Protestant mission. He perceives as a child that while his father and mother are constantly preaching "the love and mercy and care of God for him and for all,"[19] the family is always hard up, never very well clothed. In Kansas City, where the Griffiths are living when the story begins, Clyde's older sister, Esta, is seduced by a handsome actor's "chemic witchery" (21); she runs away with him to St. Louis where, instead of marrying her as he had promised, he deserts her. Although Clyde's parents conceal from him and his younger sister and brother the details of what has happened, including Esta's pregnancy, Clyde realizes that sex is involved, and concludes that "all this religious emotion and talk . . . hadn't saved Esta" (26). Fifteen years old, wanting to quit school and make his way in the glamorous world outside the drab mission, he finds a job at the Hotel Green-Davidson. Here his senses and imagination are stirred by glimpses of fashionably dressed, evidently successful and happy young men and women and by the stories he hears of sexual adventures, some of them involving bellboys and women staying at the hotel. His own initiation, by a "Venus" (70), occurs in a brothel that Dreiser calls an "erotic temple" (71), and it actually seems to be the most sacred place in the coldly secular world of *An American Tragedy*.

This experience leads Clyde to look for "a free pagan girl of his own" (70) on whom he can spend some of the money he is making at the hotel. He soon thinks he has found one in Hortense Briggs, who will, however, behave as calculatingly toward him as the actor has done toward Esta. Clyde is completely confused when he finds that Esta has returned to Kansas City and that his mother has secretly been visiting her—and thus deceiving him. Yet this deception, and Esta's confession to him of her own foolishness in getting into trouble, permit him to rationalize any misadventure that he imagines might come to Hortense through a liaison with him. Even though Clyde does not lack sympathy for his sister, the law of the survival of the fittest is impressing itself strongly on his mind.

Hortense, who is quite "fit," controls Clyde by hinting she will be "nice" to him if he buys her a fur jacket that she has seen in a store window. Completely bewitched by her, he makes a down payment on the jacket, but an accident suddenly changes his life. An automobile in which he and Hortense are riding with hotel bellboys and their dates hits a little girl, then smashes into some paving stones. Hortense, concerned only that her beauty may have been marred by facial cuts, runs home. Clyde, fearful of capture by the police, but somewhat less selfish than she, helps to place the injured driver and an injured girl in more comfortable positions in the car before running toward an open field, where he begins to crawl away to safety.

After fleeing to St. Louis, he reads in a newspaper about the little girl's death and the hospitalization and arrest of the driver, who has charged the passengers with being as guilty as he, "since they had urged him to make speed at the time and against his will—a claim which was true enough, as Clyde knew" (161). Three years later, while living in Chicago as "Harry Tenet," Clyde meets one of the other passengers, Ratterer, who tells him that the driver had been sentenced to a year in jail, " 'not so much for killing the little girl, but for taking the car' " (which belonged to his father's wealthy employer) and " 'running it without a license and not stopping when signaled' " (166).

This subliminal message to Clyde about the relative importance of property and human life is supplemented by a somewhat analogous message from his mother. Writing to "Harry Tenet" from Denver, where the family now lives, she urges Clyde to " 'cling to the teachings of our Saviour,' " always remembering that " 'right is might' "; but almost in the same breath she advises him to write to his " 'rich and successful' " uncle in Lycurgus, New York, to ask for a job in his collar business (163–65). There is no indication that Clyde is troubled by this suggestion that he serve both God and Mammon. But his later inability, in his relationship with Roberta, to act in either a steadily compassionate or a single-mindedly ruthless way seems due in part to his mother's unconsciously ambivalent teaching.

At the Chicago Union League Club, where Ratterer has found him a bellboy job and later noticed that the rich uncle is a guest, Clyde contrives to meet Samuel Griffiths. Somewhat remorseful because his ineffectual brother, Asa, had been all but disinherited by their father, Griffiths is also impressed by Clyde's apparent intelligence and ambition, and writes to him soon after their meeting to offer him a position. Clyde accepts it.

Walking about Lycurgus shortly after arriving there, he is struck by the contrast between a miserable slum, "the like of which . . . he had not seen outside of Chicago or Kansas City" (187), and the "arresting company of houses" on the same residential street. One of these homes, which he especially admires, has "trees, walks, newly groomed if bloomless flower beds, a large garage at the rear, a large fountain to the left of the house as he faced it, in the center of which was a boy holding a swan in his arms, and to the right of the house one lone cast iron stag pursued by some cast iron dogs . . ." (188).

He learns that this is Samuel Griffiths's house, and although he does not suspect that he himself will become the hunted stag rather than the possessor of a beautiful swan, his thoughts evince his "unfitness." For he fears an investigation by his "uncle or his cousin or some friend or agent of theirs," of his past life: "The matter of that slain child in Kansas City! His parents' miserable makeshift life! Esta!" (189).

The cousin he is thinking of is his uncle's son, Gilbert, whom he strongly resembles, and who as secretary of the Griffiths Collar and Shirt Company has coldly informed him that he will be starting in the "shrinking room" of the factory (182). A major motif in *An American Tragedy* is the characters' intense interest in their positions on the social scale. Clyde, contemptuously treated by Gilbert, feels inferior to him, and looks down in his turn on the collar-factory employees—who respect and fear him simply because of his surname—and on the people he meets at his "commonplace" boarding house. Dreiser has none of Molière's deftness, but he makes Clyde behave like a kind of minor-league Tartuffe when, after Samuel Griffiths has ordered Gilbert to promote Clyde to a twenty-five-dollar position as an assistant foreman, he begins to attend a Presbyterian Church, to which the Griffiths occasionally go.

People "know" each other, in the urban society Dreiser depicts, almost entirely in terms of their supposed status, as this is indicated by dress, speech, and the presence or absence of self-assurance. Clyde's rise in the factory hierarchy, which enables him to buy new clothes and move to a better boarding house, where his landlady offers a special rate because of his striking resemblance to his well-known cousin, makes him especially attractive to the female employees he now supervises. Sternly instructed though he has been by Gilbert not to associate personally with any of these women, he enjoys erotic fantasies in which his new status plays a key part. He muses about some of the employees who are of a "pagan and pleasure-loving turn" (238) in a way that foreshadows his shallow relationship with Roberta that

> it might be possible . . . without detection . . . for him to play with one or another of them—or all of them in turn if his interest should eventually carry him so far—without being found out, particularly if beforehand he chose to impress on them the fact that he was condescending when he noticed them at all. (239)

Instead of becoming a Don Juan, however, he finds himself especially drawn to a young woman who has been hired on a trial basis and whom Clyde, now elevated to stamping room supervisor, decides to retain in her job. It is notable that although Dreiser's description of Roberta Alden's background immediately recalls Clyde's to us—her parents are poor, her father is a "nebulous" blunderer (244), like Clyde's father—she thinks of him from the beginning as a glamorous Griffiths. The Clyde she falls in love with is largely a fiction created by her conventional, impressionable mind. And Clyde's strong feeling for her is inseparable from his conviction that he can dominate her, as he had not been able to dominate Hortense Briggs. Darwin's observations on sexual selection are pertinent to the genesis of this romance: Clyde's bright plumage, for Roberta, is his Griffiths name; Roberta's sexual appeal for Clyde is not only her gracefulness and vulnerability, but her obvious adulation of him.

Corresponding in power to Roberta's illusion about Clyde is his fantasy about a young friend of one of the Griffiths daughters—Sondra Finchley. He has met her on the evening of the supper at the Griffiths house. The vain, self-assured daughter of a newly rich industrialist, Sondra has had an "electric," tormenting effect on him. Clearly unattainable, as he imagines, she becomes a goddess of Beauty-and-Wealth in his mind.

Clyde's passiveness and timidity, which prevent him from attempting to win Sondra, are evident at the beginning of his acquaintance with Roberta. For it is she who initiates a conversation with him at work. In spite of her initiative, however, their first meeting outside the factory is accidental—at a lake on a Sunday afternoon, while he is thinking of "that beautiful Sondra Finchley," and then of the poor but attractive Roberta, "and the world which she as well as he was occupying here" (257). Once the fortuitous meeting occurs, Clyde's "chemisms" do send him in hot pursuit of Roberta, despite the Griffiths edict against fraternization with female workers. He becomes her initiator, teaching her—overcoming religious scruples like his own mother's—to dance, then persuading her to move from the house of one of her friends where her every move is watched to a lodging with a separate entrance. There, by promising never to desert her, he overcomes her last hesitations. Dreiser effectively evokes the mixture of guilt feelings and erotic exhilaration in both Clyde and Roberta; and, later, Clyde's cock-of-the-walk attitude that since she was "willing to sacrifice herself for him in this fashion, must there not be others?" (300).

Repeatedly, Dreiser presents human behavior, not as relatively autonomous, as writers in the ethical natural law tradition—like Dante, William Langland, Lope de Vega, Voltaire—had conceived it, but as determined by drives, or inhibitions, or environmental forces, or accidents. A chance meeting one evening with Sondra shapes Clyde's life decisively: after mistaking him in the dark for Gilbert, whose indifference to her has wounded her vanity, she finds Clyde quite interesting. She relishes the thought of both striking back at Gil and exercising her sway over his cousin. Clyde, his confidence buoyed by sexual success with Roberta, and by a recent invitation from a factory official to join an important golf club, decides not to visit Roberta that evening. During the following months, he keeps breaking appointments with her in order to accept Sondra's heady social invitations.

He is made keenly aware, however, that his relative poverty is a handicap among the sleek young beasts of Lycurgus. A wealthy girl tells him at a party that although some people think he is better looking than Gil, " 'that won't help you much . . . unless you have money—that is, if you want to run with people who have. . . . People like money even more than they do looks' " (320).

This lapidary truth is brought strongly home to him after Roberta finds herself pregnant. Clyde has been continuing the clandestine affair with her only because he cannot find a creditable way to end it. A fit Darwinian would contrive to desert the pregnant woman he no longer loves, then brazenly deny any charge that he was responsible for her condition. Clyde, however, sensitive as he is to "conventional or moral stimuli" (371), and pressed hard by the desperate Roberta to help her, obtains some pills—which do not work, then finds a doctor who, he has heard, might be to willing to perform an abortion. In a pathetic scene, Roberta goes alone to Dr. Glenn's office, Clyde having insisted that his name " 'can't be pulled into this without trouble for both of us' " (387). When she tells Glenn of her problem, he refuses on moral grounds to do what she asks and tries to persuade her to discuss the predicament with her parents. But the heart of the matter is clearly her lack of the money that people "like even more than they do looks." For the doctor,

> in several cases in the past ten years where family and other neighborhood and religious considerations had made it seem quite advisable, . . . had assisted in extricating from the consequences of their folly several young girls of good family who had fallen from grace and could not otherwise be rescued, [but] he was opposed to

aiding . . . any lapses or tangles not heavily sponsored by others. It was too dangerous. (400)

Dreiser observes, after Roberta has made a second visit to Glenn, and again been turned down, that the doctor gave no hint that he could be induced to act "as indeed he could act. It was against his prejudices and ethics" (410).

Clyde keeps playing for time with the terrified Roberta, who grows increasingly insistent on marriage. Although unable to avoid comparing Roberta's situation to Esta's some years earlier, he still coolly asks himself: who had come to Esta's rescue? And after all, if only he could get out of this mess and marry Sondra, he would be "the equal, if not the superior, of Gilbert Griffiths himself and all those others who originally had ignored him here—joint heir [with Sondra's brother] to all the Finchley means" (425).

When Roberta is four months' pregnant, he receives two letters—one a baby-talk invitation from "Sonda" to "Clydie-My-die" (Hortense, also using baby-talk narcissistically, had addressed it to the fur jacket she coveted) to visit her at the Finchleys' summer place, where " 'we'd ride and drive and swim and dance' " (433); the other from Roberta, who is anxiously waiting at her parents' home for him to take her on the wedding trip he has hinted at. Her predicament, which he has managed to hide from her family, causes Clyde "one of his old time twinges of remorse and pity"—he is able "to sympathize deeply, if gloomily" with her (434)—but the weight of her dependence on him makes him long to run away with and marry Sondra.

At this point Clyde happens to read a newspaper report of an "Accidental Double Tragedy" at a western Massachusetts lake. A rowboat that had been rented by a man and a girl had been found, upside-down, near the shore. The girl's body had eventually been discovered, but there was still no trace of the man's. Pondering the news item as he goes to bed that night, "he was struck by the thought . . . supposing that he and Roberta—no, say he and Sondra—(no, Sondra could swim so well, and so could he)—he and Roberta were in a small boat somewhere and it should capsize at the very time, say, of this dreadful complication which was so harassing him?" (440).

Clyde's brief flirtation here with the idea of dying along with Sondra ("Double Tragedy," the newspaper headline says) is consistent with his general passiveness and indicates, particularly when taken together with his complete bungling of the eventual murder plan, that his grasp of realities is much weaker than his fantasies.

Although Clyde feels that even to think of such a solution as drowning Roberta is to commit "a horrible, terrible crime" (440), the dark thought returns after an excursion with Sondra and her friends to Big Bittern, a virtually uninhabited Adirondack region dotted with "lonesome lakes" (458). A new letter from Roberta, threatening to let the world know how he has treated her (469), prompts a telephone call in which he promises to take her away, vaguely mentioning a little trip, "somewhere before they got married or after" (470).

Roberta's death comes about in a manner sufficiently different from what Clyde has envisioned to make him (and many readers of the novel) uncertain about the extent of his guilt. Dreiser's depiction of the death scene on the lonely lake epitomizes that combination of chance, "chemisms," psychological factors, and material circumstances that constitutes for him—in contrast to the relatively clear-cut tales that the prosecution and defense attorneys will tell in court—the human situation. The crucial events in the rowboat result from Clyde's sudden inability to do what he has planned: to "turn swiftly and savagely to one side or the other— leap up—upon the left wale or right and upset the boat; or failing that, rock it swiftly, and if Roberta protested too much, strike her with the camera in his hand, or one of the oars at his right." Instead, he suffers a "sudden palsy of the will" (491). His tormented facial expression frightens Roberta, who cries out and, by crawling along the keel, attempts to approach him, since he seems about to fall either into the boat or into the water. As she draws near him, "seeking to take his hand in hers and the camera from him in order to put it in the boat," Clyde strikes out at her, "but not even then with any intention to do other than free himself of her—. . . her presence forever—. . . !" This description of his intention, and the passage that follows it, convey an impression of the event that differs, as we shall see, from the impression that Clyde himself gives to the Reverend Duncan McMillan later in the novel. (It will, however, be a crucial element of Clyde's deliberately untruthful courtroom testimony that Roberta's face or hand might accidentally have struck his camera when she stumbled in coming toward him "in a burst of tenderness and gratefulness" for his having just offered to "make amends" and marry her [698–700]).

Dreiser, after telling us that Clyde's sole intention was to "free himself" from Roberta "forever," continues:

> Yet (the camera still unconsciously held tight) pushing at her with so much vehemence as not only to strike her lips and nose and chin with it, but to throw her back sidewise toward the left wale which caused the boat to career to the very water's edge. And then he, stirred by her sharp scream, (as much due to the lurch of the boat, as the cut on her nose and lip), rising and reaching half to assist and recapture her and half to apologize for the unintended blow—yet in so doing completely capsizing the boat—himself and Roberta being as instantly thrown into the water. And the left wale of the boat as it turned, striking Roberta on the head as she sank and then rose for the first time, her frantic, contorted face turned to Clyde, who by now had righted himself. (492–93)

Dreiser's language indicates that what has happened so far is an accident, for the boat's capsizing is due to Clyde's effort "to assist and recapture her and . . . to apologize for the unintended blow." What happens next, however, is described in such a way that even in the heavily "determined" world of Dreiser's novel, it strikes us as moral wrongdoing on Clyde's part. Roberta, unable to swim, calls for help, but a "voice at his ear" tells him that an accident is saving him the labor of what he has sought. "And then Clyde, with the sound of Roberta's cries still in his ears, that last frantic, white, appealing look in her eyes, swimming heavily, gloomily and darkly to shore" (493–94).

Among Clyde's many blunders in planning Roberta's death was his failure to realize that she might leave incriminating evidence at the lakeside inn where they registered. There, soon after her drowned body is recovered, a letter to her mother is found in her coat, saying, " 'We're up here and we're going to be married, but this is for your eyes alone' " (499). The County District Attorney, when shown this letter by the County Coroner—who mentions other suspicious aspects of the event, one of which is that the man's body has not yet been found—agrees tacitly with his view that the case has good political potentialities. For the District Attorney, who hopes to win a judgeship in a forthcoming election, stands to benefit among prospective voters from a timely, important criminal conviction. But as his attention focuses increasingly on Clyde—who will be arrested at Twelfth Lake, where Sondra and her friends are vacationing—he comes to have additional reasons for zealously prosecuting the case. "The son of a poor farmer's widow," District Attorney Mason had denied himself all pleasures in childhood in order to help his mother; and as an adult, he looked upon those "with whom life had dealt more kindly as too favorably treated" (504). Clyde Griffiths, although Mason soon learns he is far from wealthy, he loathes because of Clyde's close association with the "wretched . . . indifferent" rich (516). And because Mason suffers from a "psychic sex scar" (504) as the result of a facial injury in adolescence, he envies and despises Clyde's evident popularity with women. Happily for Mason, another of Clyde's blunders has been to leave in a trunk in his Lycurgus room the final fifteen letters that Roberta had sent him, as well as many notes and invitations from Sondra and letters from his mother that include two addressed to Harry Tenet in Chicago. When newspaper editors from all over the United States ask Mason for more information about the case, and especially about the "beautiful wealthy girl with whom it was said this Griffiths was in love," the District Attorney, "over-awed by the wealth of the Finchleys and the Griffiths," simply replies that she is "the daughter of a very wealthy manufacturer of Lycurgus, whose name he did not care to furnish—. . . ." But Mason does not hesitate to show reporters the bundle of letters from Roberta, or even to describe some of them in detail—for, as Dreiser mordantly observes, "who was there to protect her" (577).

As far as Clyde's relationship to the Samuel Griffiths family is concerned, he suffers more than he benefits from it. On the one hand, pre-trial press reports (622) emphasize his connections with the well-to-do:

> "CLYDE GRIFFITHS, NEPHEW OF THE WEALTHY
> COLLAR MANUFACTURER OF LYCURGUS,
> NEW YORK."

On the other hand, no member of the wealthy Griffiths family gets in touch with him or makes any public statement about him. Samuel Griffiths is honest enough to wonder whether his having ignored Clyde for eight months after putting him to work in the factory basement might have been "at least a contributing cause of all this horror" (586). And, although chiefly because "some sort of a defense on the part of the Griffiths would . . . be expected by the public," he does authorize the engagement and payment of competent lawyers to defend his nephew. Griffiths knew, however, of other criminal lawyers, "very distinguished" ones, who "for sufficient retainer," "via change of venue, motions, appeals, etc., . . . might and no doubt would be able to delay and eventually effect an ultimate verdict of something less than death, if such were the wish of the head of this very important family." But such a "hotly contested trial as this" would result in a great deal of publicity, "and did Mr. Samuel Griffiths want that" (589)?

Dreiser thus indicates that in this world where the unfit fail, Clyde is condemned to die because money is not available to him to hire the most "distinguished" lawyers—just as Roberta was condemned to continue her pregnancy because neither she nor Clyde could afford to pay enough to buy an abortion. Neither the Golden Rule, that most compassionate commandment of the Judeo-Christian version of ethical natural law, nor the golden suggestion competes effectively in *An American Tragedy* with hard Darwinian law.

In Clyde's trial, the "truths" presented to the jury by lawyers for the prosecution and the defense differ—through deceptive and distorted presentations of evidence, and through the suppression of some important details—from the truth that Dreiser, as omniscient narrator, has communicated to us. In effect, each side in the case creates its own artwork or fiction, in the hope that the jury will accept it as a conclusive marshalling of "the facts."

The prosecution has a strong evidential case. The eagerness, however, of one of Mason's assistants to prevent Clyde from escaping "justice" leads him to practice what he considers an excusable deception. He threads a strand of Roberta's hair through the lens of the camera that had caused the bruises about her head. This maneuver—of which Mason himself is apparently unaware— is calculated to have a powerful effect in a courtroom where feeling against Clyde is already high. For the printing in newspapers, before the trial, of excerpts from Roberta's "more poetic and gloomy" letters has produced "a wave of hatred for Clyde as well as a wave of pity for her—the poor, lonely country girl who has had no one but him—and he cruel, faithless, a murderer even" (577).

The smash hit of the trial is the dramatic, occasionally lachry-mose reading by Mason—who has told local newspapermen how strongly he has been moved—of her letters. Dreiser remarks that "the moist eyes and the handkerchiefs and the coughs in the audience and among the jurors attested their import" (661). As for Sondra's letters to Clyde, Mason has considered them vital to his case until her father puts pressure on him through the chairman of the Republican Party's State Central Committee not in any way to use either the girl's name or her letters. Since Clyde himself does not want the name of his goddess to be mentioned in the trial, an agreement is reached to refer to her only as "Miss X." Thus, a mysterious element is introduced into the courtroom, where it might have been in Clyde's interest for his attorneys to deal more openly with his obsession.

Just as Sondra Finchley's well-connected father is able to force Mason to keep her name out of the trial, Samuel Griffiths can prevent Belknap and Jephson, the lawyers who have been retained for Clyde, from using as they had hoped to do the defense of insanity, or "brain storm"—"a temporary aberration due to love and an illusion of grandeur aroused in Clyde by Sondra Finchley and the threatened disruption by Roberta of all his dreams and plans." This argument, which at least has the merit of analyzing more accurately Clyde's mental condition when he planned the murder than does the defense finally settled upon, is vetoed by Griffiths both because it would require perjured testimony that Clyde was of unsound mind and because it would reflect on "the Griffiths' blood and brain" (607).

Consequently, as a line of defense that Samuel Griffiths will pay for, Clyde's lawyers come up with the notion of a "change of heart." Neither believing the sincere account Clyde has given them of what happened in the boat, nor thinking that the jury will believe it, Jephson, the shrewder of his two attorneys, tells him that he must tell an effective lie in order to convince the jury of the essential truth of his "not guilty" plea. Clyde must say on the witness stand that when he went away with Roberta, he intended only to try to persuade her to free him because of his love for "Miss X"; that after spending two nights with Roberta during the trip he had a change of heart, became ashamed of himself, and decided to offer to marry her if she felt she could not let him go; that he actually made this offer in the boat, and that the accident was precipitated by Roberta's jumping up in excitement, or gratitude, to come toward him.

It is true that this ingenious piece of fiction does not account for Clyde's swimming fifty feet to shore, instead of thirty-five feet to rescue the drowning Roberta. Nor does it explain his having earlier buried a camera tripod which he took time to dig up while Roberta drowned. But it turns out that with respect to his failure to help Roberta, the judge's charge to the jury appears to favor him: " 'If the jury finds that Roberta Alden accidentally or involuntarily fell out of the boat and that the defendant made no attempt to rescue her, that does not make the defendant guilty and the jury must find the defendant "not guilty." ' " For that matter, the judge's only other reference in his charge to what happened in the boat should have favored Clyde had the jury known what Dreiser as narrator has said about Clyde's striking out at Roberta—"but not even then with any intention to do other than free himself of her— . . . her presence forever—. . . !" For the judge's instruction with respect to the "fatal accident" is: " 'if the jury finds that the defendant in any way, intentionally, there and then brought about or contributed to that fatal accident, either by a blow or otherwise, it must find the defendant guilty' " (736).

With the exception of one of its members, however, the all-male jury has been "convinced of Clyde's guilt before ever they sat down" (638–39) in the courtroom. Thus, when Clyde re-enacts, on Mason's orders during cross-examination, the way he had pushed at Roberta with the camera, the jurors—recalling the testimony of five doctors that the injuries to Roberta showed she had at least been stunned—assume that Clyde has deliberately been minimizing the force he had used.

It is also significant, as far as the atmosphere in the courtroom is concerned, that after Mason forces Clyde to admit to having continued his sexual liaison with Roberta even after seeking "Miss

X's" company, an irate woodsman cries out vengefully, " 'Why don't they kill the God-damned bastard and be done with him?' " (721). During the jury's deliberations, one man—politically opposed to Mason (who has won his judgeship during the trial)—holds out against convicting Clyde until "he was threatened with exposure and the public rage and obloquy which was sure to follow in case the jury was hung. . . . Whereupon, having a satisfactory drug business in North Mansfield, he at once decided that it was best to pocket this opposition to Mason and agree" (737).

Ironically, after the failure of his phony "change of heart" defense leads to his being condemned to die, Clyde acts in such a way as to help ensure his own execution. Through his mother, who in a sad and grotesque turn of events has come east as a paid special newspaper correspondent in order to earn money for an appeal of Clyde's case—he meets an evangelical lay preacher, the Reverend Duncan McMillan. This high-minded though sexually "repressed or sublimated" man has been persuaded by Mrs. Griffiths that Clyde is about to be unjustly executed "by the pitiful but none-the-less romantic and poetic letters of [Roberta] which should never have been poured forth upon a jury of men at all" (777). McMillan visits Clyde in jail, quotes the Bible to him, and becomes his confidant. Although the zealous McMillan is the type of person who would not have moved him at all earlier in his life, Clyde responds strongly to him in these new, desperate circumstances. Needing to confess, and to discover the extent of his actual guilt, he rejects as "shabby, false" the thought that while his appeal is pending it would be impolitic to go back on the lying testimony he had given in court (786). At last pouring out his story to the evangelist, he admits that he had had no "change of heart" (786). In the boat, just before Roberta rose to come to him, "there had been a complex, troubled state, bordering, as he now saw it, almost upon trance or palsy." Perhaps, he says, this was partly due to "the shame of so much cruelty" in connection with his plan to strike her. But at the same time "there was anger, too,—hate maybe—because of her determination to force him to do what he did not wish to do. . . ."

He goes on to tell McMillan that "perhaps"—for he is not sure even now—that anger had given the blow with the camera "its so destructive force." Despite his immediate qualification that "in rising he was seeking to save her" (792–93), the minister concludes from Clyde's further admission that he had not wanted to save Roberta from drowning, that " 'in your heart was murder then.' " And Clyde reflectively replies, " 'Yes, yes . . . I have thought since it must have been that way' " (795).

Consequently, when after the appeal of Clyde's conviction has been turned down, McMillan goes to plead for mercy with the New York State Governor, the preacher says only that Clyde has "come into a new understanding of life, duty, his obligations to man and God" (802–03). And although McMillan asks—at least partly because he opposes capital punishment—that the sentence be commuted to life imprisonment, the Governor refuses, having decided "from something in McMillan's manner that he, like all others, apparently was satisfied as to Clyde's guilt" (803).

It is clear to the reader that McMillan has concluded, not in terms of the "law" as it was conveyed in the trial judge's charge to the jury, but in terms of morality, or ethical natural law, that Clyde was guilty of premeditated murder. His conclusion is understandable; but as far as the circumstances of Roberta's death are concerned, there is a detail that presents the reader with a problem. For Clyde's account in his confession to McMillan of what happened in the boat differs subtly from Dreiser's "omniscient" account. Clyde says that there had been some anger "that had given the blow its so destructive force." In the omniscient description, Clyde yielded—as Roberta attempted to approach him—"to a tide of submerged hate, not only for himself, but Roberta . . . ," but he feared "to act in any way." Then, as she drew near him, "seeking to take his hand in hers and the camera from him in order to put it in the boat, he flinging out at her, but not even then with any intention to do other than free himself of her—her touch—her pleading—consoling sympathy—her presence forever—God!" (492). The key difference between the two accounts is that Clyde's accentuates the possibility of a link between his anger and the blow's "destructive force," while the omniscient one emphasizes the absence of any intention on his part, in vehemently pushing the camera at Roberta, "to do other than free himself of her." Why is Clyde harder on himself than the all-knowing narrator is?

The answer, I believe, is that Clyde's moral impulse (or "super-ego"), which has been weak during the long period of "pagan" rebellion against his parents' intense religious moralizing, becomes unusually strong when he is with McMillan, who, while as forceful as his mother, is more sympathetic than either she or his father. It is not accurate to say, as one critic of *An American Tragedy* does, that "at the last crucial moment Dreiser gives Clyde a hitherto undemonstrated moral sense which recoils at a hitherto undemonstrated principle of internal evil." [20] For Clyde's moral sense has certainly been demonstrated earlier in the novel. Just before Roberta told him of her pregnancy, he felt guilty over "his recent treatment of her," and Dreiser remarks: "Being sensitive to conventional or moral stimuli as he still was, he could not quite achieve a discreditable thing, even where his own highest ambitions were involved, without a measure of regret or at least shame" (371). And while reading the letter from Roberta, whose tone contrasts so strongly with that of the note he has just received from Sondra, Clyde "experienced one of his old time twinges of remorse and pity in regard to her": "For after all, this was not her fault. She had so little to look forward to—nothing but her work or a commonplace marriage. For the first time in many days, really, . . . he was able to . . . sympathize deeply, if gloomily" (434). Furthermore, after Clyde has deserted the drowning Roberta, and swum to shore, he cannot escape the thought of his moral responsibility: "For had he not refused to go to her rescue, and when he might have saved her, and when the fault for casting her in the water, however accidentally, was so truly his? And yet—and yet—. . ." (494).

The essential point about his moral sense is that it manifests itself only in reaction to particular situations. It is too weak to serve as a guide to the conduct of his life. His most powerful guides have been his "chemisms" and the values of a society that teaches him that "money makes the mare go." Only to McMillan does he attempt to tell the truth about what he did to Roberta and how he had come to do it. But the hardness on himself of his confession—is it his mother's moral sense (rather than her tough practicality) within him that speaks of the force of the anger behind the blow?—militates against his last chance to survive.

On direct examination during his trial, Clyde explains that the name "Tenet," beneath which he hid for a time, was that of a boy he once knew. When Jephson asks him if he hadn't thought that he might be doing an injustice in using that name " 'to cover the identity of a fellow who was running away,' " Clyde answers, " 'No, sir, I thought there were lots of Tenets.' " Obviously alluding to Clyde's unintentional pun, Dreiser remarks that although an "indulgent smile might have been expected at this point, . . . so antagonistic and bitter was the general public toward Clyde that such levity was out of the question in this courtroom" (674–75). So while Clyde, without intending to do so, points to the relativism that is a cultural incidence of Darwinian thought, the audience at the trial enacts a ritual of condemnation of the man they have come to regard "absolutely" as a criminal. There are indeed in the world Dreiser depicts many opinions that are held to be true; and as Dreiser shows life in *An American Tragedy*, we do not determine as free agents the tenets we live by; rather, those tenets are determined for us in ways we cannot adequately understand.

For this reason, Dreiser's sense of "injustice" in *An American Tragedy* can only be a sense of the unfairness of life itself. For injustice is an ethical concept, and in order to discuss a character in ethical terms we must believe in his relative autonomy. The whole tendency of this novel, however, is to show how "forces" within and outside Clyde drive him to the actions he takes at Big Bittern and afterward. Dreiser notes that the more sympathetic of Clyde's two lawyers, Belknap, had, when young, been caught between a pregnant girl he had been amusing himself with and a girl he wanted to marry. He had been extricated by his wealthy father's timely engagement of "the services of the family doctor" (592–93). In the world that Dreiser depicts, an adherence to either "conventional" morality or to a "golden suggestion" that derives from ethical natural law seems to subvert the individual's efforts to succeed, or sometimes even to survive. Thrasymachus's cynical definition of justice in Plato's *Republic* must be amended a little in order to be fully pertinent to *An American Tragedy*: justice is the interest of the stronger "organisms."

BRECHT'S *The Caucasian Chalk Circle*

Brecht's play *The Caucasian Chalk Circle* (*Der kaukasische Kreide-kreis*)[21] differs by virtue of its Marxist perspective from both Martin du Gard's *Jean Barois* and Dreiser's *An American Tragedy*. Martin du Gard is torn between his qualified faith in man's ability to evolve to a higher ethical level and his disenchantment over the legal and social outcomes of the Dreyfus Affair. Dreiser, focusing not on the evolutionary aspect of Darwinism, but on the struggle for existence, presents the result of Clyde Griffiths's trial as the triumph of the strong over the weak. Brecht transforms into revolutionary terms the Darwinian ideas that influenced Martin du Gard and Dreiser. His play points to the eventual emergence, through violent revolution informed by reason and agape, of a just society. Brecht differs significantly from writers in the natural law tradition by suggesting that, with exceptions, human beings are no more than *potentially* rational animals.

The Caucasian Chalk Circle, as Brecht wrote it—though not as it has always been performed in the United States—is preceded by a Prologue,[22] whose didacticism contrasts with the subtle ironies of the play itself. When we look back upon the Prologue after the final scene of the play, it makes clear the "positive" import of what from a propagandistic, if not from a complex Marxist, standpoint would seem a regrettably ambiguous work.

Set in "the ruins of a war-ravaged Caucasian village" (19) in the Soviet Union just after World War II, the Prologue concerns two collective farms that are contending for the same piece of land. One of the collectives had moved eastward on government orders at the approach of Hitler's armies. The other collective, "Galinsk," proposes to convert the former grazing land of "Rosa Luxemburg," where grass grows poorly, into orchards and vineyards. The members of "Rosa Luxemburg" are understandably attached to what they regard as their own soil. An old man from "Luxemburg" declares, "The valley has belonged to us from all eternity." But a soldier from "Galinsk" replies: "What does *that* mean—from all eternity? Nothing belongs to anyone from all eternity. When you were young you didn't even belong to yourself. You belonged to the Kazbeki princes" (21).

The soldier's point, typically Brechtian, is that reality changes ceaselessly. What is "right" or "true" in one set of circumstances—when, for example, serfs "belonged" to feudal lords—is irrelevant in other circumstances, like the present ones: a delegate of the State Reconstruction Commission has asked two collectives to decide between themselves which one is to cultivate the land. As Brecht dramatizes the argument, utilitarian reason wins: the members of "Luxemburg" are persuaded by the drawings and calculations of the "Galinsk" agriculturist that the orchard-vineyard project will be more helpful to the country as a whole than their own farming efforts could be. Anticipating the outcome of the discussion, a "girl tractorist" from "Galinsk" has enthusiastically declared, "As the poet Mayakovsky said: 'The home of the Soviet people shall also be the home of Reason!' "[23] Although Eric Bentley emphasizes in an appendix to his translation of *The Caucasian Chalk Circle*, that "the verb is *shall be*, not *is*" (130), Brecht's essential meaning clearly is that under socialism conflicts can be resolved peaceably, in the interests of a community that embraces contending parties.

Implicit in the Prologue is Brecht's acceptance—since nothing in his view is absolutely right or wrong—of the use of violence or deceit by revolutionaries in their struggle against the oppressors' violence and deceit. Here is the crux of the conflict between Brecht's concept of justice and that of writers in the natural law tradition. For with respect to the specific end that Brecht evokes—the resolution of differences through reasonable accommodation—writers like Langland, More, and Kleist would agree with him. It is the notion that toward the accomplishment of this end "everything is permitted" (in the words of Dostoevsky's Ivan Karamazov) that exponents of natural law would reject. For they assume that there are ethical imperatives that transcend history, while Brecht indicates that it is only in the course of history that man becomes an ethical being.

The Prologue ends with the announcement that in honor of the delegates from "Rosa Luxemburg" (this is a gracious bow to the collective that has yielded), the Singer Arkadi Tscheidse will present, after an evening meal, the old Chinese story "The Chalk Circle" in a "changed version" (24–25). This version is set "in olden times, in a bloody time," in an oppressively ruled Caucasian "City of the Damned" (27). There a Grand Duke and the enormously wealthy Governor Abashwili rule over a populace heavily taxed to support an army perpetually bled in foreign wars. While the Governor, with his family and retinue, attends the Easter church service, a palace revolt led by a Hermann Goering-like "Fat Prince" breaks out. The Governor, having returned from church to arrange for the conversion of a wretched slum into a garden for his child, is arrested. And the narrator of the play, or "Singer," makes a comment, reminiscent of a Greek chorus, on the "blindness of the great," who go their ways like gods, trusting to their power which has lasted so long:

> But long is not forever.
> O change from age to age!
> Thou hope of the people! (35)

It is "progressive" social change, however, not the kind of coup effected by the Fat Prince, that Brecht sees as the true "hope of the people." On his last appearance in Act I, the Prince blithely gives his Ironshirt followers gruesome instructions on how to fasten the Governor's decapitated head to the palace wall:

> Here! In the middle! . . . That's not the middle.
> Farther to the right. That's it. . . . (45)

The Governor's wife, Natella Abashwili, hurrying to escape with her brocade dresses, her hot water bottles, her "little saffron-colored boots" (41), completely forgets about her child, Michael. Left behind in the burning city, and in immediate danger from the Prince's men, he is rescued by Grusha, a kind kitchen maid. Although warned by the other servants that she would be killed if found with the baby, she cannot bring herself to abandon him. The "seductive power of goodness," the Singer tells us, is "fearful," and Grusha sits with the child

> Till evening came, till night came, till dawn came.
> . . . .
> Till toward morning the seduction was complete
> And she rose, and bent down, and, sighing, took
>   the child
> And carried it away. (46)

In saving Michael, she is risking both her life and her prospective marriage to Simon Shashava, a soldier she has just become engaged to, who has promised to return when the war with Persia (one of the wars that Grusinia seems always to be waging) is over. Like Simon, Grusha is an unreflective patriot. Although Brecht means us to like her for her goodness and emotional warmth, he also satirizes, through her "Song of the Four Generals," the nationalism that perpetuates her own subjugation, and Simon's, by Abashwilis and Fat Princes:

> Four generals
> Set out for Iran.
> With the first one, war did not agree.
> The second never won a victory.
> For the third the weather never was right.
> For the fourth the men could never fight.
> Four generals and not a single man!
> Sosso Robakidse went marching to Iran
>
> . . . .
> For him the men would always fight.
> Sosso Robakidse,
> He is our man! (47)

If Grusha's naïveté could help to encourage jingoistic slaughters, her warmheartedness makes her vulnerable to exploitation during her flight with Michael into the Northern Mountains: knowing how desperately she needs milk for the child, a peasant charges her exorbitantly for it. There comes a point at which, exhausted, and believing that she has taken Michael so far from the city that the Ironshirts would no longer find him, she lays him down on the threshold of a peasant woman's house. Although this woman is one of the good people who are found, as the Chorus says, "in the bloodiest of times" (54), her courage fails when the Ironshirts appear. Grusha, seeing them approach, has run to her and made her promise to claim that the baby is her own. But under pressure, the woman blurts out to them that she herself "had nothing to do with it. She left it on the doorstep, I swear it!" (56) An Ironshirt corporal sees Michael, in fine linen, in a crib, but the fiercely protective Grusha hits the soldier from behind with a log and rushes off with the baby. These acts on Michael's behalf bind her irrevocably to him, and, as the Singer tells us, after twenty-two days of journeying, "Grusha Vashnadze decided to adopt the child" (57).

In one of the most absorbing scenes of the play, she escapes from the pursuing Ironshirts by crossing a dangerously rotten mountain bridge. Refusing to give Michael to a woman who offers to hide him, she cries, "We belong together." Her "Song of the Rotten Bridge" epitomizes her emotional generosity:

> Deep is the abyss, son,
> I see the weak bridge sway
> But it's not for us, son,
> To choose the way.
>
> The way I know
> Is the one you must tread,
> And all you will eat
> Is my bit of bread.
>
> Of every four pieces
> You shall have three.
> Would that I knew
> How big they will be! (60)

Upon arriving (in Act III) at her brother Lavrenti's home, she is treated by her sister-in-law as if she has a contagious disease. As soon as Aniko is out of earshot, the pusillanimous Lavrenti asks, "Is there a father?" When Grusha shakes her head, he says, "We must think up something. She's religious" (63). Only Grusha's collapse from illness permits her and Michael to remain through the winter. In the spring, she reluctantly agrees to marry the reputedly dying son of a neighboring peasant woman because, as Lavrenti explains, she doesn't need a man in bed: she needs a man "on paper." Grusha concedes that she "could use a document with stamps on it for Michael" (67–68).

There follows a wonderfully farcical wedding scene in which the monk hired for the occasion asks the mother of the "dying" peasant, immediately after the ceremony, "How about extreme unction" (71)? Minutes later, having heard the wedding guests say that the war, and consequently the draft, is over, the malingering peasant jumps out of bed, throws the astonished guests out of the house, and remarks to Grusha, "I've upset the apple cart, huh?" (75–76).

For Michael's sake, Grusha stays with her brutal husband until, seven years later, Simon appears in a shabby soldier's uniform.

Grusha, weeping, cannot find words to explain her apparent betrayal. The Singer, however, movingly conveys her thought— that she has had to "break" herself "for that which was not mine" (83).

As Simon leaves, bitterly telling her to throw away his engagement pledge, a cross, two Ironshirts approach, with Michael between them. They are taking him back to the city as the suspected son of the late Governor. The judge who will decide whose child Michael is, we learn as Act III ends, is a certain Azdak.

This man, a village scrivener, has become a judge in bizarre circumstances. On the Easter Sunday of the Fat Prince's coup, the Grand Duke had to flee for his life. Shortly thereafter, Azdak found a fugitive in the woods whom he hid in his hut; although suspecting he was a peasant-flogging landlord, Azdak refrained from handling him over to the police. The scrivener's remarks to the frightened fugitive reveal the paradoxical judicial sense that will make him a remarkable judge:

> They're after you, which speaks in your favor, but how can we make sure they're not mistaken about you? In Tiflis one time they hanged a landowner, a Turk, who could prove he quartered his peasants instead of merely cutting them in half, as is the custom, and he squeezed twice the usual amount of taxes out of them; his zeal was above suspicion. And yet they hanged him like a common criminal—because he was a Turk—a thing he couldn't do much about. What an injustice! He got onto the gallows by a sheer fluke. In short, I don't trust you.

Detesting the regime under which he has been living, Azdak depicts it here as having hanged a landowner who, though brutal enough to his peasants to have won its approval, was executed because he was a hated foreigner. (The same chauvinism that blinds Grusha to the senselessness of Grusinia's wars blinds the war-makers themselves to the cruel "virtues" of the Turk.) Azdak's radicalism prevents him from turning the fugitive over to the police. But after feeding him and letting him go, the scrivener discovers that the runaway was "the old butcher, the Grand Duke himself" (88). He mistakenly concludes that a popular revolt, rather than the military coup we know it to be, has occurred; and, remorseful for having committed what he regards as a counter-

revolutionary act, he denounces himself to a policeman, demand-
ing to be taken to the capital to be publicly tried and judged.

In the courtroom, surrounded by Ironshirts—whom he believes
to be his "brothers"—he sings a revolutionary song, before they
tell him of having beaten up the weavers of the capital, whose
revolutionary zeal had led them to string up the city judge, the
one hanging from a courtroom beam. The now-terrified Azdak
seems to the Ironshirts to be an amusing buffoon. They install
him as the new judge, one of them remarking cynically, "The
judge was always a rascal! Now the rascal shall be a judge" (98)!

He proves to be an odd Robin Hood. His characteristic pro-
nouncement before beginning a case, "I accept," is an open
invitation to bribery, in contrast to what Brecht implies is the
concealed purchasing of "justice" that is endemic in this society.
Azdak's venality is further distinguished from the customary sort
by his rendering judgments against those who offer big bribes and
in favor of people who pay only small ones, or none at all. The
most amusing instance of this idiosyncratic dishonesty is his
handling of the case of an innkeeper who brings an action, "on
behalf of my son," for the rape of the son's wife. The person
accused is the innkeeper's stableman, whom the daughter-in-
law—"well schooled," according to Brecht's stage direction—
denounces for violating her in the stable. "It was all over," she
says, "when my father-in-law entered and accidentally trod on
me." Her father-in-law hastily adds, "on my son's behalf." Azdak, who in accordance with his custom has accepted money from
the innkeeper, and also observed meaningfully that he liked "the
little roan" in the stable, elicits an admission from the stableman
that he had "started it"—hardly a confession of rape. Azdak then
dramatically reveals that the girl herself, Ludovica, is the criminal:

> Public Prosecutor, drop your knife—there on the ground. . . .
> Ludovica, pick up that knife. (Ludovica, *swaying her hips, does so*).
> See that? (*He points at her.*) The way it moves? The rape is now
> proven. By eating too much—sweet things, especially—by lying
> too long in the warm water, by laziness and too soft a skin, you
> have raped that unfortunate man. . . . This is a case of intentional
> assault with a dangerous weapon!

Ludovica is sentenced to give "the Court" the little roan which,
Azdak leeringly remarks, "Your father liked to ride 'on his son's

behalf,' " and she is instructed to "come with me to the stables, so the Court can examine the scene of the crime . . ." (102–04).

The Singer and Chorus celebrate Azdak's way of rendering equity:

> When the sharks the shark devour
> Little fishes have their hour.
> For a while the load is off their back.
> On Grusinia's highways faring
> Fixed-up scales of justice bearing
> Strode the poor man's magistrate: Azdak. (104)

In another trial, an Alice-in-Wonderland one with a Marxist twist, an invalid alleges that he had a stroke upon learning that a doctor whose medical studies he had paid for had treated a patient without charging him a fee. Azdak reprimands the doctor, who can cite no circumstances extenuating his "unpardonable" oversight, but acquits him (101).

Azdak's most clearly revolutionary judgment concerns an old peasant woman accused of stealing a cow and a ham and of killing several cows belonging to a landlord who had just asked her to pay the rent on a piece of land. "Granny," as Azdak calls her, explains that one night a bearded man identifying himself as "the miracle-working Saint Banditus" had brought her a cow because her son had been killed in the war; a few days later, when the farmer's servants came to take the cow away again, "bumps as big as a fist sprouted on their heads. So I knew that Saint Banditus had changed their hearts and turned them into friendly people." The next one, she says, to become a good man was the farmer Shutoff: Saint Banditus "arranged it so he let me off the rent on the little piece of land."

The miracle-working saint proves to be "Granny's" brother-in-law, the bandit Irakli, whose entrance into the tavern which had been converted into a courtroom has elicited execrations from the rich farmer-plaintiffs and a demand for his beheading. Irakli, who is carrying a huge ax, laughs as the old woman explains how she came by her allegedly stolen ham: one morning it came flying in at her window: "It hit me in the small of the back. I'm still lame, Your Honor, look. (*She limps a few steps. . . .*) Your Honor, was there ever a time when a poor old woman could get a ham *without* a miracle" (105–06)?

Azdak responds by rising from his chair, declaring, "Granny, that's a question that strikes straight at the Court's heart." Then, after installing her in his own chair, he sits on the floor and eulogizes her as "The Woebegone / The Bereaved Mother / Whose sons have gone to war":

> On us
> Who are already damned
> May you render a merciful verdict
> Granny Grusinia!

Shouting at the farmers, Azdak sardonically demands that they admit to being atheists who don't believe in miracles. After fining each of them five hundred piasters for godlessness, he invites Granny and the "pious man," Irakli, to drink some wine with him and the Public Prosecutor.

For two years, the Singer and the Chorus tell us, Azdak "broke the rules to save" the poor and lowly:

> Broken laws like bread he gave them,
> Brought them to shore upon his crooked back. (107)

The image of Azdak bringing the poor to shore upon his back recalls the legend of St. Christopher's carrying Jesus, as a child, across a river. But lines that have been sung by the Singer and Chorus as an introduction to the case of the peasant woman and the "saint" indicate clearly that the "broken-law" justice dispensed by Azdak would need, in order to endure, the axes of many Iraklis:

> All mankind should love each other
> But when visiting your brother
> Take an ax along and hold it fast.
> Not in theory but in practice
> Miracles are wrought with axes
> And the age of miracles is not past. (104)

Azdak's quirky, revolutionary magistracy flourishes in the anarchic climate after the Fat Prince's coup, but eventually the Grand Duke and the Governor's widow take power again. The people's quarters are burned once more. The Fat Prince who had beheaded the Governor is himself beheaded—and Azdak is confronted by Natella, who is looking for her son, Michael. Azdak, like Falstaff preferring survival to heroism, obsequiously promises her that the child will be returned and that the "former servant" who had taken him away "will be beheaded, Your Highness, at your service" (110–11).

Despite his fawning, however, the Governor's widow detests him; the three rich farmers at whose expense St. Banditus performed his miracles join the Ironshirts in tearing off his gown; and the Ironshirts, now "loyal" to Natella, rough him up before dragging him under a hangman's noose. Farcically, however, he is saved: a messenger brings a dispatch from the Grand Duke, appointing as magistrate "a man whom we have to thank for saving a life indispensable to the country's welfare [the Grand Duke's, of course]—a certain Azdak . . ." (116).

His aplomb restored, Azdak sits on a statute book to cushion his sore backside, and opens—with his customary "I accept"—the case opposing the biologically maternal claims of Natella, whose lawyers pay him a generous bribe, to the humanely maternal appeal of the penniless, lawyerless Grusha. Natella speaks of "the tortures of a bereaved mother's soul," and one of her lawyers says that she conceived Michael "in the holy ecstasies of love." But her other attorney gives away the show by blurting out that the revenue of her estates is blocked: it's "tied to the heir," Michael, without whom Natella cannot even pay her lawyers. The first lawyer's attempt to cover up his colleague's blunder by remarking that even if Michael were not the heir he "would still be the dearly beloved child of my client," is interrupted by Azdak. "Stop," shouts the judge. "The Court is touched by the mention of estates. It's a proof of human feeling" (117–20).

Evidently practicing a tactical cruelty in order to prepare the way for his final decision, Azdak is very hard on both Simon, who, accompanying Grusha in court, claims to be Michael's father, and on Grusha, who says that she hasn't looked out for her own comfort, but brought Michael up "to be friendly with everyone" (119). The judge fines Simon for using indecent language in court, and tells Grusha she is a silly girl for not wiggling her backside at him (122–23). To her furious attack on him as a bribe-taking servant of the rich, he replies by asking her a straightforward question: "I don't believe he's your child, but if he *were* yours, woman, wouldn't you want him to be rich? You'd only have to say he wasn't yours, and he'd have a palace and many horses in his stable and . . . many soldiers in his service . . ." (124). Thereupon, the Singer tells us what Grusha, who remains silent, is thinking: if Michael had "golden shoes to wear / He'd be cruel as a bear," and "Being powerful and bad / Is hard on a lad." Therefore, "let hunger"—but not hungry men and women—"be his foe!" (125). Azdak, after telling the mute Grusha that he thinks he understands her, declares that since he is unable to decide who Michael's real (*wirkliche* in the German text[24]) mother is, he is obliged as judge to choose a mother for him. His method proves to be a "changed version," in the words of the Singer in the Prologue, of the method used in a twelfth- or thirteenth-century Chinese play *The Chalk Circle*.[25] Michael is placed in the center of a circle drawn on the floor, and Azdak decrees that the true (*richtige*) mother is the one who can pull him out of the circle. After Grusha, in two successive tests against Natella, lets go of the child to avoid tearing him to bits, Azdak names her the true mother (126–27).

In the original Chinese play, the same test is used to ascertain who the child's birth-mother (*wirkliche Mutter*, as Azdak puts it) is—the assumption being that only the birth-mother would loosen her grip in order to avoid dismembering the child. Given Brecht's taste for paradox, it is quite possible that he adapted to his Marxist purpose the Confucian idea of "rectification of names," whereby names were to be applied only to persons or institutions deserving them. Thus Natella, whose name closely resembles the German *nachteilig*—"hurtful"—proves herself as unfit to be called "mother" as Grusha proves deserving of the name.

The last judicial act of the crookedly straight Azdak is to divorce, by "mistake," Grusha and her brutal peasant husband rather than an elderly couple who earlier in the day have actually requested a divorce. With his usual effrontery, Azdak remarks, "Divorced the wrong couple? What a pity! And I never retract." He collects forty piasters from Simon, who happily cries, "Cheap at the price, your Honor"; and Grusha tells Simon that she had taken Michael "because on that Easter Sunday I got engaged to you. So he's a child of love" (127–28).

The play ends with a dance during which Azdak gradually fades from view; and the Singer tells us:

The people did not forget him but long remembered
The period as a brief golden age,
Almost an age of justice.

. . . .

But you, who have listened to the story of the
        Chalk Circle,
Take note of what men of old concluded:
That what there is shall go to those who are good
        for it,
Children to the motherly, that they prosper,
Carts to good drivers, that they be driven well,
The valley to the waterers, that it yield fruit. (128)

The play's ending, however, is ambiguous unless it is read with the Prologue in mind. For while a child raised by Grusha and Simon would probably be kind, brave, hard-working, what would become of Michael in a country run by tyrants who continually draft men for their mad wars? The Singer's advice that children should go "to the motherly," the valley "to the waterers," makes full sense from Brecht's perspective only in the setting of a transformed society. In a society untransformed, such selfless love as the motherly Grusha displays is of limited social value. And any fruit that the valley yields to waterers is likely to be appropriated by self-serving landlords. The Prologue points to the Soviet Union as a land where it either is or eventually will be possible for love to be "socially useful" and for utilitarian projects to be pursued in a spirit of generosity toward the larger community. It is important to keep in mind, however, that the historical route from the unjust society of Grusinia to the presumably rational society of the Soviet Union is the revolutionary one symbolized by the ax of "St. Banditus."

The violent overthrow of a tyrant by the people when they have no other recourse was permitted, according to Aquinas, by natural law. And both the American and the French revolutions were fought in the name of the natural rights that derived from natural law. But while the advocacy of revolutionary violence in *The Caucasian Chalk Circle* should present, except to pacifist readers or auditors of the play, no major problem, Brecht's easy evocation of bright, rational post-revolutionary tomorrows is difficult to accept. The thorniest problem, however, that the play raises is the implicit one—for Brecht does not address it—of the relationship between justice in the transformed society and justice as conceived by adherents of a natural law that "everyone to some extent divines." *The Caucasian Chalk Circle*, brilliantly lucid in dramatizing injustice, is simplistic and rather unclear in adumbrating a just society.

KOESTLER'S *Darkness at Noon*

Shortly after quitting the Communist Party in 1938, Arthur Koestler outlined the synopsis for a novel one of whose characters "was to be a member of the old Bolshevik guard, his manner of thinking modeled on Nikolai Bukharin's, his personality and physical appearance a synthesis of Leon Trotsky and Karl Radek. . . ." This character's surname, "Rubashov," Koestler chose because it sounded like *roubashka*, the high-necked, embroidered Russian shirt "in which I sometimes dressed him up for a Sunday."[26] But for readers of the novel eventually published in English as *Darkness at Noon* (1941), Rubashov's patronymic "Salmanovich" has more significant reverberations. Koestler's "son of Solomon" is one of the revolutionaries who have renounced the "fathers' " morality, of which the Bible was a main source, in favor of a utilitarian social code. Utility they have defined in terms of the construction of a communitarian society where, at last, human relationships would be authentic and just. The factitious individualism of pre-bourgeois and bourgeois societies, of men whose birth or money gave them status—while millions of wretched people went without food or dignity—would be supplanted by a true humanism.

For the attainment of this end, the revolutionary "sons" considered all means justifiable. Any traditional moral law could, indeed must, be broken in the interest of the Revolution, as that interest was defined by the Party. Rubashov, like other "Old Bolsheviks," loyally served the Party from his youth at the turn of the century through the 1917 revolution and the first "proletarian" dictatorship (obviously Lenin's, although Koestler makes no reference by name to Soviet leaders, or to the Soviet Union); and then through the first decade of the dictatorship of "No. 1," until Rubashov could no longer suppress what the Party perceived as a "counter-revolutionary" revulsion from his duties. As *Darkness at Noon* begins, the cell door of a Moscow prison slams behind him. He has been jailed in 1938, during No. 1's great purge. The most startling feature of the public trials ordered by Stalin was the abject confessions of treason by a succession of highly placed Communists. Koestler's novel is an attempt to interpret the complex reality that lay behind these courtroom melodramas.

The epigraphs for the novel are well chosen to underscore ideas that conflict with one another throughout the work. Juxtaposed with Machiavelli's observation that "He who establishes a dictatorship and does not kill Brutus, or he who founds a republic and does not kill the sons of Brutus, will reign only a short time," is Dostoevsky's cry, "Man, man, one cannot live quite without pity." Then, letting the pendulum swing again toward Machiavelli's viewpoint, Koestler quotes, as epigraph for the first segment of the novel, Saint-Just's apothegm "Nobody can rule guiltlessly."[27] In short, imperatives that derive on the one hand from natural law—Dostoevsky's exhortation recalls the Golden Rule—and on the other hand from Thrasymachus's dictum that justice is the interest of the stronger are kept in tension with each other in *Darkness at Noon*. Never does Koestler permit the reader, or his protagonist, to rest in any certainties. Rubashov's eventual decision, after grueling interrogations and the deprivation of sleep, to denounce himself in a public trial is based on a belief that the one sure judge of "right" and "wrong" is history. From this perspective, only "in the long run" can it be determined whether a Caesar, a Napoleon, a Stalin has been chiefly a benefactor or a tyrant. Rubashov decides—but has grave doubts as soon as he has acted upon the decision—that No. 1's "liquidations" of opponents and cruelly opportunistic changes of the Party line may have enabled the Soviet state to survive and thus opened the way to the classless society. But—*Darkness at Noon* is crammed with "buts," "howevers," and "nevertheless"—Rubashov was arrested in the first place because of his inability to suppress extreme remorse over his participation in political murders and his acquiescence in the Party's vertiginous flip-flops. He has mused in his prison cell:

> The old disease. . . . Revolutionaries should not think through other people's minds.

Or, perhaps they should? Or even ought to?

How can one change the world if one identifies oneself with
everybody?

How else can one change it? (18)

In purely intellectual terms, Rubashov cannot solve this problem, for there is no common denominator to two different values
that he holds: that of a mankind that must be brought to birth,
and that of the flesh-and-blood worth of an actual man's or
woman's life.

Three flashback episodes, during the earlier days of Rubashov's
imprisonment, correspond to his memories of what in traditional
ethical terms are awful injustices that he has committed on behalf
of the Party. The first episode begins with his appointed meeting
with a young Party member, Richard, in a German museum
during the Nazi terror of 1933. The Communist movement has
been defeated; "its members were outlawed and hunted and beaten
to death." The Party was "nothing but a thousand-armed and
thousand-headed mass of bleeding flesh" (24). Richard, fully
aware of the situation, stammeringly explains to Rubashov that he
has not distributed the official Party organ because the " 't-tone
of your propaganda material was wrong . . .' " (30). Rubashov
himself must realize, he says, that nobody would believe in the
Party's " 'unbroken will to victory.' " Although Rubashov knows
it well, he tells Richard that by spreading " 'an atmosphere of
panic,' " he has become a danger to the movement (33). Hence, in
accordance with the Central Committee's decision, Richard is no
longer a member of the Party. And despite Richard's plea that he
not be thrown "to the wolves," Rubashov's demeanor indicates
that this is exactly what will occur.

Just before informing Richard of his expulsion, Rubashov has
felt the toothache that is to signify his consciousness of guilt
throughout *Darkness at Noon*. The allusion to "a tooth for a tooth"
is one of many references to the Bible and the ethical tradition that
is closely related to it. It is Rubashov's thought, in his Moscow
prison cell, of the imploring, protective gesture in the *Pietà* he had
seen in the German museum, that sparks his recollection of the
meeting with Richard. Later, shortly before Rubashov's second
flashback episode, he thinks of the Party's "warm, breathing

body" as "covered with sores . . . bleeding stigmata" and wonders when in history there had "ever been such defective saints" (46). Perhaps more than any other passage in the novel, this one—where he conceives the failure of the Party which has been his very life in terms of Christian symbolism—dramatizes his insoluble problem. He exists partly in the "fathers' " world of individual moral responsibility, partly in the "sons' " world of revolutionary, utilitarian morality—and feels an alien in both.

The second flashback episode occurs in a Belgian port two years after Richard's expulsion and following his own arrest by the Nazis, his brutal beatings at their hands which have impaired his hearing, and his triumphal return to his native country, where No. 1 often appeared in public with him. When Rubashov departed again, for Antwerp, it was with the knowledge that half the associates of the "old man" (Lenin) no longer were alive and that those who remained were "worn out and disillusioned, full of cynical melancholy."

> From time to time No. 1 reached out for a new victim amongst them. Then they all beat their breasts and repented in chorus of their sins. After a fortnight, when he was still walking on crutches, Rubashov had asked for a new mission abroad. "You seem to be in rather a hurry," said No. 1, looking at him from behind clouds of smoke. (48–49)

The new mission is even more sickening, from a traditional moral viewpoint—which the Party would call "petty bourgeois"—than the sacrifice of Richard. It is now 1935; Mussolini has invaded Abyssinia. The Party has called for a boycott of fascist Italy; governments throughout the world have "decided to cut off the aggressor's supply of raw materials" (56). But Rubashov is in Antwerp to explain to the dockworkers' section of the Party that the world boycott has failed, because of the hypocrisy and greed of the bourgeois governments; and that if the Country of the Revolution now stopped sending petrol to Italy, those governments would "spring into the breach," thus hampering the development of industry "Over There." One of the dockers, grasping immediately what Rubashov is driving at, bitterly recalls a similar occasion two years before, when having boycotted on Party orders cargoes from or bound for Nazi Germany, these same dockworkers were ordered by the Party to unload from No. 1's ships material destined for Hitler's war industry. " 'Couldn't you choose another harbor this time,' " he asks, " 'for your little transactions' " (57–59)? It is, however, the leader of the dockworker's section, Little Loewy, whom the imprisoned Rubashov most painfully remembers.

After performing clandestine Party duties in pre-Hitler Germany, from which he had had to flee, he stayed alive by eating tree barks and killing and eating cats. Ejected from France several times by gendarmes, only to be sent back by Belgian border guards, he eventually met in a Belgian jail a Communist who after their release obtained his reintegration into the Party. Before telling the dockworkers the repellent news about the boycott, Rubashov has found himself thinking that just as Little Loewy had killed cats, "he must take [him] by his ears and legs and break him over his knee . . ." (55). A week after the meeting, which ended with Little Loewy's concurrence in his bitter fellow-dockworker's accusation of Soviet "blacklegging," Loewy was denounced by the Party as an *agent provocateur*. Three days later he hanged himself (60).

After this second flashback, Rubashov is interviewed by the Examining Magistrate, Ivanov, an old friend from the days of the post-Revolutionary Civil War, whom he had dissuaded from committing suicide after a leg operation. Koestler stresses the ideological twinship of the two men: "They had the same moral standard, the same philosophy; they thought in the same terms. Their positions might just as well have been the other way round." Rubashov can easily see himself, through Ivanov's eyes, in the position of the "accused" in which he himself had placed Richard and Little Loewy. But Rubashov has also become intensely aware, during mental dialogues with himself in prison, of a "silent" partner whom the "other, against all grammatical rules, addresses . . . as 'I' instead of 'you,' in order to creep into his confidence and to fathom his intentions. . . ." This silent partner, "a grammatical abstraction called the first person singular" exists disconnectedly in the form of a toothache, the hands of the *Pietà*, Little Loewy's cats, and it expresses itself in "the compulsion to rub one's pince-nez on one's sleeve, . . . the uncontrollable movement of the lips which murmured such senseless sentences as 'I shall pay,' and the dazed state induced by daydreams of past episodes in one's life" (88–90).

Rubashov "knows" that all this subjectivism is bourgeois hogwash. When in the interview with Ivanov, the Examining Magistrate tells him that the Party holds "proofs" of a planned attempt by Rubashov on No. 1's life, Rubashov readily understands the Party's reasoning: before his arrest he has repeatedly showed signs of disagreeing with Party policy, thus endangering the Country of the Revolution; "objectively," therefore, he is guilty of whatever he is accused of. The standard of "justice" is purely utilitarian. It matters not at all that he had no plan whatever to kill No. 1. While he tells Ivanov that the charge is idiotic, he knows well that his kind of "innocence" is irrelevant, just as mere "subjective" innocence was irrelevant in the cases of Richard and Little Loewy when Rubashov disposed of their lives.

Ivanov, in return for Rubashov's having dissuaded him from suicide, wants to save Rubashov's life now; he offers him the chance to avoid a fatal public trial by making "a partial confession" and pleading guilty "within certain carefully defined limits." The practical consequence of such cooperation with Ivanov would be a relatively brief imprisonment, then a return "to the ring again" (74–77). Rubashov's third flashback memory, however, conflicts violently with the part of himself that is vulnerable to Ivanov's logic.

Immediately after the Little Loewy episode, he had been sent to the country of "B" to lead a trade mission attached to No. 1's legation. His secretary, Arlova, had in her "slow, passive way" a quieting effect on his nerves (91). After weeks of dictating letters to her, he took her to bed. At that point, she made a comment that remained as fixed in Rubashov's memory as "the folded hands of the *Pietà*, and the smell of seaweed in the harbor town": " 'You will always be able to do what you like with me.' " Relaxing completely in her presence, he gave vent to his "heretical witticisms." Only when he made a particularly dangerous joke about No. 1's personal habits did she warn him that he ought not to say such things to other people, that he " 'ought to be more careful altogether' " (93–94). Then, during the period when No. 1 was preparing a second great trial of the "opposition . . . over there," Arlova was given political responsibility for the contents of the

Trade Delegation library. Soon, however, she was attacked at a
Party cell meeting for not weeding out of the library certain
oppositional works and for not putting into it some of No. 1's
most important speeches. When summoned to make a statement,
she said that she had followed every instruction given to her; while
speaking, "she let her glance rest a long time on Rubashov" (96)—
something she normally did not do in public. Calamity came
quickly. She was dismissed as librarian at a cell meeting that a bad
toothache kept Rubashov from attending. A short time later she
was recalled. The scent of "her large, lazy body clung to the
walls" of Rubashov's room until his own recall several months
afterward (98).

Abruptly Koestler ends the third flashback here, as if Rubashov
has suppressed his memory of how the episode ended. Later, we
learn that during Arlova's trial she constantly called on him as her
chief witness and that his public disavowal of her ensured her
condemnation and execution. He sacrificed her, because, as his
friends had persuasively argued, his own existence was more
valuable to the Revolution than hers and "more important than
the commandments of petty bourgeois morality" (103).

Now in jail, however, Rubashov witnesses a scene that at least
for a time makes his past mode of thought seem "lunacy" (116).
His friend Bogrov, a former sailor on the Potemkin, later the
commander of the Eastern Fleet (Bogrov, whom he himself had
taught to read and write) is dragged past his cell, moaning
Rubashov's name, as his legs scrape along the floor. "Had Arlova," Rubashov wonders, "whimpered in the same way when she
was dragged"—her legs trailing—along the corridor?" (116)

When Ivanov visits him in his cell in hopes of a "yes" to the
proposition that Rubashov cop a plea, Rubashov greets him with
contempt. But Ivanov refutes the accusation that he himself had
ordered Bogrov to be taken past Rubashov's cell in order to soften
him up for a confession. This "filthy trick"—Ivanov obviously
accepts Rubashov's term—had actually been arranged by an assistant, Gletkin, "against my express instructions." A young man,
an *apparatchik* with no "umbilical" ties to the Revolutionary generation, Gletkin has insisted that only "hard" methods would
work with Rubashov (120). But Ivanov, trying to retain control of
his friend's case, engages Rubashov in an argument reminiscent of

Ivan's attempt to persuade Alyosha, and himself, that desirable ends justify repugnant means. Ivanov, Ivan's Dostoevskian namesake, although admitting that he himself drinks in order to avoid "the vice of pity" (123–24), eloquently states the case for what he calls "vivisection morality" against "cricket morality," or natural law. " 'Do you know,' " he asks Rubashov, " 'a single example of a state which really followed a Christian policy? You can't point out one. In times of need—and politics are chronically in a time of need—the rulers were always able to "evoke exceptional circumstances," which demanded exceptional measures of defense . . .' " (128). Ivanov's point, as he knows, is the one that Rubashov has made in his prison diary: since Machiavelli, whose *Prince* reportedly lies permanently at No. 1's bedside, " 'nothing really important has been said about the rules of political ethics' " (78). And for years both Rubashov and Ivanov have justified the actions of the Communist Party on the grounds that, as distinguished from other, purely selfish machiavellianisms, theirs, like some surgical procedures, will cure a desperate illness.

The most intense moment of argument between these ideological twins occurs when Rubashov, unable to get Arlova out of his mind, brings up the case of Raskolnikov in *Crime and Punishment*. The problem, he recalls, is whether the young student has the right to kill the old pawnbroker. Raskolnikov is young, talented; she is old, useless to the world. But, Rubashov notes, "the equation does not stand." Raskolnikov finds himself, unforeseeably, obliged to murder a second person; and ultimately he discovers that "twice two are not four when the mathematical units are human beings. . . ." Ivan replies that all copies of Dostoevsky's novel should be burned: it distorts, he argues, the problem of ends and means. For if Raskolnikov, instead of committing a crime " 'in his personal interest,' " had " 'bumped off the old woman at the command of the Party, for example, to increase strike funds or to install an illegal Press—then the equation would stand, and the novel with its misleading problem would never have been written . . .' " (126–27).

Rubashov rebuts this by saying that the Party's strategy and commands are resulting in the sacrifice of millions of lives today in order to attain " 'a theoretical future happiness, which only we can see.' " Picking up Ivanov's phrase "vivisection morality," he remarks bitterly that it sometimes seems to him that " 'the experimenters had torn the skin off the victim and left it standing with bared tissues, muscles and nerves . . .' " (130). Yet Ivanov's rejoinder, which is the response that a part of Rubashov has often made to his own objections, is that " 'every year several million people are killed quite pointlessly by epidemics and other natural catastrophes. And we should shrink from sacrificing a few hundred thousand for the most promising experiment in history' " (131)?

Strongly affected by this articulation of what he himself had long argued, Rubashov decides before going to sleep that night that it cannot be called betrayal if he keeps "faith with the living" rather than the dead (133).

Accordingly he sends a letter to the Public Prosecutor, declaring his intention to renounce completely his oppositional attitude " 'and to denounce publicly his errors' " (141). Yet he smiles in anticipation of the "agony" with which Party theoreticians will read the letter as a whole; for he has set forth an "heretical" theory that justifies his confession on the grounds that the masses are at the moment insufficiently "mature" to permit the establishment of a democratic form of government (134–37). Not until several generations have passed will the people be able to understand the new economic system, and hence govern themselves.

Three days later when he is brought before the Examining Magistrate, Gletkin, not Ivanov, is playing that role. The bright lighting in the room indicates what awaits Rubashov: Gletkin despises subtle methods of dealing with "criminals." To Rubashov's comment that he prefers to be examined by Ivanov, Gletkin replies that a refusal to make a statement now would constitute a disavowal of his written declaration of willingness to confess. In consequence, Rubashov's sentence would then be pronounced "administratively." Certain that something has happened to Ivanov, and knowing that silence would ensure his own death, Rubashov offers to make a statement if Gletkin puts out the "dazzle light." But the new Examining Magistrate makes it plain that Rubashov has no bargaining power. And Rubashov, at this moment of humiliation, reflects that although the "swine," Gletkin, is too young to have known the pre-Revolutionary world, his generation had "right on its side." It really was necessary, he tells himself, to "deny the last tie which bound one" to "vain conceptions of honor" and hypocritical "decency" (148–49).

So Rubashov, sitting in a chair across a desk from Gletkin, behind whom is a glaring light, begins what will be a long, almost sleepless journey. He has been prepared to make a "confession" in very general terms. The specific charges that Gletkin reads to him "surpassed his worst expectations in absurdity" (151). The accusation that he had instigated the murder, by poison, of No. 1 is the crowning feature of the weird indictment. But Rubashov's attempt to avoid pleading guilty to these charges, by confessing instead to "sentimentalism" and "humanitarian weakness" (153), is crushingly defeated. Gletkin's most powerful weapon is Rubashov's consciousness of guilt toward Arlova; the Examining Magistrate forces him to admit that she had been executed " 'as a consequence of the lying declaration you made, with the object of saving your head' " (156). Thus, Gletkin, the functionary of a regime based on utilitarian morality, cleverly exploits Rubashov's ethical ambivalence. For Rubashov is torn between his feelings of remorse, derived from "natural law," for having sent Arlova to her death, and his "revolutionary" belief in strictly consequential, or utilitarian, morality. Thus, in addition to his longing to be allowed to sleep, Rubashov's capitulation to Gletkin has two causes: the desire to "keep faith with the living," with the Party that for forty years had been his life; and the need to pay the price which his "old" conscience—the grammatical fiction, the "I"—demands for the betrayal of a human being who had given herself to him completely.

It is the "old" conscience that compels him to wage this contest with Gletkin, which affords him only the satisfaction of the chess player with a losing game who staves off defeat as long as possible. One of Rubashov's little victories occurs when his interrogator brings into the room a frightened fellow-prisoner, "Harelip," who has recently been tortured. Mechanically, "Harelip" speaks of having been instigated by Rubashov to poison No. 1. When "Harelip" gives a circumstantial account of meeting Rubashov in 1937, Rubashov remembers him as the son of an old comrade, Professor Kieffer, historian of the Revolution. The son recounts accurately a conversation between his father and Rubashov which, Rubashov admits to himself, might have led young Kieffer to infer

that he was actually advocating No. 1's assassination. But Rubashov decisively disproves Kieffer's accusation, obviously inspired
by Kieffer's torturers, of subornation to poisoning. Unabashed—
since unadorned "facts" are of no more importance to Gletkin
than they are to the prosecutors or defenders of Clyde Griffiths in
An American Tragedy—Gletkin indicates that he will change the
original charge of "instigation to murder by poison" to "instigation to murder." Rubashov wearily, lyingly, confesses (168).

The rest of the interrogation exemplifies the difference between
the "petty bourgeois" notion of guilt—that it consists in having
performed the criminal acts one is accused of having performed—
and the Revolutionary idea of "objective" guilt: that it consists in
criminal acts one would logically have performed in consequence
of one's beliefs. A grim game is played in which both Rubashov
and Gletkin tacitly accept the rule that if Gletkin can prove that
the root of a charge is right, even if this root is "only of a logical,
abstract nature," he is free to insert the missing details.

Gletkin acquires a certain respect for his tenacious opponent
and even replies at length to Rubashov's comment that the Party
is populating the world with saboteurs and devils: just as early
Christianity, according to a Party outline of history, " 'realized an
objective progress for mankind,' " although its doctrine that Jesus
was the son of God and a virgin " 'is said to be symbolical,' " so
the Party is achieving progress by inventing " 'useful symbols
which the peasants take literally' " (184). When Rubashov remarks
sardonically that Gletkin's reasoning sometimes reminds him of
Ivanov's, Gletkin replies that Ivanov was a " 'cynic,' " and had
been " 'shot last night, in execution of an administrative decision' " (184–85).

Just as Koestler's characterization of Ivanov, the intellectual
revolutionary, is inspired by Dostoevsky's depiction of Ivan, the
characterization of Gletkin is a variation on Dostoevsky's treatment of Smerdyakov, Ivan's "disciple." Unlike the epileptic Smerdyakov, Gletkin is physically very strong; and as an unquestioning
follower of the Party line, he approves of Ivanov's execution, while
Smerdyakov has nothing to live for when Ivan disavows him. But
there is a notable similarity between Dostoevsky's depiction of
Smerdyakov's murder of Fyodor Pavlovich as the outcome of
Ivan's teaching that "everything is permitted" and Koestler's attri-

bution of Gletkin's brutalities to the Marxist relativism of Old
Bolsheviks like Ivanov and Rubashov. The essential difference, of
course, between Dostoevsky's world view and Koestler's is that
Dostoevsky believes faith in a loving God to be man's only hope,
while Koestler can conceive—as the conclusion of *Darkness at Noon*
will indicate—a reconciliation between ultimate Marxist goals and
humane means that accord with natural law.

That all may be consummated for Rubashov, he must perform
at a public trial—for Gletkin does not once refer to the "deal"
offered by Ivanov—the task he himself described in his prison
diary: to gild the Right, to blacken the Wrong. Assigning Rubashov this role, he calls him "Comrade" for the first time since
they have met (193). And before Rubashov signs the statement
confessing to having committed his crimes through counter-
revolutionary motives "and in the service of a foreign power," the
Examining Magistrate promises, on behalf of the Party, that "after
the victory, one day when it can do no more harm, the material
of the secret archives will be published. Then the world will learn
what was in the background of this Punch and Judy show—as you
called it—which we had to act to them according to history's
textbook" (194).

As the final segment of the novel begins, the daughter of the
janitor of Rubashov's dwelling is reading to her father the newspaper report of Rubashov's trial testimony. The accused man has
faithfully performed his role as Devil, in a speech that Koestler
was later to describe as a paraphrase of Bukharin's at his show
trial.[28] The old janitor has served under Rubashov during the Civil
War. As his Gletkin-like daughter continues to read to him about
Rubashov's humiliation, which includes the judge's contemptuous
agreement to his request for a brief suspension of the trial because
of an " 'intolerable toothache,' " the janitor thinks of the New
Testament passage: "And they clothed him with purple and they
smote him on the head with a reed and did spit upon him" (199).
The old man, however, risks being condemned by his daughter to
abandon his porter's lodge to her and her husband-to-be if he
does not play Peter to Rubashov's Jesus: he signs the worker's
resolution she is circulating, which calls for the merciless extermination of traitors (199–200).

Rubashov, back in his prison cell, has for companionship what

he has named the "grammatical fiction," the "I" of his silent
dialogues. He reflects that for forty years—"forty years," the
period spent by the Biblical Israelites in the desert, is a preoccu-
pation of Rubashov's throughout the novel—he has fought against
"economic fatality" in accordance with the vows of his secular
"order" (208–09). But he has lately discovered not only an elusive
"I" that responds unexpectedly to the memory of the *Pietà*, or of
certain childhood scenes, but also a state that mystics call ecstasy
and that Freud named the "oceanic sense": "one's personality
dissolved as a grain of salt in the sea; but at the same time the
infinite sea seems to be contained in the grain of salt. The grain
could no longer be localized in time and space" (206–07).

Rubashov's "order," the Party, considers the oceanic sense at
best an escapist notion, and at worst a counter-revolutionary one.
But as his death, a sacrifice to the Party, approaches, he reflects
that there is a mistake in the Party's system: "What had he once
written in his diary? 'We have thrown overboard all conventions,
our sole guiding principle is that of consequent logic; we are
sailing without ethical ballast' " (210). No certainties are left him.
In virtually his last coherent thoughts before receiving a bullet in
the head, the word "perhaps" recurs as frequently as an affirmative
chord at the end of a Beethoven symphony:

> Perhaps it did not suit mankind to sail without ballast. And perhaps
> reason alone was a defective compass, which led one on such a
> winding, twisted course that the goal finally disappeared in the
> mist.
>
> Perhaps now would come the time of great darkness.
>
> Perhaps later, . . . the new movement would arise—with new
> flags, a new spirit knowing of both: of economic fatality *and* the
> "oceanic sense." Perhaps the members of the new party will wear
> monks' cowls and preach that only purity of means can justify the
> ends. (210–11)

The judicial process that Koestler depicts at work in No. 1's
ostensibly socialist state is at least as corrupt as any shown in the
non-socialist societies evoked by Martin du Gard, Dreiser, and
Brecht. Through Rubashov, however, Koestler expresses a hope
for the development of an ethical socialism. He comes closer than
any of the other writers discussed in this chapter to an explicit
recognition of natural law—especially its injunctions against mur-

der and against bearing false witness—as a necessary basis of a more equitable society. Instead of resigning himself to a world where only the "fittest" survive, as Dreiser seems to do in *An American Tragedy*, or envisaging, as Martin du Gard tentatively does in *Jean Barois*, the supersession of current conceptions of truth and justice, or suggesting—like Brecht in *The Caucasian Chalk Circle*—that the good society has been brought to birth by violent revolution, Koestler indicates that only a revolution guided by ethical standards "that all men to some extent divine" could make real headway against injustice.

Notes

1. Émile Zola, *Thérèse Raquin* (Paris [?]: Fasquelle, n.d.) 8.

2. Hippolyte Taine, *History of English Literature*, trans. H. Van Laun, vol. 1 (New York: Ungar, 1965) 11.

3. Harry Levin, *The Gates of Horn: A Study of Five French Realists* (New York: Oxford UP, 1966) 371. Levin remarks that Zola's "cycle of life and work had revolved from science to conscience, from natural to social history, and from sociological observation to socialistic action."

4. Charles Darwin, *The Origin of Species by Means of Natural Selection; or, the Preservation of Favored Races in the Struggle for Life; and The Descent of Man, and Selection in Relation to Sex* (New York: Modern Library, n.d.) 64.

5. David L. Schalk, *Roger Martin du Gard, The Novelist and History* (Ithaca, NY: Cornell UP, 1967) 19.

6. Schalk 8, quoting Henri Peyre, *The Contemporary French Novel* (New York: Oxford UP, 1955).

7. Eugen Weber, Introduction, *Jean Barois*, by Roger Martin du Gard, trans. Stuart Gilbert (Indianpolis: Bobbs, 1969) x.

8. Charles Péguy, "Notre Jeunesse," *Trois Fragments: Notre Jeunesse, Victor Marie, Comte Hugo, Le Mystère des saints innocents* (Lausanne: La Guilde du Livre, n.d.) 35.

9. Roger Martin de Gard, *Jean Barois*, trans. Stuart Gilbert (1949; Indianapolis: Bobbs, 1969) 237.

10. Weber xvi–xvii.

11. Martin du Gard does not quote Zola's piquant sentence, "I accuse the handwriting experts, Messrs. Belhomme, Varinard, and Couard, of having made lying and fraudulent reports, unless a medical examination reveals that they are suffering from impaired eyesight and judgment."

See Patrice Boussel, *L'Affaire Dreyfus et la presse* (Paris: Colin, 1960) 165. My translation.

12. *Letters of Marcel Proust*, ed. and trans. Mina Curtiss (New York: Random, 1949) 51.

13. Henry Adams, *The Education of Henry Adams* (Boston: Houghton, 1918) 379–90.

14. W. A. Swanberg, *Dreiser* (New York: Scribner's, 1965) 7.

15. Donald Pizer, *The Novels of Theodore Dreiser: A Critical Study* (Minneapolis: U of Minnesota P, 1976) 10, 212–13.

16. Pizer, 212, says that Ellen Moers showed that Dreiser derived the term "chemisms" from Freud but used it "principally with a mechanistic intent."

17. Herbert Spencer, *The Principles of Ethics*, vol. 1 (New York, 1895) 147–48. C. R. B. Dunlop, in "Human Law and Natural Law in the Novels of Theodore Dreiser," *Amer. J. of Jurisprudence* 61 (1974), observes that Dreiser tried to modify his complete negation of morality by adding to it Spencer's idea of "the great equation." This equation provides for a certain equilibrium in the universe, so that if—as in the case of Dreiser's protagonist in the novel *The Financier*—"a strong man becomes too powerful, he will be brought down . . . by the principle of balance or equation which operates throughout the universe of animals and men. . . ." Dunlop does not, however, find this great equation—or any other principle that mitigates Dreiser's denial of moral order in the universe—in *An American Tragedy*, even though Dreiser "seems to have spent much of his life searching for a substitute for a God-given natural law. See "Law and Justice in Dreiser's *An American Tragedy*," *U of British Columbia L. Review* 6 (1972) 379. Both of Dunlop's articles are thoughtful contributions to law-and-literature scholarship.

18. *Theodore Dreiser: A Selection of Uncollected Prose*, ed. Donald Pizer (Detroit: Wayne State UP, 1977) 226.

19. Theodore Dreiser, *An American Tragedy* (New York: NAL, 1964) 9.

20. Charles Thomas Samuels, "Mr. Trilling, Mr. Warren and *An American Tragedy*," in *Dreiser: A Collection of Critical Essays*, ed. John Lynenberg (Englewood Cliffs, NJ: Prentice, 1971) 169.

21. *The Caucasian Chalk Circle*, trans. Eric Bentley (New York: Grove, 1966).

22. Eric Bentley says in his introduction to the Grove Press edition of *The Caucasian Chalk Circle* that the Prologue "did not appear in English until the *Tulane Drama Review* printed it at my request in 1959. Soon thereafter, it turned up in the Grove Evergreen paperback edition of the play" (11). It seems sensible to infer from this comment that most, if not all, productions of the play in English before 1959, omitted the Prologue.

23. It seems impossible to determine whether Brecht's citation of Mayakovsky here is "Stalinist" or, as Eric Bentley suggests by emphasizing Brecht's use of the future tense—"shall be," to some extent "anti-Stalinist." Mayakovsky, it has been observed, "had the remarkable tribute of being praised both by Stalin and by Pasternak. . . . His work contained remarkable contradictions, and the best of it rose from a struggle in himself, which was in the end to prove his ruin." Herbert Marshall, Foreword, *Mayakovsky*, ed. and trans. Herbert Marshall (New York: Hill & Wang, 1965), 13.

24. For Brecht's use of the terms *"wirkliche Mutter"* and *"richtige Mutter,"* see Bertolt Brecht, *Der kaukasische Kreidekreis* (Berlin: Suhrkampf, 1955) 137–38.

25. See *The Chalk Circle, World Drama: Ancient Greece, Rome, India, China, Japan, Medieval Europe, and England*, ed. Barrett Clark (New York: Dover, 1960) 227–58.

26. Arthur Koestler, *The Invisible Writing: The Second Volume of an Autobiography* (New York: Stein and Day, 1984) 479.

27. Arthur Koestler, *Darkness at Noon*, trans. Daphne Hardy (New York: Bantam, 1977), precedes 1.

28. Koestler, *Invisible Writing* 493. Koestler says that in 1952, when Otto Katz was being "liquidated" in Czechoslovakia on charges of being a British spy, a saboteur, and a Zionist agent, he quoted Rubashov's speech, thus alluding to Bukharin.

4

The Sense of Injustice in Modern Absurdist Fiction

DOSTOEVSKY'S IVAN KARAMAZOV declares that if there is no God, everything is permitted. But he finds the thought unbearable, and in the end there seem to be only two possible outcomes for him: madness or a religious conversion. Dostoevsky's intentional perspective in *The Brothers Karamazov* is conveyed not through Ivan but through Alyosha, for whom compassionate love toward one's fellows is the only "saving" response to the human suffering the thought of which torments Ivan. It is because Alyosha fears that Dmitry will become bitter, and incapable of feeling this love if he goes to prison after being unjustly convicted of murder, that Alyosha urges him to run away.

Alyosha's belief that injustice can be transcended by love was not shared by Dostoevsky's contemporary Nietzsche, who passionately proclaimed the very absurdist views that Ivan is haunted by. Nietzsche exalts the "free spirits" to whom " '[n]othing is true, everything is allowed' ";[1] and he accepts the senselessness of suffering. This vision of the abyss (although not Nietzsche's idea of the superman) animates absurdist works like Melville's *Billy Budd*, Kafka's *Trial*, Camus's *Outsider*, and Kundera's *Joke*. The injustice that is done in a courtroom or a hearing in each of these fictions is but an aspect of the irrationality that governs the human condition. There is, of course, a paradox at the heart of every absurdist work: an evidently rational writer is communicating a sense of pervasive irrationality to readers who presumably are rational to some degree. But it is true that in life itself our reason is constantly assaulted by what it calls "atrocities" and "nightmares." The great question is whether, after the outburst of irrationalism in modern thought and literature as well as in life, ethical reason can again become potent, and injustice be imaginatively conceived as mitigable.

MELVILLE's *Billy Budd*

Herman Melville is the North American writer whose works most closely resemble Dostoevsky's. But although Melville's Ahab is comparable to Dostoevsky's absurdist rebel, Ivan, who finds God guilty of permitting the torture of children, the author of *Moby-Dick* provides no counterpart to the saintly Alyosha. Melville's closest approximation to that Karamazov brother is Billy Budd. However, while the actively compassionate Alyosha conveys Dostoevsky's Christian viewpoint, naïve Billy is essentially a victim of injustice in an absurd world. He is framed by a malevolent nautical police chief, and court-martialed and hanged at the behest of a naval captain who sacrifices Billy on the altar of British *raison d'état*. The story of Billy also differs, by reason of its absurdism, from the story of Rubashov in Koestler's social novel *Darkness at Noon*. In Koestler's work, the Party is diverted from the noble goal it seeks to attain by the foul means, including the show trial of Rubashov, it uses to attain it. But in Melville's novella, the very goal that Captain Vere is striving to reach—victory in war over revolutionary France—seems clearly good only from a conservative British perspective at a particular historical moment. Moral chaos rules in *Billy Budd, Sailor*, as it does in absurdist fiction generally.

Billy's physical strength, his beauty, and his guileless goodness have made him the most popular sailor aboard the English merchantman *Rights-of-Man*, whose captain says that the "virtue" that "went out of" the young foretopman has converted a "rat-pit of quarrels" into a peaceful forecastle.[2] But England in 1797 is at war with France under the Directory, and Billy is seized by a naval lieutenant and impressed into the King's service in the H.M.S. *Bellipotent*. This violation of what contemporary radicals would have regarded as Billy's natural rights is "just" only in Thrasymachean terms: it is the will of the stronger. Billy's farewell shout to the merchantman, " 'And good-bye to you too, old *Rights-of-Man*,' " was, says Melville, satire only "in effect," and not by intention (49). For it is foreign to Billy's simple, candid nature to deal in double meanings of any kind. There is, however, an atmosphere of tension in the British fleet. Earlier that year, serious grievances including the imprisonment of seamen, boiled into a commotion at Spithead, then into "the Great Mutiny" at the Nore:

> It was indeed a demonstration more menacing to England than the contemporary manifestoes and conquering and proselyting armies of the French Directory. . . . the bluejackets, to be numbered by thousands, ran up with huzzas, the British colors with the union and cross wiped out; by that cancellation transmuting the flag of founded law and freedom defined, into the enemy's red meteor of unbridled and unbounded revolt. (54)

Melville notes that after the quelling of the mutiny some grievances were addressed, but impressment continued. Discontent, therefore, "lurkingly" survived both the Spithead and the Nore uprisings (59).

It is the conjunction of these historical circumstances with the extraordinary beauty and innocence of Billy—a kind of "upright barbarian," much like Adam before his seduction by the serpent—that impels and permits the *Bellipotent*'s depraved master-at-arms, Claggart, to destroy him. Budd and Claggart, not so much "characters" as allegorical figures, have in common only the mystery of their origins. Billy is a foundling, "a presumable by-blow, and, evidently, no ignoble one" (52), while nothing is known of Claggart's life, which is the subject of unsavory rumor and surmise. The beardless master-at-arms, the police chief of the ship, harbors a "spontaneous and profound" antipathy (74) toward the cheerful Budd, whose nature, "as Claggart magnetically felt, had in its simplicity never willed malice or experienced the reactionary bite of that serpent" (78). Mingled with Claggart's hatred and disdain of the young sailor's innocence are homoerotic feelings: "a touch of yearning, as if Claggart would even have loved Billy but for fate and ban" (88).

Budd begins to be harassed in petty ways by the ship's corporals. Unaware that these men are Claggart's "cat's paws," he asks an old Dansker, a veteran of Lord Nelson's *Agamemnon*, for advice. To the Dansker's explanation that the master-at-arms " 'is down on you,' " the surprised Billy replies, " 'I seldom pass him but there comes a pleasant word.' " With the tragic wisdom of the ages, the former *Agamemnon* man replies, " 'And that's because he's down upon you, Baby Budd' " (71).

Soon after this conversation, one of Claggart's provocateurs tries under cover of darkness to bribe Budd into a pretended conspiracy of impressed seamen. Stuttering, as he tends to do under severe emotional strain, Billy threatens to throw him over the rail if he does not go away. But Billy's repugnance to being an informer prevents him from reporting the incident to anyone; and after finally revealing to the Dansker a part of what has happened, he again fails to understand a grim warning about the master-at-arm's enmity.

Claggart cleverly chooses the moment for a decisive move against the object of his envy and frustrated love. The *Bellipotent*, dispatched on a mission at some distance from the English fleet, has just tried unsuccessfully to overtake an enemy ship. Vere, the aristocratic captain, is standing pensively on the quarter-deck, "doubtless somewhat chafed at the failure of the pursuit," when Claggart appears, seemingly unhappy to be the bearer of bad news, but obliged to report his belief that "at least one sailor was a dangerous character" in a crew that included some participants in the recent mutinies and other sailors who, "like the man in question, had entered His Majesty's service under another form than enlistment." Annoyed at the circumlocution, Vere says, " 'Be direct . . . say *impressed men*' " (91–92).

Unctuously, Claggart tells him about the suspicious behavior he claims to have observed, linking it with the recent experience of another ship whose commander's life had been put in jeopardy. Vere abruptly cuts off discussion of the tabooed mutiny, demands the "dangerous" man's name, and is astonished to hear Billy's. The Captain doubts Claggart's honesty. Warning him that a hanging is in store for him if he is bearing false witness, Vere demands proof. When Claggart alleges words and acts which, if credited, would condemn Billy, Vere decides against seeking immediate corroboration. That procedure, he thinks, might, by publicizing the affair, "undesirably affect the ship's company" (96). Instead, by shifting the scene to his own cabin, Vere plans to test the accuser. Within minutes, behind the Captain's closed door, Claggart is "mesmerically" looking Billy in the eye, and repeating his charge. Overwhelmed by the powerful emotion that brings on his stutter, Budd stands "like one impaled and gagged." When he responds only with strange gesturing and gurgling to

Vere's plea that he defend himself, the Captain realizes what is wrong and urges him to take his time. This fatherly advice, however, only prompts "more violent efforts at utterance, efforts soon ending for the time in confirming the paralysis, and bringing to his face an expression which was as a crucifixion to behold. The next instant, quick as the flame from a discharged cannon at night, his right arm shot out. . . ." Struck on the forehead, Claggart falls and lies still. Vere's quasi-whisper, " 'Fated boy, what have you done!' " sounds almost like a confession of complicity. But the captain's demeanor is soon transformed:

> with one hand covering his face [Vere] stood to all appearance as impassive as the object at his feet. . . . Slowly he uncovered his face; and the effect was as if the moon emerging from eclipse should reappear with quite another aspect than that which had gone into hiding. The father in him was replaced by the military disciplinarian. (98–100)

Sending Billy to a stateroom aft, Vere summons the ship's surgeon, who immediately pronounces Claggart dead. The Captain's impassioned utterance upon hearing this—" 'Struck dead by an angel of God! Yet the angel must hang!' " (101)—poses the central problem of *Billy Budd*. The "angel" who, with a blow of his arm has carried God's message to the lying Claggart (Vere has called the master-at-arms "Ananias"), must, in Vere's utilitarian view, be sacrificed in order to forestall a new mutiny in the fleet. The drumhead court that the Captain immediately decides to summon is thus destined to enact Vere's will.

The surgeon, to whom Vere briefly recounts the events leading up to Claggart's death, is troubled by both the Captain's agitated exclamation about the angel who must hang and Vere's intention to call a drumhead court. It seems to the surgeon that the thing to do is to place Budd in confinement and postpone further action until the *Bellipotent* rejoins the squadron. The ship's officers, to whom, on Vere's instructions, he reports what has happened, apparently agree with the surgeon that the matter should be "referred to the admiral" (101–02).

As for Vere's agitation, it is so at variance with his normal manner that the surgeon wonders whether he has become unhinged. Melville's own comments here are ambiguous. He notes the difficulty in many cases of drawing an exact line between sanity and insanity, and says that whether Vere "was really the sudden victim of any degree of aberration, every one must determine for himself by such light as this narrative may afford" (102).

Few readers are likely to regard the Captain as clinically "mad" at any point in the story. The truly disturbing question, however—and it is implicit in this absurdist work—is whether a clinical definition of madness is adequate in a world where the mass slaughter of war occurs regularly and the sacrifice of human beings for reasons of state is common.

Vere, Melville tells us, would gladly have done what the surgeon thinks should be done: defer action until the matter could be referred to the admiral. But the Captain fears that unless he acts rapidly, Claggart's death at Billy's hands will become known to the crew and tend to awaken "slumbering embers of the Nore" (104). Vere's own role will therefore be a somber enactment of Lewis Carroll's " 'I'll be judge, / I'll be jury, / . . . I'll try the whole cause / And condemn you to death.' " The Captain himself chooses three officers, none of them his intellectual equal, who along with Vere are to try the case. And Vere subtly accentuates his superior rank by testifying—he is the sole witness—from the ship's weather side, "having caused the court to sit on the lee side."

The Captain's testimony about Claggart's accusation and Budd's act is immediately confirmed by Billy, who explains that, unable to use his tongue to answer Claggart's lie " 'in presence of my captain,' " he could answer it only with a blow—" 'God help me!' " To the three officers, who were surprised to hear anything against Billy in the first place, his sincerity and innocence of intention are obvious. The slight hesitation that preceded his "no" to the question whether "he knew or suspected aught savoring of incipient trouble (meaning mutiny . . .) going on in any section of the ship's company" (105–06), they attribute to "the same vocal embarrassment which had retarded or obstructed previous answers." Yet here Billy is lying, or at least equivocating, partly because of his "repugnance" to playing an informer's part against his shipmates—"the same erring sense of uninstructed honor which had stood in the way of his reporting the matter at the time . . ." (106).

The phrase "erring sense of uninstructed honor" is significant. It points to a conflict between loyalty to a code of conduct that confers a sacred privacy upon words spoken to one in confidence and fidelity to the community of which one is a part. According to naval law, the law of his community, Billy has "erred" in not reporting an apparent effort to engage him in a mutinous enterprise; and his failure to report it, "if charged against him and proved, would have subjected him to the heaviest of penalties" (107). Yet not only does Melville solicit our respect for Billy's refusal to inform on a shipmate, but he implicitly invites us to contrast Billy's essential innocence with the tortuous complexity of "civilized" life aboard the *Bellipotent*, where the very person to whom Billy "should have" reported the unsavory incident was the police officer who—we know, though Billy does not—was seeking to entrap him.

Billy's equivocal response to the question about a mutiny derives from both "the same uninstructed sense of honor" which had originally kept him silent and something else—his "blind feeling now . . . that nothing really was being hatched . . ." (107). There is fine irony in this phrasing; for the blindness of Billy's feeling evinces both his common sense and his guilelessness. He correctly intuits that no mutiny had been intended, but is unaware of the "incipient trouble" that Claggart was fomenting against him.

While Melville's treatment of Billy's attitude toward the murky incident at least partly validates the young sailor's sense of "honor" and his "blind feeling," Vere's testimony before the drumhead court depreciates those subjective considerations of which he himself is aware. Although he concedes that " 'natural justice' " would take into account Billy's intent when he struck Claggart, as well as the deed itself, the Captain insists that the drumhead court's allegiance is not to " 'nature,' " but to the King. The King's law, the Articles of War, he argues, makes it clear that if in wartime at sea a man-of-war's man strikes his superior in grade, the blow itself, " 'apart from its effect,' " is a capital crime. The officers, however, are uneasy. One of them asks if they cannot " 'convict and yet mitigate the penalty.' " Vere's reply goes to the pith of the matter, the utilitarian need that he sees for Billy's execution. To " 'the people' " (the ship's company), he says, Billy's act " 'will be plain homicide committed in a flagrant act of mutiny.' " They know what penalty should follow it. If it does not follow, they will wonder why: " 'Your clement sentence they would account pusillanimous. They would think that we flinch, that we are afraid of them—afraid of practicing a lawful rigor . . . lest it should provoke new troubles. What shame to us such a conjecture on their part, and how deadly to discipline' " (110–13). It is this argument, Melville indicates, that most powerfully influences the officers. Billy is convicted that night, and sentenced to be hanged at the yardarm in the morning.

Melville treats sympathetically enough Vere's conservative viewpoint. Of the Captain's settled anti-revolutionary convictions, he says that while other members of Vere's aristocratic class hated the revolutionaries' theories because those theories threatened their privileges, the Captain opposed them "not alone because they seemed to him insusceptible of embodiment in lasting institutions, but at war with the peace of the world and the true welfare of mankind" (62–63).

Up to a point, Melville's own remarks on the Nore mutiny accord with Vere's philosophy. For example, Melville observes that "Reasonable discontent growing out of practical grievances in the fleet had been ignited into irrational combustion as by live cinders blown across the Channel from France in flames" (54) and that "To some extent the Nore Mutiny may be regarded as analogous to the distempering irruption of contagious fever in a frame constitutionally sound, and which anon throws it off" (55). Nevertheless, it is noteworthy that Melville makes Billy Budd a sailor in the British fleet during a war between an England from which the American colonists had recently won independence and a France that had helped them achieve it. What, we should ask, is Melville saying to the prospective reader of *Billy Budd* when he remarks that Vere had been promoted "for his gallantry in the West Indian waters as flag lieutenant under Rodney in that admiral's crowning victory over De Grasse" (60) in 1782? De Grasse, shortly before this defeat by the British admiral Baron Rodney, had played a crucial role in the American Revolutionary War. In August 1781, while General George Washington was considering a campaign against the British in the South, "a letter from Grasse came to Rochambeau [the French general who was aiding the

Americans]—a clear, concise and definite letter that cleared the air, resolved all doubts, and determined the course of the war."³ The letter prepared the way for the collaboration between the Americans and the French fleet under De Grasse, which resulted in the Americans' climactic victory over Cornwallis at Yorktown.

It is true that France in 1781 had been under the Royalist rather than the Revolutionary regime, but the key point is that Melville displays a keen awareness of how our way of evaluating an event depends upon the historical context in which we see it. Certainly, the historically aware American reader of *Billy Budd* is somewhat distanced from Vere by Melville's reference to his service "under Rodney in that admiral's crowning victory over De Grasse." It is also clear that the mutinous aspect of American history in the later eighteenth and earlier nineteenth centuries was vividly in Melville's mind when he was writing *Billy Budd*. The *Rights-of-Man*, the merchantman from which Billy was impressed into service aboard the *Bellipotent*, belonged to an admirer of Tom Paine, who had propagandized in the colonies for the Revolutionary War, and whose rejoinder, *The Rights of Man*, "to Burke's arraignment of the French Revolution had then [1797] been published for some time and gone everywhere." Melville notes that in christening the *Rights-of-Man* after the title of Paine's work, the owner "was something like his contemporary ship-owner, Stephen Girard of Philadelphia, whose sympathies alike with his native land and its liberal philosophers, he evinced by naming his ships after Voltaire, Diderot, and so forth" (48). Girard later helped finance the United States in the War of 1812, a war one of whose chief causes was the British impressment of American seamen. That conflict is glancingly alluded to by Melville in a paragraph celebrating the "nobler qualities" of past naval magnates—"Don John of Austria, Doria, Van Tromp, Jean Bart, the long line of British admirals, and the American Decaturs of 1812 . . ." (56).

These references to American history should help focus our attention upon the fact that the condemnation and execution of Billy Budd are dictated by specifically British utilitarian considerations. It is in the sole interests of the British navy and nation, as Vere perceives those interests, that the "angel of God" must hang.

The text of Melville's story that I have been citing was prepared by Harrison Hayford and Merton Sealts, Jr., from a manuscript which Melville had not completed at the time of his death in 1891. In the manuscript is a passage that Hayford and Sealts are convinced he had intended to excise. On the first of what they call "three discarded leaves" containing this passage is a handwritten penciled query, "Preface for / Billy Budd?" Because, according to Hayford and Sealts, the editors of the incomplete story who preceded them took this handwriting to be Melville's although it is in fact that of his widow, a "Preface" appears in all their versions of the novella—which before the Hayford-Sealts *Billy Budd, Sailor* (1962) had always been called *Billy Budd, Foretopman*. It is indicative, however, of continuing disagreement among scholars over Melville's editorial intentions that Milton R. Stern's edition of *Billy Budd, Sailor* (1975), while generally following Hayford and Sealts's text, restores, not as a preface but in chapter 22, the passage that they omit. If we compare the language of this passage, about which so much controversy swirls, with Melville's references, quoted earlier in this chapter, to the rebellions of 1797 as the igniting into "irrational combustion" of "reasonable discontent" and as "the distempering irruption of contagious fever in a frame constitutionally sound," we must conclude that he was of two minds about the historical significance of both the French Revolution and the Great Mutiny. Here is the passage:

> The year 1797, the year of this narrative, belongs to a period which, as every thinker now feels, involved a crisis for Christendom not exceeded in its undetermined momentousness at the time by any other era whereof there is record. The opening proposition made by the Spirit of that Age involved the rectification of the Old World's hereditary wrongs. In France this was bloodily effected. But what then? Straightaway the Revolution regency as righter of wrongs itself became a wrongdoer, one more oppressive than the Kings. Under Napoleon it enthroned upstart kings, and initiated that prolonged agony of continual war whose final throe was at Waterloo. During those years not the wisest could have foreseen that the outcome of all would be what to some thinkers apparently it has since turned out to be, a political advance along nearly the whole line for Europeans.
>
> Now, as elsewhere hinted, it was something caught from the Revolutionary Spirit that at Spithead emboldened the man-of-war's men to rise against real abuses, long-standing ones, and afterwards at the Nore to make inordinate and aggressive demands, successful

resistance to which was confirmed only when the ringleaders were hung for an admonitory spectacle to the anchored fleet. Yet in a way analogous to the operation of the Revolution at large, the Great Mutiny, though by Englishmen naturally deemed monstrous at the time, doubtless gave the first latent promptings to most important reforms in the British navy.[4]

This passage, when included in the novella, intensifies its ambiguity by contrasting two perspectives on both the French Revolution and the 1797 uprisings: the perspective of contemporaries opposed to these events and the historical viewpoint of the later nineteenth century, from which, at least to "some thinkers,"the Revolution appears to be a European "political advance," and the Great Mutiny "doubtless"—and here Melville's statement is unqualified—led directly to important reforms in the British navy. By the light of this passage, Billy's execution looks as absurd as the philosophic assumption of Captain Vere that revolutionary ideas were "incapable of embodiment in lasting institutions."

Apart from the question of what Melville would have done with the controversial passage had he been able to complete *Billy Budd*, his treatment of Vere's role after the execution underlines the absurd injustice of Billy's fate.

A few weeks following the hanging, an "authorized" naval publication prints a grossly distorted account of Claggart's death: " 'discovering that some sort of plot was incipient among an inferior section of the ship's company, and that the ringleader was one William Budd; he, Claggart, in the act of arraigning the man before the Captain, was vindictively stabbed to the heart by the suddenly drawn sheath knife of Budd' " (130). Vere's role as Billy's symbolic father, a role which Melville emphasizes by imagining a scene in which the Captain, "old enough to have been Billy's father . . . may in end have caught Billy to his heart even as Abraham may have caught young Isaac on the brink of offering him up in obedience to the exacting behest" (115), makes the Captain's failure to protect the executed sailor's reputation seem strange. Why did not Vere, immediately after the court-martial, have an accurate report of the proceedings prepared? His failure to do so appears especially odd in view of Melville's hint that Vere is Billy's actual father. Mortally wounded in a battle with a French ship while the *Bellipotent* is returning to the English fleet, he murmurs to an attendant before dying, " 'Billy Budd, Billy Budd.' " "That these were not the accents of remorse would seem clear from what the attendant said to the *Bellipotent*'s senior officer of marines, who, as the most reluctant to condemn of the members of the drumhead court, too well knew, though here he kept the knowledge to himself, who Billy Budd was" (129).

Let us assume the truth of what this permits us to infer. If Vere's haste to condemn his own son to death is, charitably, to be excused by his zealous devotion to duty, what defense can be made of his neglecting to guard Billy against a posthumous slander? Billy, whose last words were " 'God bless Captain Vere!' "

Another aspect of the story that underscores the absurdity of Billy's fate is the young sailor's symbolic relationship to Jesus. Billy had been a peacemaker aboard the merchant ship from which he was impressed; and the beatitude concerning peacemakers is jovially cited by the lieutenant who removes him to the *Bellipotent*. The most important pointers from Billy to Jesus, however, are those in the account of Billy's hanging and in the final chapter of the novella. In the death scene,

> the vapory fleece hanging low in the East was shot through with a soft glory as of the fleece of the Lamb of God seen in mystical vision, watched by the wedged mass of upturned faces, Billy ascended; and, ascending, took the full rose of the dawn.
>
> In the pinioned figure arrived at the yard-end, to the wonder of all no motion was apparent, none save that created by the slow roll of the hull in moderate weather, so majestic in a great ship ponderously cannoned. (124)

The combination of the reference to the Lamb of God, with the allusion to the wondrous non-occurrence of a seminal ejaculation at the instant of Billy's hanging, calls to mind a divine Jesus. In the final chapter, Melville tells us that the spar from which Billy was suspended was for some years kept track of by the sailors, who regarded a chip of it "as a piece of the Cross." And the ballad "Billy in the Darbies," which, composed by a poetic sailor and eventually circulated in printed form, perpetuates the memory of one who "was gone, and in a measure mysteriously gone" (131) is analogous to a Christian legend.

Billy's imperfections—his stutter, his extraordinary naïveté—militate against our "identifying" him with Jesus. But the trial and death of Melville's innocent sailor symbolize the gap between brutally utilitarian law and what Melville had evidently come to think of as a mere dream of "natural justice."

KAFKA'S *The Trial*

The Marxist critic Evgeniya Knipovich notes in an essay on Kafka that he devoted one of only two public appearances in his whole life to reading passages from Heinrich von Kleist's novella "Michael Kohlhaas." Kafka said that he "could not even think of" this work "without being moved to tears and enthusiasm." The protagonist of Kleist's story is a horse dealer who becomes a violent outlaw after his repeated efforts to obtain justice in civil courts are frustrated, and after his dear wife dies of injuries she has sustained during an attempt to petition a government official on his behalf. With the aid of a people's army he has recruited, he finally achieves his original goal, then happily proceeds to his own beheading to pay for the deaths and destruction he has caused. Knipovich observes that Michael Kohlhaas's "force of conviction and frenzied defense of justice" was unfortunately, for Kafka, "only a tale." "And if his contemporaries tirelessly spoke about the possibility and necessity of aiming at justice, Kafka, with the conviction of desperation, over and over repeated the opposite: that today in the world of capitalism such a struggle was worse than hopeless."[5]

Hopelessness is at the heart of *The Trial* (*Der Prozess*, 1925), which evokes an absurdity even more unqualified than Melville's in *Billy Budd*: Captain Vere can at least imagine a "just," if impracticable, alternative to the condemnation of Billy that he brings about and implements. There is no conceivable alternative in *The Trial*, or in Kafka stories like "The Judgment" or "In the Penal Colony," to ukases and "laws" that emanate from an inscrutable, invisible authority.

Albert Camus, calling *The Trial* a completely successful "absurd" work, maintains that "unexpressed revolt" is what is writing it.[6] I think it is more accurate, however, to say that revolt is the reader's likely reaction to *The Trial*. For as Günther Anders trenchantly remarks, Kafka himself evidently acquiesces in the humiliations of his fictional alter ego.[7] Kafka's attitude toward the world, which he renders in eerily flat, "official" prose, resembles that of a prisoner in a death camp who, habituated to it, can imagine no escape.

It is true that the opening pages of *The Trial* suggest conflict of a sort. "Someone," we are told in the first sentence, "must have been telling lies about Joseph K., for without having done anything wrong he was arrested one fine morning."[8] Further on, writing apparently from K.'s viewpoint about the two men who have invaded his boarding house, the narrator asks who these men could be, what they were talking about, what authority they could represent: "K. lived in a country with a legal constitution, there was universal peace, all the laws were in force; who dared seize him in his own dwelling?" (4).

Despite his apparently astonished indignation, K. looks for his birth certificate and presents it to the intruders before asking them for their warrant for arresting him. When they refuse to show or discuss any papers, and declare that " 'our officials . . . are drawn toward the guilty and must then send out us warders' " because that is the Law, K. retorts that he does not know this Law, which " 'probably exists nowhere but in your own head.' " Yet Kafka immediately observes that "he wanted in some way to enter into the thoughts of the warders and twist them to his own advantage or else try to acclimatize himself to them" (6). A troubling variation, this, on the theme of "tout comprendre, c'est tout pardonner." For K. not merely is attempting to understand his persecutors' strange ideas, but is already envisioning acceptance of them as the rules of the game: the "Law" will exist as much in his mind as in theirs.

Waiting in his room, as one of the warders has advised him to do, " 'for what may be decided about you,' " he is startled by a sudden summons: " 'The Inspector wants you' " (7, 9). He hurries into the next room, only to be rebuked for imagining that he can appear before the Inspector in his shirt. " 'Silly formalities!' " he growls,

> but immediately lifted a coat from a chair and held it up for a little while in both hands, as if displaying it to the warders for their

approval. They shook their heads. "It must be a black coat," they said. Thereupon K. flung the coat on the floor and said—he did not himself know in what sense he meant the words—"But this isn't the capital charge yet." (9)

The dreamlike phrase "he did not himself know in what sense he meant the words," makes clear that K.'s sense of guilt is beneath the conscious level. But it is very strong: why else would he conceive of being charged with a crime for which the penalty is death? Kafka once said of his own tuberculosis that his brain and lungs "must have conspired in secret."[9] K.'s deep-seated guilt is already conspiring with the mysterious Law to torment and ultimately to kill him.

After returning home from his work in a bank—for in Kafka's sinister comedy, an "arrest" is far from being equated with physical detention[10]—K. makes a point of apologizing to Frau Grubach, his landlady, " 'for giving you extra work today.' " This curious allusion to the warders' visit elicits an apparently reassuring reply from her. Yet to K., "she seems to think it is not quite right that I should mention it," and he reiterates the apology: " 'It must certainly have made more work, . . . but it won't happen again.' " It is as if he has participated, along with the warders, in his own arrest. This is a key to *The Trial*: K. is both accused and accuser, both victim and, at least psychologically, eventual self-executioner.

The nightmare world he lives in is full of people who play somewhat analogous double roles. Frau Grubach, for example, behaves as if she has inside knowledge when, "reassuringly, with an almost sorrowful smile, she tells him that what happened on this occasion of his arrest, 'can't happen again.' " But a moment later, she sounds like an unintelligent "good citizen," awed by authority: " 'You are under arrest, certainly, but not as a thief is under arrest. . . . It gives me the feeling of something very learned, forgive me if what I say is stupid, it gives me the feeling of something very learned which I don't understand, but which there is no need to understand' " (19).

The behavior of Fräulein Bürstner, his fellow-boarder, to whom he also wants to apologize—for having, as he oddly puts it to the landlady, " 'borrowed her room today' " (21)—is as ambiguous as Frau Grubach's language. When K. accosts her that evening by whispering her name through the chink of his door, she responds by whispering an invitation to enter. After he has come in, she " 'freely' " grants the pardon he begs for the " 'slight confusion' " into which " 'strange people' " had thrown her room that morning. Yet suddenly, upon discovering that her photographs are all mixed up, she inconsistently administers the rebuke that K.'s self-accusing manner invites: it is curious, she says, that she must now forbid him to do something " 'which you ought to forbid yourself to do, that is, to enter my room in my absence.' " His response is a typical "K." combination of self-defense and self-incrimination. He reminds her that it was not he who had interfered with her photographs, but goes on to "confess" that the Court of Inquiry had brought three bank clerks here, " 'one of whom, and I shall have him dismissed at the first opportunity, must have meddled with your photographs.' "

The earnest expression " 'and I shall have him dismissed at the first opportunity' " almost anticipates the surrealistic wit of Groucho Marx. But Fräulein Bürstner is interested only in his reference to a Court of Inquiry. When he insists that it had really been there on his account, she laughingly remarks, " 'No!' " (24–25). This ambiguous reaction introduces a new variation on Kafka's theme of guilt in *The Trial*; for it soon is obvious that the Fräulein is indirectly accusing him of sexual incapacity. The whole scene between them is full of erotic innuendo: the whispering before he enters her room; her slowly caressing her hip while reclining on the sofa; her saying, when he asks permission to move her night-table, in order to re-enact the events of the morning: " 'I'm so tired that I'm letting you take too many liberties' " (27). Her remark that he " 'couldn't really have committed a serious crime' "—coming as it does just after her laughing " 'No!' "—sounds like a slur on his virility. K. is thus in the position of attempting to clear himself of this implicit, contemptuous accusation, while at the same time trying to mitigate his "guilt" vis-à-vis the Court of Inquiry. Hence his contorted reply: " 'but the Court . . . might have discovered, not that I was innocent, but that I was not so guilty as they had assumed' " (25).

His attempt to convince her of his sexual potency takes the form of an offer—when she asks him to leave the room because

she fears that Frau Grubach's nephew can hear everything—to
" 'have it announced that I assaulted you.' " As she silently stares
at the floor, he nervously asks, " 'Why shouldn't Frau Graubach
believe that I assaulted you?' " Her evasive reply and whispered
insistence that he leave, induce a frenzy in him. He "seized her,
and kissed her first on the lips, then all over her face, like some
thirsty animal lapping greedily at a spring of long-sought fresh
water. Finally he kissed her on the neck, right on the throat, and
kept his lips there a long time" (28–29).

Thus the first chapter of *The Trial*, which began with K.'s arrest
on an unstated charge whose validity he oddly seems to concede,
ends with his desperate embrace of a provocative woman who has
impugned his manliness. We have learned that once a week K.
visits a cabaret waitress who "during the day receives her visitors
in bed" (17). This habitual intercourse with a prostitute clearly
does not bring him emotional fulfillment. His behavior with
Fräulein Bürstner—kissing her "like some thirsty animal lapping
greedily at a spring of long-sought fresh water"—indicates not
only a desire to prove himself sexually, but also a desperate
emotional need. The "trial" of K. in Kafka's sinister allegory is in
part an outward show of his overwhelming sense of frustration,
defeat, and, consequently, guilt.

It is indicative of Kafka's intent that there is no clear distinction
in the book between the public domain of the Court and the trial
and the private space of bedroom and office. When, in Chapter 2,
K. seeks in a suburban house the Court of Inquiry to which he
has been summoned, he feels that he cannot ask about the Court
by name; he therefore invents "a joiner named Lanz"—the name
suggests the German word for "lance" or "spear"—and "began to
inquire at all the doors if [Lanz] lived there, so as to get a chance
to look into the rooms" (36). This strategy is unproductive until,
in one of the flats to which he has been admitted, a woman
responds by saying, " 'Please go through' " (37). When K. does,
he finds himself in the courtroom. Thus the word "Lanz" that he
has used for a private reason suddenly becomes a semi-public
password.

The distinction between the public and the private is also
blurred in the courtroom that K. has entered. The Examining
Magistrate, turning over the leaves of a small notebook, remarks

authoritatively, " 'You are a house painter?' " When K. replies
that he is the " 'chief clerk of a large bank,' " there is "such a
hearty outburst of laughter from the right-hand side of the room
that he has to laugh too. People doubled up with their hands on
their knees and shook as if in spasms of coughing. There were
even a few guffaws in the gallery." But when K. solemnly addresses the Court, he is convinced that he is representing the
"point of view" of the people on the left-hand side of the room,
who have remained silent. He says that the Examining Magistrate's
assumption that he is a house painter " 'is typical of the whole
character of this trial that is being foisted on me. You may object
that it is not a trial at all; you are quite right, for it is only a trial if
I recognize it as such. But for the moment I do recognize it, on
grounds of compassion, as it were' " (40).

Here, instead of the transformation of the apparently private
into the public, as in the case of K.'s use of the name "Lanz," we
find a metamorphosis of the ostensibly public into the private: the
trial *is* a trial only by virtue of K.'s recognition of it. But K. has
no real will to withhold that recognition. His "heroic" courtroom
speech attacking " 'a misguided policy which is being directed
against many other people' " (42) for whom he says he is taking a
stand is no more genuine than the enthusiastic response to his
speech which he at first detects in a segment of his audience. All
his apparent supporters turn out to be wearing "official" badges
(47). K. indignantly denounces this deception, and dramatically
leaves the courtroom. But at the beginning of the next chapter we
learn that he waited day after day for a new summons, "would not
believe that his refusal to be interrogated had been taken literally,
and when no appointment was made by Saturday evening, . . .
assumed that he was tacitly expected to report himself again at the
same address and at the same time" (49).

Kafka emphasizes the abjectness of K.'s surrender to his own
"recognition" of the trial by having him discover, when he returns
to the courtroom building, that there is no session that day. He
learns this from the washerwoman who had immediately deci-
phered his question about "Lanz." Now, identifying herself as a
court usher's wife, she offers to give the Examining Magistrate a
message from K. The next scene illustrates the connection between K.'s crushing sense of inadequacy and the trial which has

become the center of his life. Despite the woman's low social standing and the fact that she had been conspicuously embracing a man during K.'s courtroom speech, K. is attracted to her as a potential instrument of "revenge on the Examining Magistrate and his henchmen." One of these henchmen is the law student who has been embracing her and who, she tells K., had brought her a pair of silk stockings from the Examining Magistrate. This student, she points out to him after displaying her stockinged legs, is even now in the doorway of the courtroom, and she says she must go to him for just a minute. Anticipating her prompt return, K. has an erotic "power" fantasy in which the Examining Magistrate, after long, arduous work on his "lying reports about K.," comes to the woman's bed and finds it empty—"Empty because she has gone off with K., because the woman now standing in the window, that supple, voluptuous, warm body under the coarse, heavy, dark dress, belonged to K. and to K. alone" (56). Then, in one of many scenes that could be superbly rendered in a silent movie, K. displays his feeling that the whispered conversation has gone on too long by "knocking on the table with his knuckles and then with his fist." The student reacts by putting his arms around the woman and kissing her loudly on the throat. When K. attempts to seize her hand, his rival lifts her up and runs to the door while the woman frustrates K.'s efforts to rescue her from " 'this little monster' " who, she says, is " 'only obeying the orders of the Examining Magistrate and carrying me to him.' " Furiously disappointed, K. punches the student in the back, but recognizes "that this was the first unequivocal defeat that he had received from these people" (57–58). "These people" is an appropriate totalizing expression: in the world of *The Trial*, everybody "belongs" to the Court, including, to a considerable extent, K. himself.

K.'s nightmarishly ambiguous role as both a victim of what he calls the "organization" and a member of it is accentuated in Chapter 5. In the lumber-room of the bank where he is employed, he comes upon the two warders, who complain that they are about to be whipped by a third man, because K. has complained about them to the Chief Magistrate. Astonished, K. protests, " 'I never complained, I only said what happened in my room. And after all, your behavior there was not exactly blameless.' " But one of the warders pleads with him—and here the post-World War II reader may imagine an eerie scene in which a Gestapo member begs for help from the Jew whom he has arrested:

> "if you only knew how badly we are paid, you wouldn't be so hard on us. I have a family to feed and Franz here wants to get married, a man tries to make whatever he can, and you don't get rich on hard work, not even if you work day and night. Your fine shirts were a temptation, of course that kind of thing is forbidden to warders, it was wrong, but it's a tradition that body-linen is the warders' perquisite. . . ." (84)

After unsuccessfully trying to persuade the brutal Whipper to spare the warders, K. leaves the lumber-room and, to prevent the bank clerks from approaching it after they hear a terrible shriek which comes from Franz as he is whipped, he tells them that the noise was " 'only a dog howling in the courtyard.' "

The chief horror of the "Whipper" episode—which frighteningly anticipates Joseph K.'s dying "[l]ike a dog!" (229)—is its repetition on the following day: K. rediscovers the three men in exactly the same postures. This freezing of the scene is an extraordinary correlative of K.'s powerlessness and feeling of guilt. Almost weeping as he runs to the clerks, he shouts, " 'Clear that lumber-room out, can't you? . . . We're being smothered in dirt!' " (90).

Later, K. considers whether to draw up and hand in to the court a kind of degrading *apologia pro vita sua*. This document would give a short account of his life, "and when he came to an event of any importance explain for what reasons he had acted as he did, intimate whether he approved or condemned his way of action in retrospect, and adduce grounds for the condemnation or approval" (113). The bizarre project bears some relation to a general human truth: we all tend, when overwhelmed by a catastrophe, to seek its cause in some sin or error we have committed. K.'s catastrophe, however, is indeterminate; it is the irruption into his life of an altogether unclear "accusation," against which he proposes to defend himself by conducting innumerable subjective "trials." Since he envisages condemning "in retrospect" at least some of his own acts, he would doubtless end by giving the Court an unsolicited confession of guilt for "crimes" of which nobody could ever have accused him. As Joost M. Meerloo observes, Kafka anticipates in *The Trial* "the age of blackmailing into confession."[11] This is true even if we interpret the book altogether as the story of a man whose sense of inadequacy provokes a nightmare in which he is arrested for no stated reason. For the most potent weapon in the armory of the totalitarian state is its understanding of ways to manipulate men's anxieties and secret consciousness of guilt. Camus's Clamence, the lawyer-narrator of *The Fall*, is the "ideal type," in Max Weber's sense, of the totalitarian. He believes that all men are, like him, guilty of some shameful act, and that his superiority to them consists in his knowing this and knowing how to make use of it in order to diminish his own sense of debasement.

When K. finally rejects the *apologia* project, he does so for reasons befitting a man whose life is almost completely absorbed into his bureaucratic role: the project, he decides, would do well enough for one's second childhood during the years of retirement: "But now, when K. should be devoting his mind entirely to work, when . . . he was still in full career and rapidly becoming a rival even to the Assistant Manager—when his evenings and nights were all too short for the pleasures of a bachelor life, this was the time when he must sit down to such a task!" (128–29). So he chooses to spend his time in the mechanical performance of joyless acts—"the pleasures of a bachelor life" is as lifeless a cliché as "he was still in full career"—rather than in the arduous effort to recollect his sins. But since his automaton-like daily behavior is inextricably entangled with his anxiety, he is simply electing one way rather than another of existing in a maze.

Just as there is a close link between K.'s anxieties and his behavior, so there is, as we have noted, a symbiotic relationship between K. and the Court that persecutes him. It is appropriate that "Justice," in the portrait on the Painter Titorelli's easel is metamorphosed before K.'s eyes, by Titorelli's crayon, into "a goddess of the Hunt in full cry" (147). As a "Court Painter," Titorelli is creating a faithful representation of his patrons' idea of justice, which is obviously that of Thrasymachus: the will of the stronger. Titorelli's ludicrously conscientious explanation of the types of acquittal which, through the painter's personal intervention with the judges K. might obtain, perfectly complements the easel portrait. After observing that " 'definite acquittal' " is not only unprocurable through personal intervention but unheard-of except in " 'very beautiful' " legendary accounts of ancient cases, Titorelli describes " 'ostensible acquittal' " and " 'indefinite post-ponement.' " The first of these results from one's persuading a sufficient number of Judges to sign an affidavit of innocence. Such an acquittal carries the drawback, however, that these Judges have no power to grant a final acquittal; that power is " 'reserved for the highest Court of all, which is quite inaccessible to you, to me, and to all of us.' " Nor can "ostensible acquittal" remove the original accusation, which continues to " 'hover above' " the defendant and can, " 'as soon as an order comes from on high, be laid on you again' " (154–58). Hence, "ostensible acquittal" is eventually followed by a second arrest—and so on indefinitely. K.'s wan reaction to this discouraging account of ostensible ac-quittal leads Titorelli to observe that " 'it doesn't seem to appeal to you.' " He therefore goes on to explain " 'indefinite postpone-ment,' " which consists of preventing the case from ever getting further than its first stages. This method demands less intense concentration of the defendant's energies than does ostensible acquittal, yet " 'it does require far greater vigilance.' " For one must never let the case out of one's sight: " '. . . you visit the Judge at regular intervals . . . and must do all that is in your power to keep him friendly; if you don't know the Judge personally, then you must try to influence him through other Judges whom you do know, but without giving up your efforts to secure a personal interview' " (160).

Clearly, neither "ostensible acquittal" nor "indefinite postpone-ment" does more than temporarily keep the Damoclean sword of "justice" from descending. But K.'s masochistic need to suffer is well served by the legal system that Titorelli has described.[12]

In Kafka's suffocatingly closed world, even the lawyer to whom K.'s uncle insists he entrust his case "belongs" to the Court, although his name, Huld (Grace), suggests spiritual autonomy. Titorelli, the Court Painter, admits that he himself talks almost like a jurist and that his " 'uninterrupted association with the gentlemen of the Court' " has greatly diminished his " '*élan* as an artist' " (151). The priest whom K. meets in the cathedral and who tells him that his " 'guilt is supposed, for the present, at least, to have been proved' " (210) is the prison chaplain, and hence also a member of the Court. It is in order to dispel the delusion which he says K. has about the Court—K. having just said, " '. . . you are an exception among those who belong to the Court. . . . With you I can speak openly' " (213)—that the priest recounts the story of a man from the country who unsuccessfully begs the " 'doorkeeper' " (213) for admittance to the law.

There is, in short, no access in *The Trial* to a realm of freedom. All thought is conscripted, and of pardon there is none.

The absence of revolt or even nonconformity is horrifically exemplified in the final chapter. Two men "in frock coats, pallid and plump, with top hats that were apparently irremovable," come to K.'s lodgings on the eve of his thirty-first birthday, exactly a year after his arrest: "Without having been informed of their visit, K. was sitting also dressed in black in an armchair near the door, slowly pulling on a pair of new gloves . . . looking as if he were expecting guests" (223). When K. was arrested in Chapter 1, and told that he must wear a black coat, he refused, declaring, " 'But this isn't the capital charge yet.' " Now, he appears to have accepted the verdict on the "capital charge," even though he "admitted to himself that he had been expecting different visitors" (223). He demurs only at their attempt to take him by the arms on the stairs of his building: " 'Wait till we're in the street, I'm not an invalid.' " But once they are outside, the men "wound their arms round his at full length, holding his hands in a methodical, practiced, irresistible grip." The passage that follows this could constitute an additional epigraph for Eliot's "The Hollow Men": "K. walked rigidly between them, the three of them were interlocked in a unity which would have brought all three down together had one of them been knocked over. It was a unity such as can hardly be formed except by lifeless matter" (224).

There does come a point at which K. says "experimentally" that he will go no farther. But then either Fräulein Bürstner, or a woman who resembles her, appears, mounting a flight of steps; and Kafka remarks that K. "suddenly realized the futility of resistance." The woman must recall to him his deep, private wound, his sense of sexual-emotional defeat. Permitted by his "warders" to lead the way, he follows the direction she has taken, "that he might not forget the lesson she had brought into his mind." This "lesson" is summed up in one of the most bitterly comic lines in *The Trial*: K. decides that the only thing for him to go on doing " 'is to keep my intelligence calm and analytical to the end' " (225). As if such intelligence could be of the slightest use! As if anything but his striking out against the thugs who are about to murder him could spare him the shame he will feel as he dies.

At the stone quarry to which the executioners lead him, there is a grisly Alphonse–Gaston parody: the thugs hand a long butcher's knife back and forth to each other. K. gets the point. "He could not," however, "completely rise to the occasion, he could not relieve the officials of all their tasks; the responsibility for this last failure of his lay with him who had not left him the remnant of strength necessary for the deed." The first "him" in this passage is disturbingly unclear. And in the passage that follows it, we cannot know who the person is who suddenly leans far out of a window, "and stretched both arms still farther." If it is, as K. thinks it may be, "a good man," or "someone who sympathized" (228), this would be the only appearance in *The Trial* of such a being. And with his last words, " 'Like a dog!' " K. condemns himself as a creature who deserves no sympathy or help; "it was as if the shame of it must outlive him."[13]

No other modern fictional work so effectively or so depressingly undermines the conception of man as a creature capable of distinguishing a law according to reason, an ethical "natural law," from a totalitarian law that is criminal.

CAMUS's *The Outsider*

If *The Trial*, where everybody, including Kafka's protagonist, collaborates in finding him guilty, evokes particularly well the suffocating atmosphere of totalitarian "justice," Camus's *The Outsider* (*L'Étranger*, 1942), in which Meursault is condemned to death by a society from which he is estranged, seems especially pertinent to bourgeois legal procedure, with its complacent claim to rationality.

Meursault, an Algerian of European descent who unpremeditatedly shoots an Arab on an Algiers beach, is unable to explain convincingly to the Examining Magistrate, or to the trial judge and jurors, why he has done it. He is condemned to die, not because of the killing, but because the prosecutor persuades the jury that Meursault's failure to have shown grief after his mother's death proves him to be a murderous monster. Writing in *The Myth of Sisyphus* about "the absurd" as it reveals itself in society, Camus notes our "discomfort in the face of man's own inhumanity," our "incalculable tumble before the image of what we are."[14] The Outsider induces just this sort of discomfort in us.

Meursault's most striking characteristic is a disinclination to tell lies. Not only does he not say what he knows not to be true, he does not express more than he feels. And what he feels sometimes seems odd. Thus, he tells us in narrating his story that when Marie, the girl he had met the day after his mother's burial, asked him if he would marry her, he "said I wouldn't mind and we could do if she wanted to." When she then asked if he loved her, his answer was similarly apathetic: "I replied as I had done once already, that it didn't mean anything, but that I probably didn't." His employer, speaking to him earlier that day of plans to establish a branch of the firm in Paris, had asked if Meursault would be interested in working there. Meursault's lackluster reply that he wasn't at all dissatisfied with his present life and that "in any case one life was as good as another" evoked the boss's retort that he lacked ambition. Many readers, especially on a first reading of the book, feel about Meursault as his employer does and are annoyed by what they see as his consistently it's-all-the-same-to-me attitude. But in the first place, Meursault tells us in his narration—although he did not tell his employer—that when he was a student, he "had plenty of that sort of ambition. But when I had to give up my studies, I very soon realized that none of it really mattered" (44). His disillusionment had evidently been as intense as his earlier yearnings.

In the second place, even in Part I of *The Outsider*—his tone will change significantly in Part II—Meursault is not always apathetic. When during the Sunday at the beach that was to end in the sudden killing, he noticed Marie laughing and chatting with their host's wife, "For the first time perhaps, I really thought I'd get married" (52). More notable, however, than this modest surge of feeling is his successful effort later in the day to prevent an act of violence. Meursault and Marie have come to the beach with Raymond, a pimp who lives in Meursault's apartment house. Raymond has some days earlier enlisted Meursault's help in a scheme of revenge against a Moorish girl who had "let him down." By punishing the girl, Raymond has incurred the enmity of her brother, with whom he now has two confrontations. First, while walking on the beach with Meursault and their host, Raymond meets his enemy, accompanied by another Arab. During a mêlée that Raymond appears to have provoked, he is knifed in the arm and mouth. Later, after being treated by a doctor, he takes another walk, followed by Meursault, who obviously fears that Raymond will get into trouble again. When they meet the two Arabs once more, Raymond puts his hand to his hip-pocket and asks Meursault, " 'Should I let him have it?' " What follows reveals a Meursault we have not seen before:

> I thought if I said no he'd get himself worked up and be bound to shoot. I simply told him, "He hasn't said anything to you yet. It'd be unfair to shoot just like that." . . . Then Raymond said, "I'll insult him then, and when he answers back, I'll let him have it." I answered, "All right. But if he doesn't draw a knife, you can't shoot."

But Raymond "started getting a bit worked up," so Meursault took a stronger stand: " 'No,' I said . . . , 'take him on hand to hand, and give me your gun. If the other one intervenes or if he draws his knife, I'll let him have it.' "

This attempt of Meursault's to avert fatal violence contrasts sharply with his earlier it's-all-the-same-to-me reactions. It is true that after Raymond handed over the gun, and as the four men remained motionless, Meursault realized "that you could either shoot or not shoot" (57). But rather than implying that he did not care whether Raymond shot or not, this phrase expresses what Camus describes in his essay on Kafka as the "void":[15] an awareness of an indifferent universe that neither punishes nor rewards our acts, and in which the sole certainty is that we shall some day die. Such a universe, devoid of ethical natural law, is the one inhabited by characters in absurd fiction and in serious modern fiction generally. What is truly noteworthy about Meursault is the contradiction between his sense (which is "ours") of the void and his effort to prevent a killing. The contradiction illustrates Camus's idea of the absurd, in one of its aspects, as the gap between an incomprehensible world and the human need for meaning and rationality.

What makes Meursault so difficult for us to understand is his display, again and again, of conflicting attitudes that Camus implies are at the heart of the human condition. Tired and at loose ends on a Saturday morning, after returning the night before from his mother's funeral, he decided to go for a swim. At the harbor pool he met Marie, who had once been a typist for his employer. He flirted and swam with her, and they made an appointment to go to the movies that evening; she wanted to see a Fernandel film. After they had dressed at the pool,

> she seemed very surprised to see me in a black tie and she asked me if I was in mourning. I told her that mother had died. She wanted to know when, so I said, "Yesterday." She recoiled slightly, but made no remark. I felt like telling her that it wasn't my fault, but I stopped myself. . . . In any case, you're always partly to blame. (24)

Meursault's wearing of a black tie on the day he began an affair recalls the story of the American insufficiently proficient in French to buy at a Parisian haberdasher's the black hat he wanted to wear at his wife's funeral. Haltingly explaining to the clerk that his wife was "morte," he asked for "un capeau [condom] noir." "Ah, monsieur," exclaimed the clerk, "quelle délicatesse!" Meursault himself made a verbal mistake, of a rather different sort, in telling Marie that his mother had died yesterday, when he should have said, *buried* yesterday. The mistake seems related to a comment he was to make much later, to his court-appointed attorney, after being arrested for killing the Arab: " 'I probably loved my mother quite a lot, but that didn't mean anything. To a certain extent all normal people sometimes wished their loved ones dead' " (65).

This "Freudian" remark, which shocks the lawyer, indicates why Meursault could not "help feeling guilty" during the poolside conversation with Marie: he had desired, "at one time or another" the death of the mother he loved. In his need to confess, without openly avowing that desire, he said that her death, not her funeral, had just taken place. The black tie, incongruous as it appears during a flirtation scene, must be the emblem of a muffled grief, mingled with remorse. As for Meursault's beginning an affair soon after his mother's death, he may have been obeying a call as strong as his guilt, though antithetical to it: a will to affirm his own vitality against what Camus elsewhere calls "the cruel mathematics that govern our condition."[16]

Just as Meursault can be at once remorseful and sensual, philosophically indifferent ("you could either shoot or not shoot") and morally committed ("if he doesn't draw his knife, you can't shoot"), he is both hypersensitive to the heat and glare of the sun and "in harmony" with external nature. His narration of two scenes involving himself and Marie presents him as a healthy human animal. First, describing the dalliance at the harbor pool: "I hoisted myself onto the buoy beside her. It was good and as if for fun, I let my head sink back on to her stomach. . . . I had the whole sky in my eyes and it was all blue and gold . . . " (24). Later, telling of a swim in the sea on the fatal Sunday: "The water was cold and I was glad to be swimming. Marie and I swam right out, moving together and feeling content together. Out in the open we lay on our backs and with my face turned towards the sky I could feel the sun peeling away the last few layers of water which trickled down into my mouth" (52).

On the other hand, Meursault as narrator refers frequently, especially in Chapter 1, where he tells of attending his mother's funeral, and Chapter 6, at the end of which he describes the shooting of the Arab, to his extreme sensitivity to the heat and light of the sun. It was "the glare of the sky reflecting off the road" (10), together with the jolting of the bus and the smell of petrol, that made him sleep during the trip to the old people's home where his mother had died. And while walking in the funeral procession, as the sun glared intolerably, "All I could feel was the blood pounding in my temples" (22). Just before describing his fatal act, Meursault makes a point of saying, "It was the same sun as on the day of mother's funeral and again it was my forehead that was hurting me most and all the veins were throbbing at once beneath the skin" (59). Earlier that day, but not long after the swim with Marie which he had enjoyed so much, he had found the sun-glare from the sea "unbearable" (54).

This virtual allergy to intense light and heat is a crucial element in the book. Meursault evokes laughter at his trial by saying, in response to the judge's question about "the motives which had inspired my crime," that it was "because of the sun" (99). But on strictly rational grounds, which are those on which the trial is supposedly being conducted, it is inexplicable that after preventing violence on Raymond's part during the second confrontation with the Arabs, Meursault used the gun he had carefully taken from his friend, to commit murder. He tells us—and we have no reason to doubt his word—that when walking along the beach toward the shade of the rock where he and Raymond had met the Arabs, he was a bit surprised to see that "Raymond's Arab had come back." For as far as Meursault was concerned, "it was all settled and I'd gone there without even thinking about it" (58–59). There followed a moment of tense silence as the Arab, who had been lying on his back, his forehead in the rock's shade, sat up slightly to put his hand in his pocket and as Meursault responded by gripping Raymond's gun inside his jacket. But Meursault was fully aware that he "only had to turn around and it would all be over." It was, he says, because he could not stand the burning feeling on his cheeks and especially on his forehead that he moved forward. Yet he knew that this was "stupid" (59)—he would not get out of the sun with one step. The Arab, without sitting up, "drew his knife and held it out towards me in the sun. The light leapt up off the steel and it was like a long, flashing sword lunging at my forehead." The sweat that had gathered in Meursault's eyebrows now became a blinding veil of salty tears: "All I could feel were the cymbals the sun was clashing against my forehead and, indistinctly, the dazzling spear still leaping off the knife in front of me. It was like a red-hot blade gnawing at my eyelashes and gouging out my stinging eyes." An hallucination was apparently brought on by the terrible pain: "That was when everything shook. The sea swept ashore a great breath of fire. The sky seemed to be splitting from end to end and raining down sheets of flame." Meursault's "whole being went tense," he tightened his grip on the gun, and "the trigger gave" (60). The killing bullet thus seems not to have been deliberately fired.

Discussing the four additional shots that Meursault emptied into the inert body, Robert Champigny suggests that Meursault's awareness of having "destroyed the balance of the day" led him to ensure his own punishment, his "undoing." Perhaps. What is more persuasive in Champigny's discussion is his comparison of Meursault to Orestes, who during his trial in the *Eumenides* is defended by Apollo,[17] the god of light, often identified with Helios, the sun god. Apollo declares that he himself was responsible for Clytemnestra's death at Orestes's hands. Hence Meursault's courtroom attribution of the murderous shot to the sun— although he realized as he said this that it sounded ridiculous— would not have seemed bizarre to the ancient Greeks. Indeed, polytheism, with its often angry and warring gods, seems to provide as satisfactory a way as human beings have discovered to "explain" the absurd.

It is interesting to compare Meursault's actual violent act, and its legal consequences, with what might very well have occurred earlier, during the two-*vs.*-two confrontation. Recall his words to Raymond: " 'If the other one starts making trouble or takes out his knife, I'll shoot.' " Had the Arab pulled his knife at that moment and had Meursault shot to kill, Raymond could subsequently have testified that Meursault had fired in order to save his, Raymond's, life. The Examining Magistrate would have taken this testimony seriously into account in recommending a charge against Meursault, and it is virtually certain that a trial would not have ended in his condemnation to death. Even if he had not been acquitted of all blame, he would probably have been regarded, in the European community of Algiers, as a "brave type." Who then would have cared that he had drunk *café au lait* at his mother's funeral?

In the actual circumstances of the story, it is, above all, Meursault's honesty about feelings that society finds unacceptable which dooms him. Shortly after his arrest, the court-appointed lawyer insisted that he not repeat to the Examining Magistrate, or at the trial, his observation about a "normal" desire for the death of beloved persons. Meursault's response was that the only thing he could say for certain was that " 'I'd rather mother hadn't died.' " When the displeased attorney asked Meursault's permission to tell the court that Meursault had controlled his "natural feelings" that day, Meursault answered, " 'No, because it's not true' " (65). The lawyer's weak performance at the trial may have been partly due to revulsion from his candid client.

The Examining Magistrate, whose task it was, before the trial, to assemble all information pertinent to the crime, was explicit about the horror which " 'Mr. Antichrist,' " as he came to call Meursault (70), inspired in him. The sobriquet derived from the first intensive interrogation of Meursault, in which the Magistrate pressed the question why he had fired at a dead body. Meursault, having no answer, said nothing. Now the Magistrate's insistence on knowing why Meursault had kept on shooting at a prostrate man is at least as comprehensible as Meursault's estrangement from his own "motives"; but Camus loads the dice against the Magistrate by making him a religious fanatic. Suddenly, brandishing a crucifix before Meursault's eyes, he passionately declared "that he believed in God, that he was convinced that no man was so guilty that God wouldn't pardon him but that he must first repent and so become like a child whose soul is empty and ready to embrace everything" (67–68). To the Magistrate, the only part of Meursault's confession that "didn't make sense, the fact that I'd paused before firing my second shot," was directly linked to the question whether he believed in God. Meursault's flat "no" evoked the indignant retort that even those who reject God believe in him and that if he, the Magistrate, ever came to doubt this, his life would lose all meaning:" 'Do you want my life to be meaningless?' " he cried. As far as I was concerned, it had nothing to do with me, and I told him so' " (68).

This scene, to my mind, is artistically unconvincing. Camus's dislike of both judges and religious bigotry overcomes his sense of verisimilitude, and turns the Examining Magistrate into a grotesque. Because of that distortion, a reader may here be more inclined than he should be to sympathize with Meursault, and perhaps to overlook a disturbing aspect of the "outsider." Meursault's response to the Magistrate's final question in the interview—whether Meursault regretted what he had done—is that, "rather than true regret, I felt a kind of annoyance" (69). This is a characteristically candid description of what he felt. But the feeling itself should be unsettling to us. We ought to be disturbed that he feels only "annoyed" by the death of a man killed by bullets that he, even if involuntarily, has fired.

Camus's artistic mastery is unquestionable, however, in Meursault's account of his long pre-trial imprisonment and his trial. In both jail and courtroom, we see him pointlessly diminished as a human being. Shortly after Marie's first and only prison visit, he received a letter from her, saying that the authorities would not let her come again, because she was not his wife. From the day he got this letter, he realized that he had lost his freedom, that his life was at a standstill. While he gradually became used to the sheer boredom of prison existence, he paid a high emotional price:

> It was the end of the day, the part I don't like talking about, the nameless part, when evening noises would rise up from every floor of the prison. . . . for the first time in several months, I clearly heard the sound of my own voice. I recognized it as the one that had been ringing in my ears for days on end and I realized that all the time I'd been talking to myself. (79)

Meursault applies to his own situation the "no-way-out" lesson he had learned during his mother's funeral procession when a nurse had remarked that if you walked slowly you risked getting sunstroke, but if you went too fast you perspired and risked catching a chill in church. It is probably because of this trapped feeling that at the beginning of his trial he seems more apathetic, more detached from what is happening around him, and to him, than ever before. To a policeman who asks if he is nervous, he says no—that "in a way it would be interesting to watch a trial," for he had never seen one. As he observes journalists, policemen, lawyers in the courtroom, behaving as if they were members of a club, he has the "peculiar impression" of being "a bit like an intruder" (81–82). Except for experiencing discomfort in the hot courtroom, and becoming "annoyed" when he realized that the judge was "going to talk about mother again" (85), he continues to feel estranged from his own trial until the warden of the old people's home testifies that Meursault had not wanted to see his own mother's body, had not cried once, and had left immediately after the funeral. The prosecutor's triumphant glance in his direction now brings him painfully alive: for the first time in years he feels like crying, "because I could tell how much all these people hated me."

The phrase "for the first time" recurs when Meursault as narrator reports his realization—after testimony about his smoking and drinking *café au lait* at the old people's home has evoked indignation in the courtroom—that he was "guilty." It is as if he has lost a kind of virginity: "for the first time" he understood feelingly, not just abstractly, that he was condemned (87). No longer would he experience his own trial almost as he were covering it for a newspaper. Startling, however, in its emotional intensity was his reaction to the testimony of the café-proprietor, Céleste, who called Meursault a "friend" as well as a customer, and said that the killing on the beach " 'was a mishap' " that you could not " 'guard against' ": "And as if all his knowledge and his goodwill could avail him no further, Céleste turned towards me. . . . He seemed to be asking me what more he could do. I didn't say anything, I didn't even move, but it was the first time in my life that I'd ever wanted to kiss a man" (89–90). None of the jurymen knew ("I didn't even move") how deeply Meursault was moved by Céleste's testimonial of friendship. If they had known, if Meursault had not maintained throughout the trial—as his narration implies he did—an extremely impassive demeanor, would their verdict have been less severe?

More muted in the narration, but no less significant a signal to the reader that Meursault's "indifference" is only one aspect of his temperament, is his response to the testimony of another defense witness, Raymond. It was, Raymond explained, he himself, not Meursault, against whom the dead man had had a grudge, because it was Raymond who had beaten up the Arab's sister. The Prosecutor then attempted to demonstrate a sordid link between Raymond and Meursault: he argued that Meursault's having written for Raymond a letter to the girl that led to violence against her, and Meursault's subsequently vouching for Raymond at the police station, were the acts of an "immoral monster." Turning to Raymond, the Prosecutor asked if Meursault was his friend. Raymond said yes, and the Prosecutor asked Meursault the same question. "I met Raymond's eyes and he didn't look away. I answered, ' "Yes" ' " (92).

A sordid episode, but one not nearly as sinister as the Prosecutor implied, did lie behind the mutual solidarity of Raymond and Meursault. Raymond had asked him to compose a letter, the kind that would bring the Arab girl back by exploiting both her guilt over her betrayal and her jealousy. The letter had worked, as had the rest of Raymond's plan: when the girl came to his room, he excited her sexually, then spat in her face and told her to get out. Unexpectedly, however, she then slapped him, so he gave her a violent beating. At Raymond's request and without knowing the girl's side of the story, Meursault subsequently testified to the police that she had been unfaithful to Raymond. It was evidently more important to Meursault to be loyal to a pal than—"coldly," he probably would have thought—to look into the "facts" of a messy case or to protect the girl against harm. Meursault's behavior in this affair had nothing to do, we know, with his killing of the Arab. Yet the Prosecutor declaimed, after Meursault's avowal of friendship for Raymond: " 'Not only did this man indulge in the most shameful debauchery on the day after his mother's death, but he needlessly killed a man in order to resolve an intrigue of unconscionable immorality' " (92).

This is defamation. But Meursault's court-appointed lawyer did not even challenge the characterization of his client's lovemaking with Marie as "shameful debauchery." Instead he virtually played into the Prosecutor's hands by asking whether Meursault was being accused of burying his mother or killing a man. With pompous but effective vehemence, the Prosecutor retorted that the defendant had buried his mother "like a heartless criminal" (93).

Similarly "rational" linkage of carefully selected details characterizes the summation of both lawyers. The Prosecutor, emphasizing that Meursault's crime was premeditated, began by describing him as insensitive: he had not known, when asked at the old people's home, his mother's age; he had gone swimming and begun an affair on the following day. Then, in words that Meursault as narrator sardonically describes as "quite plausible," the Prosecutor accused the defendant of having "provoked Raymond's adversaries on the beach": "Raymond had been wounded. I'd asked him for his gun. I'd gone back with the intention of using it. I'd shot the Arab as I'd planned. I'd waited. And 'to make sure I'd done the job properly,' I'd fired four more shots, deliberately and at point-blank range and with some kind of forethought" (96).

Although Camus attacks courtroom rationalism from a perspective different from Dostoevsky's—Camus sees life as essentially absurd, while Dostoevsky sees it as absurd unless one

believes in God—the French writer may well have had Dostoevsky's Kirillovich, the prosecutor of Dmitri Karamazov, in mind
when he composed his own trial episode. For Camus's prosecutor
not only uses a plausible but simplistic logic, like his Dostoevskian
counterpart, but also professes to see ominous social implications
in the defendant's behavior. He asserts that Meursault, who has
not shown the least contrition for this crime, lacks a soul; then,
after observing that tomorrow the court would be trying a man
for parricide, he suggests to the jury that Meursault is also guilty
of that crime. For "any man who was morally responsible for his
mother's death thereby cut himself off from the society of men to
no lesser extent than one who raised a murderous hand against
the author of his days" (98). Meursault's own lawyer, whom
Meursault as narrator calls "ridiculous," plays the same kind of
courtroom game as his adversary. He "made a quick plea of
provocation and then he too started talking about my soul. But he
didn't seem to have nearly as much talent as the prosecutor."
According to the defense attorney, Meursault was an ideal em-
ployee, faithful to the company that employed him, and " 'a
model son who had supported his mother for as long as he
could.' " Meursault, recalling these observations and noting that
the only thing his lawyer did not talk about was the funeral, adds
with deadpan gallows humor, "and I felt that this was an important omission in his speech." The lawyer's ineptness is epitomized
by his fatuous plea that the surest punishment for Meursault's
crime "was the eternal remorse with which I was already stricken"
(100–01).

Conor Cruise O'Brien, making an alert criticism of the defense
counsel's conduct of the case, observes that an actual lawyer in
French-ruled Algeria

> would have made his central plea that of self-defense, turning on
> the frightening picture of the Arab with a knife. There is no
> reference to the use of any such defense or even to the bare
> possibility of an appeal to European solidarity in a case of this kind.
> This is as unrealistic as to suppose that in an American court, where
> a white man was charged with killing a black man who had pulled
> a knife, the defense counsel would not evoke, or the court be moved
> by, white fear of blacks.

O'Brien errs slightly in saying that there is no reference to a self-defense plea: the defense attorney did make "a quick plea of provocation." But his criticism is essentially sound. O'Brien may also be right in arguing that Camus, himself an Algerian, could not come to grips with the social aspect of the story he was telling. French justice in Algeria, O'Brien asserts, "would almost certainly not have condemned a European to death for shooting an Arab who had drawn a knife on him and who had shortly before stabbed another European."[18]

The only reasonable reply to this criticism is that even a European jury in French Algeria might have condemned to death a "soulless" monster who not only had failed to mourn publicly for his mother, but had attributed his crime to the sun and refused to say he regretted having killed the Arab. O'Brien's rationalism, far more intelligent than that of either of the lawyers in Camus's story, does not take into account the intense fear that the members of a socially dominant community may have of one of their "own" who has violated certain taboos.

Camus's protagonist is, in a profound sense, a modern man. He sees himself neither as part of a polis to which he owes allegiance nor as having a soul that belongs to God. As narrator, Meursault treats scornfully the representatives of the judicial system—Examining Magistrate, trial judge, defense attorney, and prosecutor—and the representative of religion, the prison chaplain who tries to convert him to Christianity. Our reactions to Meursault, if we read *The Outsider* carefully, are bound to be mixed. How can we not be horrified, and mystified, by his sudden killing of another man and by his mere feeling of "annoyance" after the act? But can we fail to sympathize with him in his passionate outburst against the priest who visited him in his condemned man's cell and promised to pray for him?

> I started shouting at the top of my voice and I insulted him and told him not to pray for me. . . . He seemed so sure of everything, didn't he? And yet none of his certainties was worth one hair of a woman's head. He couldn't even be sure he was alive because he was living like a dead man. I might seem to be empty-handed. But I was sure of myself, . . . sure of my life and sure of the death that was coming to me. . . . (115)

Up to a point, Meursault's view, that because death equalizes us all, it mocks the judgments that human beings pass on each other, is persuasive. His declaration, in the final paragraph of *The Outsider*, that he now felt he understood why at the end of her life his mother had taken "a fiancé," and that "no one had any right to cry over her," movingly rebuts the accusation that he had behaved callously after her death. He cares far more for her than the hypocrites do who have condemned him for not going through the conventional motions of grief.

On the other hand, his fervent embrace of nature in the same paragraph, and, especially, his intense misanthropy, exhibit the extremism, the lack of "measure," that Camus would describe in later writings as a deep sickness of our time. Meursault, in saying that he "looked up at the mass of signs and stars in the night sky and laid myself open for the first time to the benign indifference of the world," seems to forget that the world had not been benign to him (*tendre* in the French text) when, blinded by sunlight reflected from a knife, he killed a man. And there is something ominous, however comprehensible in view of his situation, in his "last wish": "that there should be a crowd of spectators at my execution and that they should greet me with cries of hatred" (117).

We assume, as *The Outsider* ends, that Meursault will be guillotined. It is conceivable, however, that his judicial appeal will succeed. If he lives, will he become a violent enemy of the society that condemned him to death for his "monstrous" failure to observe the proprieties after his mother's death? In any case, his nihilism is a danger signal of the hollowness of strictly bourgeois "ideals" and the hypocrisy of much bourgeois "justice."

KUNDERA'S *The Joke*

Milan Kundera, whose writings were long proscribed in his native Czechoslovakia, shows the absurdity of the Communists' legalism after their takeover of the country in 1948. Like the authors of *Billy Budd*, *The Trial*, and *The Outsider*, however, Kundera indicates that the human condition itself is absurd, under whatever sky. A fundamental theme in his fiction is the many-faceted, ever-changing nature of reality: what has once seemed "just" or "true" to individuals or to large groups of people is later perceived in very different terms. A notable example of such a metamorphosis is provided by the Czech government's reconstruction of history, as Kundera recounts it in the opening chapter of *The Book of Laughter and Forgetting* (*Kniha smíchu a zapomnění*, first published in France as *Le Livre du Rire et de l'Oubli*, 1979):

> In February 1948, Communist leader Klement Gottwald stepped out on the balcony of a Baroque palace in Prague to address the hundreds of thousands of his fellow citizens packed into Old Town Square. It was a crucial moment in Czech history—a fateful moment of the kind that occurs once or twice in a millennium.
>
> Gottwald was flanked by his comrades, with Clementis standing next to him. There were snow flurries, it was cold, and Gottwald was bareheaded. The solicitous Clementis took off his own fur cap and set it on Gottwald's head.
>
> The Party propaganda section put out hundreds of thousands of copies of a photograph of that balcony with Gottwald, a fur cap on his head and comrades at his side, speaking to the nation. On that balcony the history of Communist Czechoslovakia was born. Every child knew the photograph from posters, schoolbooks, and museums.
>
> Four years later Clementis was charged with treason and hanged. The propaganda section immediately airbrushed him out of history, and, obviously, out of all the photographs as well. Ever since, Gottwald has stood on that balcony alone. Where Clementis once stood, there is only bare palace wall. All that remains of Clementis is the cap on Gottwald's head.[19]

The immediate cause of Kundera's first expulsion from the Party, in 1950 (the second, in 1970, led eventually to his exile), was his restiveness over the Stalinism evoked in the quoted passage. There was also, however, a basic philosophic conflict between the Party and the young man who had joined it out of sympathy for its economic and social aims. The Party insisted that consciousness reflected "objective conditions" and that justice— here the ideology recalls Plato's, minus Platonic transcendence— consisted in the harmonious orchestration, by the Party, of all elements of society. Intellectual individualism, from this perspective, was a counter-revolutionary crime. Kundera's viewpoint, as we can readily infer from his fiction, is that consciousness not only reflects but creates reality, and that intellectual individualism is both an aspect of and a confrontation with man's absurd situation. His novel *The Joke* (*Zert*, Prague, 1967), is in part a satire on the Party's humorless shackling of its members' minds.

Ludvik Jahn, one of the four narrators and characters in the novel, recounts his expulsion from the Party and from the university where he has been studying and the ridiculous flop of his attempt, fifteen years later, to avenge himself on his chief persecutor. His troubles originate in a postcard he sends to a girlfriend who, while taking a summer course in revolutionary techniques, has written to him, praising the "healthy atmosphere" around her and enthusiastically predicting an early social revolution in the West. Annoyed in his loneliness that Marketa is happy, Ludvik replies, in order to "hurt, shock, and confuse her": "Optimism is the opium of the people. A healthy atmosphere stinks of stupidity! Long live Trotsky!"[20]

He is summoned, when the fall term begins, to a meeting of three members of the Party University Committee. He knows them all well, but they greet him coldly and ask questions revealing their knowledge of his correspondence with Marketa, including many unanswered letters he sent her after the postcard. Focusing on his travesty of Marx's dictum that religion is "the opium of the people," Ludvik's inquisitors attack his excuse that the card was simply a joke on a girl who took everything seriously and whom everybody enjoyed trying to shock. One Committee member observes, reasonably enough, that his other letters did not indicate any failure to take Marketa seriously (29). There is truth as well in another inquisitor's accusation that the things Marketa takes seriously—the Party, optimism, duty—are just a joke to Ludvik. As narrator he has mordantly remarked that the years immediately following the Communist coup of February 1948 "told the world that they were the most radiant of years, and anyone who failed to rejoice was immediately suspected of lamenting the victory of the working class or (what was equally criminal) giving way *individualistically* to inner sorrow" (23).

Even before the postcard brouhaha, he has been reproved in meetings of the League of University Students, in which he holds an important post, for lingering " 'traces of individualism.' " The evidence of this, he was told, was his " 'strange kind of smile . . . as though you were thinking to yourself' " (24). Ludvik realizes that smiles and jokes are both masks, and he points out in his narration that young people are especially inclined to hide their uncertainties and to convey an attitude of worldly wisdom. He says of the student he had been, "I had several faces because I wasn't young and didn't know who I was or wanted to be" (25). But if it is apparent to the reader of *The Joke* that Ludvik's face when he wrote the postcard was that of a sexually jealous youth with an irreverent sense of humor, the Committee members see before them a Trotskyite conspirator's face. They therefore fire him from his League of Students post despite his insistence that he knows no Trotskyites and has read no Trotsky. His case, they tell him, will be handled by the Party branch at the Natural Sciences Division of the university.

Now comes the blow that changes his life, and, eventually, his attitude toward other human beings. The Party chairman of his department, Zemanek, knows both Ludvik and Marketa very well. He has even displayed a sense of humor by solemnly confirming to Marketa a fantastic story of Ludvik's about a tribe of Czech dwarfs whose existence bourgeois scholarship had suppressed, and who, in great demand abroad because of their extraordinary virility, had been exported for hard currency by the pre-Communist Czech government," especially to France, where they were hired by aging capitalist ladies as servants, though obviously used for different purposes altogether" (32).

Ludvik assumes that Zemanek will immediately understand the humorous intent of the "Trotskyite" postcard. But at the plenary session of the Party branch at the science faculty, it is Zemanek who, in what Ludvik parodically describes as "a highly effective, brilliant, unforgettable" address, recommends his expulsion from the Party (38). By this time, the pressures put on Ludvik have made him feel that his postcard words, "though genuinely intended as a joke, were still a transgression of sorts," and "torrents" of self-criticism have been whirling through his head (37). In consequence he recites a self-criticism and a plea for mercy. But nobody supports him. Everyone present, "including my teachers and closest friends," approves his expulsion, not only from the Party, but from the university as well (38).

Marketa has prepared him, up to a point, for Zemanek's role at the plenary session. She has sought Ludvik out, after avoiding him for months, to say that she had showed his postcard to the Comrades when they asked to see it—and had subsequently showed them his letters—and that Zemanek had warned her to stay away from Ludvik. She has added, however, that, having received permission from the Comrade who had run her training session, she was ready to emulate the wife in the Soviet film *Court of Honor*: after her scientist husband's condemnation by his colleagues for placing a discovery at the disposal of a foreign country, she stays with him and tries to help him atone for his wrong. Marketa was clearly prepared to "give herself to me body and soul," on the single condition that "the object of her salvation (I, myself, alas) would have to concede his profound, his innermost guilt" (37).

While, inwardly, Ludvik is still enough of a Party member to share the Comrades' suspicions of what lies behind the "façade" of his postcard joke, he refuses to assume the mask of guilt that he would have to wear in order to keep Marketa. So he finds himself alone. The most damaging effect of the experience is to be his eventual incapacity for any intimate relationship:

> the image of that lecture hall with a hundred people raising their hands, giving the order to destroy my life, comes back to me again and again. . . . I've made up numerous variations on the situation; what it would have been like, for example, if instead of expulsion from the Party, the verdict had been hanging by the neck. . . . I can't see them doing anything but raising their hands again, especially if the utility of my hanging had been movingly argued in the opening address. Since then, whenever I make new acquaintances, men or women with the potential of becoming friends or lovers, I project them back into . . . that place, and ask myself whether they would have raised their hands; no one has ever passed the test. (65)

The despairing cynicism of this passage recalls Meursault's hatred of his fellow-humans at the end of *The Outsider*. And the image of a hundred people mechanically raising their hands "to destroy my life" is somewhat reminiscent of Kafka's description of the "lifeless unity" in which the two executioners and K. are locked toward the end of *The Trial*. The classical and Judeo-Christian beliefs in ethical natural law were articulated by writers who assumed that members of the polis were reflective individuals. The absurdists, however, show us a world where human beings tend to act like automata controlled by "the Law," or rigid conventions, or a Party.

Ludvik does not actually lose his faith in other people immediately after his public ordeal at the plenary session. On the contrary, while serving in the penal division of the army, he meets a girl who revives his *joie de vivre*. With Lucie, a drably dressed factory worker whom he first saw outside a provincial movie—where *Court of Honor* was playing, he "for once . . . started a conversation naturally without a joke or an ironic remark." He was surprised at how easy this was after hiding behind masks for so long (58). Between Lucie and him, there is a reciprocal sympathy for each other's depression about life. For several months, they enjoy an innocently affectionate relationship. Ludvik, who has never recited poetry to anyone, moves her to tears by reading her the lyrical verse of the late poet Halas, recently denounced officially for "morbidity, depression, bad faith, existentialism" (63). Lucie begins to give him bunches of flowers to thank him for the letters he has written her when he could not get away from his penal labor in the Ostrava mines. She tells him she left her school and her home four years earlier to escape being beaten by her stepmother and stepfather. Her evident trust of Ludvik and appreciation of everything he says leave him completely unprepared for her reaction when he finally attempts to make love to her. She resists furiously, first in her hostel room that she has strewn with flowers as if to make it a fragrant bridal chamber and later in a private home where he thinks she will be more at ease. Finally, as she fights him, weeping and telling him that he does not love her, he suddenly feels that a "supernatural force," the same one "that had robbed me of my Party, my Comrades, my university degree," was tearing out of his hands "everything I longed for, everything that by rights was mine" (99). He tells her to get out.

What he does not know at this point, what she conceals beneath her own mask, will be revealed to him fifteen years later, in the mid–1960s, by his friend, Kostka, whose narrative sounds like a confessional monologue overheard by the reader. A fervent Christian, Kostka has been a lecturer at Ludvik's university. Despite his sympathy for the social aspects of Communism, complaints were made after the February 1948 coup that his religious faith disqualified him from educating Socialist youth. Ludvik stood up for him at a plenary meeting of the Party and Kostka subsequently thanked him, although he plainly said that he would never "outgrow"—as Ludvik had assured the Communists he would—his Christianity. Kostka left not only the university, but also his wife and child, in order to follow Christ by working for "the people" on a state farm. Ironically, his decision was misinterpreted by the Communists, who regarded it in terms of their own faith, not his, "as an unprecedented example of self-criticism" (181–84).

While Kostka was working in Bohemia, Lucie—who had wandered there after the ugly scene with Ludvik—was found in a barn by local officials, and employed as Kostka's greenhouse assistant. He treated her kindly, taught her about Jesus, and elicited from her an account of having been beaten regularly at home, of having given herself repeatedly at the age of sixteen to a gang of fellow-laborers whom she had thought of as her real father and mother, and of having spent a year in a reformatory before going to Ostrava. There she had met a soldier—Kostka did not learn his name—who turned out to be as nasty and vicious as the gang had become (195).

When Ludvik reflects on what Kostka has told him about Lucie's life, he realizes that he had regarded her simply as "*a function of my situation*; everything beyond that concrete situation, everything she was in her own right, had escaped me entirely" (210).

This existential analysis is a key passage in the novel. Ludvik had found it easy to spot self-deceptions in the judgments made by others—notably the Party members' judgment of him. Now, however, he sees that his own "trial" and punishment of Lucie resulted from a similar blindness to her as a human being.

It was many years before coming to this awareness that he had fallen into misanthopy after a nightmarish experience following his dismissal of Lucie. He and other penal conscripts found one of their group dead in his bed. This was Alexej, an ardent young Communist who had remained loyal to the Party even after being sent to the penal division, but then lost all desire to live when he learned that the Party had expelled him. Ludvik had never liked him—the son of "a highly placed Communist official who had been recently arrested," Alexej "had renounced his father for betraying and defiling the most sacred thing in his life" (77, 89)—but still respected the zealotry that made him a scapegoat within the penal system itself. It was when Alexej committed suicide, Ludvik reflects in his narration, that he himself lost any chance of regaining his trust in people. For he had come to realize that the penal collective "was as capable of bullying a man (making him an outcast, hounding him to death) as the collective in that lecture hall, as any collective" (102).

Desperately attempting now to find Lucie, he had gone AWOL, and been arrested, court-martialed, and sentenced to a jail term for desertion. After serving one year as a "political," then three years as a civilian in the mines, he was reintegrated into the Party. Almost a decade later, he found what seemed a perfect opportunity to avenge himself on Pavel Zamanek.

The apparent godsend was Zemanek's wife, Helena. Another of the four narrators of *The Joke*, she reveals in her recital, which evidently consists of diary entries, that she has met the now-rehabilitated Ludvik at his "institute," where she went to interview him for Czechoslovak radio. Not especially attractive, and emotionally starved because Pavel—who once told her that they had married, not for love, but *"out of Party discipline"* (13)—beds other women, she was excited at the prospect of a second meeting with Ludvik. She planned to see him again in his Moravian hometown, where she was to do a radio feature on a folklore event.

Unaware of Pavel's indifference to Helena, Ludvik relished the prospect of cuckolding him. Having borrowed Kostka's flat for the purpose, he easily persuaded Helena to accompany him there. Just before making love to her, he remembered the horribly painful plenary meeting: altogether forgetting his self-criticism and plea for clemency, he recalled only refusing "to play the role played at hundreds of meetings, hundreds of disciplinary proceedings, and before long, at hundreds of court cases: the role of the accused who accuses himself and by the very ardor of his self-accusation (his complete identification with the accusers) begs for mercy" (168).

His appetite, not exactly for Helena, but for revenge against Zemanek, whetted by this selective recollection, he possessed her—only to experience moments later the detumescence of his pride: Helena, passionately in love with Ludvik, assured him she had not even lived with Pavel for three years.

The climactic joke of the novel comes when Ludvik suddenly meets Zamanek at the folklore festival. With an insouciant " 'God, man, it's been years,' " Zemanek introduces him to an attractive brunette; and Ludvik, instead of punching him in the face, plays the conversational game. The young woman, a student of Zemanek's, says he is one of the most popular teachers at the university: students worship him for the very intellectual courage and independence that gets on the Administration's nerves (228). To Ludvik's dismay it becomes clear that Zemanek has completely abandoned the views he held fifteen years ago; that

> if a conflict of a political nature were to arise, I would find myself on his side, like it or not. That was what was so horrible; that was what I least expected; though there was nothing miraculous about his aboutface; on the contrary, it was quite usual; great numbers of individuals had done it, and the whole country was actually doing it gradually. The point was that I hadn't counted on it in Zemanek: he was petrified in my memory in the form in which I'd last seen him, and I was damned if I'd grant him the right to change in the least detail. (228–229)

There is an additional joke within the joke of Zemanek's reversal of his politics of 1950; the attractive girlfriend he has chosen, during this post-Stalinist period, has the same surname as that celebrated rebel against Stalin, Tito of Yugoslavia: she is "Miss Broz."

Overcome by shame, feeling that he has acted despicably toward Helena by turning her into a "rock he'd tried (and failed) to throw at somebody else," he tells her that he won't be seeing her again, that he doesn't love her (237). His "rock" immediately becomes a terrible boomerang—before being metamorphosed into the custard pie of farce. Helena reacts to what he has said by going to her office at the folklore festival and swallowing all the pills in a bottle labeled "aspirin" that she has found in her assistant's overcoat pocket. Ludvik, to whom she then sends the assistant with a farewell note, races to the rescue, and finds that she has actually swallowed a bottle of laxatives. She will live, and Ludvik will be afflicted with remorse for the cramps his inept attempt at revenge has induced in Helena.

The final episode in *The Joke* underlines the protean, uncertain nature of reality which, Kundera indicates, subverts our judgments of others and ourselves. Jaroslav, the fourth narrator of the novel, and an old musician friend of Ludvik's, has fervently described to us the plans for a folklore event called *The Ride of the Kings*. An ancient legend is to be enacted in which a pauper king, disguised as a woman, with opaque ribbons across his face, and accompanied by a retinue, returns on horseback to the land which had exiled him and which now welcomes him with gifts and rejoicing as the rightful monarch. Devoted though he is to the poetic spirit of the legend, Jaroslav realizes that folk art is almost dead: "What all those folk instrument orchestras and folk ensembles played was more opera or operetta or hit tunes than folk music." Yet in his ardor for the "dream" (here, Kundera implies, he resembles other self-deluded persons) instead of saying what he thinks of the "blasphemy" (214), he finds himself making falsely enthusiastic comments during a radio interview. But in addition to masking his own feelings at the festival, he discovers that the "King," the disguised horseback rider whom he proudly assumed to be his son, Vladimir, is actually another boy. Vladimir, with his mother's connivance, has gone to the city to watch the motorcycle race. Dejectedly thinking of himself as the "last king," a king "with no heir" (258), Jaroslav goes to lie down by the river, to be soothed by the flowing water. The equally depressed Ludvik finds him there and asks whether he may "sit in" with Jaroslav's folk music quartet that afternoon. In the last scene of the novel, which Ludvik narrates, he plays the clarinet as he had in his youth, and Jaroslav plays first violin in a band performing in an open-air restaurant.

By chance Ludvik had met Lucie soon after returning to his hometown; but she had pretended not to recognize him. Thinking of her as he played the first song with the band, he believes he finally understood why she had again appeared to him after so many years, and why on the following day he had heard about her from Kostka—in an account that mixed "legend" with truth, because Kostka did not know the truth of Ludvik's relationship with Lucie. Perhaps, he reflects, Lucie had wanted to tell him that her fate, that of a rape victim, was much like his; that although "we'd failed to understand each other and were lost for each other, our life stories were twinned, intertwined, . . . because they were both *stories of devastation.*" Just as Lucie had been devastated by physical love, although such love is in itself "innocent," so he had been robbed of values pure and innocent in origin: the word "comrade," for example, and the word "future." The blame lay, he reflects, elsewhere, "and was so great that its shadow had fallen over a vast area, over the world of innocent things (and words) and was devastating them" (262).

The shadow falls, too, over the folk music concert being played by Jaroslav's ensemble. As the few elderly people listening attentively are joined by more and more youths, it seemed to Ludvik that "those long-haired small fry spitting out saliva and words indiscriminately and with great ostentation" were bad actors "wearing masks of mindless virility and arrogant brutishness" (263). Jaroslav, evidently feeling much the same way, suddenly says that he does not want to perform for this kind of audience. But the bass player (who is "the inspector for cultural affairs") reminds him that the band has agreed to play into the evening. So as the crowd becomes increasingly rude, the musicians turn inward, creating "a magic circle of music" (264) within which Ludvik feels he has found his "only real home" (265). Suddenly, however, Jaroslav stops playing, stricken by a heart attack. Ludvik tries to comfort him while waiting for an ambulance. But he reflects that even if Jaroslav recovers, his life from now on will be "without passionate devotion, without jam sessions." And Ludvik envisions the ironic end of his own journey home—which he had undertaken to wreak vengeance on Zemanek: "holding [Jaroslav] and carrying him, carrying him, big and heavy as he was, carrying my own obscure guilt . . ." (266).

Kundera points here to man's exile from a "kingdom" that can be perceived only by the imagination and possessed only in art, like that of Jaroslav's band—or a novel like *The Joke*. Injustice, Ludvik has come to see, consists not only in the social wrongs that once led him to join the Communist Party, but in the blindness that induces us all to mistake a partial, ever-changing reality, which is all we can ever glimpse, for the "truth." Absurdly, the Communists punished Ludvik's joke as a counter-revolutionary act. Absurdly, Ludvik punished Lucie for a frigidity whose cause he came too late to understand. Absurdly, he made the pitiful Helena suffer by trying to avenge the wrong that her husband had done him.

Kundera's perspective on injustice differs markedly from that of another ex-Communist, Koestler, in that it does not derive from a belief, however qualified Koestler's seems to be, in the possibility of progress toward a fairer, more rational society. Koestler has strong affinities with writers in the natural law tradition, like Langland, Voltaire, Kleist. Kundera, on the other hand, is philosophically, if not temperamentally, in accord with his fellow-Czech Kafka, who was deeply moved by the passion for justice of Kleist's Michael Kohlhaas, but could not believe in justice himself. For the author of *The Joke*, too, injustice, whether in courtrooms or in our judgments of others, is at the heart of an irremediably absurd human condition.

Notes

1. Friedrich Nietzsche, "The Genealogy of Morals," *The Philosophy of Nietzsche*, trans. Horace B. Samuel (New York: Modern Library, n.d.) 780.

2. Herman Melville, *Billy Budd, Sailor (An Inside Narrative)*, ed. Harrison Hayford and Merton M. Sealts, Jr. (Chicago: U of Chicago P, 1962) 46–47.

3. Christopher Ward, *The War of the Revolution*, ed. John Richard Alden, vol. 1 (New York: Macmillan, 1952) 881–82.

4. Herman Melville, *Billy Budd, Sailor: An Inside Narrative*, ed. Milton R. Stern (Indianapolis: Bobbs, 1975) 97–98.

5. Evgeniya Knipovich, "Frants Kafka," *Inostrannaya Literatura*, 1 (1964) 195–204, and passages from her *Sila Pravdy: Literaturnokriticheskie stat'i* (Moscow: Sovetskii Pisatel', 1965), 343–45, 349–54; rpt. in *Franz Kafka: An Anthology of Marxist Criticism*, ed. and trans. Kenneth Hughes (Hanover: UP of New England, 1981) 192.

6. Albert Camus, Appendix: "Hope and the Absurd in the Work of Franz Kafka," *The Myth of Sisyphus and Other Essays*, trans. Justin O'Brien (New York: Vintage, 1955) 96.

7. Günther Anders, *Kafka*, trans. A. Steer and A. Thorlby (London: Bowes, 1960) 40.

8. Franz Kafka, *The Trial*, trans. Willa and Edwin Muir, rev. and with additional material trans. E. M. Butler (1968; New York: Schocken, 1974) 1.

9. Allan Blunden, "A Chronology of Kafka'a Life," in *The World of Franz Kafka*, ed. J. P. Stern (New York: Holt, 1980) 23. Three weeks after bringing up blood from his lungs, Kafka knew he had tuberculosis and saw the disease as the symptom of "a more general failure." Kafka wrote, in a letter, "I sometimes think that my brain and my lungs must have conspired in secret. 'Things can't go on like this,' said the brain, and now, five years later, the lungs have agreed to help."

10. Martha S. Robinson, "The Law of the State in Kafka'a *The Trial*," *ALSA Forum*, 6.2 (1982): 129. The author argues that it is "the Austro-Hungarian system of courts and court officialdom in pre-war Czechoslovakia," in caricature, "that has enmeshed" Joseph K. "In part, [the] apprehension and arrest scene has parodied what might actually have happened, and in some details it follows the law quite accurately."

11. Joost M. Meerloo, *The Rape of the Mind: The Psychology of Thought Control, Menticide, and Brainwashing* (New York: Grosset, 1961) 70.

12. Walter H. Sokel, "Freud and the Magic of Kafka'a Writing," in *World of Franz Kafka* 146–47. In contrast to Freud and Freudian analysis, "Kafka saw emotional illness not as something remediable and extrinsic to human existence," but as a manifestation of "a spiritual or existential anguish, inseparable from the whole being of the one who suffered it." When Kafka said, " 'There is only one illness,' " he meant "the individual existence itself."

13. Hannah Arendt, "Franz Kafka," *Sechs Essays* (Heidelberg: Schneider, 1948) 128–49, excerpted in *Franz Kafka* 3–11, says (4) that the "shame" referred to at the end of *The Trial* is the shame "that this is the world order and that he, Joseph K., even if its victim, is its obedient member."

14. Camus, *Myth* 11.

15. Camus, "Hope and the Absurd," 97.

16. Camus, *Myth* 12. I have substituted "govern our condition" for O'Brien's "command our condition."

17. Robert Champigny, *A Pagan Hero: An Interpretation of Meursault in Camus'* The Stranger, trans. Rowe Portis (Philadelphia: U of Pennsylvania P, 1969) 58–60, 53–54.

18. Conor Cruise O'Brien, *Albert Camus of Europe and Africa* (New York: Viking, 1970) 22.

19. Milan Kundera, *The Book of Laughter and Forgetting*, trans. Michael Henry Heim (Harmondsworth: Penguin, 1981) 1.

20. Milan Kundera, *The Joke*, trans. Michael Henry Heim (Harmondsworth: Penguin, 1983) 26. Mr. Kundera paid tribute to Mr. Heim's translation, first published in the United States by Harper & Row (New York, 1982), as "the first valid and authentic version of a book that has

. . . so often been violated" by mistranslation (Penguin edition, xvi). Early in 1992, having changed his mind about the Heim translation—as he explained in a somewhat embarrassed passage of his preface to a new version of *The Joke*—Mr. Kundera issued a Definitive Version, Fully Revised by the Author (HarperCollins). I cannot read Czech, but after carefully comparing the rendering in the Definitive Version with that by Mr. Heim of those passages I had planned to quote in *Dark Mirror*, I decided that I preferred Mr. Heim's translation.

5

A "Dissenting" Perspective

SERIOUS MODERN EUROPEAN AND AMERICAN FICTION, I have argued, frequently expresses a sense of injustice, but rarely points to clear standards of justice. I have related this murkiness about standards—often a rejection of standards—to the decay, since the later nineteenth century, of ethical natural law, which presupposed agreement, "from China to Peru," on at least some fundamental principles. Despite the decay, however, there are modern works that show the criminal trial as capable of revealing at least approximate truths and of producing a pretty clearly definable justice. In James Gould Cozzens's *The Just and the Unjust* (1942), for example, an American jury does not doubt that a defendant accused of participating in a kidnapping and murder has actually had a role in these crimes; but the jurors refuse, on grounds of an equity or fairness that conflicts with "the law" as enunciated by the presiding judge, to convict the defendant of murder in the first degree. They evidently believe that torture was used to extract his pretrial confession, and they do not think that he took a direct part in the killing. In C. P. Snow's *The Sleep of Reason* (1968), an English jury declines to accept the defense's psychiatric argument that two women accused of savagely murdering a boy had "diminished responsibility" when engaged in their brutal behavior. Instead, the jury decides that the defendants are morally responsible, "in the sense that you are for what you do," as the judge has put it in his disinterested charge. The women are consequently found to be guilty and, in a Britain that has eliminated execution, are sentenced to life imprisonment.

Both these novels are works of social realism. But neither Cozzens nor Snow is especially concerned with the economic inequities, or the racial or ethnic prejudices, which in so much social fiction is intertwined with the alleged crimes or with the trials they lead to. The authors of *The Just and the Unjust* and *The Sleep of Reason* are so intent upon affixing personal responsibility for crime that they virtually neglect the truths about squalid and hostile environmental influences that writers like Martin du Gard, Dreiser, Brecht, and Koestler emphasize. I shall be discussing, in a concluding chapter, a few modern fictions that attempt to reconcile a belief in ethical imperatives derived from natural law with an awareness of the importance of social conditions in determining how people act. But the Cozzens and Snow novels, with their distant echoes of eighteenth-century "rationalist" writers like Fielding and Voltaire, are well worth reading in a cultural climate in which reason is denigrated, except when it is put at the service of professional expertise.

COZZENS'S *The Just and the Unjust*

A philosophic conservative, James Gould Cozzens sets a high value in his fiction on the preservation of social order. In what one of his critics calls his "mature novels"[1] each of the protagonists is a professional man whose institutional commitment, whether to the Episcopal priesthood in *Men and Brethren*, to the army air force in *Guard of Honor*, or to the law in *The Just and the Unjust* and *By Love Possessed*, is accompanied by a commitment to reason and prudence and by a willingness—however slowly acquired—to compromise in a world where there seem to be few moral absolutes.

Writing about *The Just and the Unjust* in the *Harvard Law Review*, Zechariah Chafee, Jr. said that it was "extraordinary that an author who is not a lawyer could have written this book."[2] I would add that it is unusual if not extraordinary to find in modern fiction a character—with whom we are evidently invited to agree—praising the law as a profession. Philander Coates, a retired judge, tells his son Abner, an assistant district attorney and the protagonist of the novel, that although there are things in the law that "seem stupid, or not right," " 'they don't matter much. It's the stronghold of what reason men ever get around to using. You ought to be proud to hold it. A man can defend himself there. It gives you a groundwork of good sense; you'll never be far wrong—' "[3]

The rather stolid, pragmatic district attorney, Martin Bunting, whom Abner is helping to prosecute a kidnapping-and-murder case, distinguishes between the kind of law that is practiced by a former classmate of theirs whom he knows Abner envies and the kind that he himself is proud to practice:

> "I was in a big office for a couple of years after I was admitted to the bar. . . . It really isn't law at all. It has nothing to do with justice or equity. What it really is, is the theory and practice of fraud, or finding ways to outsmart people who're trying to outsmart you. . . . Sure, they'll pay you anything if you can do it for them. But you only have one life." (166)

Especially interesting in Cozzens's depiction of the trial of two men in a small town in a northeastern American state is the conflict between the applicable statutory law—as it is defined both by the presiding judge in his charge to the jury, and by the President Judge, who rebukes the jurors for their verdict—and the sense of fairness that is represented by the jury's decision. Cozzens finally implies, through the comments of Philander Coates toward the end of the novel, that justice in American criminal trials is accomplished through a dialectic between the rationality of judges and the intuitive judgments of juries. This implicit generalization, of course, tells us nothing about the quality of the jury, or the judge, in a particular trial. And it is notable that the jurors at Childerstown are altogether unexceptional. In a passage describing the murdered man's wife, Mrs. Frederick Zollicoffer, as speaking on the witness stand in a tough and uneducated way, Cozzens notes that the jurors listened with irritation to her and the other "foreigners"—defendants and witnesses who came "from somewhere else":

> Justice for all was a principle [the jurors] understood and believed in; but by "all" they did not perhaps really mean persons low-down and no good. They meant that any accused person should be given a fair, open hearing, so that a man might explain, if he could, the appearances that seemed to be against him. If his reputation and presence were good, he was presumed to be innocent; if they were bad, he was presumed to be guilty. If the law presumed differently, the law presumed alone. (57–58)

Later, while the judge is charging the jury, Abner Coates reflects on its members in uncomplimentary terms:

The truth was, it would never cross your mind to ask the opinion of any one of them on a matter of importance. Old Man Daniels was a plain fool. . . . Genevieve Shute had the face of a silly middle-aged woman. . . . All Abner knew about [Perry Vandermost] was that he was not one of the "good" [house] painters in Childerstown. . . . (375)

Yet, however inclined these jurors are to prejudge witnesses on the basis of their presence and reputation, and however unintelligent or incompetent Abner considers the jurors to be as individuals, they are not obviously unqualified to pass collective judgment on the defendants. Compare what we are told about them in the above passages with what Dreiser says about the twelve men chosen to hear Clyde Griffiths' case in *An American Tragedy*:

with but one exception, all religious, if not moral, and all convinced of Clyde's guilt before ever they sat down, but still because of their almost unanimous conception of themselves as fair and open-minded men, and because they were so interested to sit as jurors on this exciting case, convinced that they could pass fairly and impartially on the facts presented to them. (638–39)

The composition of the Griffiths jury makes it certain that Clyde will not get a fair trial. Dreiser depicts this judicial proceeding more as a ritual sacrifice to an angry god than as a struggle in which the defendant has a chance of saving his life. Cozzens's jurors, however botched a crew, are described as ready to hear a man explain "if he could, the appearance that seemed to be against him."

As far as appearance is concerned, the death of the man who had been kidnapped, Frederick Zollicoffer, might, District Attorney Bunting realizes, strike the jury as such a gain to society at large that they would "do something silly, like deciding the defendants were not so bad after all" (49). For Zollicoffer had peddled drugs, taken them himself, and compiled a despicable criminal record. Bunting has hoped, before meeting his widow, that her demeanor and testimony would counter the jury's feelings about Zollicoffer himself. Unfortunately for the prosecution, however, "Mrs. Zollicoffer had a mind of her own, and it was a poor one" (50). Before the trial, she has told Abner the obvious lie that she didn't know what her husband's business was. Bunting

knows that Harry Wurts, the able attorney for one of the defendants, will expose her lie during his cross-examination. This he
proceeds to do; when to Wurts's question as to whether her
husband was selling opium and narcotics, Mrs. Zollicoffer answers " 'No. He wasn't,' " Wurts slightly rephrases his question,
elicits a " 'Not that I know of,' " and goes on to "insinuate
derision, to invite her and everyone else to join him in contempt
for the deceased. Harry had seen where and how to wound her
without doing himself any damage . . ." (113–14).

The key witness for the prosecution, Roy Leming, also presents
Martin Bunting and Abner Coates with an "appearance" problem.
He participated in the kidnapping, but Bunting has obtained a
severance of his trial from that of the other defendants because
Leming, in order to get life imprisonment instead of the electric
chair, has agreed to testify for the Commonwealth. Crucial as his
testimony is, it is tainted because it comes from a turncoat—as
well as a drug addict and a criminal, who had met one of the
defendants while serving time for a prior offense.

The Just and the Unjust is in part a *Bildungsroman*, the story of
Abner Coates's education by life itself. The trial of Stanley Howell
and Robert Basso is his first murder case, but he has come,
"through a lengthening experience" (38), to realize how cruel such
men as the defendants, and Leming, actually are. Cozzens, while
noting that Howell experienced "misery and poverty and, probably, hunger" during his youth, has emphasized "the things he had
done to himself, and the consequences of those things," in his
long "war with the law" (23). Abner reflects that criminals like
him, and Basso and Leming, "might be victims of circumstance
in the sense that few of them ever had a fair chance; but it was a
mistake to forget that the only 'fair chance' they ever wanted was
a chance for easy money" (38).

This viewpoint is strikingly different from that of writers like
Dreiser, Koestler, and Brecht, who stress the power of circumstances to turn people to what their societies define as crime.
Cozzens, in his novel *Men and Brethren* (1936), explicitly condemns
that perspective through the reply of the Episcopal vicar, Ernest
Cudlipp, to what an ordained graduate student, Wilber Quinn,
says about a fellow they both know who is in jail:

"I think Jimmy's a bad egg," Wilber said. "But he's never had a chance. . . . He's the natural product of a society in which property is the source of privilege—until we change that, we won't get anywhere."

"Until we get somewhere, how will we change that?" asked Ernest, exasperated. "Your friends downtown aren't getting anywhere, Wilber. They're sentimentalists. They don't believe in the doctrine of original sin. Realists are the only people who get things done."[4]

Bunting and Abner are realists, in Cozzens's sense of the term, in their attitude toward both Leming and the defendants. But Leming, although he provides indispensable details about the kidnapping, in which he played only a minor part, and the planning and accomplishment of the murder—all of which he heard discussed but did not participate in—also makes two revelations that harm the Commonwealth's case because of the light they throw upon him and the police of the county in which the kidnapping occurred. During direct examination by Abner, he first reveals that one night while he himself was out of the state, the two defendants and a friend of Basso's named Mike Bailey, the leader of the gang, had, according to what Bailey told Leming, set out to kidnap Zollicoffer. But when they came to the road that led to Zollicoffer's place, they saw two men get out of an automobile that had pulled down the street with the lights out. The subsequent behavior of these two men—lighting matches and looking at the different houses for a quarter of an hour—led Bailey to indicate angrily to Leming the gang's suspicion that he was a stool pigeon. Although this vivid report by Leming fails to make clear why Bailey did not get rid of him, in one way or another, it does tell the jury that Leming's confederates distrusted him long before he became an open turncoat.

His second revelation concerns Zollicoffer's reported reaction when he was actually kidnapped: " '[Howell] said when they first grabbed him, Zolly thought they were the cops. He pulled out a can with some opium, and about fifty or sixty dollars, and said, 'Here is the money,' as much as to say, leave him go for it." This testimony is vividly embarrassing for the prosecution. The jury stirs at the thought that "down there"—in the county where the kidnapping took place—"policemen could be bribed." Abner,

Cozzens observes, felt like telling the jurors, whose impulse would be to drop everything and haul in the corrupt cops, "that the detail, for what it was worth, had been brought to the attention of the district attorney's office in that county; and this was all they could do; and all that would be done, too. It was one thing to learn of irregularities on third-hand evidence; it was another to prove that they ever took place" (136).

Harry Wurts's cross-examination of Leming seeks to implicate him as much as possible in the kidnapping, suggests that the "sleeping pills" that Leming has been given in jail are actually narcotics to feed his habit, and establishes that one of his businesses had been the manufacture of dice, including loaded ones. Despite this effective performance, however, the prosecution's case against the defendants seems very solid: Leming has testified that Zollicoffer was kept imprisoned in a bungalow, that the gang was dissatisfied with the size of a ransom paid by a Zollicoffer associate, and that Leming was told by Bailey and Howell how the murder was done and how the weighted body was thrown into a creek—in the county where the case is being tried.

Stanley Howell, the only kidnapper to testify at the trial—Basso stands mute, and Bailey, mortally injured in a fall while trying to avoid arrest, has died in a hospital after naming his confederates to the police—seems, when he takes the stand, to be in a juridically hopeless situation. As soon as Bailey's story was on the wire, the F.B.I. had arrested Howell, on suspicion of involvement a few years before in the shooting of an F.B.I. agent during the investigation of a mail robbery. Wanting to turn over to the Commonwealth a case that would stick against him, the F.B.I. obtained a signed confession from Howell about his part in the Zollicoffer kidnapping. But Wurts "plays" his client with the adroitness of a card shark who has been dealt a poor hand.

> To pretend to be defending an innocent man only invited scorn, if the jurors believed him sincere, because he was such a fool; and if they believed him insincere, he invited their anger, because he showed that he thought he was smarter than they were. Harry's tactic was to put it to the jurors that he was a shrewd man, and they were shrewd, too; and they all disliked Howell; but more than they disliked Howell, they loved justice, he and they. (309)

Howell obviously hates his attorney for this attitude, not understanding that Wurts can help him only by evincing feelings like
those of the jury. Harry knows he must deliberately frown, for
example, when Howell replies, " 'My mind was a blank,' " to a
question about how much time he had spent in F.B.I. custody:
"for the phrase, as Howell offered it, would not be acceptable to
anyone in his right senses. That was something [Howell] had read
somewhere; and so he naturally spoke it like a liar. Harry cut in,
'Do you recall the time of day or night when you signed [the
confession]?' " (310). Howell's reply, " 'It was around one o'clock
in the morning,' " provides from Wurts's viewpoint an appropriately sinister prelude to the witness's description of how he had
been treated before confessing: the F.B.I. man, Howell testifies,
put shackles on his legs, handcuffed him, " 'and then they got to
working around.' " They hit him in the chin, twisting his ears
and arms, and using hoses on him. What he says, jerkily, "expel-
ling the phrases with bitter little grunts," rings true to Abner
Coates: Howell "spoke what he knew" (311).

Wurts's questions draw a compelling account from Howell of a
beating over the kidneys with hoses so that " 'for twenty-four
hours I urinated blood.' " When he asked for a doctor, he was
told, " 'We will doctor you.' " This testimony establishes a close
rapport between Wurts and the jury:

> Harry . . . took a turn down past the jury, looking at the floor, his
> face morose, making to them the simple appeal of his troubled
> mind. Leaving Howell aside, and no matter whether Howell repelled
> them or not, or whether he told the exact truth or not, the law was
> aspersed. They could joke about the law, and speak of it disrespect-
> fully; and say that there was no justice, or that the rich could get
> away with murder, or that political influence was what counted;
> but, in fact, they never believed it. It could not be true because they
> had the final say. When they swore that they would well and truly
> try and true deliverance make between the Commonwealth and the
> prisoner at the bar, they meant it. Their minds shared Harry's
> trouble. They did not like any of this. (313)

This indirect discourse conveys what the jurors believe, and Cozzens's tone suggests that he shares their belief. Contrast his clear
indication that a small-town lawyer like Harry Wurts may very
effectively defend a poor man like Howell, with Dreiser's equally

clear implication in *An American Tragedy* that Clyde fails to escape
the electric chair because his rich uncle has not engaged powerful,
celebrated lawyers to argue his case.

The passage on the jury's reaction to Howell's testimony is
more arresting than it would have been had Cozzens not earlier
described the jurors as provincial people who resent the defendants
as "urban foreigners." Their very parochialism makes their revulsion from the torture of Howell particularly impressive.

After Howell identifies Kinsolving, an F.B.I. agent and prosecution witness, as one of his torturers, and says of his own signed
confession that he would have " 'told them anything' " to avoid
further pain, Wurts attempts to show that under duress his client
" 'allowed it to appear that he had taken a larger part in the
business than . . . he did take' " (314–16). Howell claims to have
argued against killing Zollicoffer, and even to have extracted from
Bailey an assurance that Zollicoffer would be released unharmed.
The shooting, according to Howell, happened suddenly in a car
he was driving, ostensibly to take the kidnapped man home, while
Bailey, Basso, and the victim were in the back seat. Howell's
further testimony that neither Basso nor he himself had a gun in
the car calls into question Leming's earlier recollection on the
witness stand. Leming said he had been told by Basso that Basso
had fired the second shot into Zollicoffer after Bailey had fired the
first. Howell also conveys a vivid impression of his own fear of
Bailey, as Bailey—who had put weights on the body—aided by
himself and Basso, took it out of the car on a bridge, and heaved
it into the creek.

Despite Abner's establishing, on cross-examination, that Howell made pretty much the same confession to him, of Howell's
own free will, as he had previously made, after torture, to the
F.B.I., it is impossible to know exactly how guilty he is. The truth
about Basso's role also remains unclear. Nevertheless, Martin
Bunting and Abner Coates believe they have won their case. Judge
Vredenburgh's point in his charge to the jury—that if they find
that the defendants took part in a kidnapping, deliberate intent in
the killing is not necessary in order to justify a verdict of first-
degree murder—seems clearly to benefit the prosecution. From
the perspective of the law, even if the jurors believe both Howell
and Basso to have been unarmed at the time of Zollicoffer's death,

both men could be convicted on the capital charge and sentenced to either life imprisonment or death.

The jury's decision, which stuns Vredenburgh (who, in the Attorneys Room, during a break, had said that the defendants "ought to be electrocuted") as well as Abner, Bunting, and President Judge Horace Irwin, is that both Howell and Basso are guilty of murder in the second degree. Leming reacts as if he has been clobbered: he knows that the maximum sentence for that crime is twenty years, while he himself "would have life imprisonment to reward him for his co-operation in pleading guilty" (402).

At this point, Judge Irwin, whom Cozzens has characterized as philosophically inclined, less insistent on the letter of the law than Vredenburgh, makes a harsh public criticism of the jury. Declaring that the court does not consider the customary thanks to be appropriate for their service, he asserts that they have not " 'properly done the duty' " for which they were summoned (405). They were bound, he emphatically states, to find the defendants guilty of first-degree murder if they had taken part in a kidnapping, and " 'if their victim was killed before he came to be released.' " He adds that to find that the accused men were not the kidnappers, " 'you would have to doubt the evidence of numerous witnesses, even including one of the defendants himself' " (408).

According to Kinsolving, in a remark after the trial to Basso's young court-appointed lawyer, the reason for the jury's verdict is simply that they did not want to "burn a man who maybe didn't actually take a gun" and shoot somebody (411). But had the jury found the defendants guilty of first-degree murder, they would have had to decide the penalty too—and they could have chosen life imprisonment instead of execution. Harry Wurts's closing statement in the trial has probably weighed heavily with the jurors. Comparing the law under which kidnappers who have not joined in a killing are nevertheless held to be murderers to " 'barbarous' " eighteenth-century laws that " 'the conscience and love of justice of members of juries made them refuse' " to enforce (346), Wurts appeals to the " 'free men and women' " before him to make their own independent decision. (346–47).

Cozzens suggests that an excess of "rationality" in Bunting, an inability to imagine that the jury could do anything other than produce the verdict he has asked for, has led him to ignore Wurts's eloquent plea. To Bunting,

> A miscarriage of justice, with some good, brave man in the inter-esting and dramatic plight of standing trial for what he never did, might get by in a book or a play where anything could be made plausible. In practical, in real life, it could be made plausible only to those ignorant of how a prisoner at the bar arrived there. (361)

It is Abner's father who, in effect, reconciles the convergent perspectives of Bunting, Vredenburgh, and Irwin, the defenders of "law," with the jury's perspective. When Abner, who has stayed late in the Attorneys Room discussing the case, arrives home, it is midnight, and Judge Coates is asleep. But he wakes up and, impressively alert even though a stroke had led him to resign as a judge of the Superior Court, he engages in an animated conversation about the case. Abner, after blurting out—and then feeling guilty for doing so—that " 'Marty may have taken it a little too much for granted,' " says that Kinsolving " 'thought the jury was jibbing at executing two men for something they argued a third man had really done.' " The judge replies that one of the uses of a jury is to be like a cylinder-head gasket: " 'Between two things that don't give any, you have to have something that does give a little, something to seal the law to the facts. There isn't any known way to legislate with an allowance for right feeling' " (426–27). His reference to "right feeling" points to the importance of an intuitive response to testimony—a response evidently based on ethical natural law—to counterbalance the rigidity of the writ-ten law that judges defend. But Judge Coates then appears to contradict himself. He says that if judges always found the verdicts, " 'Resentment would build up every time the findings didn't go with current notions or prejudices.' " This observation, taken together with his comment that " 'the jury is the public itself,' " seems to identify the kind of justice upheld by the jury not with ethical natural law but with what the ancient Greeks called *nomos*— custom or convention. However, when the judge reverts to the expression "right feeling," saying that while entrapment is per-fectly legal, he doesn't think that " 'right feeling can ever stoop to it,' " and adding that although compounding a felony is an indictable offense, " 'a man feels that he has a right to forgive those who injure him' " (428), he is invoking, once again, natural law. For he is implying that a revulsion from entrapment and an inclination toward forgiveness are not simply "current notions or prejudices" that change with time or place, but attitudes deeply rooted in our civilized selves, under whatever sky.

Judge Coates is talking informally, not giving a lecture, so it is understandable that he should not make precise distinctions between a jury's adherence to essentially local or customary laws (such as the one, we might recall, which in Harper Lee's *To Kill a Mockingbird* permits a Negro to be condemned to die, solely on the lying word of a girl who claims he raped her[5]) and its articulation of "right feeling." What does emerge clearly from his comments is his sense, which presumably is Cozzens's too, that in the American criminal trial the jury's right to be "wrong" can protect the public against the tyranny of a necessary but narrow legal expertise.

I have pointed to differences between Dreiser (and other "environmentalist" writers) and Cozzens with respect to two issues: (*a*) the treatment of the link between a character's adverse circumstances and his criminality; and (*b*) the depiction of the relationship between the criminal trial and the passions and prejudices in the world outside the courtroom. On the second issue, one more specific comparison may be helpful. Cozzens indicates at the beginning of the Childerstown trial that from Judge Vredenburgh's perspective most of the reporters present are there with the intention of manufacturing and printing "sensational rubbish prejudicial to the dignity of the law" (15). Since there is no indication, however, anywhere in the novel that reportage has corrupted the trial, we may conclude that the law's dignity has been prejudiced only outside the courtroom doors. In *An American Tragedy*, on the other hand, cries of " 'Peanuts!' " " 'Popcorn!'" " 'Hot dogs!'" " 'Get the story of Clyde Griffiths, with all the letters of Roberta Alden. Only twenty-five cents!' " (630) are heard just outside the courthouse at the beginning of the trial. And Clyde's mother has read in the *Rocky Mountain News* a story about him, under the blatantly prejudicial headline "Boy Slayer of Working Girl Indicted," which says in part, " 'Griffiths, . . . in spite of almost overwhelming evidence, has persisted in asserting that the alleged crime was an accident . . .' " (620). There are additional suggestions in Dreiser's novel that the press has helped to stimulate a public hatred of Clyde which affects the jury's perception of him.

Cozzens's positive view of the trial distinguishes him, of course, not only from an environmentalist writer like Dreiser, but also from religiously oriented authors like Dostoevsky and Mauriac and absurdist ones such as Melville and Camus. For from the religious perspective, judicial error is a foreseeable result of reliance on man's corrupt or erring reason rather than on God. And from the absurdist point of view, there is no common measure between an act allegedly "criminal," but originating in an intention either innocent or obscure, and the judgment of that act by representatives of a society whose chief aim is the maintenance of order. Cozzens is, I believe, narrower in his social interests, less generously responsive to human diversity, than any of the writers I have mentioned in this paragraph. But *The Just and the Unjust* strikes me as significant for its intimation, heterodox in modern trial literature, that something like justice may emerge from a dialectic between "the law" and "right feeling."

C. P. SNOW's *Sleep of Reason*

There is a scene in *The Just and the Unjust* in which Abner Coates, relaxing at a party, hears a mandolin accompanied by voices singing, " 'Every time my honey leaves me, I get the blues.' " It occurs to him that the mandolinist's husband, although he might once have been her honey, has certainly left her, to her relief and joy. In all the actions for divorce with which Abner is familiar, the chief cause of trouble is the same: those about to marry avoided real knowledge of each other, "and were satisfied if, among their feelings, they discovered some truth, such as: every time my honey leaves me, I get the blues" (96–97).

While less acerbic than Cozzens, C. P. Snow shares his distrust of emotion uncontrolled by reflective intelligence. Like Cozzens, he finds in the courtroom trial an exemplification of man's ability to impose some order on the chaos of existence, to seek justice in a rational, disinterested way.

Snow's wife, the writer Pamela Hansford Johnson, was asked

by the *Sunday Telegraph* in 1966 to set down her impressions of the
trial at Chester, England, of Ian Brady, twenty-seven, and Esther
Hindley, twenty-three, on charges that between December 26,
1964, and October 7, 1965, they had deliberately murdered a
seventeen-year-old man, a ten-year-old girl, and a twelve-year-old
boy. After composing these impressions, she felt a need "to write
at some length about the social implications I believed to exist,
and to try to explore whether there was not, in our increasingly
permissive society, some compost-heap of rottenness out of which
such ugly weeds could flourish and grow lush." The result of her
exploration was *On Iniquity: Some Personal Reflections Arising out of
the Moors Murder Trial* (1967). It suggested, in part, that we too
readily comfort ourselves by believing there is "no such thing as
wickedness"—only sickness, for which the subject bears no responsibility. Johnson, on the other hand, believed that some of us
are capable of being "fairly wicked"; and she tried to determine
whether "there are things which may encourage us in wickedness,
or else break down those proper inhibitions which have hitherto
kept the tendency to it under restraint."[6]

She points out that both Brady and Hindley admired Nazism,
that he had taken her to a film of the Nuremberg rallies, and that
there was a passage in the Marquis de Sade's works—Brady owned
about fifty volumes of sado-masochism—that Brady used to
brood upon:

> "Is Murder a crime in the eyes of Nature?" . . . Destruction is
> Nature's method of progress, and she prompts the murderer to
> destruction, so that his action shall be the same as plague or famine.
> . . . In a word, murder is a horror, but a horror often necessary,
> never criminal, and essential to tolerate in a republic." (58)

Johnson observes that this couple, who in court did not seem mad
to her, and for whom no plea of diminished responsibility was
made at the trial, had tape-recorded their sadistic slaughter of the
ten-year-old girl.

Johnson believes that Brady and Hindley "drifted into a kind of
corporate wickedness" (102), Hindley doing anything Brady
asked her to because, as she said, " 'I loved him . . . I love him
still' " (26).

> If the condition of this couple is madness at all, it would seem to be
> a case of *folie à deux*, and to approximate most nearly to the case of

the lesbian Papin sisters, cook and housemaid in Le Mans to
Madame and Mademoiselle Lancelin, who, in 1933, murdered their
employers in circumstances of Gothic atrocity. (106)

While she has no solution for the problem of sadistic violence,
which she links with "permissiveness" in contemporary literature,
sub-literature, and the popular arts, Johnson urges rejection of
William Blake's idea that it is better to strangle an infant in its
cradle than to nurse unacted desires. We must, she says, "nurse"
such desires, "since if we indulged them it would be to the danger
and misery of our fellow men" (57).

Snow's *The Sleep of Reason* (1968), the next-to-last volume in
his *Strangers and Brothers* series, expresses concerns similar to those
of Johnson in *On Iniquity*. Snow's narrator, ex-barrister Lewis
Eliot, recounts two trials, the first of which—a disciplinary hearing which he has taken part in as a member of a university
Executive Court—is not causally related, yet is "atmospherically"
linked, to the second, the prosecution of two women for the
killing of an eight-year-old boy. What both judicial procedures
reveal is a flight from personal responsibility that Snow implies is
epidemic in modern society.

The university hearing is an appellate one for four students
whom a disciplinary committee has decided to expel for fornicating in the sitting room of a women's dormitory. One naked
couple had been discovered at three a.m. on a sofa, the other
couple on an improvised bed. At the student body's request, these
students are being permitted to testify before the court. Eliot's
role is to see that they get a fair hearing. The first student to make
a statement, a stockbroker's daughter for whom, as she candidly
says, expulsion would not create much of a problem, does not
concede that she has done anything wrong; she is sorry only that
others, who are concerned about careers, got " 'dragged in. That
wasn't so good.' "[7] The second woman says little but that she had
been influenced by " 'the rest of them.' " The most capable
member of the group, a promising physicist, ascribes his behavior
that night to " 'collective hysteria' " (36), though he admits that
the party in the sitting room was inexcusable. The last of the
students to testify, Dick Pateman, denies the right of the university authorities " 'to impose their own laws unilaterally on the

students.' " Matters of discipline, he argues, should be settled by
" 'mutual consent." For him, the practical thing for the court to
consider is simply " 'whether you want to ruin us' " (38–39).

The Executive Court, after hearing the appellants, eventually
adopts Eliot's suggestion—over the protest of the university's
vice-chancellor, a stern moralist who advocates immediate expulsion—that formal action be delayed for two months. This would
save some chance for the student's careers if faculty members
could arrange placements at other universities. As narrator, Eliot
concedes that his compromise solution was not even, as the vice-
chancellor complained, a "rational" one. Yet Eliot had felt "quite
pleased with the morning's work" (46–47). The reader of the
novel who is persuaded at this point that Eliot's sense of satisfaction is justified may be less sure of that by the end of *The Sleep of
Reason.*

In the fall of 1963, several months after the students' hearing,
Dick Pateman's sister, Katherine ("Kitty"), and the woman with
whom she has been living, Cora Ross, are arrested for the murder
of young Eric Antony Mawby. Dick's reaction to this news,
which he expresses to Lewis Eliot, is essentially identical to his
reaction at the university hearing: " 'The whole wretched set-
up,' " the establishment, the society, were to blame. Look at what
" 'they' " were doing to him. (He was evidently having trouble
with examinations at the university to which he had transferred.)
Kitty would be happy in a decent society. As for Cora, anything
she had done was "their fault: no one had looked after her . . ."
(267).

What Kitty and Cora did, according to the police account, was
to pick up Eric Mawby at random, take him to a cottage in the
country, play cat-and-mouse with him for a weekend, then beat
him to death.

Eliot becomes involved in the horrific situation because Cora
Ross's uncle, George Passant, is his oldest friend. For many years,
George has led a group of younger people whose watchword is
"freedom" from warping, hypocritical Victorian rules. While
disagreeing with his philosophy, Eliot likes and admires him for
his courage, and is concerned lest, sixtyish and in failing health,
he be injured by the trial. George tells him that Cora had been
" 'on the fringe of our crowd' "; but he refuses to take responsi-

bility for either her or the Pateman girl: " 'I told them what I've told everyone else, that they ought to make the best of their lives and not worry about all the neutered rubbish round them who've denied whatever feeble bit of instinct they might conceivably have been endowed with.' " Emphatically he denies that if they had not been told this, " 'they'd have been just as safe as everyone else' " (247–48).

Snow's setting of the stage at the beginning of the murder trial contrasts markedly with the setting in works by modern writers like Dostoevsky, Dreiser, and Camus, who criticize, from a religious, a social, or an absurdist perspective, the trial as an institution. In Camus's *The Outsider*, for example, Meursault's account of his own trial evokes a disquieting atmosphere reminiscent of a George Grosz painting. He tells us that he was led by two policemen into "a small room" from which "we could hear people talking and shouting, chairs scraping and a whole commotion which reminded me of one of those local festivals where, after the concert, they clear the room for dancing" (80). In the prisoner's dock, Meursault had the impression that the jury looking at him, objectifying him, were anonymous passengers on the opposite side of a tram who "were scrutinizing the new arrival to find his peculiarities" (81). Just before three judges came into the stifling courtroom, two huge fans began whirring around. The presiding magistrate "wiped his little bald head with a handkerchief and announced that the court was in session" (83).

Snow's narrator, on the other hand, is disposed to see the trial as a relatively rational, civilized process. Eliot describes a "small and handsome" courtroom that might almost have been "a miniature Georgian theater in a county town"; the heads of spectators pushing forward, "trying to get a glimpse" of the defendants whom they knew to be lesbians and the savage killers of a small boy; and the "old judge" whose bearing is that of "a strong and active man" and whose bow to the court and the jury is accompanied by "an amiable and Punchlike smile." Eliot's comments on the judge's appearance, temperament, and character, especially the remark that "he had tried more criminal cases than anyone on the bench, and no one had been more compassionate" (281–83), prepare us for a trial that will not be "absurd," or corrupted by an economic or political bias, or vitiated by man's inability to

discover a truth that only God knows. If, along with the spectators, the readers of Snow's novel objectify these defendants at the
outset, we feel we could not do otherwise; they have put themselves beyond the pale of our sympathy by torturing a child to
death.

In addition to Lewis Eliot's tone in setting the scene, and in
describing the trial as a whole, there is a specifically legal aspect
of this proceeding that helps to make it seem relatively rational.
Because of a recent change in English law, there was no chance of
Cora's and Kitty's being executed; Eliot observes that when he
was a young barrister, it was the possibility that a defendant might
in fact be condemned to die that had "at least in part, enticed us
to the courts. Yes, young lawyers like myself had gone there to
pick up something about the trade; yes, there was the drama: but
we had also gone there as men might go, lurking, ashamed of
themselves, into a pornographic bookshop. Into the mephitic air,
the sentence would be coming nearer" (283–84).

By contrast, Eliot notes that at the trial of these two women
there seemed to be an attempt on the part of the prosecution as
well as the judge to avoid appealing to people's sensations. The
prosecuting attorney "was as quiet and factual as if he were
proposing an amendment to the Rent Act." The judge, in determining the timetable for the trial, had taken into consideration
medical advice that Miss Pateman had had an attack of rheumatism. He "was being elaborately considerate: just as when he called
her Miss he seemed to be rebuking the old custom of the courts,
which the clerk had had to follow, of charging prisoners by their
bare surnames" (284).

This courtesy appears to be that of a human species different
from the one to which the defendants belong. For, according to
the prosecuting attorney, Bosanquet, Eric Mawby's skull had
been battered in, and there were also signs of lacerations and other
wounds on his body, " 'which may have been inflicted many
hours before death' " (287). Bosanquet goes on to cite Kitty
Pateman's admission that she and Cora Ross had long wanted
" 'to have a child alone, . . . to be in control of. . . . They wanted
to teach it to behave' " (296).

Eliot, reflecting on all the evidence presented that afternoon,
recalls seeing, with his brother Martin, the films of the German

concentration camps just after the Allied troops had entered. His and Martin's reactions had been strangely mixed: on the one hand, the brothers had vowed that if people like themselves had any part in action, "this couldn't happen again." On the other, "while we watched those films, we had, as well as being appalled, felt a shameful and disgusting pleasure. . . . We were fascinated (the sensation was as affectless as that) because men could do these things to other men" (326). In the courtroom, he realizes, it had been the same for himself and for everyone around him.

This passage, and the one on Eliot's recollection of the "pornographic" pleasure he and other lawyers had once taken in anticipating the announcement of a death sentence, show Snow's awareness of the most appalling aspect of "the brotherhood of man." Implicit here is the recognition of an underground kinship between even the most considerate trial judge and the defendants who have committed acts uniquely human in their hideousness. Yet despite Snow's knowledge of what Dostoevsky, and Freud knew, the predominant impression we get from his account of the Pateman-Ross trial is that of a modest victory for reason over the hellish impulses we all share.

A sudden change in the defense's strategy occurs as the result of a detective's testimony about Kitty Pateman's account of what she and Cora had done with Eric after picking him up on a Friday evening. According to the detective, " 'Miss Pateman stated that they hadn't any knowledge themselves of what did happen to him' " (337). Asked by Bosanquet to clarify this startling testimony, the detective has quoted Kitty directly: " 'I've given you the story as far as I remember it. I don't remember much about anything that Sunday night.' "

Cora's attorney, Benskin, now tries to concede the facts about the murder, but he claims that because of the defendants' condition at the time of the killing, their responsibility was "diminished," and their crime should therefore be regarded as manslaughter. As if in perverse, or perhaps canny, support of this new strategy, Cora bursts out against her own lawyer: " 'What the hell do you think you're doing with us? . . . We'll answer for ourselves. . . . Do you think we need to explain ourselves to a set of——?' " (338–39).

In the corridor, at the end of this trial session, lawyers disagree as to whether Cora's outcry was sincere. More disturbing to Eliot, however, than the possibility that she was putting on an act, is Kitty's mother's reaction when he explains to her that if Kitty were to be sent to a mental hospital, she couldn't be released until the authorities were satisfied she'd present no danger to anyone else. Mrs. Pateman vehemently replies that Kitty's " 'got her head screwed on. . . . she won't let the police get hold of her again' " (343). Clearly, the moral vacuum that this comment betokens to Eliot is, from Snow's viewpoint, a great illness of our time.

Opening for the defense the next morning, Benskin explains that his plea is not based on the old, nineteenth-century M'Naughten rules under which a defendant was free from guilt only if at the time of his offense he could not tell right from wrong. Rather, he is taking his stand on the definition of "diminished responsibility" in the Homicide Act of 1957: " '[A person] shall not be guilty of murder if he was suffering from such abnormality of mind (whether arising from a condition or arrested or retarded development of mind or any inherent causes or induced by disease or injury) as substantially impaired his mental responsibility. . . .' " (346). In short, the defense argues that the women in the dock could not help doing what they did to Eric Mawby.

According to Adam Cornford, Benskin's chief psychiatric witness, Miss Ross has called her relationship with Kitty Pateman "all she lived for" (349). Both women, like many heterosexual couples, were living in a world made for two; but their relationship, loaded with guilt, had a component of "bad sex," which got expressed in the form of a " 'folie à deux' ": they incited each other to fantasies which neither would have indulged if left to herself. The crucial difference, Cornford stresses, between these women and many other lovers who share fantasies is that Miss Pateman's and Miss Ross's fantasies about "having children in their charge" and about "ultimate freedom"—Eliot recognizes the latter as a slogan among George Passant's group—have been converted into action. Cornford's theory about how the line got crossed between fantasy and action is that guilty relationships, especially when the guilt is unconscious, tend to lead to further guilt. But the central point that Benskin elicits from him is that both defendants had much less responsibility while planning and performing their criminal actions than " 'most of the people' " he meets in everyday life (351–55).

The drama inherent in the subsequent cross-examination is heightened by the contrast between Cornford, the upper-class, Cambridge-educated psychiatrist, sure of his own enlightenment, and Bosanquet, the son of a poor family, who had gone to a north-country grammar school and who, after living in the criminal courts for thirty years, was sure neither of "his own enlightenment [n]or of anyone else's" (356). The verbal battle between Cornford and the prosecutor epitomizes the modern argument about the relationship between crime and mental illness. When the psychiatrist concedes that he would be likely to consider any case in which morbid fantasies were carried out in action an example of diminished responsibility, Bosanquet pounces upon him: " 'I should like to suggest to you that this is a curiously circular position.' " What it amounts to, he argues, is that the very fact of people's committing certain terrible crimes implies they are acting with diminished responsibility. Cornford says that he's not prepared to generalize in this way. To Bosanquet's question, " 'Don't you see that, . . . if we accept that people don't commit crimes when they are responsible, we can dispense with a good deal of our law?' " Cornford answers that he cannot talk about the law but only, as a psychiatrist, about specific persons whom he examines (358).

The "heavy-weight" psychiatrist for the prosecution, Matthew Gough, seems early in his testimony to be concurring in Cornford's view rather than rebutting it. For when Bosanquet, addressing the defendants' claim that they had forgotten what they did to Eric Mawby after Sunday afternoon, suggests to Gough, " 'That is, they were concealing it?' " Gough responds—to Bosanquet's surprise—that he believes it was genuine amnesia: " 'It is quite common for someone to forget the act of killing.' " The psychiatrist goes on, however, to testify, in reply to Bosanquet's questions, that he does not believe the women's planned cruelty and killing to be a proof of impaired responsibility. In each defendant, he carefully states, there is " 'a degree of abnormality.' " But not enough, in terms of the 1957 Act, to diminish responsibility (377–79).

Benskin's cross-examination seeks to establish that Gough's

expert opinion is just one among many, and that the forgetting by both of the defendants of the act af murder indicates " 'to most of us' " an abnormal state of mind. Gough counters with the assertion that in the case of the killing of a child, he has not known the murderer who could recall such an act (381–82). This testimony, despite Benskin's effort to depict Gough as predisposed to hold the women responsible because they are intelligent, evidently impresses the jurors deeply.

Comments made by Cora as a witness remind us, uneasily, of some of the things said during or after the students' hearing earlier in the novel. On direct examination by Benskin, who hopes that her testimony will convince the jurors of her irresponsibility, Cora concedes that though she does not remember the boy's death, she does know that " 'something happened.' " Pressed to explain why she set out to do "something," she says, " 'I suppose you get carried away,' " the same explanation that one of the students had given for fornicating in the sitting room of the university hostel. Cora's answer to Benskin's question whether she was sorry for what she did—" 'I'm sorry that I dragged [Kitty] into it' " (400–02)—recalls the same student's remark that she was only " 'sorry other people get dragged in. That wasn't so good.' " Snow is a scrupulous writer. He does not tendentiously liken the case of child-torturers and murderers to that of students who have copulated semi-publicly. What he does do is evoke a mid-twentieth-century climate of feeling, of which Lewis Eliot, who has delayed the expulsion of the students from the university, and George Passant, who believed in "ultimate freedom"—as well as the students and the criminals—are in their diverse ways a part. In this climate, the sense of personal responsibility has significantly diminished.

Unlike Pamela Hansford Johnson in her non-fictional On Iniquity, Snow does not point to sadistic literature or sub-literature as an aid in the creation of such a climate. Cora's responses in the witness box to Bosanquet's questions indicate that she reads no books, and scarcely a newspaper. She has been "drenched and saturated with sound"; she listens to all kinds of music, often watches television the whole evening through, but in her life there are few printed words (404). As for Kitty, of whom Eliot says that she could not quite bring off her attempt to sound unbalanced as a witness (though she has had one medically attested breakdown and claims to have had a second), she supposedly " 'read a lot.' " But Eliot suspects her of having lied when she gave Camus as an example of the " 'deeper' " authors she had read. And her comment on those authors, " 'Oh, they go to the limit, don't they, I like them when they go to the limit,' " sounds to Eliot like something she has "half-read" (417). Snow's narrator doubts that she has been influenced by her reading. Malignant and shallow, she has evidently wanted to feel cleverer than anyone else in "going to the limit" and getting away with it.

The trial judge, after reviewing for the jury the diametrically opposed testimony of prosecution and defense psychiatrists, emphasizes that the outcome of the trial must not be decided by doctors. In the end, he tells the jurors, they are the judges:

> It is for you to reach a decision as to whether these young women . . . are or are not responsible for these criminal actions, in the sense that you are yourselves for what you do. . . . You will have to be guided by your experience of life, your knowledge of human nature, and I must say, by something we sometimes undervalue, by your common sense. (429)

The jury's verdict is that both Katherine Pateman and Cora Ross are guilty; and the judge imposes the statutory sentence of imprisonment for life. Snow, however, raises a difficult question about the assigned punishment. Eliot has dismissed as boring brightness the remark of one of his acquaintances before the verdict that if the women were sane, they would never do anything of the kind again, in which case there was no justification for keeping them in jail. But in Eliot's account of his visit to Cora in prison after the trial, Snow implicitly asks what should be done with the two killers. Cora wanted to know when Kitty and she would be set free. Eliot explained that the authorities would eventually review their cases, and that the women might be released in about ten years, if there was thought to be no danger.

> "What are you talking about, danger?"
> "They'll need to be sure you won't do anything of the same kind again."
> She gave a short despising laugh.

"They needn't worry themselves. We shan't do anything like that again."

For an instant, I recalled that [acquaintance], too clever by half, making bright remarks before the verdict. . . .

"We shan't do anything like that again," said Cora.

She added: "Why should we?" (454–55)

The only appropriate response to Cora's question is Lear's agonizing question about what "makes these hard hearts." Is there *any* adequate solution to the problem of what to do in the long run with the murderers of Eric Mawby?

Snow's final word on the implications of the case is conveyed through Eliot's telling of George Passant's decision to leave town because his enemies could now smear everything he did, " 'control every step' " he took (440). George's departure, sad because he was more honest and brave than most of those who denounced him, seems nevertheless to confirm the illusiveness of his belief that complete freedom is the highest human good. Eliot's own wife, the narrator observes, has been brought up among people whose rationalism, she used to think, made life too hygienic and thin. Yet she has come to believe that even their way was better than the glorification of unreason. Paraphrasing Goya's title for one of his *caprichos*, "El sueño de la razón produce monstruos" ("The sleep of reason begets monsters"), Eliot says grimly: "Put reason to sleep, and all the stronger forces were let loose. We had seen that happen in our own lifetimes. In the world: and close to us. We knew, we couldn't get out of knowing, that it meant a chance of hell" (445).

While Cozzens's *The Just and the Unjust* scouts the idea that criminals are criminals because of circumstances beyond their control, *The Sleep of Reason* addresses at length the conflict between the belief in individual moral accountability and the attribution of "diminished responsibility" to the perpetrators of hideously lawless acts. Through Lewis Eliot's account of the trial, Snow slants against the defense attorney's argument that the child-murderers should be regarded as ill rather than evil. But despite the horrible fascination with which Eliot himself, the judge, the lawyers, and the audience react to descriptions of the accused women's treatment of Eric Mawby, the courtroom atmosphere seems oddly antiseptic: except perhaps for Cora's outburst, there is no uncontrolled shout of anger, no cry of pain. If in most modern trial fiction reason is subverted by the implication that the struggle for existence, or moral evolution, or revolutionary violence, or God's labyrinthine way, or "the absurd," ultimately determines what is called "justice," calm reason dominates the trial in this novel.

The thoughtful reader in our age, however, might be said to long not merely for the victory of common sense over sophisticated "excuses" for crime but also for a convincing intimation that common sense—or "right reason" that knows natural law—is an integral part of the universe, even as craziness or evil is. Snow and Cozzens do not satisfy this desire because their rationality is rather desiccated; it is not combined with a lively sympathy for human beings, a generosity of spirit. Nevertheless, *The Sleep of Reason* and *The Just and the Unjust* constitute provocative dissents from the overwhelming condemnation of the criminal trial in modern fiction.

NOTES

1. Pierre Michel, *James Gould Cozzens* (New York: Twayne, 1974) 8.

2. Zechariah Chafee, Jr., *Harvard Law Review*, 61.5 (March 1943): 836.

3. James Gould Cozzens, *The Just and the Unjust* (New York: Harcourt, 1942) 109.

4. James Gould Cozzens, *Men and Brethren* (1936; New York: Harcourt, n.d.) 139–40.

5. Harper Lee, *To Kill a Mockingbird* (New York: Warner, 1982).

6. Pamela Hansford Johnson, *On Iniquity: Some Personal Reflections Arising out of the Moors Murder Trial* (London: Macmillan, 1967) 7.

7. C. P. Snow, *The Sleep of Reason* (New York: Scribner's, 1968) 34.

Conclusion:

Toward a Renewal of the Dialogue

IT IS BECAUSE IMAGINATIVE LITERATURE reveals the values and attitudes of the society that gives it birth that I find the rarity of clear ethical standards of justice in modern European and American trial fiction so disturbing. Roland Barthes takes 1850 as the approximate date at which the writer ceased to be "a witness of the universal" and became an "unhappy conscience."[1] For me, 1880 roughly divides pre-modern literature, with its dialectic between an idealistic notion of justice based on belief in universal natural law and a cynical Thrasymachean conception of justice as "the interest of the stronger," from a modern literature almost devoid of lucid idealism. When modern trial fiction does not articulate Thrasymachus's view, it tends to define justice in murky evolutionary or revolutionary terms, or to posit a mysterious, loving God as compensation for a lack of earthly justice, or to see justice as impossible in an absurd world. Rare are the modern trial fictions that point with some clarity to an ethical standard derived from natural law—which, as a contemporary philosopher of natural law, Yves R. Simon, points out, can be interpreted in terms of social justice as well as justice to the individual.[2] I shall return to the subject of exceptions to the modern fictional trend. But first I want to discuss some modern Western works not dealt with earlier in this book, whose treatments of the trial accord with the contemporary anti-idealistic orthodoxy.

Ugo Betti's drama *The Landslide* (*Frana allo scalo Nord*, 1932; first performed, in Rome, in 1936) emphasizes in a manner reminiscent of religiously oriented fiction by Tolstoy, Dostoevsky, and Mauriac the weakness or unreliability of reason. The play focuses on the effort of a judge in an unnamed city to affix responsibility for an accident at a railway construction site that has caused several deaths and cases of insanity. Parsc, the judge, is at first confident that "the facts" pertinent to the catastrophe will readily be discovered. But his interrogations of laborers at the site, and members of their families, as well as the entrepreneur who had employed the laborers, and the head of the electric railroad that had contracted out the work, produce utterly contradictory and confused versions of the accident. Mutual recriminations among witnesses modulate into bewildering confessions of personal guilt—until Parsc himself finally avows that for most of his life he has been "a pleasure-seeking pig and an egotist" who has kept himself going "by pretending to believe in so many fine things," although he "didn't really believe in anything at all. Justice, the law, . . . ha! I'm sick to death of sitting up here playing the fool." Telling the prosecutor-general to "take your stupid papers," he scatters documents about the floor. But everyone in the courtroom, after gathering around the papers, replaces them on the judge's table and in his hands, saying, "We have undoubtediy sinned, Your Honor. We want to be punished." The prosecutor-general now argues persuasively that "they"—including himself and Parsc— "want to be punished so they can be certain that they are walking together and that their journey is not in vain." Soon the judge, continually prompted by the prosecutor general, intones:

> In the name of God; in the name of the law; we declare that these men . . . have themselves pronounced their just and proper sentence. They pronounce it every day, in the lives that they lead and the torments that they suffer. We declare that by themselves they have found their certainty. And perhaps from the hands of the judge they will need to have something else, something higher: compassion. Compassion.

All in the courtroom join in as if in response to prayer: "Compassion. Compassion."[3]

One commentator on Betti's plays believes that in *The Landslide* the playwright is simply indicating the "need for reciprocal compassion" in consequence of "the terrible inadequacy of human justice."[4] But surely Parsc's reference to the judge from whose hands "they will need . . . compassion" evokes the God in whose name he delivers his "verdict," a God on whom human beings in their moral feebleness must depend for understanding. Betti's perspective in *The Landslide* resembles Tolstoy's denial, in "God Sees the Truth, But Waits," of man's capacity to know truth or justice, Dostoevsky's subversion of rationality in Dmitri's trial in

The Brothers Karamazov, and Mauriac's contrast between the corrupt acquittal of the poisoner-protagonist of *Thérèse Desqueyroux* and Thérèse's hunger to know a compassionate, loving God.

While modern religious trial fiction recalls Augustine's insistence on sinful man's need to rely absolutely on God, and tends to reject the Thomistic notion of a polity in which rational human beings can approximate justice by following natural law, modern social trial fiction commonly depicts the courtroom as a Darwinian jungle. Some social writers, like Dreiser, in *An American Tragedy*, see this jungle as unreclaimable. Others, like Martin du Gard and Brecht, present it as susceptible of either evolutionary or revolutionary transformation. What is not clear in the works of such relatively hopeful writers is the ethical grounding of the "just" polity to come. Richard Wright, for example, lets the reader of *Native Son* (1940) infer that the racial oppression responsible for creating a killer like Bigger Thomas might end if the Marxist views of Bigger's lawyer were translated into revolutionary action.[5] But while Wright's analysis of American racism, including its contamination of the trial of a black man like Bigger, is telling, the novel leaves us in as much doubt as does Brecht's Marxist play *The Caucasian Chalk Circle* about the criteria of justice in a revolutionized society. I do not mean, in saying this, to asperse the artistry of either Wright's novel or Brecht's drama any more than I intend to denigrate that of Dostoevsky's *The Brothers Karamazov* by emphasizing its subversion of rationalism. I am simply emphasizing that some of the most important modern writers exhibit in their treatment of justice an uncertainty about ethical standards that pervades European and American culture.

Susan Glaspell's "A Jury of Her Peers" is a Darwinian story that evokes the structural injustice of the American legal system toward women in the early twentieth century. Published in 1917, "A Jury" concerns a woman who is revealed to have strangled her stingy, cold, uncommunicative husband. Two other women, one of them married to "the law" as the sheriff's wife, infer Minnie Wright's guilt and the reason for her violent act from evidence overlooked by the men investigating the case.[6] These women constitute themselves, in effect, a jury of her peers at a time when, in the United States, women were generally excluded from jury service.[7] Drawn together by the contempt expressed for their "petty" female concerns by the county district attorney and the sheriff, the women discover in Minnie's kitchen a mutilated songbird that they conclude must have been killed by Mr. Wright. The mutilation, they intuit, was the immediate cause of Minnie's murder of a man whose persistent meanness has destroyed her vitality and sanity during years of rural isolation. As the story ends, the two women conceal from the investigators, who strongly suspect Minnie's guilt, the circumstantial evidence—the body of the dead canary—which would have been needed in court to demonstrate her motive for committing the crime.

Glaspell arouses our sympathy for both Minnie and her female protectors, our dislike for the complacent male characters and for the judicial system which deems women "unfit" to serve as jurors. The ad hoc "jury of her peers" is actuated by what Carol Gilligan, in her book on women's moral development, calls "an ethic of care."[8] But Glaspell's sardonic tale points to no clear reconciliation of conflicting "male" and "female" perspectives on justice.

The Soviet writer Vladimir Tendryakov's story "Justice" ("Sud," 1961) is a more complex variation on the Darwinian "fitness" theme. The protagonist, Simon Teterin, is a hunter in northern Russia who discovers evidence that would clear his friend, Mityagin, of the accidental shooting of a man during a hunt, and would incriminate a powerful, generally respected industrialist, Dudyrev. The evidence, a bullet fired from Mityagin's gun that Simon finds in the body of a dead bear, strongly indicates that the other bullet, fatal to the man, must have been fired by Dudyrev. But when Simon brings his evidence to the industrialist, Dudyrev turns down his plea to clarify the matter, and suggests that the hunter bring the bullet to the public prosecutor. The prosecutor, however, unwilling to investigate further, puts it to Simon that he has simply made up a story to protect Mityagin's name. Confused and frightened, Simon finally recants in the court his original story, and Dudyrev "magnanimously" declares, in view of the impossibility of knowing who had fired the fatal bullet, that he and Mityagin must share the blame.[9]

This post-Stalinist story is "Thrasymachean" in that the "interest of the stronger," Dudyrev, determines the justice that is publicly rendered. Privately, Dudyrev is troubled by doubts, which he tries to repress, about his responsibility for the accident;

but the prosecutor is chiefly concerned to avoid a conflict with the popular industrialist. And Simon, although completely at home in the woods of northern Russia, cannot deal adequately with the moral sinuosities of civilized life. His situation invites a contrast with Michael Kohlhaas's in Kleist's early nineteenth-century, pre-Darwinian novella. For Kohlhaas persists in adhering to ethical natural law even after he has been denied due process in the eourts. It is true that he violates natural law while defending it—and the incendiary violence he has committed leads to his being executed after his vindication in a civil suit with respect to his own demand for justice. Despite the complexity of Kohlhaas's situation, however, the reader can believe in the reality of both the justice that he invokes and the justice that he ultimately consents to be judged by. In Simon's case, on the other hand, his tragic inability to remain loyal to the truth he knows—because such loyalty would undoubtedly have led to his reputation's being smeared in court by the prosecutor—results in our seeing justice as a kind of orphan. It exists, but only abstractly, for there is finally nobody in the world of "Justice" who defends it rather than his own interests.

While modern social writers tend either, like Dreiser in *An American Tragedy* or Tendryakov in "Justice," to indicate no alternative to a bleakly Darwinian "justice," or, like Martin du Gard in *Jean Barois*, Brecht in *The Caucasian Chalk Circle*, Wright in *Native Son*, and possibly Glaspell in "A Jury of Her Peers," to project "true" justice into a vaguely defined future to be reached by evolution or revolution, the absurdist writers—Melville, Kafka, Camus, Kundera—are those most typical of the modern age. They reject the possibility of a rational standard of justice in a world they perceive as utterly chaotic and irrational.

Katherine Anne Porter's "Noon Wine" (1936) is as absurdist in its way as Camus's *The Outsider*. All the major characters in this disturbing American novella exhibit, at times, symptoms of irrationality; and the climactic episode—the ax-killing by a Texas farmer of a bounty hunter who has tried to arrest, for a reward, his "loony" handyman, seems to be the result of an hallucination brought on by the farmer's anger and the extreme August heat. The handyman, Olaf Helton, is a silent, competent, harmonica-playing Swede who has been doing nearly all the work on Royal

Earle Thompson's farm for nine years. He has brought order out of the chaos into which Thompson, whose sickly wife, Ellie, cannot work much, has let the farm fall. Except for one incident that troubled Ellie, although her husband angrily blamed it entirely on their two young sons—Helton's violently shaking the boys after they dirtied his harmonicas by blowing into them—the family and Helton have lived together on excellent terms. One hot day, the bounty-hunter, Homer T. Hatch, arrives, conceals his purpose awhile beneath aggressive pleasantries, then tells Thompson that Helton had escaped from a North Dakota insane asylum where he had been confined after going "crazy with the heat"[10] and killing with a pitchfork his brother, who had lost and refused to replace Olaf's new harmonica. Hatch has tracked Helton down with the aid of a letter, enclosing a check for $850.00 (probably, we realize, all of Helton's savings), which the handyman had recently sent to his old mother in North Dakota. Worried by Hatch's story—would Helton go crazy again?—but loyal to the handyman, and angry at this "dirty low-down hound" (194) for prying into other people's business, Thompson refuses to cooperate with Hatch in handcuffing and arresting Helton. Telling the bounty-hunter that *he* is the crazy one, Thompson threatens to knock him down for trespassing if he doesn't immediately go away. What happens next, in the intense heat, Thompson later cannot make "come straight" (196–97). He remembers seeing Helton running toward him and Hatch, his eyes wild, and coming between them with his fists doubled up. Then Thompson recalls Hatch's driving at Helton with a long bowie knife; and Thompson can see, in his mind's eye, the knife going into Helton's stomach. The farmer also remembers seizing an ax from a stump and bringing it down on Hatch's head, "as if he were stunning a beef."

At that moment, Thompson thought that Helton had been killed. But Ellie, arriving on the scene after hearing the men's shouts, screamed, "Why, yonder goes Mr. Helton" (197), as the handyman ran through the orchard like one pursued by dogs. She also saw a man whom she did not know, lying doubled up with his bloody head smashed in.

Helton, when finally overtaken by the sheriff and his men, hadn't a scratch on him, but his violent resistance to being captured led to their injuring him mortally; he died after flinging himself against the walls and floor of a prison cell.

Thompson, his case presented by an adroit lawyer, is acquitted on grounds of self-defense. But he can convince neither himself nor the neighbors he visits, seriatim, in the company of an uncomfortable, though publicly loyal Ellie, that he has not committed murder. Ellie, missing the sweetly plaintive harmonica tune that Helton used to play over and over, bitterly condemns men's violence, especially her husband's; she thinks, "he has to be a murderer and ruin his boy's lives and cause Mr. Helton to be killed like a mad dog" (201). One night, she has a terrible fit, rolling on the bed and screaming; when the older son, summoned by Thompson's shouts, bursts into the bedroom, he furiously blames his father for scaring his mother to death: " 'What did you do to her? . . . You touch her again, and I'll blow your heart out!' "

Demoralized, Thompson tells his boys that " 'I never did your mother any harm in my life, on purpose.' " Then, after writing a note solemnly swearing that he " 'did not take the life of Mr. Homer T. Hatch on purpose,' " but that Hatch " 'came to do wrong to a harmless man,' " he kills himself with his shotgun (210–12).

The sudden violent acts, "fits," and bitter verbal assaults in "Noon Wine" contrast eerily with the apparent calm of life in a rural Texas community. When the reader reflects on the story, however, Thompson's hallucination (his going "crazy with the heat"?) becomes emblematic of a madness that seems to infect human existence. The courtroom acquittal—the trial itself, for that matter—appears to be as meaningless as the judicial process culminating in Meursault's condemnation in *The Outsider*. In both these fictional works, human beings seem not to be rational animals, as Aristotle, Aquinas, Voltaire, and other writers in the natural law tradition had perceived them, but creatures of tempestuous impulses that they can neither understand nor control.

In Jean Anouilh's absurdist *Antigone* (1944), written after France's occupation by the Nazis, the eternal laws that the heroine of Sophocles's *Antigone* invokes in defense of her violation of Creon's edict forbidding the burial of Polyneices, are ultimately unimportant to the protagonist. For although at first she states that she must bury Polynice, whom Créon has denounced as a traitor to Thebes, in order to prevent him from wandering restlessly through eternity, she is soon disenchanted by Créon's argument that Polynice was a worthless fellow: after gambling away a large sum of money, he had reviled and struck his own father, Oedipus. Stunned, Antigone agrees to stop defying her uncle and to marry his son, Hémon, whom she loves. But Créon's complacent praise of "happiness" immediately disgusts her: this happiness strikes her as the ignominious acceptance of pretense, of compromise, of the disappearance from life of all freshness and beauty. Fearful now that even Hémon's love for her will eventually disappear—she has always felt that she is far less attractive than her conventional sister, Ismene—she refuses the opportunity Créon gives her to save her life, even though, as she write to Hémon, she does not know what she is dying for.

Anouilh's treatment of Créon's reluctant decision to condemn his niece to death for reasons of state agrees with the author's existentialist perspective on Antigone's decision to die. For Créon's "justice" is simply the working of his will in the interest of keeping Thebes united. While he regards the two brothers who had died together on the battlefield, Etéocle and Polynice, as equally disloyal to Thebes, he is determined to give the people what he believes they need: a hero, on the one hand; a traitor, on the other. Antigone's choice of death is a gratuitous act, dictated by sheer contempt of life itself. Créon's choice is motivated entirely by political pragmatism. There is no transcendent law, as there is in Sophocles's drama, which anybody in this version of *Antigone* feels bound to obey.[11]

In a manner differently absurdist from Anouilh's, the Swiss writer Adolf Muschg evokes in the short story "Reparations or Making Good" ("Der Wiedergutmacher," in *Der blaue Mann*, 1974) the failure of a trial to render a justice that can be ethically defined. Armin Bleuler, a fifty-year-old Swiss civil servant employed by a crematorium in the early 1940s, pleads guilty to "corpse-looting." When mourners indicated, on an official form, their desire that any wedding ring found on the corpse should remain there, rather than be handed over to them before the cremation, Armin had appropriated the ring. On the other hand—and this puzzles the court—never has he pocketed a ring which had been specifically requested by a mourner, even when it was too deeply embedded in the corpse's flesh to be removed with the aid of a piece of soap. In such cases, Armin would tell the mourner that "the dear departed would not give up the ring but be faithful beyond fire and the grave." For Armin, who "did not want to know"—the author sardonically remarks—that you could be unfaithful with a ring on your finger, "honored fidelity under all circumstances."[12]

The story emphasizes the disjunction between a rigid private morality, or rather a sense of "respectability," which Armin has imbibed from his father, and what the narrator implies is the indifference of Armin, his family, and their contemporaries generally, to the social and political horrors of the pre-World War II and World War II periods. Armin's father, a foundry laborer frequently unemployed during the 1920s and early 1930s—his sense of manhood had been saved only by his wife's many childbirths—had suddenly become employable "beyond expectation" when, after the Nazis' takeover of Germany, the Swiss generals' demands for weapons, "accompanied by the mothers' prayers," once more rewarded loyalty and fitness with hard cash." Father Bleuler, who had sometimes reproached his own children as the "children of drunkenness," was now rid of "all inclinations toward alcohol, coitus, or rebellion" (54–55). And Armin learned from this harsh father, whom he had come to hate, that anything in life would be preferable to manual labor.

Armin's corpse-looting was directly related to this socio-economic lesson and to what he had recently been told by the wealthy Swiss who employed him—while he was also working at the cemetery—as a gardener: that the maid, Armin's fiancée Sabine, was pregnant; that other people might not believe what the astonished Armin now stated—that he had never had intercourse with her; and that the employer was prepared to make a christening gift of 10,000 francs if Armin quickly married Sabine; the employer "would even be willing to have the pavilion near the rose-garden cleaned out and prepared as a live-in apartment . . . without Armin having to give up his position with the city administration" (63–64).

Suppressing both his shock and his urge to murder the employer, Armin had not replied, but had immediately sought out

Sabine, slapped her face, torn off the engagement ring from her finger, and possessed her on top of the laundry basket. Then his rage at her for having surrendered to their employer "with my ring on your finger" had inspired him—to his own horror at his sexual athleticism—to a second tumbling of "the faithless one." After this feat, his persistent questioning of Sabine drew from her a gratifying comparison of his lovemaking with the boss's, which emboldened him to up the ante to the employer: "15,000 francs for the woman, no further services whatsoever." From then on, Armin was driven by a determintion to "climb" in the world, by any means, as well as by a desire to humiliate Sabine, whose pregnancy terminated in a stillbirth which he attributed to her "selfishness": she "just hadn't wanted to part with the child to whom he would have been a good father" (64–66).

The court, sympathetic to Armin for the delicate discrimination of his corpse-looting, nevertheless feels compelled to give him four months' probation, and to impose on Sabine—whom we know Armin has vengefully involved in the ring sales—a short suspended sentence for receiving stolen property. His social climbing, however, is only temporarily impeded, for the trial judge's influence with the police superintendent gets Armin, after a discreet surveillance period, a job on the police force. As for Sabine, she dies at forty-six of what "they say" was cancer of the uterus. "Nothing you can do about that" (69–72).

Muschg attributes Armin's behavior and attitudes to his acculturation in a family and society that regard sexual pleasure as wrong and that make no moral response to the cruelties of unemployment and war. The tone of Muschg's observation, for example, that Armin "became engaged to a decent girl [Sabine] in the fall of 1942, after Hitler's assault on Russia" (60), evokes an atmosphere of ethical listlessness. It would be possible for an author to treat the contrast between rigid private respectability and the abdication of humane social responsibility in the vein of social criticism. But Muschg belongs not to the family of Martin du Gard, Glaspell, Dreiser, Wright, Brecht, and Koestler, but the absurdist family of Kafka, Porter, Camus, Anouilh, and Kundera. For he indicates that human rationality is far too weak and occasional for us to place any reliance upon it. We live, he seems to imply, amid moral chaos: the notion of a "good society" is a myth, and whatever relatively good sense manifests itself in a trial, or anywhere else, is insignificant.

Overwhelming as the tendency of modern trial literature is to suggest that there are no clear ethical standards of justice, a small number of serious fictions depart to some extent from this orthodoxy. I have indicated my sense of the limitations of novels by Cozzens and Snow as such "dissenting" works: both *The Just and the Unjust* and *The Sleep of Reason* present the courtroom as a haven for rationality in a world of great violence and unreason, but neither work recognizes sufficiently the importance of social circumstances in impelling a person to lead either a "straight" life or one classified by the law as criminal. Among the modern fictions I have discussed so far, the one that seems to me to adumbrate most persuasively the idea of justice as ethical reason is Koestler's *Darkness at Noon*. For the "old Bolshevik" protagonist, Rubashov, realizes after playing his assigned role in a 1930s "show" trial that the Party has produced disaster by throwing overboard all "ethical ballast." He wonders, just before being shot, whether a new Party will arise some day, wearing monks' cowls and preaching not only "economic fatality" but also the truth that moral ends can be reached only through moral means. Although Koestler does not develop the thought further at this point, earlier passages in the novel make it plain that Koestler conceives of morality, hence justice, in terms of the injunctions of Judeo-Christian natural law. It is true that Rubashov can only hope that "perhaps" (a word that often recurs during his final minutes) a decent new Party will arise. In the dismal weather of the twentieth century, however, *Darkness at Noon* is at least a faint beacon.

Another somewhat heterodox modern novel, and one of the rare fictions by a Western writer to describe a trial in a colonial setting, is E. M. Forster's *A Passage to India* (1924). The trial is brought about by a young British woman's charge of attempted rape against a Moslem doctor who had invited her and her fiancé's mother to visit the famous Marabar caves. Even before the trial begins, Adela Quested has come to doubt that Aziz, the doctor, had actually made advances to her in one of the caves. But she is confused by a persistent echo in her head that she first heard at Marabar, and the members of the Anglo-Indian community put such heavy pressure on her to punish Aziz that only when giving

testimony in court does she muster the courageous clarity to say
that she has made a mistake. Aziz is consequently acquitted, and
justice is done in the sense that a particular Indian, after undergo-
ing a painful ordeal, has received his due from a court established
under British authority. But Aziz's escape from an unjust verdict
is fortuitous: the case has not been carefully or impartially inves-
tigated by the government, and Anglo-Indian prejudice against
"niggers" has come close to carrying the day. Forster clearly
indicates that British-controlled "justice" is strongly skewed
toward the community that holds political power. Whatever hope
he lets us entertain that the judicial situation will ever change
markedly arises from the attitudes and behavior toward the Indians
of two British characters—Cyril Fielding, the Principal of the
Government College, and Mrs. Moore, the mother of Adela's
fiancé. Fielding, rational and kind, represents the English, at least
the male English, at their best. He likes and trusts Aziz, and writes
to Adela before the trial to say that the doctor is innocent. Mrs.
Moore, intuitive rather than rational, has met Aziz by chance in a
mosque shortly after arriving with Adela in India. She has immediately taken to him, and he to her, and she later declares flatly to
Adela that he is innocent. By the time she says this, however, she
herself has had a strangely disagreeable experience in one of the
caves, and been left with a sense of the insignificance of human
concerns. Although willing to attend Adela's wedding to her
son—which never occurs—she refuses to testify at the trial, telling
her civil servant son that she has "nothing to do with your
ludicrous law courts."[13] When he criticizes this attitude, she cries
out petulantly that " 'The human race would have become a single
person centuries ago if marriage was of any use.' " And she goes
on to denounce " 'all this rubbish about love, love in a church,
love in a cave, as if there is the least difference . . .' " (201–02). Yet
Mrs. Moore, who rejects Adela's description of her as " 'so
good,' " and calls herself " 'bad,' " (205) is much loved by the
Indians. When she leaves for England at her son's behest, they
suspect that she has been gotten out of the way to prevent her
from testifying for Aziz. Her death at sea helps to elevate her, in
their eyes, to the status of a god.

Perhaps Forster is suggesting that a combination of Fielding's
sturdy, intelligent good will and Mrs. Moore's almost mystical

empathy and virtual self-identification with a people whose cultures and ethnic backgrounds differ so much from her own, could effect a real "passage to India." Were such a reconciliation to occur, trials like the one described in the novel would never take place; for the mutual respect called for by the Golden Rule, a cardinal tenet of natural law, would largely govern human relationships. One hardly believes, at the end of *A Passage to India*— where Aziz, wanting the British out of his country, cannot, despite his affection for Fielding, regard him as a friend—that such a reconciliation will occur. But Forster, aware as he is of everything that militates against justice in colonial India, points with some clarity to the idea of a polity more just.

A slighter work than *A Passage to India*, and published a generation after it, Harper Lee's *To Kill a Mockingbird* (1960) has in common with Forster's novel a milieu in which strong color prejudice poisons the atmosphere of a trial.[14] Alabama in the 1930s—a few years after the "Scottsboro boys" were tried for allegedly raping two white girls—is the setting of Lee's story about the condemnation to death of a Negro who is innocent of the rape with which he has been charged. The black man, Robinson, is eventually shot and killed when he makes a desperate attempt to escape from the death house. Yet Robinson's white lawyer, Atticus Finch, sees in some aspects of the trial reasons to believe that the community from which the prejudiced white male jury was chosen is gradually gaining respect for the legal rights of colored persons. The fact that instead of assigning a run-of-the-mill lawyer to Robinson's defense, the judge had chosen Finch, notorious in the county for his advocacy of equal rights for blacks, is one reason for his hopefulness. Another reason is that the jury took a comparatively long time to report its shameful verdict: the jurymen were evidently troubled by the bias that was dictating their decision. In short, this miscarriage of justice in a small Southern town is perceived by Lee's lawyer-protagonist as a short step in a too-slow advance toward judicial fairness.

Despite its vivid dramatizations, some of them finely satirical, of anti-black prejudice, and its evocation of a few whites' bravely decent acts—which the white community in general regards at best as eccentricities—*To Kill a Mockingbird* seems to me too pat in its liberalism to confront the racial issue as a complex phenome-

non. Lee does not probe deeply enough into the social circumstances that have kept ugly anti-black feeling intensely alive in the
South (as well as elsewhere in the United States) a generation after
her book was published. Still, the novel suggests possibilities for
a fiction animated by a sense of justice as well as of injustice.

The interdependence between fiction and the attitudes and
values of the culture that shapes it is complex. But the pervasive
cynicism about trials and justice in modern imaginative literature
is surely to some extent a reaction against smug pieties in the
Western world about "justice for all." It would be ridiculous to
suggest that any writer has a "duty" to compose in a hopeful
vein. André Gide aptly observed that it is not with good senti-
ments that one makes good literature. For the sake, however, of
the dangerously decaying society we live in, we should hope that
fiction writers will want to go beyond the delineation of injustice,
to intimate what they believe justice might be. It is possible, after
all, to conceive of absurdities in the world without conceiving of
the world as altogether absurd; or to see that most human beings
have "better" natures as well as the ones that they exhibit in the
heat of the struggle for existence. The idea of ethical natural law,
adapted to our age by a strong emphasis on distributive as well as
humane retributive justice at the global level, could provide us
with a worthy goal. But before indicating in specific terms what I
mean, I must address the chief criticisms that have been made of
the concept of natural law.

They have been effectively marshaled by John Hart Ely in
Democracy and Distrust: A Theory of Judicial Review (1980).[15] After
quoting Blackstone's assertion that the " 'law of nature . . . is
binding over the whole globe, and in all countries and at all
times' " (48), Ely undercuts it by citing Benjamin Wright's attack
on natural law for having had as its content

> whatever the individual in question desired to advocate. This has
> varied from a defence of theocracy to a defence of the complete
> separation of church and state, from revolutionary rights in 1776 to
> liberty of contract in recent judicial opinions, from the advocacy of
> universal adult suffrage to a defence of rigid limitations upon the
> voting power, from philosophical anarchy in 1849 with Thoreau to
> strict paternalism five years later with Fitzhugh, from the advocacy
> of the inalienable right to secession to the assertion of the natural

law of judicial supremacy, from the right of majority rule to the rights of vested interests.[16]

Ely follows up Wright's indictment by quoting what he says may be "the most explicit invocation of natural law" in a United States Supreme Court opinion: Justice Bradley's in *Bradwell* v. *Illinois* (1872), denying a woman's application to become a lawyer:

"[T]he civil law, as well as nature herself, has always recognized a wide difference in the respective spheres of men and women. . . . The constitution of the family organization, which is founded in the divine ordinance, as well as in the nature of things, indicates the domestic sphere as that which properly belongs to the domains and functions of womanhood. . . . The paramount destiny and mission of woman are to fulfill the noble and benign offices of wife and mother. This is the law of the creator."

" 'Reliance on the nature of things,' " Ely remarks, "recurs in *Plessy* v. *Ferguson*" (51). This, of course, was the 1896 case in which the Supreme Court ruled that the railroad segregation of blacks and whites was permissible as long as the facilities provided to Negroes and whites were "equal."

Finally, as if to drive a nail into the coffin of ethical natural law, Ely quotes Unger's disdainful contemptuous comments in *Knowledge and Politics* (1975):

"[A]ll the many attempts to build a moral and political doctrine upon the conception of a universal human nature have failed. They are repeatedly trapped in a dilemma. Either the allegedly universal ends are too few and abstract to give content to the idea of the good, or they are too numerous and concrete to be truly universal. One has to choose between triviality and implausibility." (Ely 51–52)

With respect to Wright's list of contradictory invocations of natural law, as well as to Bradley's Victorian opinion, and the Plessy decision, it seems to me that natural law has been poorly served by those of its advocates who have cited it in contexts in which it is not applicable. There are many aspects of human behavior and public policy that can be effectively and fairly regulated only by positive laws that do vary from time to time, from place to place. Here, the discussion of natural law during the Clarence Thomas Supreme Court confirmation hearings is to the point. Thomas had seen the Constitution, in many speeches and articles, in the light of natural law. In 1987, he had praised an article attacking the *Roe* v. *Wade* decision on abortion as a violation of natural law. Yet, during the hearings in 1991, he insisted in response to repeated questioning that he had simply been expressing his views on a "political theory," not speaking as a "judge who would actually decide cases by reference to natural law "[17]

Clearly, adjudication or legislation based on what is alleged to be natural law may constitute what many jurists today would regard as an illegitimate intrusion into people's private lives. H. L. A. Hart, in *Law, Liberty, and Morality* (1963), quotes approvingly both the English Wolfenden Commission's view that " 'There must remain a realm of private morality and immorality which is, in brief and crude terms, not the law's business' " and the recommendation of the American Law Institute's Penal Code " 'that all consensual relations between adults in private should be excluded from the scope of criminal law.' "[18] My own argument in favor of an adaptation to modern conditions of natural law should not be misconstrued: I reject the notion of regulating private, intimate behavior that involves only adults. At the heart of the natural law tradition—which, as we have seen, is secular as well as religious—is a concern for the common weal, not with individuals' sexual appetites and passions.

That a natural law does exist which is neither, *pace* Unger, trivial nor implausible, is indicated by the important distinction between *malum in se* and *malum prohibitum*. *Malum in se*, which has been defined as " 'naturally evil, as adjudged by the sense of a civilized community,' " refers to an " 'act or case involving illegality from the very transaction, upon principles of natural, moral and public law.' " "For example, murder is 'malum in se' because even without a specific criminal prohibition the community would think it to be an evil and wrongful act." *Malum prohibitum*, on the other hand, refers to "an act which is wrong only because it is so by statute." An example would be "speeding" along the highway, as contrasted with reckless driving, which would be considered *malum in se*.[19] Marriage between first cousins is prohibited in some jurisdictions, permitted in others. But laws against kidnapping, rape, robbery, and defamation are based on natural law—a general and profound aversion to these acts. It is notable that Oliver Wendell Holmes, one of the best-known modern adversaries of the natural law tradition, a jurist for whom "the law" was nothing but prophecy as to "what the courts will do in fact," conceded that there was a "wider point of view from which the distinction between law and morals becomes of little or no importance."[20] It is a "wider point of view" that I want to take in suggesting some ways in which the natural law tradition might become more vigorously pertinent to modern circumstances, and to the literature of today and tomorrow.

The human repugnance to murder, while universal, obviously conflicts with a powerful tendency in human beings to butcher their fellows, in wars declared and undeclared. The contradiction between the repugnance and the attraction to violence is pointed up by the disjunction between the sentencing to death, notably in the United States, of some persons convicted of murder, and the awarding of honors to members of the armed forces who in wartime have been especially successful in killing the country's enemies. Not only killing, however, but also torture, kidnapping, and libel and slander in the form of "disinformation" are regularly employed by national states, in both hot and cold wars. While international law—which is based on natural law—reproves such national behavior, that law is egregiously flouted by national states except when they find it in their interest to abide by decisions of an international judicial body. In short, there is a striking contrast between the enforcement, however inadequate and inequitable, of ethical rules (natural law) within particular societies, and the sheer chaos that reigns in the international arena. Gerald and Patricia Mische point out, in *Toward a Human World Order* (1977), that under the global system of absolute national sovereignty, political prisoners have no effective recourse to any higher law than that of the very government that imprisons them.[21] What we urgently need, as our fellow-humans are slaughtered and violated, is the intelligence and the will to implement internationally the ethical prohibitions that have traditionally been enforced, to some extent, within national borders.

"Utopia" is the mocking murmur I hear—but even more is required of us if we are to adapt traditional natural law to the conditions of our planet today. In addition to extending effectively to the international sphere the prohibitions against the crimes of murder, torture, kidnapping, bearing false witness, we need to internationalize distributive justice. As I write, starvation in Somalia is evidently the severest problem in this domain that has recently caught the attention of the world community. There are other places, however, where people are in comparably desperate circumstances. Simply at the practical level, even the technologically "developed" peoples will have to overcome taxing problems in order to help effectively their ill and poorly nourished fellows in other lands. But we cannot do that until we acquire a more lively sense than we now have of that universal fraternity on which the Stoics laid stress, and which became one of the watchwords of the French Revolution.[22]

Yves R. Simon has pointed out that in the twentieth century there is the opportunity (which was not available in earlier, less technologically advanced societies) and the necessity to recognize, as part of natural law, society's duty to help ill or aged people who cannot help themselves.[23] I would emphasize that we must extend our moral vision beyond national frontiers—as groups like the medical personnel "without borders" are doing—in order to relieve hunger and illness, and to help enable the education of persons who are truly the wretched of the earth. Ecological consciousness and conscience should also be an essential part of a reformulated natural law. To put the matter too briefly: the injunction not to kill needs to be made thoughtfully applicable to the land, the air, the seas around us, the elements that we share with other animals.

Clearly, it is extremely difficult to say how much we must do, and in what ways to do it, in order to satisfy the demands of distributive justice throughout the world. What we surely can do, however, is to recognize the urgent need to act in the spirit of global fraternity.

The reaction of some readers to what I am saying will be that it takes insufficient account of the selfishness of "human nature." Others will feel that the predominance of corporate power throughout the world would prevent the implementation of a renewed version of natural law. These readers are, in their diverse ways, the descendants of Thrasymachus, whose trenchant definition of justice as the interest of the stronger has overwhelmingly dominated literature since the late nineteenth century. In expressing cynicism about the possibility of *true* legal and social justice, most modern imaginative writers have been, to paraphrase Balzac, the secretaries of a cynical society. Writers, however, have a certain power to shape—not simply to reflect or refract—the attitudes and feelings of their age. Perhaps, increasingly, writers who refuse to accept the death of justice (or of literature) will take seriously the idea of natural law, in something like the form I have tried to delineate. Perhaps there will gradually be re-established a kind of dialogue between the spiritual progeny of Socrates and those of Thrasymachus. Trial fiction can address absorbingly the complex relationships between legal processes and the rendering of justice as fairness, equity, reconciliation. My secular prayer is that fiction writers, who have so compellingly dramatized the corruptions, cruelties, and absurdities of our barbarous time, will speak to us in their disparate voices of new paths to be made, and taken.

NOTES

1. Roland Barthes, *Le Degré Zéro de L'Ecriture; suivi de Eléments de Sémiologie* (1953; 1964; Paris: Gonthier, n.d.) 10. My translation. In Barthes's phrase, "malheureuse conscience," "conscience" seems more appropriately rendered into English by "conscience" than by "consciousness."

2. Simon 163–66.

3. Ugo Betti, *Three Plays on Justice: Landslide, Struggle Till Dawn, The Fugitive*, trans. G. H. McWilliam (San Francisco: Chandler, 1964) 54–58.

4. G. H. McWilliam, "Introduction," in Betti x.

5. Richard Wright, *Native Son* (1940; New York: Literary Classics of the United States, 1991).

6. Susan Glaspell, "A Jury of Her Peers," in *The Best Short Stories of 1917* (Boston: Small, Maynard, 1918) 256–82.

7. See Albie Sachs and Joan Hoff Wilson, *Sexism and the Law: A Study of Male Beliefs and Legal Bias in Britain and the United States* (New York: Free Press, 1978) 122–24.

8. Carol Gilligan, *In a Different Voice: Psychological Theory and Women's Development* (Cambridge: Harvard UP, 1982) 164.

9. See chap. 2, n. 8, above.

10. Katherine Anne Porter, "Noon Wine" (1936) in *Six Great Modern Novels* (New York: Dell, 1967) 191. For a way of reading "Noon Wine"

that differs from mine, see James Boyd White, "Telling Stories in the Law and in Ordinary Life: *The Oresteia* and "Noon Wine," in *Heracles' Bow: Essays on the Rhetoric and Poetics of the Law* (Madison: U of Wisconsin P, 1985) 168–91.

11. Jean Anouilh, *Antigone* (Paris: La Table Ronde, 1946).

12. Adolf Muschg, "Reparations or Making Good," *The Blue Man and Other Stories*, trans. Markis Zeller Cambon and Michael Hamburger (New York: Braziller, 1985) 52.

13. E. M. Forster, *A Passage to India* (1924; New York, Harcourt, n.d.) 200.

14. See chap. 5, n. 5, above.

15. John Hart Ely, *Democracy and Distrust: A Theory of Judicial Review* (Cambridge: Harvard UP, 1980).

16. Ely, *Democracy*, p. 51, citing Benjamin Wright, *American Interpretations of Natural Law* (1931), 339–40n30.

17. *New York Times*, 3 July 1991: 1, and 12 Sept. 1991: A21.

18. H. L. A. Hart, *Law, Liberty and Morality* (Stanford: Stanford UP, 1963) 14–15.

19. Steven H. Gifis, *Law Dictionary* (Woodbury, NY: Barron's, 1975) 123–24.

20. Oliver Wendell Holmes, "The Path of the Law," *American Thought: Civil War to World War I*, ed. Perry Miller (New York: Rinehart, 1954) 186.

21. Gerald and Patricia Mische, *Toward a Human World Order: Beyond the National Security Strait-Jacket* (New York: Paulist, 1977) 192.

22. The German Marxist Ernst Bloch, in *Natural Law and Human Dignity*, trans. Dennis J. Schmidt (Cambridge: MIT P, 1986), remarks that "the Stoic thesis of the unity of the human race, . . . provided the first basis for the ideal of equality" (167), and asserts that "Freedom, equality, fraternity, the orthopedia of the upright carriage, of human pride, and of human dignity, point far beyond the horizon of the bourgeois world" (174).

23. Simon 165.

LIST OF WORKS CITED

Abraham, Henry J. *The Judicial Process: An Introductory Analysis of the Courts of the United States, England, and France.* 3rd ed. New York: Oxford UP, 1975.

Adams, Henry. *The Education of Henry Adams.* Boston: Houghton, 1918.

Aeschylus. *The Oresteia.* Trans. Robert Fagles. New York: Bantam, 1977.

Aguirre, José M. "El alcalde de Zalamea: '¿Venganza o justicia?'" *Estudios filologicos* 7 (1971): 119–32.

Albright, William Foxwell. *From the Stone Age to Christianity: Monotheism and the Historical Process.* New York: Doubleday, 1957.

Anders, Günther. *Kafka.* Trans. A. Steer and A. Thorlby. London: Bowes, 1960.

Anglo-Saxon Poetry. Trans. R. K. Gordon. London: Dent, 1926.

Anouilh, Jean. *Antigone.* Paris: La Table Ronde, 1946.

Arendt, Hannah. "Franz Kafka." *Sechs Essays.* Heidelberg: Schneider, 1948. 128–49. Excerpted in *Franz Kafka* 3–11.

Aristotle. *The Ethics of Aristotle: The Nicomachean Ethics.* Trans. J. A. K. Thompson. Rev. Hugh Tredennick. New York: Penguin, 1976.

——. *Rhetoric.* Trans. W. Rhys Roberts. *Rhetoric and Poetics.* Trans. W. Rhys Roberts and Ingram Bywater. 1954. New York: Modern Library, 1984.

Augustine, St. *The City of God.* Trans. Marcus Dods. New York: Modern Library, 1950.

Balzac, Honoré de. "The Red Inn." *Novels: The Unknown Masterpiece, The Maranas, A Seashore Drama, The Red Inn, Master Cornelius.* Trans. G. Burnham Ives. Philadelphia, 1899. 181–238.

Barthes, Roland. *Le Degré Zéro de l'écriture: Suivi de Éléments de sémiologie.* 1953, 1964. Paris: Gonthier, n.d.

Barton, Anne. Introduction. *Measure for Measure. Riverside Shakespeare* 545–49.

Bayley, John. *Tolstoy and the Novel.* New York: Viking, 1967.

Bentley, Eric. Introduction. Brecht, *Caucasian* 5–14.

Berlin, Isaiah. "Tolstoy and the Enlightenment." *Mightier Than the Sword.* London: Macmillan, 1964. 99–128. Rpt. in *Tolstoy: A Collection of Critical Essays.* Ed. Ralph E. Matlaw. Englewood Cliffs, NJ: Prentice, 1964. 28–51.

Betti, Ugo. *Landslide. Three Plays on Justice: Landslide, Struggle Till Dawn, The Fugitive.* Trans. G. H. McWilliam. San Francisco: Chandler, 1964. 1–58.

Bloch, Ernst. *Natural Law and Human Dignity*. Trans. Dennis J. Schmidt. Cambridge: MIT P, 1986.

Blunden, Allen. "A Chronology of Kafka's Life." *World of Franz Kafka* 11–29.

Boussel, Patrice. *L'Affaire Dreyfus et la presse*. Paris: Colin, 1960.

Brecht, Bertolt. *The Caucasian Chalk Circle*. Trans. Eric Bentley. New York: Grove, 1966.

——. *Der kaukasische Kreidekreis*. Berlin: Suhrkampf, 1955.

Calderón de la Barca, Pedro. *The Mayor of Zalamea*. *Four Plays*. Trans. Edwin Honig. New York: Hill & Wang, 1961. 141–215.

Camus, Albert. Appendix: "Hope and the Absurd in the Work of Franz Kafka." Camus, *Myth* 92–102.

——. *The Fall*. Trans. Justin O'Brien. New York: Vintage, 1956.

——. *The Myth of Sisyphus*. *The Myth of Sisyphus and Other Essays*. Trans. Justin O'Brien. New York: Vintage, 1955. 1–91.

——. *The Outsider*. Trans. Joseph Laredo. 1982. New York: Penguin, 1983.

Chafee, Zechariah, Jr. Rev. of *The Just and the Unjust*, by James Gould Cozzens. *Harvard Law Review* 56 (March 1943): 833–36.

The Chalk Circle. *World Drama* 227–58.

Champigny, Robert. *A Pagan Hero: An Interpretation of Meursault in Camus'* The Stranger. Trans. Rowe Portis. Philadelphia: U of Penn P, 1969.

Chapters in Western Civilization. Ed. Contemporary Civilization Staff of Columbia College, Columbia University. Vol. 1. New York: Columbia UP, 1948. 2 vols.

Chaucer, Geoffrey. "The Tale of Melibee." *The Poetical Works of Chaucer*. Ed. F. N. Robinson. Boston: Houghton, 1933.

Cicero. *On the Laws*. *Selected Works of Cicero*. Roslyn, NY: Black. 218–47.

Clagett, Marshall. "The Medieval Heritage: Political and Economic." *Chapters* 3–73.

Corneille, Pierre. *Cinna*. *Théâtre choisi de Corneille*. Ed. Maurice Rat. Paris: Garnier, 1961. 147–205.

Cozzens, James Gould. *The Just and the Unjust*. New York: Harcourt, 1942.

——. *Men and Brethren*. 1936. New York: Harcourt, n.d.

Dante Alighieri. *The Divine Comedy*. Trans. Laurence Binyon. *The Portable Dante*. Ed. Paolo Milano. New York: Viking, 1947. 3–544.

Darwin, Charles. *The Origin of Species by Means of Natural Selection; or, The Preservation of Favored Races in the Struggle for Life; and The Descent of Man, and Selection in Relation to Sex*. New York: Modern Library, n.d.

DeMoss, William Fenn. *The Influence of Aristotle's "Politics" and "Ethics" on Spenser*. Chicago, 1920. Excerpted in "Appendix I: The Virtue of Justice and the Plan of Book 5." *The Faerie Queene: Book Five*. Ed. Ray Hefner. Vol. 5 of *The Works of Edmund Spenser: A Variorum Edition*. 269–98. Ed. Edwin Greenlaw. 11 vols. Baltimore: Johns Hopkins UP, 1936. 269–98.

Diderot, Denis. *Le Neveu de Rameau*. *Oeuvres Romanesques*. Ed. Henri Bénac. Paris: Garnier, 1962. 395–492.

———. *La Religieuse*. *Oeuvres Romanesques*. 235–393.

Doctorow, E. L. *Ragtime*. 1975. New York: Bantam, 1976.

Dostoevsky, Fyodor. *The Brothers Karamazov*. Trans. Andrew Mac-Andrew. New York: Bantam, 1970.

———. *Notes from Underground, and The Grand Inquisitor, With Relevant Works by Chernyshevsky, Shchedrin, and Dostoevsky*. Sel. and trans. by Ralph E. Matlaw. New York: Dutton, 1960. 3–115.

Dreiser, Theodore. *An American Tragedy*. 1925. New York: NAL, 1964.

———. *Theodore Dreiser: A Selection of Uncollected Prose*. Ed. Donald Pizer. Detroit: Wayne State UP, 1977.

Dumbauld, Edward. *The Life and Legal Writings of Hugo Grotius*. Norman: U of Oklahoma P, 1980.

Dunlop, C. P. B. "Human Law and Natural Law in the Novels of Theodore Dreiser." *Amer. J of Jurisprudence*, 61 (1974): 61–86.

———. "Law and Justice in Dreiser's *An American Tragedy*." *U of British Columbia Law Review* 6 (1972): 379–403.

Earlier English Drama from Robin Hood to Everyman. Ed. Thomas Whitfield Baldwin. New York: Thomas, 1929.

Eliot, George. *Felix Holt, the Radical*. Ed. Fred C. Thomson. Oxford: Oxford UP, 1980.

Ely, John Hart. *Democracy and Distrust: A Theory of Judicial Review*. Cambridge: Harvard UP, 1980.

d'Entrèves, A. P. *Natural Law: An Introduction to Legal Philosophy*. London: Hutchinson, 1951.

Euripides. *Orestes*. Trans. William Arrowsmith. *The Complete Greek Tragedies*. Ed. David Grene and Richmond Lattimore. Vol. 7. New York: Oxford UP, 1945. 11–105. 7 vols.

La Farce de Maistre Pierre Pathelin. Ed. C. E. Pickford. Paris: Bordas, 1967.

The Farce of the Worthy Master, Pierre Patelin, the Lawyer. Trans. Moritz Jagendorf. *The World of Law*. Ed. Ephraim London. Vol. 1. New York: Simon & Schuster, 1960. 472–94. 2 vols.

Fielding, Henry. *The History of Tom Jones, a Foundling*. New York: Modern Library, n.d.

Fiore, Robert L. *Natural-Law Ethics in Spanish Golden Age Theatre*. Lexington: UP of Kentucky, 1975.

Forster, E. M. *A Passage to India*. 1924. New York: Harcourt, n.d.

Fox, Dian. *Kings in Calderón: A Study in Characterization and Political Theory*. London: Tamesis, 1986.

Frankel, Charles, and Donald O'Connell, "The Enlightenment." *Chapters* 336–88.

Franz Kafka: An Anthology of Marxist Criticism. Ed. and trans. Kenneth Hughes. Hanover: UP of New England, 1981.

Frazer, Sir James George. *The Golden Bough: A Study in Magic and Religion*. Abr. ed. in 1 vol. New York: Macmillan, 1942.

Gifis, Steven H. *Law Dictionary*. Woodbury, NY: Barron, 1975.

Gilbert, Allan A. *Dante's Conception of Justice*. Durham, NC: Duke UP, 1925.

Gilligan, Carol. *In a Different Voice: Psychological Theory and Women's Development*. Cambridge: Harvard UP, 1982.

Glaspell, Susan. "A Jury of Her Peers." *The Best Short Stories of 1917*. Boston: Small, Maynard, 1918. 256–82.

Gordis, Robert. "Natural Law and Religion." John Cogley, Robert J. Hutchins, John Courtney Murray, s.j., Scott Buchanan, Philip Selznick, Harvey Wheeler, Robert Gordis. *Natural Law and Modern Society*. Cleveland: World, 1963. 240–76.

Greene, Graham. *The Heart of the Matter*. New York: Viking, 1948.

Greenhouse, Linda. "Sticking to the Script." *New York Times* 12 Sept. 1991: A21.

Greenlaw, Edwin. "Spenser and British Imperialism." *Mod. Philol.* 9 (Jan. 1912): 347–70. Rpt. in *Spenser's Critics: Changing Currents in Literary Taste*. Ed. William R. Mueller. Syracuse: Syracuse UP, 1959. 128–47.

Groethuysen, Bernard. *Origines de l'esprit bourgeois en France*. Paris: Gallimard, 1927.

Hart, H. L. A. *Law, Liberty, and Morality*. Stanford: Stanford UP, 1963.

Havelock, Eric A. *The Greek Concept of Justice, from Its Shadow in Homer to Its Substance in Plato*. Cambridge: Harvard UP, 1978.

Hazard, Paul. *The European Mind: The Critical Years (1680–1715)*. Trans. J. Lewis May. New Haven: Yale UP, 1953. Rpt. New York: Fordham UP, 1992.

Heilman, Robert Bechtold. *This Great Stage: Image and Structure in King Lear*. Seattle: U of Washington P, 1963.

Herndl, George C. *The High Design: English Renaissance Tragedy and the Natural Law*. Lexington: UP of Kentucky, 1970.

Hesiod. *Works and Days*. Trans. Richmond Lattimore. Ann Arbor: U of Michigan P, 1959.

A History of the Western World: Early Modern Times. Ed. Shepard B. Clough. Lexington, MA: Heath, 1969.

Holmes, Oliver Wendell. "The Path of the Law." *Collected Legal Papers.* New York: Harcourt, 1920. 167–202. Rpt. in *American Thought: Civil War to World War I.* Ed. Perry Miller. New York: Rinehart, 1954. 184–206.

Homer. *The Iliad.* Trans. A. T. Murray. 2 vols. Cambridge: Harvard UP, 1976.

——. *The Odyssey.* Trans. A. T. Murray. 2 vols. Cambridge: Harvard UP, 1975.

Ihering, Rodolphe. *Le Combat pour le droit.* Trans. François Maydieu. Paris, 1875.

Introduction to Contemporary Civilization in the West: A Source Book. Ed. Contemporary Civilization Staff, Columbia College, Columbia University. Vol 1. New York: Columbia University Press, 1946. 2 vols.

Jaeger, Werner. "Euripides and His Age." *Paideia: The Ideals of Greek Culture.* Trans. Gilbert Highet. Vol. 1. New York: Oxford UP, 1945. 329–54. 3 vols.

James I. *The Trew Law of Free Monarchies, or, The Reciprock and Mutuall Dutie Betwixt a Free King and His Naturall Subjects.* Rpt. in *Introduction,* 694–710.

Johnson, Pamela Hansford. *On Iniquity: Some Personal Reflections Arising out of the Moors Murder Trial.* London: Macmillan, 1967.

Jonson, Ben. *Volpone. The Selected Works of Ben Jonson.* Ed. Harry Levin. New York: Random, 1938. 209–337.

Kafka, Franz. *The Trial.* Trans. Willa and Edwin Muir. Rev. ed. with addit. material trans. by E. M. Butler, 1968. New York: Schocken, 1974.

Kamen, Henry. *The Spanish Inquisition.* 1965. New York: NAL, 1975.

Kermode, Frank. "The Faerie Queene, I and V." *Bull. of the John Rylands Library,* 47 (1965): 123–50. Rpt. in *Essential Articles for the Study of Spenser.* Ed. A. C. Hamilton. Hamden, CT: Archon, 1972. 267–88.

Kleist, Heinrich von. "Michael Kohlhaas." *The Marquise of O—and Other Stories.* Trans. David Luke and Michael Reeves. Harmondsworth: Penguin, 1978. 114–213.

Knipovich, Evgeniya. "Frants Kafka: *Inostrannaya Literatura.* 1964. No. 1. 195–204. Rpt., with two passages from her *Sila Pravdy: Literaturnokriticheskie stat'i* (Moscow: Sovetskii Pisatel', 1965), 343–45 and 349–54 in *Franz Kafka* 186–205.

Koestler, Arthur. *Darkness at Noon.* Trans. Daphne Hardy. 1941. New York: Bantam, 1977.

——. *The Invisible Writing: The Second Volume of an Autobiography, 1932–40.* New York: Stein and Day, 1984.

Kroeber, Karl. *Romantic Narrative Art*. Madison: U of Wisconsin P, 1961.

Kucherow, Samuel. *Courts, Lawyers, and Trials Under the Three Tsars*. New York: Praeger, 1953.

Kundera, Milan. *The Book of Laughter and Forgetting*. Trans. Michael Henry Heim. Harmondsworth: Penguin, 1981.

———. *The Joke*. Trans. Michael Henry Heim. Harmondsworth: Penguin, 1983.

Langland, William. *Piers the Ploughman*. Trans. J. F. Goodridge. Harmondsworth: Penguin, 1966.

Lee, Harper. *To Kill a Mockingbird*. 1960. New York: Warner, 1982.

Lever, J. W. Introduction. *Measure for Measure*, by William Shakespeare. London: Methuen, 1965. xi–xcviii.

Levin, Harry. *The Gates of Horn: A Study of Five French Realists*. New York: Oxford UP, 1966.

———. Introduction. *The Selected Works of Ben Jonson*. See Jonson. 1–36.

Lewis, Neil A. "Court Nominee Is Linked to Anti-Abortion Stand." *New York Times* 3 July 1991: 1+.

Locke, John. *An Essay Concerning the True Original, Extent, and End of Civil Government*. *The English Philosophers from Bacon to Mill*. Ed. Edwin A. Burtt. New York: Modern Library, 1939. 403–503.

Lockert, Lacy, trans. *The Chief Rivals of Corneille and Racine*. Nashville, TN: Vanderbilt UP, 1956.

Lope de Vega. *Fuente Ovejuna (The Sheep Well)*. *Four Plays*. Trans. John Garrett Underhill. 1936. Westport, CT: Hyperion, 1978. 277–355.

Lucretius. *On the Nature of Things*. Trans. H. A. J. Munro. London: Bell, 1929.

Machiavelli, Nicolò. *The Prince and the Discourses*. New York: Modern Library, 1940. 3–98.

McWilliam, G. H. Introduction. See Betti vii–xvi.

Magnusson, Magnuss, and Herman Pálsson, trans. *Njal's Saga*. Harmondsworth: Penguin, 1960.

Maritain, Jacques. *The Rights of Man and Natural Law*. London: Bles, 1958.

Marlowe, Christopher. *The Jew of Malta*. *Five Plays*. Ed. Havelock Ellis. New York: Hill & Wang, 1956. 197–266.

Marshall, Herbert. Foreword. *Mayakovsky*. Ed. and trans. Herbert Marshall. New York: Hill & Wang, 1965.

Martin du Gard, Roger. *Jean Barois*. Trans. Stuart Gilbert. 1949. Indianapolis: Bobbs, 1969.

Martinenche, E. *La Comédie espagnole en France de Hardy à Racine*. Paris, 1900.

Mauriac, François. *The End of the Night*. *Thérèse* 191–383.

——. *The Inner Presence: Recollections of My Spiritual Life*. Trans. Herma Briffault. Indianapolis: Bobbs, 1968.

——. Preface. *Cinq Années de ma vie (1894–1899)*, by Alfred Dreyfus. Paris (?): Fasquelle, 1962. 11–21.

——. *Thérèse Desqueyroux. Thérèse: A Portrait in Four Parts*. Trans. Gerard Hopkins. New York: Farrar, 1974.

——. *Vipers' Tangle*. Trans. Warre B. Wells. Garden City, NY: Doubleday, 1968.

Maurois, André. *From Proust to Camus: Profiles of Modern French Writers*. Trans. Carl Morse and Renaud Bruce. 1966. New York: Doubleday, 1968.

Meerloo, Joost M. *The Rape of the Mind: The Psychology of Thought Control, Menticide, and Brainwashing*. New York: Grosset, 1961.

Melville, Herman. *Billy Budd, Sailor (An Inside Narrative)*. Ed. Harrison Hayford and Merton M. Sealts, Jr. Chicago: U of Chicago P, 1962.

——. *Billy Budd, Sailor: An Inside Narrative*. Ed. Milton R. Stern. Indianapolis: Bobbs, 1975.

Michel, Pierre. *James Gould Cozzens*. New York: Twayne, 1974.

Mische, Gerald, and Patricia Mische. *Toward a Human World Order: Beyond the National Security Strait-Jacket*. New York: Paulist P, 1986.

Montaigne, Michel de. "Of Experience." *The Essayes of Montaigne*. Trans. John Florio. New York: Modern Library, n.d. 963–1013.

More, Sir Thomas. *Utopia*. [Trans. Ralph Robinson.] *Utopia and a Dialogue of Comfort*. London: Dent, 1951. 13–142.

Muschg, Adolf. "Reparations or Making Good." *The Blue Man and Other Stories*. Trans. Markis Zeller Gambon and Michael Hamburger. New York: Braziller, 1985. 52–72.

Nietzsche, Friedrich. "The Genealogy of Morals." *The Philosophy of Nietzsche*. Trans. Horace B. Samuel. New York: Modern Library, n.d. 617–807

O'Brien, Conor Cruise. *Albert Camus of Europe and Africa*. New York: Viking, 1970.

Orwell, George. "Inside the Whale." *A Collection of Essays*. 1946. San Diego: Harcourt, 1981. 210–52.

Péguy, Charles. "Notre Jeunesse." *Trois Fragments: Notre Jeunesse, Marie, Comte Hugo, Le Mystère des Saints Innocents*. Lausanne: La Guilde du Livre, n.d. 13–113.

The Penguin Companion to European Literature. Ed. Anthony Thorlby. New York: McGraw-Hill, 1969.

Pizer, Donald. *The Novels of Theodore Dreiser: A Critical Study*. Minneapolis: U of Minnesota P, 1976.

Plato. *Crito. Apology, Crito, Republic* I–II. Chicago: Great Books Foundation, n.d. 31–46.

——. *The Republic. The Portable Plato: Protagoras, Symposium, Phaedo, and The Republic.* Trans. Benjamin Jowett. Ed. Scott Buchanan. New York: Viking, 1948. 281–696.

Porter, Katherine Anne. "Noon Wine." *Six Great Modern Novels.* New York: Dell, 1967. 157–212.

Posner, Richard. *Law and Literature: A Misunderstood Relation.* Cambridge: Harvard UP, 1988.

Proust, Marcel. *Letters of Marcel Proust.* Ed. and trans. Mina Curtiss. New York: Random, 1949.

——. *La Prisonnière. À La Recherche du temps perdu.* Ed. Pierre Clarac and André Ferré. Vol. 3. Paris: Gallimard, 1954. 7–415. 3 vols.

Rabinowitz, Isaac. "Towards a Valid Theory of Biblical Hebrew Literature." *The Classical Tradition: Literary and Historical Studies in Honor of Harry Caplan.* Ed. Luitpold Wallach. Ithaca, N.Y.: Cornell UP, 1966. 315–28.

Racine, Jean. *Athaliah. Complete Plays.* Trans. Samuel Solomon. Vol. 2. New York: Random, 1964. 371–459. 2 vols.

The Riverside Shakespeare. Ed. G. Blakemore Evans. Boston: Houghton, 1974.

Robinson, Martha S. "The Law of the State in Kafka's *The Trial.*" *ALSA Forum* 6.2 (1982): 127–48.

Robson, William A. *Civilization and the Growth of Law: A Study of the Relations Between Men's Ideas About the Universe, and the Institutions of Law and Government.* New York: Macmillan, 1935.

Roeder, Ralph. *The Man of the Renaissance: Four Lawgivers—Savonarola, Machiavelli, Castiglione, Aretino.* New York: Viking, 1935.

Sachs, Albie, and Joan Hoff Wilson. *Sexism and the Law: A Study of Male Beliefs and Legal Bias in Britain and the United States.* New York: Free Press, 1978.

Samuels, Charles Thomas. "Mr. Trilling, Mr. Warren and *An American Tragedy.*" *Yale Review* 53 (Summer, 1964): 624–40. Rpt. in *Dreiser: A Collection of Critical Essays.* Ed. John Lydenberg. Englewood Cliffs, NJ: Prentice, 1971. 163–73.

Schalk, David. *Roger Martin du Gard, The Novelist and History.* Ithaca, NY: Cornell UP, 1967.

Schiller, Friedrich. *Mary Stuart.* Adapt. and trans. Stephen Spender. New Haven: Ticknor & Fields, 1980.

Scott, Sir Walter. *The Heart of Midlothian.* London: Dent, 1956.

Shakespeare, William. *Hamlet. Riverside Shakespeare* 1141–97.

——. *King Lear. Riverside Shakepeare* 1255–1305.

——. *Measure for Measure. Riverside Shakespeare* 550–86.

——. *The Merchant of Venice. Riverside Shakespeare* 254–85.

——. *Troilus and Cressida. Riverside Shakespeare* 448–94.

Simon, Yves R. *The Tradition of Natural Law: A Philosopher's Reflections.* Ed. Vukan Kuic. 1965. New York: Fordham UP, 1992.

Snow, C. P. *The Sleep of Reason.* New York: Scribner's, 1968.

Sokel, Walter H. "Freud and the Magic of Kafka's Writing." *World of Franz Kafka* 145–58.

Sophocles. *Antigone. The Oedipus Cycle: An English Version.* Trans. Dudley Fitts and Robert Fitzgerald. New York: Harcourt, n.d. 183–238.

Spencer, Herbert. *The Principles of Ethics.* Vol. 1. New York, 1895. 2 vols.

Spenser, Edmund. *The Poetical Works of Edmund Spenser.* Ed. J. C. Smith and E. de Selincourt. London: Oxford UP, 1916.

——. *The Works of Edmund Spenser: A Variorum Edition.* Ed. Edwin Greenlaw. 11 vols. Baltimore: Johns Hopkins UP, 1936.

Steiner, George. *Antigones.* New York: Oxford UP, 1984.

——. *Tolstoy or Dostoevsky: An Essay in the Old Criticism.* New York: Knopf, 1959.

Sterne, Richard. "Reconciliation and Alienation in Kleist's 'Michael Kohlhaas' and Doctorow's *Ragtime.*" *Legal Studies Forum* 12.1 (1988): 5–22.

Stone, Julius. *Human Law and Human Justice.* Stanford: Stanford UP, 1965.

Swanberg, W. A. *Dreiser.* New York: Scribner's, 1965.

Swift, Jonathan. "A Voyage to Brobdingnag." *Gulliver's Travels and Other Writings.* New York: Modern Library, 1958. 57–116.

Taine, Hippolyte. *History of English Literature.* Trans. H. Van Laun. Vol. 1. New York: Ungar, 1965. 4 vols.

Tendryakov, Vladimir. "Justice." Trans. Olive Stevens. *Three, Seven, Ace, and Other Stories.* Trans. David Alger, Olive Stevens, and Paul Falla. New York: Harper, 1973. 71–159.

Thomas, Calvin. *The Life and Works of Friedrich Schiller.* New York: Holt, 1901.

Thompson, E. P. *The Making of the English Working Class.* New York: Knopf, 1966.

Tolstoy, Leo. "God Sees the Truth, But Waits." *Twenty-Three Tales.* Trans. Louise and Aylmer Maude. London: Oxford UP, 1906. 1–10.

——. *Resurrection.* Trans. Rosemary Edmunds. Harmondsworth: Penguin, 1966.

Torrey, Norman L., ed. *Les Philosophes: The Philosophers of the Enlightenment and Modern Democracy.* New York: Capricorn, 1960.

Troyat, Henri. *Tolstoy.* Trans. Nancy Amphoux. New York: Doubleday, 1967.

Turnell, Martin. *The Classical Moment: Studies of Corneille, Molière, and Racine.* Norwalk, CT: New Directions, n.d.

Voltaire. "Essay on Toleration." Trans. Joseph McCabe. New York: Putnam's, 1912. Rpt. in part, in *Introduction* 840–44.

———. "Natural Law." *Philosophical Dictionary*. Trans. H. I. Woolf. New York: Knopf, 1924. Rpt. in *Introduction* 833–35.

Ward, Christopher. *The War of the Revolution*. Ed. John Richard Alden. 2 vols. New York: Macmillan, 1952.

Weber, Eugen. Introduction. *Jean Barois*. See Martin du Gard.

Webster, John. *The Duchess of Malfi*. *Eight Famous Elizabethan Plays*. New York: Modern Library, 1932. 435–543.

White, James Boyd. "Telling Stories in the Law and in Ordinary Life: *The Oresteia* and 'Noon Wine.' " *Heracles' Bow: Essays on the Rhetoric and Poetics of the Law*. Madison: U of Wisconsin P, 1985. 168–91.

Willey, Basil. *The Eighteenth Century Background: Studies on the Idea of Nature in the Thought of the Period*. New York: Columbia UP, 1940.

Williams, Raymond. "The Industrial Novels." *Culture and Society, 1780–1950*. New York: Doubleday, 1960. 94–118.

Wilson, Margaret. *Spanish Drama of the Golden Age*. New York: Pergamon, 1969.

World Drama: Ancient Greece, Rome, India, China, Japan, Medieval Europe, and England. Vol. 1 of *World Drama*. 2 vols. Ed. Barrett H. Clark. New York: Dover, 1960.

The World of Franz Kafka. Ed. J. P. Stern. New York: Holt, 1980.

Wright, Richard. *Native Son*. 1940. *Early Works: Lawd Today! Uncle Tom's Children, Native Son*. New York: Literary Classics of the United States, 1991. 443–850.

Zola, Emile. *Thérèse Raquin*. Paris (?): Fasquelle, n.d.

INDEX

Abraham, 13, 178
Absurdism, 56, 201–02, 247, 252
Absurdist literature
  and human condition, 194, 201–02,
    204, 206
  and madness, 172–73
  Book of Job, 14–15
  by Porter, 247–49
  Sense of injustice in, 168–215
Adams, Henry, 119
Aeschylus, 4–5, 7, 12, 16, 23
Agape
  in Brecht, 140, 142
  in Dostoevsky, 86, 88, 95
  in Mauriac, 102
  in Tolstoy, 80, 108–09
Aguirre, José M., 45
Alcalde de Zalamea, El, SEE *Mayor of*
  Zalamea, The
Allegory, 170
Ambiguity, in Kafka, 182–87
American Revolution, 175–76
American Tragedy, An (Dreiser), xviii,
  110, 121–39, 162, 165, 166*n*17,
  221, 226, 229–30
Anders, Günther, 180–81
Anouilh, Jean, 62*n*6, 249–50, 252
Antigone (Anouilh), 62*n*6, 249–50
Antigone (Sophocles), xi, 6, 12, 71, 93,
  249–50
Anti–hero, 122–23; see also Dreiser,
  Theodore
Antinomianism, 68, 71, 81–83; see also
  Tolstoy, Leo
Anti–Semitism, 99, 112; see also Drey-
  fus Affair
Antonio (*The Merchant of Venice*), 31–
  34, 89
Aquinas, St. Thomas, xiii, 18–20, 28,
  41–43, 48–49, 108, 151
Aristophanes, 12, 23

Aristotle, xi–xiv, 16, 18–19, 27, 106
Asceticism, in Tolstoy, 79–80, 81
Athaliah (Racine), xv, 47–48
Attorneys, in literature
  French, 23–24
  Greek, 4
  in Brecht, 146–50
  in Camus, 194, 196–98, 200–03,
    234
  in Cozzens, 221–28
  in Diderot, 53
  in Dostoevsky, 87–95
  in Dreiser, 131–36
  in Kafka, 185–86
  in Koestler, 157, 160–63
  in Lee, 255
  in Martin du Gard, 117
  in Mauriac, 96–97
  in Melville, 169, 173
  in Porter, 249
  in Scott, 57
  in Snow, 234–39
  in Spenser, 29
Augustine, St., xiii, 17–18, 20, 86,
  108, 245

Bacon, Francis, 41
Balzac, Honoré de, xvii, 57–61, 67,
  70–71, 261
Barristers, in literature, *see* Attorneys,
  in literature
Barthes, Roland, 243
Baudelaire, Charles–Pierre, 102
Bayle, Pierre, 47–49
Bayley, John, 79
"Bed trick," 37
Bentley, Eric, 141, 166*n*22
Berlin, Isaiah, 71, 75
Betti, Ugo, 243–44
Bible, 62–63*n*16, 154, 164; *see also*
  Book of Job

Bigotry, Religious, in Camus, 198
Billy Budd (Melville), xx, 168–80, 204
Blake, William, 106, 232
Bloch, Ernst, 262
Book about Myself, A (Dreiser), 121
Book of Job, 14–15
Book of Laughter and Forgetting, The (Kundera), 205
Bourgeoisie, 204
  and natural law, 55–61
Bradwell v. Illinois, 257
Brecht, Bertolt, xix, 110–11, 140–52 (passim), 164, 167*n*23, 219, 245
Brothers Karamazov, The (Dostoevsky), xviii, 68, 84–96, 106, 168, 202, 245
Burke, Edmund, 57, 176

Calderón de la Barca, Pedro, 43, 45
Camus, Albert, xx, xxii, 14, 168, 180, 188, 230, 234, 240, 247, 252
Catherine the Great (czarina of Russia), 52
Catholic Church, 26, 66*n*74
  in Dostoevsky, 87
Caucasian Chalk Circle, The (Brecht), xviii, 110, 140–52, 165
  German text of, 150
Chafee, Zechariah, Jr., 219
Chalk Circle, The (Chinese), 150
Champigny, Robert, 196–97
Charity, 34, 38
Charles I (king of England), 47
Chaucer, Geoffrey, 15
Chekhov, Anton, 83
Chemism, 110, 122, 130
Christianity, 18
  and Jews, 31–34
  in Mauriac, 101–02, 104–05
  in Tolstoy, 70–71
Cicero, xii–xiii, 16, 19, 35
Cinna (P. Corneille), xiv, 46
City of God, The (St. Augustine), 17
City–state/polis, 9, 19–20
"Coalhouse Walker" (Doctorow), 66*n*83
Colonialism, 253–55
Comédie humaine (Balzac), 57, 67
Commedia (Dante), 20, 23, 67

Compassion, 88–89, 244
Concentration camps, 235–36
Corneille, Pierre, 46
Corneille, Thomas, 46
Counter-Reformation, 41
Court-martial, *see* Trials, in literature
Court of Inquiry, *see* Trials, in literature
Cozzens, James Gould, xx, 218–30 (passim), 241, 253
Crime and Punishment (Dostoevsky), 159
Cupidity, 19
Cynicism, 26, 149
  and trials, 256
  in Euripides, 6–9
  in Kundera, 208
  in *Patelin* farce, 23

Dante, xiii, 19–24, 67, 86, 127
Darkness at Noon (Koestler), xix, 110–11, 152–65 (passim), 169, 253
Darwin, Charles, 67, 109–10, 127
Darwinism, xviii, xx, 67, 122–23, 133, 139, 245–47
De monarchia (Dante), 19, 21
Descartes, René, 41
Diderot, Denis, xvi, 52–54
Discourses (Machiavelli), 24
Divine love, in Dostoevsky, 84–86
Divine right of kings, xiv, 22, 27–28, 46–47
Doctorow, E. L., 66*n*83
Dostoevsky, Fyodor, xvii, 84–96 (passim), 98, 108, 162–63, 168–69, 201–02, 230, 234, 236, 243–45
Dreiser, Theodore, xviii, 110, 121–40 (passim), 164–65, 166*n*17, 219, 222, 225–26, 229–30, 234, 245, 247
Dreyfus, Alfred, xviii, 96–97, 99, 109, 111, 113–14, 116–20
Dreyfus Affair, 109, 111–20
Duchess of Malfi, The (Webster), 41
Dunlop, C. R. B., 166
Duns Scotus, 28

Earl of Essex, The (T. Corneille), 46
Eliot, George, xvii, 58, 60–61, 67

Elizabeth I (queen of England), xiv, 27–30
Ely, John Hart, 256–57
End of the Night, The (Mauriac), 105
Ennius, 16
Entrèves, A. P. d', xv–xvii, 51
Environment, Influence of, in Cozzens and others, 222–23, 229
Eroticism/sexuality, 94, 109, 126–27, 237
  in Camus, 200–01
  in Kafka, 183–84, 190
  in Melville, 170–71
  in Muschg, 251–52
  in Snow, 237
Ethics, in Brecht, 140
Eumenides (Aeschylus), 4–5, 7, 197
Euripides, 6–7, 9, 12, 16
Executive Court, *see* Trials, in literature
Existentialism, in Anouilh, 250
"Ex machina," 8

Faerie Queene, The (Spenser), xiv, 26–27, 30
Faith, Religious, in Martin du Gard, 113
Fall, The (Camus), 188
Farce of the Worthy Master Patelin (anon.), xii, 23–24
Felix Holt (Eliot), xvii, 58, 60, 67
Fielding, Henry, 51
Fiore, Robert L., 42–43
Flaubert, Gustave, 100, 109
Forster, E. M., 253–55
Fox, Dian, 65n52
Freedom, 241, 262n22
  Religious, 49–51
French Revolution, 177–78
Freud, Sigmund, 94, 116, 122, 164, 216n12, 236
Fuenteovejuna, SEE *Sheep Well, The*

Gentiles, 31–34, 89
George, Henry, 78
Gide, André, 256
Gilligan, Carol, 246
Glaspell, Susan, 245–47
God, xiii, 12–16, 27, 48, 71, 86, 97, 101–02, 106, 244–45

Gods, and justice, 1–5, 7
"God Sees the Truth, But Waits" (Tolstoy), xviii, 68–71, 106, 244
Golden Rule, 33, 122, 133, 153, 255
Gordis, Robert, 62–63n16
Greenlaw, Edwin, 28
Groethuysen, Bernard, 66n74
Grotius, 12, 19, 48–49
Guilt, Sense of
  in Camus, 194
  in Kafka, 182–84, 187, 189–90
  in Koestler, 162
  in Snow, 237

Hamlet (Shakespeare), 11, 39
Harrington, James, 49
Hart, H. L. A., 258
Havelock, Erik A., 62n10
Hayford, Harrison, 176–77
Hazard, Paul, 48
Heart of Midlothian, The (Scott), xvii, 56–57, 60, 71, 93
Hegel, Georg, 6
Heilman, Robert, 39
Hesiod, 3, 5, 12
History, as judge, 153
Holmes, Oliver Wendell, 259
Homer, 1–5, 12
Honesty, in Camus, 197
Horace, 54
Human condition
  Absurdity of, 201–02, 204, 215
  and Camus, 194
Hume, David, 54

Idealism, xii, 17, 34
  Christian, 17, 28
  of Dante, 20, 24
  of St. Augustine, 17–18
Ihering, Rudolphe von [Ihering, Rodolphe], 33
Iliad (Homer), 2
Individualism, in Kundera, 206–07
Inferno (Dante), 20
Injustice, Sense of
  and human condition, 215
  as ethical concept, 139
  Greek, 7, 10, 31
  in Brecht, 152

in Dostoevsky, 88, 92–93
in *King Lear*, xii, 40
in Koestler, 111
in Kundera, 214–15
in Mauriac, 98, 101–02
in modern absurdist fiction, 168–215
in the polis, 19–20
in religious fiction, 67–106
in social fiction, 108–65
in Tolstoy, 71–82, 84
Social, 71–82
International law, 259–60
Irrationality, 168
Isaac, 13–14, 178

Jaeger, Werner, 6
James VI (king of Scotland), 27–29
Jean Barois (Martin du Gard), xviii–xix, xxii, 109–21, 165, 247
Jennie Gerhardt (Dreiser), 122
Jesus, in Melville, 179–80
Jew of Malta, The (Marlowe), 30, 32
Jews, 44, 55, 99, 187; *see also* Anti-Semitism, Dreyfus Affair
in Martin du Gard, 113–14, 117
in Mauriac, 97, 99
in Shakespeare, 31–35, 89
Job, 14–15, 62*n*16
Johnson, Pamela Hansford, 230–32, 239
Joke, The (Kundera), xx, 168, 204–15
Jonson, Ben, 30–31
Judeo–Christian tradition, 15, 63*n*16, 133, 208–09, 253
Judges, in literature, *see* Attorneys, in literature
Judicial error, 98, 101
Jury/jurors, in literature
Greek, 5
in Camus, 203, 234
in Cozzens, 220–21, 225–29
in Dreiser, 133, 135–36, 221
in Glaspell, 245–46
in Lee, 255
in Tolstoy, 72–74
Jury of Her Peers, A (Glaspell), 245–47
Just and the Unjust, The (Cozzens), xx, 218–30, 241, 253

Justice, Sense of
and law, 112
and the Party, 205
as undefinable, 218
Decay of, 70
definable, 218, 220
Distributive, 259–60
Earthly, 20–23
Greek, 1–5, 9–12
Heavenly, 18
Idealistic, 11–12, 34, 54, 61
in Anouilh, 250
in Aristotle, xi, 19
in Betti, 244
in Brecht, 140–41, 245
in Forster, 254–55
in Kafka, 187
in Koestler, 157, 253
in Martin du Gard, 115
in Melville, 180
Rational, 230, 236
Realistic (Thrasymachean), xii, 9–12, 54, 61, 169, 243, 246, 260
Roman, xiii, 16–17
Totalitarian, 191
"Justice" (Tendryakov), 246–47

Kafka, Franz, 54, 56, 180–91 (passim), 208, 215, 216*n*12, 247, 252
Kant, Immanuel, 55–56
Kaukasische Kreidekreis, Der (Brecht), 167*n*24
Kermode, Frank, 28–29
King Lear (Shakespeare), xii, 3, 34–41, 241
King's law, 174
Kleist, Heinrich von, xvii, 55–57, 59–61, 66*n*83, 71, 111, 141, 180, 215, 247
Knipovich, Evgeniya, 180
Koestler, Arthur, xix, 110–11, 152–65 (passim), 169, 219, 222, 252–53
Kundera, Milan, xx, 168, 204–15 (passim), 247, 252

Landslide, The (Betti), 243–44
Langland, William, xii, 20–23, 29, 67, 86, 111, 127, 141, 215
Law, in Kafka, 216*n*10
Law, *vs.* morals, 259

Lawyers, in literature, *see* Attorneys, in literature
Lee, Harper, 229, 255–56
Levin, Harry, 30
Libation Bearers (Aeschylus), 4
Liberty, Religious, *see* Freedom, Religious
Locke, John, xiv–xv, 47–49, 51–52, 55
Lope de Vega, xiv, 42, 45, 67, 127
Louis XIII (king of France), 46
Louis XIV (king of France), 46–47
Lucretius, 17

Machiavelli, xiii, 12, 24–26, 29, 159
Madame Bovary (Flaubert), 100, 109
Madness, 249
  and absurdity, 173, 216n12
Magistrates, in literature, *see* Attorneys, in literature
Malum in se vs. *malum prohibitum*, 258
Maritain, Jacques, xviii, xxi, 19
Marlowe, Christopher, 30
Martin du Gard, Roger, xviii–xix, 109, 111–21 (passim), 140, 164–65, 219, 245, 247
Marx, Groucho, 183
Marx, Karl, 12
Marxism, 110, 163, 206
  in Brecht, 140–52 (passim)
Mary, Queen of Scots, xiv, 28–29
Mary Stuart, 29–30
Mauriac, François, xvii, 68, 96–106 (passim), 108, 112–13, 243, 245
Mayakovsky, Vladimir, 141, 167n23
Mayor of Zalamea, The (Calderón), 43–46
Measure for Measure (Shakespeare), 34–39, 56
Medieval literature, Christian, 13–15
Meerloo, Joost N., 188
Melville, Herman, xx, 168–80 (passim), 230, 247
Men and Brethren (Cozzens), 222
Mental illness, and crime, in Snow, 238
Merchant of Venice, The (Shakespeare), 31–34, 89, 93
Mercy, 34–35, 38, 89
"Michael Kohlhaas" (Kleist), xvii, 55–57, 59–60, 66n83, 71, 180, 247

Middle class, 55, 58; *see also* Bourgeoisie
Misanthropy
  in Camus, 204
  in Kundera, 210
Mische, Gerald, 259
Mische, Patricia, 259
Moby-Dick (Melville), 169
Molière, 126
Monarchs, 19, 21, 25–26; *see also* names of individual monarchs
  English, 47
  French, 46
  Renaissance, 25–26
  Russian, 83
  Spanish, 41–42, 44
Money
  in Brecht, 146
  in Cozzens, 222
  in Dostoevsky, 91
  in Dreiser, 128
Montaigne, Michel de, 26
Montesquieu, 49–50
Morality, 253
  in Tolstoy, 71–72, 81, 83
Morals, *vs.* law, 259
Moral sense, in Dreiser, 138
More, Sir Thomas, xiii, 25–26, 86, 111, 141
Moses, 12
Murder, in literature, 108
  Greek, 2–4, 7
  in Balzac, 70
  in Cozzens, 218
  in Dostoevsky, 86, 94, 168
  in Dreiser, 123, 130, 137
  in French drama, 46–47
  in Johnson, 231–32
  in Porter, 247–48
  in Scott, 56–57
  in Snow, 218, 233–35, 239
  in Tolstoy, 69–70
Muschg, Adolf, 250–52
Myth of Sisyphus, The (Camus), 192

Native Son (R. Wright), 245, 257
Natural law, xi–xxi, 18–19, 41, 159, 163, 242, 245
  Absence of, 193–94
  and bourgeoisie, 55–61

and Dante, 20
and English literature, 30, 49, 51
and French literature, 50
and Golden Rule, 33
and justice, 152
and Langland, 21–23
and liberty, 51
and natural rights, 48–55
and Spanish drama, 41–43, 46
and St. Thomas Aquinas, 18–19, 48–49
Ethical, 18–19, 23, 38, 67–68, 108, 110–13, 122–23, 127, 133, 137, 191, 208–09, 218, 228–29, 256–58
in Greek literature, 6, 19
in Kleist, 247
in Koestler, 164–65
in Renaissance literature, 24–31
in Shakespeare, 38–41
Rational, 71, 79, 86, 95–96
Repudiation of, 30–31
Scientific, xv, 121
to Romans, 16–17, 63n16
Natural rights, 48–55, 151
Naturalism, 109
Nature, in Shakespeare, 34, 41
Neveu de Rameau, Le (Diderot), 53–54
New Testament, 35, 71, 82, 179
Nicholas II (czar of Russia), 83
Nicomachean Ethics (Aristotle), 18–19, 27
Nietzsche, Friedrich, 12, 168
"Noon Wine," 247–49
Notes from Underground (Dostoevsky), 87
Nun, The, SEE Religieuse, La

O'Brien, Conor Cruise, 202–03
Odyssey (Homer), 1–4
Oedipus complex, 94
Old Testament, 12–15, 17
On Iniquity: Some Personal Reflections Arising out of the Moors Murder Trial (Johnson), 231–32, 239
Oresteia (Aeschylus), 4–5
Orestes (Euripides), 7–9
Origin of Species (Darwin), 109
Orthodox Church, and Tolstoy, 80–81, 83

Orwell, George, xx, 58
Outsider, The (Camus), xx, 168, 191–204, 208, 234, 247

Paine, Thomas, 176
Party (Communist)
in Koestler, 111, 153–59, 169
in Kundera, 206–11
Pascal, Blaise, 113
Passage to India, A (Forster), 253–55
Péguy, Charles, xvii–xviii, 96, 102
Peloponnesian War, 9
Philip IV (king of Spain), 44
Piers the Ploughman (Langland), xii, 20–23, 67, 71
Plato, xii, 2, 6, 9–12, 25, 62n10, 139, 205
Play of Coventry, The (anon.), 18
Plessy v. Ferguson, 257
Polis, see City-state/polis
Politics, 16–20
Pope, Alexander, 73
Porter, Katherine Anne, 247–49, 252
Portia (The Merchant of Venice), 33–35, 89
Posner, Richard A., xxiin1
Prince, The (Machiavelli), xiii, 25
Prosecutors, in literature, see Attorneys, in literature
Protestants, 26–27, 41
Proust, Marcel, 84, 118–19
Punishment
in Betti, 244
in Muschg, 252
in Snow, 240
Purgatorio (Dante), 20

Quevedo, Francisco de, 44

Rabinowitz, Isaac, 15
Racine, Jean, xv, 47–48
Racism, 66n83, 245, 254, 255–56
in Lee, 255–56
Rameau's Nephew, SEE Neveu de Rameau, Le
Rationalism, 90, 95–96
Rationality, Weakness of, 252–53
Realism, 109
Social, 218–19
Reality, in Kundera, 204–05

"Red Inn, The" (Balzac), xvii, 57–58, 60, 70–71

Reformation, 41

Religieuse, La (Diderot), xvi, 52–54

Religious fiction, 108–09
   Sense of injustice in, 67–106, 111

"Reparations or Making Good" (Muschg), 250–52

Republic (Plato), xii, 11, 16, 25, 139

Responsibility
   Diminished, 238, 241
   Personal, 218–19, 232, 239, 241

Resurrection, xviii, xxii, 68, 71–84, 95, 106, 109

Revenge, in literature, 45
   Greek, 5–7
   in French drama, 46
   in Kundera, 211–12

"Right feeling," 228–30

Roe v. *Wade*, 258

Rotrou, Jean, 47

Rousseau, Jean-Jacques, 52, 75

Samuels, Charles Thomas, 166n20

Satire, 23–24, 143

Schiller, Friedrich, 29, 116

Scott, Sir Walter, xvii, 56–57, 59, 61, 67, 71, 93

Sealts, Merton, 176–77

Seneca, 35

Sexuality, *see* Eroticism/sexuality

Sexual selection, 127

Shakespeare, Willliam, xiv, 31–41, 89

Sheep Well, The (Lope de Vega), xiv, 42–45, 68, 71

Shylock (*The Merchant of Venice*), 31–35, 89

Simon, Yves R., xii, xviii, 243, 260

Sister Carrie (Dreiser), 122

Sleep of Reason, The (Snow), xxi, 218–19, 230–42, 253

Snow, C. P., xx, 218–19, 230–42, 253

Social scale, 126

Society, Duties of, 260

Socrates, xii, 9–12, 26, 31, 54, 261

Sophists, 6–7, 9; *see also* Thrasymachus

Sophocles, 6, 12, 93, 249–50

Spanish Inquisition, xiv, 41, 43–44

Spencer, Herbert, 74, 121–22, 166n17

Spenser, Edmund, xiv, 26–30

Steiner, George, 62n6, 107n12

Stern, Milton R., 177

Stoics, 26, 116

Stone, Julius, xiii

Survival of the fittest, 123–24, 165, 246

Swift, Jonathan, 49

Symbolism, Christian
   in Koestler, 154–57
   in Melville, 179–80

Sympathy, in Dreiser, 122, 129, 138

Taine, Hippolyte, 109

Tendryakov, Vladimir, 246–47

Thérèse Desqueyroux (Mauriac), xviii, 68, 96–106, 112, 245

Thérèse Raquin (Zola), 109

Thomas, Clarence, 257–58

Thoreau, Henry David, xvi, 81

Thrasymachus, xi, xxi, 9–12, 23, 26, 54, 61, 69, 153, 188, 260–61

To Kill a Mockingbird (Lee), 229, 255–56

Tolstoy, Leo, xvii–xviii, xxii, 68–84 (passim), 108–09, 243–44

Tom Jones (Fielding), 51

Transcendental intervention, 59–60, 71

Trial, The (Kafka), xx, 168, 180–91, 204, 208

Trials, in literature, 68, 84
   and cynicism, 256
   as genre, 261
   Greek, 3–4
   in Betti, 243–44
   in Brecht, 146–50
   in Camus, 196, 198–203, 234
   in Cozzens, 220–27
   in Dostoevsky, 87–95, 244–45
   in Dreiser, 133–36, 139
   in Forster, 253–54
   in Kafka, 184–87
   in Langland, 21
   in Lee, 255
   in Martin du Gard, 116–19
   in Melville, 173–75
   in Muschg, 250, 252
   in Porter, 249
   in Shakespeare, 32–34